Cracking the New

GRE

with DVD

2012 Edition

The Princeton Review

Cracking the New
GRE
with DVD

2012 Edition

The Staff of The Princeton Review

PrincetonReview.com

Random House, Inc. New York

The Princeton Review, Inc.
111 Speen Street, Suite 550
Framingham, MA 01701
E-mail: editorialsupport@review.com

ISBN: 978-0-375-42819-7
ISSN: 1938-7210

GRE is a registered trademark of the Educational Testing Service.

Editors: Laura Braswell and Neill Seltzer
Production Editor: Kathy G. Carter
Production Coordinator: Deborah A. Silvestrini

Printed in the United States of America on partially recycled paper.

10 9 8 7 6 5 4 3 2 1

2012 Edition

Editorial

Seamus Mullarkey, Associate Publisher
Laura Braswell, Senior Editor
Selena Coppock, Editor
Heather Brady, Editor

Random House Publishing Team

Tom Russell, Publisher
Nicole Benhabib, Publishing Manager
Ellen L. Reed, Production Manager
Alison Stoltzfus, Associate Managing Editor

Acknowledgements

The following people deserve thanks for their help with this book:

Thanks to Ellen Mendlow, Rachel Warren, Briana Gordon, Mariwyn Curtin, Katie O'Neill, Neill Seltzer, Curtis Retherford, and the staff and students of The Princeton Review.

Special thanks to Adam Robinson, who conceived of and perfected the Joe Bloggs approach to standardized tests and many of the other successful techniques used by The Princeton Review.

Contents

Using Your Resources

The DVD and online tools that accompany *Cracking the New GRE with DVD* are specifically designed to enhance your book's presentation. Here's how you can make the most of these resources.

DVD: Start Out Strong

A great way to begin your preparation for the GRE is to watch the enclosed DVD. Our expert instructors will give you an overview of what's on the test and will identify some of the most critical issues to look out for as you prepare. Armed with this information, you'll be in great shape to begin your studies.

You can return to the DVD at any point during your preparation to refresh your memory or to reinforce key concepts that give you trouble. Look for the DVD icon in the book, which indicates the topics that are also covered in your DVD.

Watch it on your DVD

Online Tools: Just a Few Clicks Away

In order to access our online tools, you must register the serial number at the bottom of the inside back cover of your book at **PrincetonReview.com/cracking**. After you receive confirmation of your registration, follow the directions to reach the site and be sure to do the following:

- **Access Your Study Plan**—Will you be ready when test day comes? Visit our website to access a customized study plan that will help you stay on track with your studies. We'll guide you through every step of your preparation based on how much time you have to study, so you'll be in top form on test day.

- **Take Full-Length Practice Tests**—By working through a full-length test early on, you'll be able to identify your strengths and weaknesses and better focus your studies. As you get closer to test day, taking simulated tests will help you practice techniques, build your stamina and confidence, and gain familiarity with the kinds of questions you're going to see.

- **Target Your Preparation**—If you come across a particular GRE concept or question type that gives you trouble, don't worry. Our online activities will allow you to quickly gain mastery over even the trickiest topics.

- **Research Schools**—Visit our Grad Schools and Careers website, where you'll find a wealth of information about schools that match your specific criteria. You can also use the site to manage your application process and even submit applications directly to schools!

Part I
Orientation

Chapter 1
Introduction

What is the GRE? Who makes the test? What's a good score? What's with this "new" GRE? The answer to these questions and many others lie within in this chapter. In the next few pages, we'll give you the lowdown on the things you need to know about the new GRE.

CRACKING THE GRE

For a lot of people, taking a standardized test like the GRE usually engenders a number of emotions—none of them positive. But here's the good news: The Princeton Review is going to make this whole ordeal a lot easier for you. We'll give you the information you will need to do well on the GRE, including our time-tested strategies and techniques.

The GRE has just been rather significantly revised. The new test supposedly allows graduate schools to get a better sense of an applicant's ability to work in a postgraduate setting—a goal that is unrealistic indeed, considering that the people who take the GRE are applying to programs as diverse as physics and anthropology.

However, it's safe to say that neither GRE—new or old—is a realistic measure of how well you'll do in grad school, or even how intelligent you are. In fact, the GRE provides a valid assessment of only one thing:

> The GRE assesses how well you take the GRE.

Need more info? Check out the DVD.

Got it? Even so, you still want to do well on the GRE, because you still want grad schools to take you seriously when they consider your application. With this in mind, there are several very important skills to cultivate when you're preparing for the test, and each of them is attainable with the right guidance (which we'll give you), a strong work ethic (which you must provide), and a healthy dose of optimism. Who knows? Maybe after working through this book and learning how to crack the test, you'll actually look forward to taking the GRE.

So what exactly *is* this test you've heard so much about?

WHAT IS THE GRE?

The Graduate Record Examination (GRE) is a 3-hour, 40-minute exam that's used to rank applicants for graduate schools. The scored portion of the new GRE consists of the following sections:

- One 30-minute Analysis of an Issue essay
- One 30-minute Analysis of an Argument essay
- Two 30-minute Verbal Reasoning sections
- Two 35-minute Quantitative Reasoning sections

The Verbal Reasoning sections test your skills on three different types of questions:

- Text Completion
- Sentence Equivalence
- Reading Comprehension

The Quantitative Reasoning sections measure your prowess in four areas:

- Basic Math
- Algebra
- Geometry
- Data Analysis

What Exactly Is New About the GRE?

The GRE has been around in one form or another for decades, and this newest version represents the latest set of "improvements" on the test. The following are the most significant differences between the current GRE and the former GRE:

- The old GRE was adaptive by question, which means that your performance on one question influenced the selection of the next one, and you couldn't skip or go back to questions. The new GRE is adaptive by section. This means that the difficulty of the second section depends upon your performance on the first, but you can jump around within a section.
- The new test is longer; while the old test was 2 hours and 30 minutes long, as we previously mentioned, the new test is a bloated 3 hours and 40 minutes—and that's without any introductory modules or an experimental section.
- You get to use an on-screen calculator on the GRE now!
- There are a bunch of new question types, including multiple-choice questions, multiple-choice questions with more than one answer, fill-in-the-blank questions, select-in-passage questions, and other strange-looking questions.
- The new test has a new scoring system; the old test was graded on the same 200–800 scale as the SAT, but the new test is graded on a 130–170 scale.
- Some of the types of questions have been eliminated, including antonyms and analogies.

Need more info? Check out the DVD.

So why was the test changed? Well, ETS, the company that makes the GRE, claims that the changes were made to "increase the validity of the test, address security concerns, increase worldwide access to the test, [and] make better use of advances in technology and psychometric design."

We at The Princeton Review are a bit reluctant to trust the word of ETS, though. While the test writers claim that the new GRE will be a more valid measure of student ability and will allow graduate schools to better gauge their applicants, we're not convinced. After all, the test is now longer and less convenient to take, and it contains a number of new question types that have yet to be tested in depth.

WHY DO SCHOOLS REQUIRE IT?

Even though you will pay ETS $160 to take the GRE, it is important to note that you are not their primary customer. Their primary customers are the admissions offices at graduate programs across the United States. ETS provides admissions professionals with two important services. The first is a number, your GRE score. Everyone who takes the test gets a number.

Applicants could come from all over the world and will certainly have an enormous range in academic and professional experience. How does one compare a senior in college with a 32-year-old professional who has been out of college working in a different industry for the past 10 years? A GRE score is the only part of the application that allows for an apples-to-apples comparison among all applicants.

The second service that ETS provides is mailing lists. That's right; they will sell your name. You can opt out, but when you sit down to take the test, ETS will ask you a whole bunch of questions about your educational experience, family background, race, and gender, as well as other biographical data. All of this information goes into their database. In fact, ETS is one of the most important sources of potential applicants that many graduate programs have.

Another reason for the GRE is that it ensures that most applicants to graduate school are qualified. It helps to weed out the people who might be considering grad school, but who can't get their act together enough to fill out applications. It is difficult for admissions committees to make a decision between a candidate with a 3.0 and a 3.2 GPA from drastically different schools and in two different majors. A GRE score, on the other hand, provides a quick and easy way for busy admissions offices to whittle a large applicant pool down to size. When you ask a program how important the GRE score is to the application, they may say, "it depends" or "not very" and that may be true as long as your score is in the top half. If your score is in the bottom half, however, it may mean that your application never gets seen.

So the GRE may have little relevance to any particular field of study you might be pursuing, but as long as it helps graduate programs uncover potential candidates, and as long as it is the only tool available to compare a diverse candidate pool, the GRE is here to stay.

WHO IS ETS?

Like most standardized tests in this country, the GRE is created and administered by the Educational Testing Service (ETS), a big, tax-exempt, private company located in New Jersey. ETS publishes the GRE under the sponsorship of the Graduate Record Examinations Board, which is an organization affiliated with the Association of Graduate Schools and the Council of Graduate Schools in the United States.

ETS is also the organization that brings you the SAT, the Test of English as a Foreign Language (TOEFL), the National Teacher Examination (NTE), and licensing and certification exams in dozens of fields, including hair styling, plumbing, and golf.

TEST DAY

The GRE is administered at Thompson Prometric Centers. This is a company that specializes in administering tests on computer. They administer citizenship exams, professional health certifications, dental exams, accounting exams, and hundreds of other exams on computer. As professional proctors, they are a particularly humorless lot. When you arrive at the center, they will check your ID, give you a clipboard with a form to fill out, and hand you a locker key. Despite the fact that they already have your information, you will be asked to fill out a long form on paper. This form includes an entire paragraph that you have to copy over—in cursive (they specify this)—that states that you are who you say you are and that you are taking the test for admissions purposes. This process will take you about ten minutes, and you can complete it while you wait for them to call you into the testing room. The locker is for all of your personal belongings, including books, bags, phones, bulky sweaters, and sometimes even watches. You are not allowed to take anything with you into the testing room.

When they call you into the testing room, they will first take a photo of you, and, in some cases, fingerprint you before you go in. They will give you four or six sheets of scratch paper and two sharpened pencils with erasers. Then they lead you into the room where someone will start your test for you. The room itself will hold three or four rows of standard corporate cubicles, each with a monitor and keyboard. There will be other people in the room taking different tests than the GRE. Some of these tests have oral components, so people may be talking into microphones. Because of the noise, you will be provided with optional headphones.

Test Day Tips

- Dress in layers, so that you'll be comfortable regardless of whether the room is cool or warm.
- Don't bother to take a calculator; you're not allowed to use your own—just the one on the screen.
- Be sure to have breakfast, or lunch, depending on when your test is scheduled (but don't eat anything weird). Take it easy on the liquids and the caffeine.
- Do a few GRE practice problems beforehand to warm up your brain. Don't try to tackle difficult new questions, but go through a few questions that you've done before to help you review the problem-solving strategies for each section of the GRE. This will also help you put your "game-face" on and get you into test mode.

What to Take to the Test Center:
1. Your registration ticket
2. A photo ID and one other form of ID
3. A reliable watch
4. Several pencils
5. A snack

 Need more info? Check out the DVD.

- Make sure to take photo identification to the test center. Acceptable forms of identification include your driver's license, photo-bearing employee ID cards, and valid passports.
- If you registered by mail, you must also take the authorization voucher sent to you by ETS.
- Stretch, drink some water, go to the bathroom, and do whatever you need to do in order to be prepared to sit for this four-hour test.

TEST STRUCTURE

While your test structure may vary, you should expect to see something like this when you sit down to take the exam:

The first section of the test collects all of your biographical information. If you fill this out, you will start getting mail from programs that have bought your name from ETS. In general, this is not a bad thing. If you don't want them to sell your name, or you don't want to spend the time answering their questions, you can click on a box that tells ETS not to share your information.

Next, you will get a tutorial. If you have taken practice tests in a similar computer setting and you feel comfortable, you can skip this section. Remember: The GRE is a four-hour exam. Save your brain-time and your eyeball-time for when it counts. The tutorial will tell you how to use a mouse, how to click on a button, and how to scroll. Chances are that you know this already. At this point, you have probably spent between ten and twenty-five minutes working at the computer, and you haven't even seen a scored question yet.

Once all of that is done, you will begin your first scored section, the essays. Your two essays will be back to back. You have thirty minutes for each essay. If you know for sure that your programs don't care about the essay score, click out of this section. Immediately after your second essay, you will get your first multiple-choice section. It may be math or verbal. You will have a one-minute break between sections. Here is the structure of the test:

Section	Time	# of Questions
Biographical Information	+/− 10 minutes	–
Tutorial	+/− 10 minutes	–
Issue Essay	30 minutes	1
Argument Essay	30 minutes	1
Section 1	30 or 35 minutes	approximately 20
Break	10 minutes	–
Section 2	30 or 35 minutes	approximately 20
Section 3	30 or 35 minutes	approximately 20
Section 4	30 or 35 minutes	approximately 20
Section 5	30 or 35 minutes	approximately 20
Possible Research Section	Optional	Depends
Select Schools/Programs	5 minutes	Up to 4
Accept Scores	1 minute	–
Receive Scores	1 minute	–

Here are some things to keep in mind:

- You will see five multiple-choice sections, but only four will count. The fifth is an "experimental" section. It can come at any time after the essays. At the end of the exam, you will know, based on the number of math or verbal sections, if the experimental section was math or verbal, but you will not know which section will not count toward your score.
- Math Sections are 35 minutes. They have approximately 20 questions. The exact number may vary by one or two. If your experimental section is math, your test will be five minutes longer than someone whose experimental section is verbal.
- Verbal sections are 30 minutes. They have approximately 20 questions. The exact number may vary by one or two.
- The 10-minute break always comes after the third section. You have a 1-minute break between each of the other sections.
- You may or may not get a research section. If you do, it will come last; it does not count toward your score, and it is optional.
- You must accept your scores and, if you choose, send your scores to selected programs prior to seeing your scores.
- If you choose not to accept your scores, neither you nor any program will ever see them.
- You may choose to send your scores to up to four graduate programs on the day of the test. This service is included in your testing fee.

The Experimental Section

When most companies want to test a new product, they provide free samples, test it on animals, or pay for some user testing. Not ETS. ETS uses the experimental section of the test to assess new questions that it will give to later testers.

Research Section

At the end of the test, you may also have an unscored Research section. At the beginning of this section, you will be told that it is an unscored Research section, and that it will be used only to help develop and test questions for the GRE. If you want to skip it, you have the option of skipping it. You may be offered some sort of prize to induce you to take it, but by that point in the test you will probably be exhausted. If you're offered a Research section, just go ahead and decline, get your scores, and go home.

The Tutorial and the 10-Minute Break

Start to finish, the GRE is about a four-hour experience. In normal life, you don't do anything for four hours straight. You get up, you go to the bathroom, you check your e-mail, you grab something to drink. You're lucky if you can sleep for four uninterrupted hours. Taking a four-hour multiple-choice test, therefore, does not come easily. Anything you can do to cut down on the amount of time you spend staring at that computer screen is a good thing. This starts with the tutorial. You should have taken practice tests prior to the real thing, so feel free to skip the tutorial altogether. Save yourself the eyeball time.

You are given one minute between sections except after section three, when you get a 10-minute break. During this break, stand up, leave the testing room, leave the testing center, and go walk around. Go the bathroom, splash water on your face, wave your arms around. You want to re-oxygenate your brain. The goal, as much as it is possible, is to hit your brain's reset button. When you sit back down for section four, you want it to be as if you are just sitting down at that computer for the first time that day. They don't give you much on this test, so you want to take full advantage of all that you can. That means making the most of your break.

Accepting and Sending Your Scores

Before you see your scores, you will be given the opportunity to cancel your scores. There are very few reasons to do so. First, if you cancel your scores, you will never see your scores and you will have to go through the whole experience (and pay another $160) again. Second, the GRE is a tough test, but scores are curved. Most people believe that they are doing worse than they actually are. And third, most programs will look at the highest scores on record. You might as well accept your scores. If you don't get the scores you need, you will have to take the test again anyway. At least give yourself a chance to get it right the first time around. If you are not sure how the admissions folks will view multiple scores, call them up beforehand and ask. This is a legitimate question. Knowing that they will look at only the highest scores also takes a ton of pressure off your first sitting. It's nice to know that if something goes wrong, you can always take the test again.

The same goes for sending your scores. The minute you walk out of the testing center, ETS will charge you $20 every time you want to send off a set of scores. You might as well max out the ones they give you on test day. You will have to send your scores before you see your scores, but again, there is little downside to sending them. If you can't get into your first-choice school with your first set of scores, you have to take the test again, no matter what. When you send your new and better scores, schools will see both sets of scores anyway.

WHAT DOES A GRE SCORE LOOK LIKE?

Every GRE score has two components: a scaled score and a percentile rank. As we previously mentioned, GRE scores fall on a 130–170 point scale. However, your percentile rank is more important than your scaled score. Your percentile rank indicates how your GRE scores compare to those of other test takers. For example, a scaled score of 150 on the GRE translates to roughly the 50th percentile, meaning that you scored better than 50 out of every 100 test takers—and worse than the other 50 percent of test takers. A score of 150 is about average, while scores of 162 and above are very competitive. Get the latest reported scores and percentiles at **PrincetonReview.com** and at **www.gre.org**, the official ETS website for the GRE.

The essays are scored a little differently than are the Verbal and Quantitative sections. All essays receive a scaled score of 0–6, in half-point increments. The corresponding percentiles are:

Score	Analytical Writing Percentile
6	96
5.5	86
5	71
4.5	52
4	32
3.5	17
3	7
2.5	3
2	1
1.5	0
1	0
0.5	0

In other words, a score of 5 on the essay portion of the GRE means you performed better than 71 percent of test takers.

Remember that the new GRE may be new for you, but it is new for the admissions folks as well. For years now they have been used to thinking about a 500-level or a 600-level applicant. Now they will have to think about a 142-level applicant. Also, scores are good for five years, so programs will be receiving both old and new scores for many years before the transition is complete. During this changeover, admissions departments are likely to rely far more heavily on percentiles than on scores.

How Much Does the GRE Matter?

The simple answer is "It depends." Some programs consider the GRE very important, while others view it as more of a formality. Because the GRE is used for such a wide range of graduate studies, the relative weight it is given will vary from field to field and from school to school. A master's program in English literature will not evaluate the GRE the same way as a PhD program in physics, but it's hard to predict what the exact differences will be. A physics department may care more about the Math score than the Verbal score, but given that nearly all of its applicants will probably have high Math scores, a strong Verbal score might make you stand out and help you gain admission.

Do Your Research

GRE scores are used in a number of different ways. The first step in figuring out how to prepare for the GRE is figuring out how your scores will be used. The only way to do that is to contact the programs to which you plan to apply. Larger programs may have many of these questions already spelled out on their websites. Smaller programs, on the other hand, may not want to be pinned down to specific answers, and the answers may change from year to year. If you are applying to a smaller program, you will have to dig a bit deeper to get answers to some of these questions. Here are some things you should be asking:

1. **What scores do I need to be accepted?** The answer to this question is always "It depends." The GRE is not the only part of the application, and the quality of the applicant pool varies from year to year. Nevertheless, you need to have a target score so you can figure out how much work you need to put in between now and test day. If the school doesn't have or won't quote you a cutoff score, see if you can at least find out the average scores for last year's incoming class.

2. **Will you look at all parts of my score?** Some programs may care about your math score, but not your verbal score, and vice versa. Many programs don't use the essay scores at all. If a program doesn't care about your math or your essay score, then you know exactly where to put your prep time.

3. **Are scores used for anything else?** If your scores are to be used for placement or for scholarship, it would be good to know that now, while you still have time to prepare.

4. **How important are my scores?** In many ways, the importance of scores is a function of how competitive the program is. The scores may not matter much, but if it is a competitive program, every number will count.

5. **What do you do with multiple scores?** Depending upon your first scores, you may have to take the test a second time. It would be good to know, however, the importance of that first score. If a school is going to take the highest score, then you can relax a bit on test one, knowing that you can take it again if you need to.

In any case, remember that the GRE is only one part of an application to grad school. Admissions officers also consider many other factors, including:

- Undergraduate transcripts (i.e., your GPA, relevant courses, and the quality of the school you attended)
- Work experience
- Any research or work you've done in that academic field
- Subject GREs (for certain programs)
- Essays (Personal Statements or other essays)
- Recommendations
- Interviews

The GRE can be a significant part of your graduate school application (which is why you bought this book), but it certainly isn't the only part.

SCHEDULING A TEST

You can schedule a test session for the GRE by calling 800-GRE-CALL or by registering online at **www.gre.org**. You can also register through a local testing center (the list of centers is available online). After you get the list of local testing centers from ETS, you can call the one nearest you and set up an appointment. You can also call ETS at 609-776-7670 or send them an email at gre-info@ets.org to ask any general questions you have about the GRE.

Students registering to take the exam in August or September of 2011 may be eligible for a 50% discount on testing fees. Check **www.gre.org** for the latest pricing details. If you are not eligible for the discount, the test fee is likely to be $160, but this may change. Again, check **www.gre.org** for the latest pricing.

Note: If you take the test between August 1 and October 31, 2011, you will not receive your official scores, nor will schools receive official scores, until mid-November.

Computer Testing Facts

- You can take the GRE almost any day—morning or afternoon, weekday or weekend. Appointments are scheduled on a first-come, first-served basis. You may take the test only once per calendar month.

- There's no real deadline for registering for the test (technically, you can register the day before). But there's a limited number of seats available on any given day and centers do fill up, sometimes weeks in advance. It's a good idea to register in advance, to give yourself at least a couple of weeks of lead time.

- The GRE is technically simple. Selecting an answer and moving to the next question involves three easy steps. All you need to do is point the mouse arrow at the answer and click, then click the "Next" button, and then click the "Answer Confirm" button to confirm your choice.

- You don't have a physical test booklet, which makes it impossible to write directly on the problems themselves (to underline text, cross out answer choices, etc.). Thus, all of your work must be done on scratch paper. Although the amount of scratch paper you may use is unlimited, requesting additional paper takes time. You should be efficient and organized in how you use it; learning to use your scratch paper effectively is one of the keys to scoring well on the GRE.

- When you've finished taking the test, you will be given the option to accept or cancel your scores. Of course, you have to make this decision before you learn what the scores are. If you choose to cancel your scores, they cannot be reinstated, and you will never learn what they were. No refunds are given for canceled scores, and your GRE report will reflect that you took the test on that day and canceled (though this shouldn't be held against you). If you choose to accept your scores, they cannot be canceled afterward. We suggest that unless you are absolutely certain you did poorly, you accept your score.

- You will receive your Verbal and Math scores the instant you finish the exam (provided that you choose not to cancel your score), but your Analytical Writing scores and "official" percentile scores for all three sections won't get to you until a few weeks later, in the mail. You will not see your actual test ever again unless you make a special effort. ETS offers the GRE Diagnostic Service (**grediagnostic.ets.org**) as a free option for test takers to have a limited review of their tests. This service allows you to see how many questions you missed and where they fell on the test, but you cannot review the actual questions. The diagnostic service also claims to let you know the difficulty of the questions you missed, but the scale used—a simple scale of 1 to 5—is not particularly useful.

Accommodated Testing

If you require accommodated testing, please see the Appendix at the end of this book. It contains information on the forms you'll need to fill out and procedures you'll need to follow to apply for accommodated testing. Be sure to start that application process well in advance of when you want to take your test, as it can take many weeks to complete.

HOW TO USE THIS BOOK

This book is chock full of our fail-safe GRE test-taking techniques, some of which, at first, might seem to go against your gut instincts. In order to take full advantage of our methods, however, you'll have to trust them and use them consistently and faithfully.

Make sure to use the techniques on all of the practice problems you do and to thoroughly review the explanations for all of the questions—even the ones you get right. That way, the techniques will become second nature to you, and you'll have no problem using them on test day.

If you want to change your score, you have to change the way you take the test.

Practice for Technique, Not for Result

There is a finite amount of GRE material available in the world. Once you have used it all up, that's it. You don't get any more. Many people will work through the books, doing problems, looking for answers. When they get a problem right, they are happy. When they get a problem wrong, they are frustrated, and then they go on to the next problem. The problem with this approach is that you can churn through lots and lots of questions without ever actually getting better at taking the GRE. The techniques you use and the way you solve a problem are what matters. The results just tell you how you did. When you are practicing, always focus on your approach. When you get good at the techniques, your score will take care of itself. If you focus on just the results, you do nothing more than reinforce the way you are taking the test right now.

Additional Resources

In addition to the material in the book, we offer a number of other resources to aid you during your GRE preparation.

This book includes a DVD, which contains a number of live instructor lessons and demonstrations of the some of the key techniques in this book.

Need more info? Check out the DVD.

With your purchase of this book, you gain access to the many helpful tools on The Princeton Review website as well as to additional lessons and practice GRE tests, which will help reinforce what you've learned in the book. Go to **PrincetonReview.com/cracking** to register. **PrincetonReview.com** also contains a ton of useful information on graduate programs, financial aid, and everything else related to graduate school.

Real GREs

The practice problems in this book are designed to simulate the questions that appear on the real GRE. Part of your preparation, however, should involve working with real GRE problems. Working with real questions from past GRE exams is the best way to practice our techniques and prepare for the test. However, the only source of real GREs is the publisher of the test, ETS, which so far has refused to let anyone (including us) license actual questions from old tests. Therefore, we strongly recommend that you obtain *GRE POWERPREP® II Software—Test Preparation for the GRE General Test*, which includes a retired question pool presented in two computer-adaptive tests. A CD-ROM version of this software is sent to all test takers when they register for the test, and you can also download *POWERPREP II* for free at **www.gre.org**. In addition, you should purchase the book *Practicing to Take the Revised GRE General Test*, which contains retired math and verbal questions from seven paper-and-pencil GREs. You can buy this book from any large bookstore or order it online at **www.gre.org**.

Of course, the GREs in the book are paper-and-pencil tests, so use them to practice content. Whatever you're using, always practice with scratch paper. As you prepare for the GRE, work through every question you do as if the question is being presented on a computer screen. This means not writing anything on the problems themselves. No crossing off answers, no circling, no underlining. Copy everything to scratch paper and do your work there. You can't give yourself a crutch in your preparation that you won't have on the actual test.

MAKING A SCHEDULE

The GRE, like other standardized tests, is not a test for which you can cram. While you may have fond memories from your college days of spending the night before the midterm with a pot of coffee and a 500-page economics textbook, that strategy won't be as effective on the GRE. Why? Because, by and large, the GRE is a test of patterns, not of facts. This book does its best to reveal those patterns to you, but without sufficient time to practice and absorb the information in this book, your GRE score is not likely to improve. Thus, you should allow an adequate amount of time to fully prepare for the GRE.

Otherwise, you should allow yourself somewhere between 4 and 12 weeks to prepare for the GRE. Obviously we can't know exactly where you are in terms of your starting score, your target score, and the amount of time you can devote to studying, but in our experience, 4 weeks is about the minimum amount of time you'd want to spend, while 12 weeks is about the maximum. There are a number of reasons for these suggested preparation times. Attempting to prepare in fewer than 4 weeks typically does not allow sufficient time to master the techniques presented in this book. As you'll see, some of our approaches are counterintuitive and take some getting used to. Without adequate practice time, you may not have full confidence in the techniques. Additionally, vocabulary is part of the Verbal section of the GRE and it's difficult to substantially increase your vocabulary in a short period of time. Finally, as mentioned before, the GRE contains a number of patterns, and the more time you spend studying the test, the better you will be at recognizing these patterns.

On the other hand, spending an inordinate amount of time preparing for the GRE can have its downside as well. The first concern is a purely practical one: There is a finite amount of GRE practice material available. Budgeting six months of preparation time is unproductive because you'll run out of materials in less than half that time. Finally, spreading the material out over a long period of time may result in your forgetting some of the lessons from the beginning of your studies. It's better to work assiduously and consistently over a shorter time period than to dilute your efforts over a long time frame.

STAY UP TO DATE

We at The Princeton Review will continue to learn all about the new GRE as it evolves. As you prepare for your GRE, make sure you periodically check both our website at **PrincetonReview.com** and the GRE website at **www.gre.org** for the latest updates and information about the test.

Summary

o The GRE is a 3-hour, 40-minute exam used by graduate schools to rank applicants.

o The GRE tests your mathematical, verbal, and writing abilities.

o The GRE has been updated to include new question types, new content, a new scoring system, and a new way of delivering the test.

o The importance of your GRE score varies from program to program. Schools also consider your undergraduate record, your personal essays, and your relevant experience.

o GRE tests can be scheduled online at **www.gre.org**.

Chapter 2
General Strategy

This chapter contains some basic advice to get you into the Princeton Review mindset. You'll learn some core test-taking strategies to help you maximize your score. In addition, you'll see some of the different question formats you will probably encounter on test day.

Need more info? Check out the DVD.

CRACKING THE SYSTEM

The GRE is not an intelligence test. Although ETS claims that the GRE measures "critical thinking, analytical writing, verbal reasoning, and quantitative reasoning skills that have been acquired over a long period of time," that isn't quite true. What the GRE really measures is how well you take the GRE. The first step to bettering your GRE score is realizing that you can improve your score, in many cases substantially, by familiarizing yourself with the test and by practicing the techniques in this book.

I Thought the GRE Was Coach-Proof

ETS would have you believe that its tests are coach-proof, but that is simply untrue. In many ways, taking a standardized test is a skill and, as with any skill, you can become more proficient at it by both practicing and following the advice of a good teacher. Think of your GRE preparation as if you were practicing for a piano recital or a track meet; you wouldn't show up at the concert hall or track field without having put in hours of practice beforehand (at least we hope you wouldn't!). If you want to get a good score on the GRE, you'll have to put in the necessary preparation time.

Why Should I Listen to The Princeton Review?

Quite simply, because we monitor the GRE. Our teaching methods were developed through exhaustive analysis of all of the available GREs and careful research into the methods by which standardized tests are constructed. Our focus is on the basic concepts that will enable you to attack any problem, strip it down to its essential components, and solve it in as little time as possible.

Think Like the Test Writers

You might be surprised to learn that the GRE isn't written by distinguished professors, renowned scholars, or graduate school admissions officers. For the most part, it's written by ordinary ETS employees, sometimes with freelance help from local graduate students. You have no reason to be intimidated by these people.

As you become more familiar with the test, you will also develop a sense of "the ETS mentality." This is a predictable kind of thinking that influences nearly every part of nearly every ETS exam. By learning to recognize the ETS mentality, you'll earn points even when you aren't sure why an answer is correct. You'll inevitably do better on the test by learning to think like the people who wrote it.

The Only "Correct" Answer Is the One That Earns You Points

The instructions on the GRE tell you to select the "best" answer to each question. ETS calls them "best" answers, or "credited" responses, instead of "correct" answers to protect itself from the complaints of test takers who might be tempted to quarrel with ETS's judgment. Remember that you have to choose from the choices ETS gives you, and sometimes, especially on the Verbal section, you might not love any of them. Your job is to find the one answer for which ETS gives credit.

Cracking the System

"Cracking the system" is our phrase for getting inside the minds of the people who write these tests. This emphasis on earning points rather than finding the "correct" answer may strike you as somewhat cynical, but it is crucial to doing well on the GRE. After all, the GRE leaves you no room to make explanations or justifications for your responses.

You'll do better on the GRE by putting aside your feelings about real education and surrendering yourself to the strange logic of the standardized test.

GENERAL STRATEGIES

Take the Easy Test First

Within a section, each question counts equally toward your score. There will inevitably be questions you are great at and questions you don't like. The beauty of the GRE is that there is no need to bow to Phoenician numerical hegemony; you can answer questions in any order you like. The question you can nail in 25 seconds is worth just as much as the question that will torture you for minutes on end. To maximize your score, leave the questions you don't like for last. If you are going to run out of time anywhere—and unless you are shooting for a 160 or higher, you should be running out of time—make sure that the questions that get chopped off are the ones you didn't want to answer anyway.

This method is called Take the Easy Test First. Skip early and skip often. Doing so will result in two passes through an individual section. On the first pass, cherry pick. Answer the questions you like. Get all of those easy points in the bank before time starts running short. You know that the hard questions—or the ones that you don't like—are going to take more time. Also, although you should never rush, everyone starts to feel the pressure of the clock as time starts running low.

This is NOT a test of intelligence!

Need more info? Check out the DVD.

This is often when mistakes happen. Leave those difficult, time-consuming questions for the end of the test. If you run out of time or make some mistakes at that point, it won't matter because these are low percentage questions for you anyway.

Use the Mark Function

On your first pass through the questions, if you see a question you don't like, a question that looks hard, or a question that looks time consuming, you're going to walk on by and leave it for the end. Sometimes, however, a question that looks easy turns out to be more troublesome than you thought. The question may be trickier than it first appeared. On the other hand, you may have simply misread the question, and it seems hard only because you're working with the wrong information. From start to finish, the GRE is nearly a four-hour test. Over four hours your brain is going to get tired. When that happens, misreading a question is virtually inevitable. Once you read a problem wrong, it is almost impossible to unread the problem and see it right. As long as you are still in the problem, you could read it ten times in a row and you will read it the same wrong way each time.

Whether a question is harder than it first appeared, or made harder by the fact that you missed a key phrase or piece of information, the approach you've taken is not working. This is where the Mark button comes in.

Reset your brain by walking away from the problem, but Mark the question before you do. Do two or three other questions, and then return to the marked problem. When you walk away, your brain doesn't just forget the problem, it keeps on processing in the back ground. The distraction of the other questions helps your brain to consider the question from some other angles. When you return to the problem, you may find that the part that gave you so much trouble the first time is now magically clear. If the problem continues to give you trouble, walk away again.

Staying with a problem when you're stuck burns time but yields no points. You might spend two, three, five, or even six minutes on a problem but still be no closer to the answer. Spending five minutes to get one point will not get you enough points on a 30- or 35-minute section. In the five minutes you spend on a problem that you've misread, you could nail three or four easier questions. When you return to the question that gave you trouble, there is a good chance that you will spot your error, and the path to the correct answer will become clear. If it doesn't become clear, walk away again. Any time you encounter resistance on the test, do not keep pushing; bend like a reed and walk away. Use the Mark button to facilitate this key skill. Skip early and often so that you always have questions to distract your brain when you get stuck.

Review

Within a single section you can mark an answered or unanswered question and return to it later. In fact you can skip any question you like and return to any question at any time you like. Navigating around a section is easy with the new Review Screen, which looks like this:

Question Number	Status	Marked
1	Not Answered	
2	Not Answered	
3	Not Answered	
4	Not Answered	
5	Not Answered	
6	Not Answered	
7	Answered	
8	Answered	
9	Answered	✔
10	Answered	✔
11	Answered	
12	Not Answered	

Simply click on a question and hit the button marked "Go To Question," and you will return directly to that question. This opens up a whole new realm of strategic opportunities for the savvy test taker.

Pacing

Speed kills on the GRE. The clock has a way of infecting your brain. Just knowing that there is a ticking clock, however, provokes mistakes. The trick is to take each section as if there is no clock. As long as you are skipping the hard ones and using the Mark button and coming back every time you run into trouble, you should get very few questions in a section wrong. Wrong answers drag your score down and often take up even more time than the right ones!

Remember that it is not the number of question that you answer that gives you your score; it is the number of questions you answer correctly. Accuracy is everything. Ignore the clock. Slow down and work for accuracy only. If you run into a brick wall, don't keep spending time; do an easier question and come back. The minute you try to go faster, however, your accuracy will go down and bring your score along with it.

Accuracy is all that matters. Walk away often.

There is only one exception to this, and that is the last two minutes of a section. A skipped question and a wrong answer count the same. In other words, there is no penalty for "guessing" on a question you don't know. When two minutes remain on your clock, stop what you're doing and bubble in answers to any remaining unanswered questions. Use the Review button to quickly see which questions you haven't answered. A few lucky guesses will pay off. If you don't get any of them right, no harm done.

To avoid careless mistakes and to make the best use of your time, we suggest the following:

1. **Be Aware of Your Personal Order of Difficulty.** Spend your time on the questions that are easiest for you. Work through them methodically and accurately and collect points.
2. **Use the Two-Pass System.** The Two-Pass system involves taking each section in two parts, or passes. During the first pass, focus on all the questions that you're comfortable with. On the second pass, return to the tougher questions and do the best you can on them in the remaining time.

GENERAL STRATEGY: POE—PROCESS OF ELIMINATION

Because there are many more wrong answers on the GRE than there are credited answers, on some of the more difficult questions (those you do on your second pass) you'll actually be better served not by trying to find the *best* answer, but instead by finding the wrong answers and using POE, Process of Elimination.

ETS Doesn't Care How You Get the Best Answer

Remember when you were in high school, and even if you got a question wrong on a test, your teacher gave you partial credit? For example, maybe you used the right formula on a math question, but miscalculated and got the wrong result, but your teacher gave you some credit because you understood the concept?

Well, those days are over. ETS doesn't care how you get an answer; it cares only about whether or not you click on the right answer choice or choices. You might as well benefit from this by getting questions right without really knowing how to do them, using POE. POE is the way to go: Learn it, live it, love it.

Also, keep in mind that on multiple-choice, multiple-answer questions, you must click on all the correct answers in order to get credit. If there are three correct responses, but you click on only two of them, you will not get any points.

The Importance of Wrong Answers

By using POE, you will be able to improve your score on the GRE by looking for wrong answers instead of right ones, on questions you find difficult. Why? Because, once you've eliminated the wrong ones, picking the right one can be a piece of cake.

Wrong answers on standardized multiple-choice tests are known in the testing industry as "distractors," or "trap answers." They are called distractors because their purpose is to distract test takers away from correct choices. Trap answers are specifically designed to appeal to test takers. Oftentimes, they're the answers that seem to scream out "pick me!" as you work through a question. However, these attractive answers are often incorrect.

Remembering this simple fact can be an enormous help to you as you sit down to take the test. By learning to recognize distractors, you will greatly improve your score.

Improve Your Odds Indirectly

Every time you're able to eliminate an incorrect choice on a GRE question, you improve your odds of finding the best answer; the more incorrect choices you eliminate, the better your odds.

For this reason, some of our test-taking strategies are aimed at helping you arrive at ETS's answer indirectly. Doing this will make you much more successful at avoiding the traps laid in your path by the test writers. This is because most of the traps are designed to catch unwary test takers who try to approach the problems directly.

POE and Guessing

If you guessed blindly on a five-choice GRE problem, you would have a 1-in-5 chance of picking ETS's answer. Eliminate one incorrect choice, and your chances improve to one in four. Eliminate three, and you have a fifty-fifty chance of earning points by guessing. Get the picture? You must answer each question to get to the next one, so you'll have to guess sometimes. Why not improve your odds?

Guess, but guess intelligently.

Use That Paper!

In order for POE to work, it's crucial that you keep track of what choices you're eliminating. By crossing out a clearly incorrect choice, you permanently eliminate it from consideration. If you don't cross it out, you'll keep considering it. Crossing out incorrect choices can make it much easier to find the "credited response," because there will be fewer places where it can hide. But how can you cross anything out on a computer screen?

By crossing out a clearly incorrect choice, you permanently eliminate it from consideration.

Even though on the GRE the answer choices have empty bubbles next to them, you're going to pretend that they are labeled A, B, C, D, and E (and so are we, throughout this book).

A B C D E	A B C D E	A B C D E	A B C D E
A B C D E	A B C D E	A B C D E	A B C D E

Carve up at least a couple of pages (front and back) like this. This will give you a bunch of distinct work areas per page, and is especially helpful for the Math section; you don't want to get confused when your work from one question runs into your work from a previous question.

By doing this, you can physically cross off choices that you're eliminating. Do it every time you do a GRE question, in this book or anywhere else. Get used to not writing near the question, since you won't be able to on test day.

More About Scratch Paper

You'll get six sheets of scratch paper at the beginning of the test. If you run out, you can request more, but be aware that the proctor will take away your old scratch paper as he or she gives you the new paper. Also, if you're in the middle of a section, you'll have to put your hand in the air and wait for a proctor to notice it, enter the testing room, and give it to you. In short, don't be profligate with your scratch paper. Use it wisely and try to refresh your supply during the break. (If you're not sure what *profligate* means, look it up! ETS likes putting that word on the GRE.)

Double-Check

By training yourself to avoid careless errors, you will raise your score.

Get into the habit of double-checking all of your answers before you click on your answer choice—or answer choices. Make sure that you reread the directions and have done everything they asked you to—don't get the answer wrong just because you chose only one answer for a question that required you to choose two or more.

The only way to reliably avoid careless errors is to adopt habits that make them less likely to occur. Always check to see that you've transcribed information correctly to your scratch paper. Always read the problem at least twice and note any important parts that you might forget later. Always check your calculations. And always read the question one last time before selecting your answer.

Let It Go

Every time you begin a new section, focus on that section and put the last section you completed behind you. Don't think about that pesky synonym from an earlier section while a geometry question is on your screen. You can't go back, and besides, your impression of how you did on a section is probably much worse than reality.

Need more info? Check out the DVD.

The Week Before the Test

The week before the test is not the time for any major life changes. This is NOT the week to quit smoking, start smoking, quit drinking coffee, start drinking coffee, start a relationship, end a relationship, or quit a job. Business as usual, okay?

Now let's get cracking!

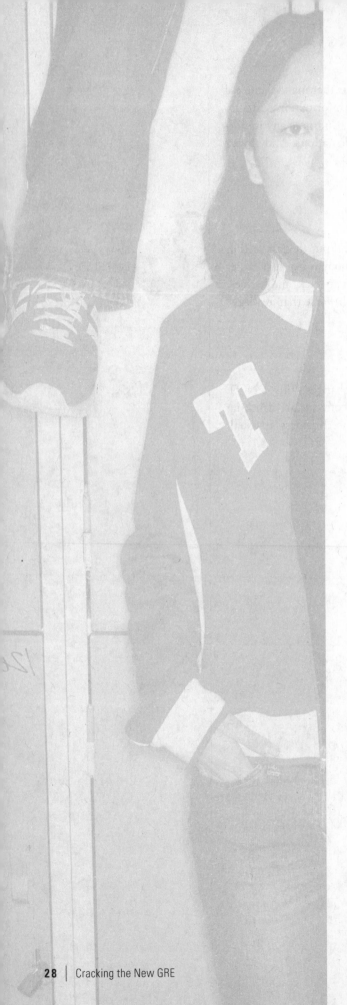

Summary

- You can increase your score on the GRE through practice and successful application of test-taking strategies.

- The GRE uses a variety of question formats throughout the test.

- Not all questions on the GRE are of equal difficulty. Your Personal Order of Difficulty should tell you which questions to spend time on and which to skip.

- Accuracy is better than speed. Slow down and focus on accumulating as many points as possible. Forcing yourself to work faster results in careless errors and lower scores.

- Process of Elimination is an extremely useful tool on the test. Use it to eliminate wrong answers and increase your odds of guessing correctly.

Part II
How to Crack the Verbal Section

Chapter 3
The Geography of
the Verbal Section

The Verbal section of the GRE is designed to test your verbal reasoning abilities. This chapter will explain what types of questions ETS uses to accomplish that. You'll also see how the concepts of Personal Order of Difficulty and Process of Elimination apply to the Verbal section. Finally, you'll learn what role vocabulary plays in achieving a good score on the Verbal section.

Need more
info? Check
out the DVD.

WHAT'S ON THE VERBAL SECTION

Now that ETS has redesigned the GRE, the company claims that the new Verbal section will accomplish the following:

- Place a greater emphasis on analytical skills and on understanding vocabulary in context rather than in isolation
- Use more text-based materials
- Contain a broader range of reading selections
- Test skills that are more closely aligned with those used in graduate school
- Expand the range of computer-enabled tasks

While those sound like lofty and admirable goals, what they really translate into are the following changes:

- There won't be questions that involve analogies or antonyms on this test, as there have been on past tests (and good riddance!).
- You'll see new question types that weren't on the old version of the test: Critical Reasoning questions and Sentence Equivalence (in which you search for synonyms—somewhat easier and more reasonable than the antonyms questions, but not by much).
- The test writers made minor tweaks to the Text Completion and Reading Comprehension questions (we'll get into how these are constructed later in this section).
- You'll see some wacky-looking question formats that you've probably never seen before.
- Though they say the new version of the test de-emphasizes vocabulary, there's no getting around the fact that the more vocabulary you know when you sit down to take the test, the better off you'll be.

Of course, ETS claims that the new GRE is a better and more valid test than the previous incarnation, but we have our doubts. For one, there hasn't been much testing done on the new question types. In other words, ETS hasn't extensively tried these questions out on test takers to see how well they evaluated knowledge or ability. Second, the new test is longer and less convenient for students—but more on that later. Suffice it to say that we're not totally convinced that this test represents an improvement over those of the past.

There are three types of questions on the verbal section of the test. They are:

Text Completions

These consist of a short section of text, between one and five sentences, with one to three blanks. A one-blank text completion will have five answer choices while a two-blank or three-blank text completion will have three choices per blank. Your job is to find the best word for each blank.

They look like this:

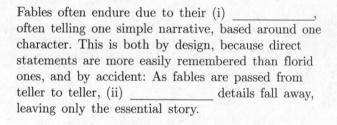

Fables often endure due to their (i) _____, often telling one simple narrative, based around one character. This is both by design, because direct statements are more easily remembered than florid ones, and by accident: As fables are passed from teller to teller, (ii) _____ details fall away, leaving only the essential story.

Blank (i)	Blank (ii)
bombast	superfluous
objectivity	requisite
simplicity	apocryphal

Reading Comprehension

Reading Comprehension makes up the lion's share of the verbal portion of the test. You will be given a passage that may vary in length from one to five paragraphs with one to five questions per passage. Reading comprehension questions might ask you for the main idea of the passage; they might ask about specific pieces of information in the passage; they might ask you about the structure or tone of a passage; they might ask you about vocabulary in the passage, the point of view of the author, or about the argument being made in the passage. The good news about reading comprehension questions is that they are rarely dependent upon vocabulary, and the answers are always in the passage.

There are three question formats:

Multiple Choice

Question 20 is based on this passage.

After examining the bodies of a dozen beached whales and finding evidence of bleeding around the animals' eyes and brains as well as lesions on their kidneys and livers, environmental groups fear that the Navy's use of sonar is causing serious harm to marine animals. A leading marine biologist reports that sonar induces whales to panic and surface too quickly, which causes nitrogen bubbles to form in their blood.

The argument above relies on which of the following assumptions?

○ Marine biologists have documented that other marine animals, including dolphins and sea turtles, have exhibited kidney and liver lesions.

○ No studies have been conducted on the possible detrimental effects of sonar on marine animals.

○ Whales in captivity panic only when exposed to man-made, rather than natural, sound waves.

○ The presence of nitrogen bubbles in the blood has been demonstrated to cause damage to various internal organs.

○ It is unlikely that the symptoms found in the beached whales could be caused by any known disease.

Select all that Apply

Questions 10 and 11 are based on this passage.

What was it about Oscar Wilde's only novel, *The Picture of Dorian Gray*, that caused it to create such an uproar when it was published in 1891? While critics attacked the quality of Wilde's formal elements, their denunciation merely masked the true concerns of many nineteenth-century critics. What these critics were actually railing against was the thematic content of Wilde's work, specifically his illustration of a lifestyle devoted to useless beauty. For many a nineteenth-century moralist, *The Picture of Dorian Gray* was nothing more than a primer for spiritual depravity. Wilde's ultimate sin was his leniency toward his protagonist, an unabashed hedonist. To the critics, allowing an evil character to escape his just desserts was an unforgivable sin. In their minds, Wilde's work was corrupting the genteel reading public by failing to show the proper consequences of immoral behavior.

Consider each of the choices separately and select **all** that apply.

The author of the passage would probably agree with which of the following statements?

☐ Most critics of Oscar Wilde's novel objected primarily to the lifestyle of its author.

☐ If *The Picture of Dorian Gray* were written in the twentieth century, the critical reaction would be less severe.

☐ Some critics of Wilde's *The Picture of Dorian Gray* believed that an author of a book had a moral responsibility to the book's audience.

Select in Passage

Question 16 is based on this passage.

Called by some the "island that time forgot," Madagascar is home to a vast array of unique, exotic creatures. One such animal is the aye-aye. First described by western science in 1782, it was initially categorized as a member of the order Rodentia. Further research then revealed that it was more closely related to the lemur, a member of the primate order. Since the aye-aye is so different from its fellow primates, however, it was given its own family: *Daubentoniidae*. The aye-aye has been listed as an endangered species and, as a result, the government of Madagascar has designated an island off the northeastern coast of Madagascar as a protected reserve for aye-ayes and other wildlife.

Click on the sentence that would most seriously weaken the author's claim that "this practice may result in the loss of a superb example of life's variety."

Sentence Equivalence

These are similar to text-completion questions. You will be given a single sentence with one blank and six answer choices. Your job is to select two words from the answer choices that could fit in the blank. Here's what they look like:

He was a man of few words, _____ around all but his closest friends.

- ☐ laconic
- ☐ garrulous
- ☐ ascetic
- ☐ taciturn
- ☐ tempestuous
- ☐ ambiguous

HOW IS THE GRE VERBAL SECTION STRUCTURED?

The GRE now has two scored multiple-choice verbal sections. Each will be 30 minutes long with 20 questions per section. The way you perform on one verbal section will affect the questions you see on the next verbal section (more on this later). Verbal sections tend to follow the same order. Roughly your first six questions will be Text Completion, your next five or six will be Reading Comprehension, followed by about four Sentence Equivalence, and then another four or five Reading Comprehension questions. In profile, your two verbal sections will look something like this:

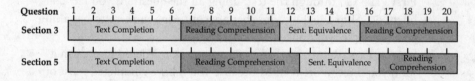

BASIC STRATEGIES FOR THE GRE VERBAL SECTION

Here are some strategies that will help you on the Verbal section. We'll show you how to use them as we go through specific question types in the chapters ahead, but for now read through the strategies and get a sense of what they are before moving on.

Scratch Paper

You may be tempted to do the verbal questions in your head. Don't. Use your scratch paper, not only for jotting down strategy, but also for POE. Always write down A, B, C, D, E on your scratch paper so you can physically cross out choices you're eliminating.

Personal Order of Difficulty

One very important thing to keep in mind as you go through the verbal section is that you can control which questions you do and when you do them. Once again, you're able to skip around the test, so do the questions in any order you like. If you come to a question that stumps you, skip it and move on to the next one. Go back to the hard ones at the end of the section if you have time—remember that all questions are worth the same number of points, so you won't get any more credit for answering a hard question than answering an easy one—use your time wisely.

We call this method the Two-Pass system. In the Two-Pass system, you do the following:

1. **First Pass:** Go through the test, doing all the questions you feel confident on. Skip any questions that are confusing or seem to be taking you a while to work out.
2. **Second Pass:** Return to the questions you skipped and give them a shot; you'll feel more relaxed because you'll have completed most of the section and done well on it, and you can settle in and give them your full attention.

Process of Elimination (POE)

One important point to keep in mind here is that on verbal questions, your goal is to find the "best" answer. Note that this doesn't mean the same thing as finding the "right" answer or the "correct" answer. On this section, it's essential that you get into the habit of considering every answer choice, even if you're pretty sure you've already found the answer. After all, there's no way of saying one answer is the "best" unless you've compared it to all the others.

Sometimes it's far easier to find the wrong answer to a verbal question than the right one; after all, statistically there are far more wrong answers on the test than correct ones. This is where the Process of Elimination comes into play. If you can recognize a bad answer and eliminate it, you will greatly increase your odds of choosing the right answer if you must guess on a question.

Intelligent guessing—guessing after eliminating at least one answer choice—is a good way to get the best GRE verbal score you can get. Consider the following question:

---

1 of 20

When studying human history, one must be aware that the _____ between historical periods are arbitrary; certainly none of the people alive at the time were aware of a shift from one era to another.

| judgments |
| ideologies |
| innovations |
| demarcations |
| episodes |

Here's How to Crack It

If you encountered this question on the GRE, you might not know what the best answer is (you'll learn how to approach questions like this in Chapter 4). However, you might see that some of the answers simply don't make sense. Choices (A), (B), and (C) don't seem to fit the sentence at all. By eliminating these wrong answers, you've suddenly given yourself a great chance of choosing the correct answer just by guessing, since only answer choices (D) and (E) are left. And if you realize that choice (E) doesn't make sense either, then you know the correct answer is (D), even if you're not sure what "demarcations" means. Sometimes it's easier to find the wrong answer than the right answer.

Need more info? Check out the DVD.

THE IMPORTANCE OF VOCABULARY

Although ETS says that vocabulary is de-emphasized on this test, having a wide vocabulary will still help you on the GRE. Text Completion questions and Sentence Equivalence questions rely heavily on vocabulary, and reading passages can and will contain some tough words in both the passages and in the answer choices.

To that end, working on improving your vocabulary can translate into higher scores on the GRE. We've provided you with the Hit Parade in Chapter 7; it's a list of words commonly used on the GRE, but that's only the beginning. As you read books and newspapers, watch movies or television, or talk to your smarter friends, keep track of any and all new vocabulary words you read or hear, write them down, look them up, and remember them. Chances are they'll come in handy on test day.

Three Kinds of Words

As you encounter difficult words throughout this book, put them in one of these three categories:

- **Words you know**—These are words you can define accurately. If you can give a definition of a word that's pretty close to the dictionary definition, then it is a word you know.
- **Words you sort of know**—These are words you've seen or heard before, or maybe even have used yourself, but can't define accurately. You may have a sense of how these words are used, but beware! Day-to-day usage is often different from the dictionary meaning of words, and the only meanings that count on the GRE are those given in the dictionary. ETS likes using words that have secondary meanings, and some of the words in this category may have secondary definitions that you're not aware of. You have to treat these words very differently from the words you can define easily and for which you know all the meanings. Every time you encounter a word you sort of know in this book, be sure to look it up in the dictionary and make it a word you know from then on.
- **Words you've never seen**—You can expect to see some words in this book you've never seen before. After you encounter a word like this, look it up! If it's been on the GRE one year, there's a good chance it will show up again.

GENERAL STRATEGIES FOR THE GRE VERBAL SECTION

Scratch Paper—Say No to Multitasking

Scratch paper is every bit as important on the verbal side of the test as it is on the math. When you answer a verbal question in your head, you are really doing two things at once. The first is evaluating each answer choice; the second is keeping track of which answer choices are still in and which ones you don't like. This is multitasking, and the problem with multitasking, studies have shown, is that you end up doing both tasks worse! Multitasking leads to inefficient use of time as you end up revisiting answer choices that you've already evaluated, and it leads to errors as you distract your brain with other tasks while making crucial choices.

The better approach is to engage your hand and take a load off your brain by parking your thinking on the page. The answer choices represent ETS's suggested answers. They are carefully designed to mislead the tired test taker. Because of this, you should always have a clear sense of what you're looking for before you get to the answer choices. When you do get to the answer choices, it's a simple assessment: Does it match your answer or not? This is an easy call to make. If the answer is a vocabulary word, either you know the word and it works, you know the word and it doesn't work, or you don't know the word. If it is a reading comprehension question, either the answer matches your answer, it does not match, or you're not sure. As you evaluate each answer choice, mark your assessment on your scratch paper. Verbal scratch paper looks like this:

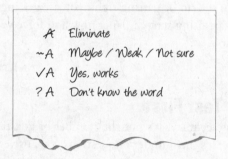

We will discuss different strategies for setting up scratch paper for specific question types later in the chapter, but there are four basic symbols you will use for all questions:

× **Eliminate**—When an answer choice is clearly wrong, get rid of it. Having it there as an option is nothing but a distraction, so make it go away.

~ **Maybe**—Don't be afraid of the Maybe. GRE students often get hung up considering a particular answer choice. On the first pass through the answer choices, this is time wasted. It is entirely possible that the other four answer choices are wrong, or that you find one that is clearly better. Before you invest too much time (too much time means more than 5 seconds) on any one answer choice, give it the *Maybe* and move on. You can always come back to it and give it more time *if* you have to, but you never want to give it more time *than* you have to. If you're not sure or you don't love it, just give it the *Maybe* and move on.

✔ **Yes, Works**—When you have one that works, give it the check mark.

? **Question Mark**—If you don't know the meaning of a word, mark it with a question mark. You must be honest with yourself here. You do yourself no favors by acting like you know a word more than you actually do. You cannot eliminate a word just because it looks bad. You don't have to pick it, but if you don't know it, you can't eliminate it.

You are taking a two-pass approach through the answer choices. On the first pass, it's a simple question of *Maybe* or *Gone?* Park your thinking on the page and nine out of ten times your scratch paper will be able to answer the question for you. If you have two question marks and a check, you're done. The check is your answer. If you have two maybes and a check, you're done; the check is your answer. If you have four eliminates and a question mark, the question mark is your answer.

Using scratch paper on the Verbal section is a habit. It's something you do every time. Over time, it should just become automatic. When you're working on a verbal question, your hand should be moving. This will save you time and mental effort. Remember that it is a four-hour exam, and over four hours, your brain will get tired. Saving mental effort makes a difference and helps to avoid mistakes. The job of the techniques is to help you with the hard problems, but it is also to ensure that the questions you should be getting right, you are getting right. Both jobs are equally important. Start using scratch paper now and force yourself to keep doing it until it becomes habit.

Take the Easy Test First

The GRE is all about accuracy. It's not the number of questions you answer that determines your score; it's the number of questions you answer correctly. It is more important to get questions correct than to get to answer all questions. Since all questions within a given section count equally toward your score, you might as well do the easy ones first. If you love text completion, but hate reading comprehension, then do the text completion first.

Work slowly. Work for accuracy. Skip often. When a question pops up that you don't like, click to the next one. You can always come back and answer it later, time provided, but take the easy test first. Invest your time in those questions you like. That way, when you run short on time, you have nothing left but the questions you don't like doing anyway. Another way to think about it is to play to your strengths. As you work through this book and learn new techniques, the types of questions you decide to skip might change. Just because they give you questions in a specific order doesn't mean you have to answer them in that order.

You are in control of question order. Take the easy test first!

Bend—Don't Push

Over a period of four hours, your brain will get tired. When that happens, you will misread a question, a sentence, or an answer choice. It is inevitable. When you go back and look at these questions later, you will smack your forehead and think, "That was so stupid! Why did I do that? That's not what it says at all. I thought…" Everyone has these moments. It happens because most of us no longer read things word for word. We read in chunks. We don't read words anymore; we recognize words. Sometimes, especially when our brains get tired, we get these chunks wrong or we recognize a different word. The problem is that once you have seen a question or a word wrong, it is all but impossible to un-see it and see it correctly.

The solution is to walk away. Distract your brain by working on a few other questions. The minute you run into any resistance, walk away. When you are left with two answer choices and you would swear that both are correct, walk away. When you have eliminated all of the answer choices, walk away. When a sentence isn't quite coming into focus, walk away. Do not continue to push on a question that is giving you problems. Walk away.

The time that you would otherwise spend struggling with a hard question, you can now invest in an easier one. Then, when you have two minutes left, use the Review screen to guess on all unanswered questions.

Got it? Now you're ready to move on and learn more about the types of questions you'll see on the Verbal section. Let's get cracking!

Summary

o The GRE Verbal section consists of two, 30-minute sections, each containing 20 questions.

o The Verbal section is made up of sentence completion, argument, reading comprehension, and synonym questions.

o Use the Two-Pass system along with your own Personal Order of Difficulty to focus your time on the questions you feel more comfortable working on.

o Success on the Verbal section of the exam involves using Process of Elimination to eliminate "worse" answer choices.

o Vocabulary is an important aspect of success on the GRE Verbal section. Classify words on the GRE in three categories: words you know, words you kind of know, and words you've never seen before. Work on your vocabulary.

Chapter 4
Text Completions

If you took the SAT, you probably remember sentence completion questions. Well, they're back, retooled and renamed for the GRE. Text-completion questions test your ability to figure out which word or words best complete a given sentence or group of sentences. On the GRE, the sentence can have one, two, or even three blanks that you must fill. This chapter will show you the Princeton Review approach to text completions, a tried-and-true approach that will help you focus on exactly the parts of the sentences that you'll need to figure out the best answer. Along the way we'll provide you with some valuable tips on using Process of Elimination to help you when you don't know all the vocabulary on a question.

THE FORMAT

On each Verbal section of the GRE you can expect to see about 6 text completions. Text-completion questions on the GRE will have one, two, or three blanks. One-blank text completions will have five answer choices, while two- and three-blank questions will have three choices for each blank.

Some blanks are designed to test vocabulary, and others are designed to test comprehension. The vocabulary blanks have hard words; the context blanks often include prepositions and trigger words.

Text Completion Directions

On the test, the directions will look something like the italicized blurb below. Make sure you learn them now so you don't waste time reading them on test day.

For the following questions, select one entry for each blank from the corresponding column of choices. Fill all blanks in the way that best completes the text.

Text-completion questions often use difficult vocabulary words. Make sure you look up any words you don't know.

The blanks may operate independently or in conjunction with each other. If they operate in conjunction, the word you select for one blank will affect the meaning of the sentence, and therefore the word that might fit in another blank. This is a big help! When you find the word for one blank, it can help you determine all of the others.

The first thing to note is that every answer choice will fit grammatically into the sentence, and quite a few of them will make a degree of sense.

The "best" answer is what ETS says is the "best" answer.

The answer choices represent ETS's suggestions for what to put into the blank. The answer choices have been carefully selected and tested by thousands of students for their ability to tempt you into the wrong answer. As a test taker, don't trust their suggestions and certainly don't rely on them. They are there to mislead you. If you plug them into the sentence to see what "sounds" the best, ETS will get the better of you. They're good at it.

> The answer choices represent ETS's suggestions for what to put into the blank. They are carefully selected to mislead you. Don't use them.

The first step, therefore, is to cover up the answer choices. That way they can't distract you while you find the story, and there will always be a story. The question above lacks a complete story. You will never see a text-completion question like this on the test.

Here's a more realistic example:

Robert Ingersoll, although virtually unknown today, was the _____ orator of the nineteenth century; people traveled hundreds of miles to hear his eloquent speeches.

domineering
consummate
unobjectionable
conventional
execrable

Here's How to Crack It

1. **Set up your scratch paper with a column of answer choices, A through E.**

2. **Cover up the answer choices.** That's right, literally take your hand, put it on the screen, and cover up your answer choices. Don't trust the answer choices; they are there to mislead you.

3. **Find the story.** Who or what is this sentence about, and what are we told about this person or thing? In this case the sentence is about Robert Ingersoll. What are we told about him? He was some kind of orator, but we don't know what kind because that is the blank. What else are we told about him? The sentence is like a small reading composition passage, and you can use only things you are specifically told in the text. Robert Ingersoll gave eloquent speeches, and people travelled hundreds of miles to hear them. That's all we know.

4. **Speak for yourself.** Use the information you're given in the sentence to come up with your own word for the blank. Be as literal as you can. If you can recycle part of the sentence, feel free to do so. In this case we can say that Robert Ingersoll was the most *sought out* or *eloquent* orator of the nineteenth century. That is all we can say because that is the only information we are given in the text.

5. **Use Process of Elimination.** Only when you have come up with your own word from the blank are you protected against the mind games in the answer choices. You now know exactly what the blank needs, and you therefore have a way of evaluating the answer choices. Use your words as a filter to eliminate wrong answers. Use your scratch paper to track your progress. Don't get hung up on any individual

answer choice at this stage. If you're not sure, just give it the maybe and move on. You are looking for a word that means the same thing or similar to "most sought after" or "eloquent."

- Does *domineering* mean the same thing or similar to *sought after* or *eloquent*? No. Eliminate it.
- Does *consummate* mean the same thing or similar to *sought after* or *eloquent*? Maybe/not sure? Don't worry; give it the maybe and move on.
- Does *unobjectionable* mean the same thing or similar to *sought after* or *eloquent*? No. Cross it off.
- Does *conventional* mean the same thing or similar to *sought after* or *eloquent*? No. Cross it off.
- Does *extensive* mean the same thing or similar to *sought after* or *eloquent*? No. Cross it off.

Now check your scratch paper. You have four crossed-off answer choices and a maybe. This is why it doesn't pay to get too hung up on an answer choice in the first pass. If it could work, leave it in. If you're not sure, give it the maybe. Eliminate only those answer choices that are clearly wrong.

———————————————◯———————————————

What if you're stuck between two answer choices? First, mark the question and walk away. As always on the GRE, the minute you encounter the least resistance, walk away. There can be only one correct answer to a text-completion question. If two answers look correct, you may have misread something. The only way to reset your brain is to distract it by doing a few other questions and coming back.

Finding the Clue

Next, check your proof. The correct answer will always have proof in the passage. The proof is the part of the text that tells you what goes into the blank. We call this the clue. All text-completion questions have them. The clue is like an arrow that points to one answer choice and one answer choice only. If you are stuck between two, the clue will break the tie.

Consider this example:

> Sophocles, who wrote the play *Oedipus Rex*, was
> one of the most _____ playwrights of ancient
> Greece.

famous
bombastic
critical
prolific
eclectic

What's your word for the blank? Not sure? That's because this sentence has no clue.
Now try it again:

> Sophocles, who wrote the play *Oedipus Rex*, was
> one of the most _____ playwrights of ancient
> Greece, completing 123 plays in his lifetime—double
> that of any of his contemporaries.

famous
bombastic
critical
prolific
eclectic

Now find the story. Who is the main character? Sophocles. What are we told
about him? He wrote 123 plays—double that of any of his other contemporaries.
Now it's easy to fill in the blank with your own word. Sophocles was a *productive,
bountiful,* or *copious* playwright. He wrote lots of plays. When you go to the
answer choices, you know you are looking for something that means the same
thing or similar to *productive* or *lots of plays,* because your clue is, "completing
123 plays in his lifetime—double that of any of his contemporaries."

More on the Clue

As you might have seen by now, finding the best answer on a text-completion question depends on your ability to find the clue. Putting it another way, there is a word or group of words in the sentence that basically tells you what the right answer is. All you have to do is find the clue and then know enough vocabulary to figure out the answer choice that matches the clue. Why would ETS put the answer to a question right in front of you? It has to, or otherwise it could reasonably be argued that there is more than one "best" answer to a question. ETS couldn't have that—it would be deluged with complaints and challenges.

One important consequence of this fact is that the clue is everything when it comes to text completions. Find the clue and the correct answer will follow from it.

Sophocles was certainly one of the most famous playwrights of ancient Greece. While this may be true, your clue talks about the number of plays he wrote. It says nothing about how well known he was or is. While you might assume that a playwright who wrote so many plays must surely be famous, keep it literal. Assumptions will get you into trouble. The clue points to one answer choice and one answer choice only. Only *prolific* describes the number of plays written. The other four answer choices may fit the sentence, but none is the best answer choice.

In some sentences, the clue will be fairly obvious, while in others, the clue will be harder to spot. If you're having difficulty finding the clue, ask yourself the following questions:

1. Who or what is the blank referring to?
2. What other information is provided about this subject?

The answer to these questions is the clue. Let's try finding the clue in the following text completion.

What is the blank referring to? What other information is provided about it?

Don't go to the answer choices until you've come up with your own word for the blank!

Because his one presidential term was marked by crisis and conflict, many historians consider the presidency of John Adams _____ .

| an expediency |
| an indulgence |
| a calamity |
| a regency |
| a sovereignty |

Here's How to Crack It

First find the story. Who or what is the main idea? The presidency of John Adams. What are we told about his presidency? It was marked by crisis and conflict. In that case, how would historians view it? (Hint: Use your clue.) Clearly, his presidency was *problematic* at best. Use the word problematic and compare it to the answer choices, marking your progress on your scratch paper as you go.

- Does *expediency* mean the same thing or similar to *problematic* or *worse*? No. Eliminate (A).
- Does *indulgence* mean the same thing or similar to *problematic* or *worse*? No. Eliminate (B).
- Does *calamity* mean the same thing or similar to *problematic* or *worse*? Hmm, possible. Leave it in.
- Does *regency* mean the same thing or similar to *problematic* or *worse*? No. Eliminate (D).
- Does *sovereignty* mean the same thing or similar to *problematic* or *worse*? No. Eliminate (E).

You've got one answer choice left on your scratch paper. No need for further work. You're done. The best answer is choice (C).

Now try using this technique to find the clue on the questions in the following practice.

Practice: Finding the Clue

Underline the clue in each of the following sentences. Then, think of your own word for the blank and write it down. Answers can be found in Part V.

Be systematic! Ask yourself who or what is the blank referring to? What other info is provided about that subject?

1 of 8

The _____ relationships in his life haunted Eugene O'Neill and are often reflected in the harrowing nature of many of his plays.

2 of 8

Mount Godwin-Austin, more commonly known as K2, is the second highest mountain in the world, with its _____ peaks reaching more than 28,000 feet high.

3 of 8

A wind-chill warning is issued when the temperature is projected to reach minus 25 degrees Fahrenheit or lower, the point at which the cold has _____ effects on living creatures.

4 of 8

Divers still stumble across unexploded shells, 70-year-old _____ from World War II, in the waters outside Tokyo.

5 of 8

Although some people use the terms interchangeably, mastodons and mammoths were quite _____ ; mammoths were hairy with long tusks, while mastodons had low-slung bodies and flatter skulls.

6 of 8

The mayor was definitely _____ ; he crafted his policies not with an eye toward their political consequences but instead toward their practical effects.

The first-year law student was amazed at the sheer _____ of the material he had to read for his classes; he imagined that he'd have to read for hours and hours each day to finish it all.

Our word "ghoul" is _____ from the Arabic word "Algol," the name for the Demon Star, a star in the constellation Perseus.

A Quick Word About Your Words

Once you've found the clue in a sentence, you've done most of the heavy lifting. Don't strain yourself trying to come up with the perfect GRE word for the blank. Simple words like *bad, good, different,* and *same* are perfectly okay, as long as they get the main idea of the word across.

Or, to make your life even easier, recycle! Many times, the clue itself can be recycled into your word for the blank.

Positive/Negative

In some cases, you might not be able to come up with a word, but you might know whether the word you're looking for is positive or negative. Look again at question 3 from the previous practice exercise:

A wind-chill warning is issued when the temperature is projected to reach minus 25 degrees Fahrenheit or lower, the point at which the cold has _____ effects on living creatures.

You might not have been able to think of a word that fit in the blank, but you probably guessed that these very low temperatures don't help living creatures in any way. So you can eliminate any answer choices that contain "positive" or beneficial adjectives, right off the bat. Every little bit helps!

However, don't rely on positive/negative connotations unless you have <u>no</u> other option. It's better to recycle the clue if at all possible.

TRIGGER WORDS

Let's take a second look at the mastodon sentence from the clue drill.

> Although some people use the terms interchangeably,
> mastodons and mammoths were quite _____;
> mammoths were hairy with long tusks, while
> mastodons had low-slung bodies and flatter skulls.

The first part of the sentence tells us that many people use the terms mastodon and mammoth interchangeably, and yet clearly the two are quite different. If our clue is *interchangeably,* the word in the blank will be opposite of the clue. The reason you know this is because of the trigger word, "Although."

> Triggers tell you whether the word for the blank should match the clue or be the opposite of the clue.

Think of it this way:

I won the lottery, *and…*
I won the lottery, *but…*

One of these stories is going to have a happy ending. One is not. Sensitize yourself to trigger words. They always play an important role in the story being told, and they always impact the meaning of the word in the blank.

Here are some of the most important text completion trigger words.

Change Direction		Same Direction
but	while	thus
although	however	similarly
unless	unfortunately	and
rather	in contrast	therefore
yet	despite	heretofore
previously		; (semicolon) and : (colon)

Note the colon and the semicolon in the preceding chart. A colon or a semicolon divides a sentence into two completely separate sentences, both of which say the exact same thing. If that sentence has a blank in it, whatever is missing from one part of the sentence will be present in the other.

Practice: Clues and Triggers

Underline the clues and circle the triggers in the following sentences; then come up with your own word for the blanks. Recycle the clues if possible. Answers can be found in Part V.

1 of 8

The star receiver is widely regarded as one of the top talents in the game, but his _____ performance as a rookie almost ended his career.

2 of 8

The prime minister received international _____ for her work; she brokered a diplomatic solution to a potential crisis.

3 of 8

While it is often assumed that drinking alcohol is detrimental to one's health, many studies have shown the _____ effects of having a glass or two of wine daily.

4 of 8

Despite the increasing technological connectivity of the modern world, many cultures still remain _____ from the global society.

5 of 8

Although many cultures view the toad as a symbol of ugliness and clumsiness, the Chinese revere the toad as a _____ symbol.

6 of 8

Stock analysts often use holiday sales to gauge future stock prices; thus, retail performance can be an important _____ of market trends.

7 of 8

It is somewhat ironic that while the population at large tends to have a negative view of the legal profession, individuals rarely display such _____ to their lawyers.

8 of 8

Methyl bromide is a pesticide that has devastating effects on insects; unfortunately some believe it has the same _____ to humans.

You probably noticed that sentences can have multiple triggers. For example, a same-direction and a change-direction trigger will cancel each other out, while two change-direction triggers in the same sentence will also negate each other. Look at the following examples:

Although extremely poisonous, the puffer fish is
also so rare that many people insist on eating the
_____ creature.

In this sentence, there is one change-direction trigger, *although*, and one same-direction trigger, *also*. But the clue is that the fish is *extremely poisonous* and *rare*. We wouldn't want to use words like *nonpoisonous* or *common* for the blank—the triggers cancel each other out.

It is somewhat ironic that while the population
at large tends to have a negative view of the
legal profession, individuals rarely display
such _____ to their lawyers.

In this sentence, there are two change-direction triggers. The clue is "negative view," and the word for the blank would also have to be something negative. Thus, the two change-direction triggers cancel out.

PUTTING IT ALL TOGETHER

Now you're ready to put all your techniques together. In the following drill, find the clue and any triggers. Come up with your own word for the blank, and then use POE to pick the best answer.

Practice your scratch paper technique.

Remember to use your scratch paper. The place to invest your time on text-completion questions is in finding the story, the clues, and the triggers. Do not look at the answer choices until you have a crystal clear idea of the story being told. Your first pass through the answer choices should take ten seconds or so. Don't get hung up on any of the answer choices. Either you know the word and it works, you know the word and it doesn't work, or you don't know the word. If you're not sure, or the word only kind of works, just give it the *maybe* and move on.

Remember to skip and come back if the sentence is not immediately clear.

Because there are words missing, the story being told in the sentence may not be immediately clear. If you are having trouble bringing the story into focus, do not continue to push. You may have misread the sentence. Further time spent at this point is time wasted. Click the Mark button; then do a few other problems and come back. Trace your finger across the screen and make sure to read every word. If it is still not clear, walk away again.

Do:

- Cover your answer choices.
- Find the story being told.
- Identify clues and note the direction of triggers.
- Walk away if the sentence is not clear.
- Read with your finger.
- Come up with your own word for the blank.
- Work quickly through the answer choices, using your scratch paper to keep track of which ones are in and which ones are out.
- If you are stuck between two choices, walk away.
- Ask yourself the question "Does the clue point to my answer choice and my answer choice only?"

Do Not:

- Stay with a sentence that you cannot fill in your own word for.
- Go to the answer choices and start plugging them in.
- Go to the answer choices until you have come up with your own word for the blank.
- Select an answer until you have a mark on your page next to each answer choice.
- Eliminate an answer choice unless you know exactly what that word means and have a good reason.

If your hand is not moving, you are getting caught thinking. Walk away and do a different question.

Text Completions Drill

Answers can be found in Part V.

Despite the smile that spread from ear to ear, her eyes relayed a certain _____ .

jubilance
sorrow
mischievousness
vision
liveliness

Some historians see the Jacksonians as little more than ruthless capitalists who had _____ regard for individual welfare.

mixed
undue
inconsistent
scant
obtrusive

One of social science's major themes is that of stability versus change; to what extent are individual personalities _____ yet different over time?

transient
maladjusted
static
disturbed
discreet

The Erie Canal's completion caused _____ economic ripples; property values and industrial output along its route rose exponentially.

persistent
invaluable
incredulous
severe
prodigious

Voters have become so inured to the fickle nature of politicians that they responded to the levy of a new tax with _____ .

amazement
stolidity
exasperation
alarm
perplexity

The division between child-rearing goals that emphasize originality and personalization and those that place emphasis on adoption of conventions and compliance with rules discloses a _____ that stems from the principles on which these goals are based.

contradiction
monotony
benefit
forseeability
genius

AN IMPORTANT WORD ABOUT USING POE

Sometimes you might do everything right—you might find the clue, identify the triggers, and come up with a great word for the blank—but you will still be stymied by the vocabulary that ETS uses in the answer choices and have no idea what any of the words means.

In these situations, it is important to make use of POE strategies:

1. **Never Eliminate a Word You Don't Know.** If you have any doubts about the meaning of a word, do not eliminate it! Never get rid of an answer that just doesn't "sound good" in the sentence.
2. **Spend Your Time Working with the Words You Do Know.** Focus your energies on the words you do know, trying to match them with the clues in the sentence.
3. **Use Positive/Negative Associations Wherever Possible.** Be aggressive. If you know you need a positive word, eliminate any negative words.

Take a look at the following example:

Years of confinement in a sunless cell had left the prisoner wan and weakened, with a shockingly _____ appearance.

sidereal
boisterous
etiolated
singular
circumscribed

Here's How to Crack It

The clue in this sentence is "wan and weakened," so we need to look for a word in the answer choices that means something like "wan and weakened." However, the answer choices are a vocabulary hater's nightmare (or a pleasant dream, for the word lovers in the audience!).

Let's go through them. Choice (A) is a tough one—if you're not sure of what this word means, you can't eliminate it. Just leave it, and we'll worry about it later. You might know that choice (B) means to be loud and noisy; if so, you can eliminate this choice. The third choice is another difficult word, so let's move on to the fourth word. You might be aware that *singular* doesn't mean weak or wan; it means being one-of-a-kind or unique, so you can safely eliminate this choice. The

Never eliminate words that you don't know.

final choice is *circumscribed*. Looking at this word, we might note it has the root *scribe* in it, which has to do with writing and drawing. Once again, it doesn't seem to match our clue so we can eliminate it. That leaves us with just two choices. At this point, you've done all you can do, so go ahead and pick one of the two. The important thing is to use careful POE to increase your odds.

By the way, the correct answer is *etiolated*, which means to cause to appear pale or sickly.

———————○———————

TWO- AND THREE-BLANK TEXT COMPLETIONS

Remember that we said earlier that not all text-completion questions on the GRE have just one blank: ETS will ratchet up the difficulty level of text-completion questions by presenting you with sentences that have as many as two or three blanks.

However, the techniques you've learned in this chapter constitute the basic approach to all types of text completions, no matter how fancy. Here's an example:

———————○———————

Multiple blanks aren't that big of a deal. Use the same approach as you do for single blanks.

8 of 20

Federal efforts to regulate standards on educational achievements have been met by (i) _____ from the states; local governments feel that government imposition represents an undue infringement on their (ii) _____ .

Blank (i)	Blank (ii)
receptivity	autonomy
intransigence	legislation
compromise	comportment

Step 1:   **Engage the hand.** Make a column on your scratch paper for blank i and blank ii.

Step 2:   **Cover the answer choices and find the story.** We have a semicolon that divides the sentence into two separate but equal parts. The first part says that the states have reacted in a particular way to federal regulation, but we don't know what that way is, so let's check the second part. In the second part we're told that the local governments feel that the regulation is an "undue infringement" and an "imposition."

Step 3:   **Come up with your own words for the blanks.** We know that the first word must be something negative so put a negative sign above your first column. For the second column, use the information in the story to come up with your own word. Federal standards would impact a state's ability to decide standards for itself, so try something like "rights" or "decision making" and jot it down on your scratch paper.

Step 4:   **Use Process of Elimination.** Put down an "x" for any answer choice that does not work. Under the first blank, *receptivity* and *compromise* are both gone because they're positive words, and we need a negative word. The middle word stays; even if you don't know what it means, it doesn't matter. No need to spend any more time on it than that. For the second blank *legislation* is tempting, since we're talking about governments, but it's meant to be tempting. Our words are *rights* and *decision making,* neither of which means *legislation,* so put an "x" in the middle slot. *Comportment* means the way you carry yourself. That's not even related, so give that one an "x" too. *Autonomy* is the closest to *rights* or *decision making;* in fact it fits quite well. We have an answer. When you're done, your scratch paper should look something like this:

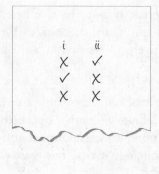

Don't try to deal with all the blanks at once. Take them one at a time.

Let's try another one.

5 of 20

Many popular musicians have (i) _____ new digital technologies that allow them unprecedented control over their music. These musicians use computers to (ii) _____ and modify their songs, resulting in a level of musical precision often unattainable naturally. Of course, though, as is often the case with new technologies, some traditionalists (iii) _____ these developments.

Blank (i)	Blank (ii)	Blank (iii)
incorporated	energize	balk at
synthesized	delineate	revel in
alleviated	recast	retaliate at

Can you come up with your own word for the blank? Are there other words that could also work?

Here's How to Crack It

Don't be intimidated by the multiple-blank sentences; just try to isolate each blank and apply the strategies we taught you. You don't have to work the blanks in order: Start with whichever one of the blanks seems easiest to you.

For this one, let's start with the second blank. The clue is *modify* and the trigger is *and*, so we need to find a word that's similar to *modify*. Let's go with *alter*. Now use POE and look at the answer choices in the second box. *Energize* doesn't match our word, so eliminate it. Neither does *delineate*, which means to outline or to depict. That leaves us with *recast* for the second blank.

You may have noticed that the first blank is related to the second blank. If the musicians are modifying their songs and also have *unprecedented control* over their modification, we need a word like *using* or *embracing* for the first blank. The only answer choice in the first box that's even close to this word is *incorporated*.

Finally, we move on to the last blank. The clue here is that we're dealing with *traditionalists*. How would traditionalists react to these *new technologies*? They would probably react negatively, so we need a word like *reject* or *dislike* for the third blank.

Look at the choices in the final box. *Revel in* is a positive sentiment, so we can eliminate it. *Retaliate at* is definitely negative, but there is nothing in the sentence that indicates that the traditionalists are taking action against those using the new technology, or the new technology itself! Thus, *balk at*, which means to resist or object to, is the best answer.

RELATIONSHIP BETWEEN THE BLANKS

Many two- and three-blank text completions hinge on the use of trigger words, and don't contain really strong or obvious clues that you can rely on. For example, look at the following sentence:

---

6 of 20

Jenkins is an artist known for engendering strong reactions in his viewers; in fact, some of his more (i) _____ paintings have caused viewers extreme (ii) _____ .

Blank (i)	Blank (ii)
ominous	discouragement
accomplished	discomposure
innovative	resoluteness

Here's How to Crack It

What if you put a positive word in that first blank, let's say *joyous,* what would happen to the second blank? You would have to put in a word such as *joy.* On the other hand, if you put in a word such as *offensive* for the first blank, you would need something along the lines of *offense* for the second blank. The very information you need for one blank is, itself, another blank. What should be a clue is another blank. In these cases all you have to go on is the relationship between the blanks.

Start by noting each answer choice on your scratch paper with a simple + or − sign. Your scratch paper should look like this:

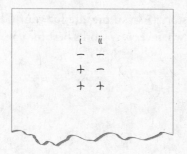

We've already determined that there is a strong relationship between the two blanks. Both words need to be "on the same side of the fence," which is to say, closely related.

The word for the first blank is negative, so it can go with only two of the second blank words. Something ominous wouldn't necessarily cause discouragement, so you can cross off discouragement. Something ominous could cause discomposure, so this pair is possible. Moving on to the positive words, something accomplished wouldn't necessarily cause resoluteness, so you can cross off accomplished. Something innovative wouldn't necessarily cause resoluteness either, so cross both off because there is no positive pair that works. You're left with ominous and discomposure as the only two that could possibly work. If you didn't know the word discomposure but could guess that it's negative, you would still get this question right because you would have eliminated all other possible pairs.

> If there is no clear clue, look for the relationship between the blanks.

THE LAST WORD—VOCABULARY

Study vocabulary every single day.

As we've seen, using the techniques, including POE, can help you a great deal on a great majority of text-completion questions. However, on some questions you hit the "vocabulary wall"—the point at which you're stuck because you don't know the meaning of the words in the question. The only cure for this predicament is to improve your vocabulary as much as you can before test day. Memorizing the Hit Parade (in Chapter 7) is a good start, but there are myriad other ways of increasing your vocabulary.

Need more info? Check out the DVD.

Here's the moral of the story: As you prepare for your GRE, try to keep learning new words every day, in whatever way works best for you.

Text Completions Practice Set

Answers can be found in Part V.

Although the concept of vegan donuts did not appeal to Sean, he actually found them to be quite _____ once he finally tasted them.

detestable
unappetizing
bland
gleeful
scrumptious

Although using recorded birdcalls makes the California gnatcatcher less (i)_____ and easier to observe, it also seems to (ii)_____ its normal mating patterns.

Blank (i)	Blank (ii)
timid	direct
approachable	increase
tameable	upset

The sparring of the two lawyers appeared (i)_____ ; however, it is well known that, outside the courtroom, the friendship between the two is (ii)_____ .

Blank (i)	Blank (ii)
pointless	obvious
lighthearted	cooperative
hostile	concealed

The notion that socialism, which emphasizes collective ownership of the means of production, (i)_____ individual expression is supported by historical studies that have shown that individualism has (ii)_____ only in societies where socialist programs have been (iii)_____ .

Blank (i)	Blank (ii)	Blank (iii)
promotes	diminished	improved
inhibits	thrived	sponsored
fosters	wallowed	abandoned

At first, humans were (i)_____ tool users, (ii)_____ convenient sticks or stones to achieve a purpose, but then (iii)_____ the tool when finished with that purpose.

Blank (i)	Blank (ii)	Blank (iii)
prehistoric	employing	annihilating
casual	contriving	concealing
adept	fashioning	discarding

Jean Jacques Rousseau, whose social philosophy was often austere, was in his personal life a surprisingly _____ man: he attended fashionable Parisian parties, wore flashy clothing, and dated other men's wives.

flamboyant
indisputable
pristine
astute
courteous

When developing a completely new skill, it is typical to feel (i)_____ . One's status as a (ii)_____ , however, is usually ephemeral, as the initial sense of awkwardness soon gives way to mastery.

Blank (i)	Blank (ii)
calumnious	dessicant
impertinent	tyro
maladroit	demagogue

The Objectivist mantra, "A is A," is of course a (i)_____ with which no logical person could disagree. The problem is that those who cite this axiom invariably proceed to substitute in different concepts for the first A and the second, in a feat of verbal (ii)_____ worthy of a stage magician, and then proceed as if the interchangeability of these concepts is indisputable.

Blank (i)	Blank (ii)
filigree	peregrination
tautology	prestidigitation
quandary	peroration

The American public venerates medical researchers because the researchers make frequent discoveries of tremendous humanitarian consequence; however, the daily routines of scientists are largely made up of result verification and statistical analysis, making their occupation seem _____ .

fascinating
quotidian
recalcitrant
experimental
amorphous

To his friends and social companions, Gomez seemed a pleasing combination of affable and (i)_____ . His employees and business associates, however, found him to be as (ii)_____ as he was officious.

Blank (i)	Blank (ii)
pernicious	meddlesome
complaisant	prescient
mercurial	puerile

Summary

- In text-completion questions, come up with your own word for the blank, using the clues and triggers in the sentence.

- If you can't find the clue, ask yourself: Who or what is the blank referring to? What other information is provided about that subject?

- Trigger words tell you whether the word in the blank should be similar to the clue or opposite of the clue.

- After you've come up with your own word for the blank, use POE to eliminate words that aren't close to your word. Don't eliminate words if you are unsure of their meanings. Focus on the words you do know.

- If the sentence has two or three blanks, do the blanks one at a time. Pick the easier (or easiest) blank to start with, find the clue, come up with a word, and use POE. Then repeat for the remaining blanks.

- Keep studying vocabulary. Make sure to look up any words you don't know.

Chapter 5
Sentence
Equivalence

This chapter details a variation on the text completions you learned about in the prior chapter. Sentence-equivalence questions still require you to find the best word to complete a sentence. For these questions, however, you'll have to pick the two answers that best complete the sentence; this means the two correct answers will be synonyms. Because both words create sentences that are equivalent—both have the same meaning—we refer to these types of questions as sentence-equivalence questions. This chapter will show you how to apply the strategies you learned last chapter and use Process of Elimination to answer these questions.

WHAT YOU WILL SEE

Remember in the last chapter when we alluded to the "other" type of text-completion question? Well, now it's time to look at these questions in a little more detail. These questions are somewhat similar to the one-blank text-completion questions we worked on in Chapter 4. However, they are different in several major respects. First, these questions always have six answer choices, not five. Second, you need to pick the two answers that complete the meaning of the sentence in the same way. Generally this will mean synonyms, but they don't need to be exact synonyms, as long as the meaning of the sentence stays the same.

You should expect to see about three to five sentence-equivalence questions on your GRE Verbal sections.

Here's What the Directions Will Tell You to Do:

*For the following questions, select the **two** answer choices that, when used to complete the sentence, fit the meaning of the sentence as a whole **and** produce completed sentences that are alike in meaning.*

How does this question differ from the text-completion questions in Chapter 4?

Now, here's what a sentence-equivalence question looks like:

2 of 20

Anthropologists contend that the ancient Mesopotamians switched from grain production to barley after excessive irrigation and salt accumulation made the soil _____ grains.

- ☐ indifferent to
- ☐ inhospitable to
- ☐ unsuitable for
- ☐ acrimonious to
- ☐ benignant to
- ☐ inured to

Need more info? Check out the DVD.

Our goal is to choose the TWO answers that produce sentences with similar meanings. In other words, you'll be clicking on two answer choices instead of one.

APPROACHING SENTENCE EQUIVALENCE

Besides being similar in appearance, sentence-equivalence questions are also very similar to text completions in their structure. Sentence-equivalence questions have clues and triggers, just like the sentences we looked at in Chapter 4.

However, sentence-equivalence questions are even more vocabulary-driven, because they require you to find two answers that are synonymous.

Remember that the meaning of the sentence must stay the same. For that to occur, the meaning of the sentence must be clear to you. Just as with text completions, the place to invest your time is in the sentence.

> You cannot go to the answer choices until you have a crystal clear understanding of the story being told by the sentence.

The good news is that you don't have to do this all in one go. Some of the sentences are tough, and, of course, there is information missing. If the sentence does not come into focus after the first or second reading, walk away. Mark that sentence and go do some easier ones. Often you will find that, when you return to a sentence after having done a few others, the meaning suddenly becomes clear. Also, the time you would otherwise have spent staring at a difficult problem in frustration, you have now spent getting a few other questions correct. You should always be spending your time *doing,* not *thinking.*

Tackling Sentence Equivalence

The approach to sentence equivalence is almost exactly the same as text completions.

1. **Set Up Your Scratch Paper.** You will see three to five sentence equivalence in a row. Each has six answer choices, so set up your scratch paper. If you don't, you will try to answer the question in your head rather than on your scratch paper. Doing questions in your head leads to harder work, wasted time, and more errors.

2. **Find the Story.** *Who* or *what* is the sentence talking about, and what are you told about that person or thing? Pay close attention to triggers; they are always significant clues to the direction of the sentence.

3. **Speak for Yourself.** Come up with your own word or phrase for the blank. It doesn't have to be a big ETS word. Any word or words will do as long as you keep it literal and don't add any concepts or ideas that aren't already in the sentence. If you can recycle your clue, do so.

4. **Use Process of Elimination.** Get your hand moving. Your pass through the answer choices should take ten or fifteen seconds only. Either you know a word and it works, you know a word and it doesn't work, or you don't know the word. If you're not sure, don't sit and think about it; give it the *maybe* and move on. You cannot eliminate a word if you don't know what it means.

Take a look at the grey box for the basic approach to sentence-equivalence questions, which is identical to the method for text completions you already learned. Then try it out on the question we just saw:

Anthropologists contend that the ancient Mesopotamians switched from grain production to barley after excessive irrigation and salt accumulation made the soil _____ grains.

- ☐ indifferent to
- ☐ inhospitable to
- ☐ unsuitable for
- ☐ acrimonious to
- ☐ benignant to
- ☐ inured to

Here's How to Crack It

First, look for the clues and triggers in the sentence. In this sentence, the clue is that the Mesopotamians "switched from grain to barley." For this reason, the word in the blank has to mean something along the lines of *bad for* or *unsuited for*. Now it's a matter of going to the answers and using POE.

Answer choice (A) doesn't match the clue; eliminate it. Choices (B) and (C) are both pretty close to the words we came up with, so leave them. How about the remaining choices? *Acrimonious to*, in choice (D), means using sharp language, so that doesn't make sense. The word in choice (E) is a positive word, so you can eliminate that as well. And finally, *inured to* means to become accustomed to something bad. That doesn't match our choices either, so eliminate it. The best answers are (B) and (C).

Keep in mind that even if you don't know what *acrimonious* or *inured* means, you can probably still get the correct answer. How? By POE of course! All the guidelines we talked about for text completions still apply here. As we said in Chapter 4, you should always work with the words you do know and leave the unknowns alone. Your scratch paper can answer the question for you. If you have two words that work and two question marks, you're done. Pick the ones that work.

Sentence Equivalence Drill

Work the following questions, using the same approach you used for text completions. Check your answers in Part V when you're done.

To any observer, ancient or _____ , the night sky appears as a hemisphere resting on the horizon.

- ☐ antiquated
- ☐ perceptive
- ☐ modern
- ☐ astute
- ☐ contemporary
- ☐ archaic

Researchers interested in the nature versus nurture debate use identical twins who were separated at birth to explore which personality characteristics are _____ compared to those that arise through experience.

- ☐ intractable
- ☐ nascent
- ☐ erudite
- ☐ innate
- ☐ predilection
- ☐ instinctive

The Canadian Prime Minister, Mackenzie King, often used séances to contact his dead pet dog for advice; despite this _____ behavior, the public had so much confidence in his ability as a leader that he was in power for 22 years.

- ☐ aberrant
- ☐ lackluster
- ☐ poised
- ☐ unconventional
- ☐ repulsive
- ☐ decorous

The circulation of the blood makes possible human adaptability to the _____ conditions of life, such as atmospheric pressure, level of physical activity, and diet.

- ☐ inveterate
- ☐ dynamic
- ☐ timorous
- ☐ cowed
- ☐ turgid
- ☐ fluctuating

Arriving in New Orleans days after Hurricane Zelda had passed and without an adequate number of vehicles of its own, the armed forces began to _____ any working form of transportation they could find, including a bus that had been chartered at great expense by a group of tourists.

- ☐ repatriate
- ☐ commandeer
- ☐ extradite
- ☐ interdict
- ☐ expurgate
- ☐ appropriate

PROCESS OF ELIMINATION STRATEGIES

With six answer choices in front of you, there are many opportunities to make effective use of Process of Elimination. Here are a few things to look for.

Positive and Negative Words

One strategy that you can use to answer sentence-equivalence questions is to separate the answer choices into positive ones and negative ones. Remember how we talked about positive and negative words in Chapter 4? You don't need to know the dictionary definition of a word if you can somewhat confidently identify the word as being positive or negative. Here's how you would use them on this type of question:

---

6 of 20

Despite the implications of their noble status, many aristocrats were virtually penniless and lived in a state of _____ .

- ☐ indigence
- ☐ opulence
- ☐ eminence
- ☐ penury
- ☐ depravity
- ☐ complacency

Can you identify any of the words as positive or negative?

Here's How to Crack It

The trigger in this sentence, *despite*, tells us that we need a word that has a meaning that's opposite to *noble status*. Also, the clue states that the aristocrats were *virtually penniless*. Therefore, we only want to consider negative words.

Let's look at the choices and see if we can figure out if they're positive or negative. The third word is *eminence*. Can you figure out if this is a positive or negative word? You might have heard the word *eminent* before, as in *an eminent doctor* or an *eminent scientist*. This is a good word, so let's eliminate choice (C). Choice (F) is *complacency*. Are there any other words you've seen that remind you of this word? You may have heard the word *placate* before. This word means to please someone. Or, how about the word *placid*? That describes someone who is calm and satisfied. Each of these words—*complacent*, *placate*, and *placid*—share the same root, *plac-*, which means to please. So it looks like we can eliminate choice (F).

We've eliminated two words, but we've still got some tough ones left. Don't give up! Look at choice (E). *Depravity* is certainly a negative word, but does it match the clue? Would you describe a penniless person as depraved? Not likely, so we can eliminate choice (E) as well. That leaves only three choices. If you were to guess at this point, you'd have a one-in-three chance of guessing correctly. Of course, if you know the meaning of just one of the remaining three words, you're in pretty good shape as well. For example, if you know that *opulence* is a positive word, then you've got the answer—it has to be choices (A) and (D), which both mean to be poor. If you know the meaning of either choice (A) or choice (D), then you have a fifty-fifty chance of guessing correctly, which is not too bad at all.

Let's move on to another strategy.

Synonym/No Synonym

If you're pretty familiar with the words in the answer choices, you can use your vocabulary to eliminate certain answers and to lump certain other answers together. You do this by looking at the choices and first eliminating any answer choice that has no synonym among the remaining choices. You can also identify pairs of words as synonyms and lump them together.

Word Roots

Learning word roots gives you the opportunity to get more bang for your vocabulary buck. You'll probably never know all the words the GRE will throw at you, but by mastering some common roots, you might know just enough about a mystery word to determine whether you should keep it or get rid of it. Here are some common roots to get you started:

- *Ben/bene*—good. Examples: *benefit, benevolent, benefactor*
- *Mal/male*—bad. Examples: *malign, malevolent, malediction*
- *Animus*—spirit, soul. Examples: *animate, magnanimous*
- *Cise/cide*—cut. Examples: *excise, homicide, circumcise*
- *Gen/gene*—type, kind. Examples: *genesis, generate, homogenous*
- *Port*—carry. Examples: *export, transport, porter*
- *Andro/anthro*—man, person. Examples: *anthropology, android*

Obviously, this list barely scratches the surface of word roots but you get the idea. Look for roots in your Hit Parade words (in Chapter 7) and any other new words you learn.

Look up words you don't know.

Consider this example:

Because mercury has a variety of innocuous uses, including in thermometers and dental fillings, few people realize that it is one of the most _____ substances on the planet.

- ☐ acidic
- ☐ irritating
- ☐ mundane
- ☐ deleterious
- ☐ disagreeable
- ☐ pernicious

Here's How to Crack It

Work with the answer choices and see if we can lump them into synonym/no synonym groupings. First, eliminate choices that have no synonyms among the answer choices.

We can start by eliminating choice (A). None of the other choices are similar in meaning to the word *acidic*, so choice (A) cannot be the correct answer. The same goes for choice (C). There is no other answer choice that's similar in meaning to *mundane*, so eliminate it.

Next, we'll group the remaining choices together. You might notice that choice (B) and choice (E) are synonyms for each other, which means if you select one of them, you'll have to select the other. The same logic applies to choices (D) and (F). With four answer choices left, you now have a fifty-fifty chance of getting the question right: you know that the correct answer is either (B) and (E) or (D) and (F).

The clue in this sentence is *innocuous uses* and this sentence also contains a trigger—"few people realize." We're looking for a word that means the opposite of *innocuous*, which means harmless. Choices (D) and (F) are the best answer.

IF YOU'VE NEVER SEEN THE WORD BEFORE

No matter how expansive your vocabulary is, at some point you'll probably run across a word you've never seen before. Don't panic! Just work with the words you do know and rely on your old friend POE. Take a look:

There's no substitute for a strong vocabulary.

---

5 of 20

Despite their outward negativity, many a cynic harbors an inner faith in the _____ of mankind.

☐ benevolence

☐ precocity

☐ parsimony

☐ ignobility

☐ antipathy

☐ probity

Here's How to Crack It

First things first. The clue for this sentence is *outward negativity*, and we also have the trigger word *despite*. Thus, we need a word meaning the opposite of negativity. This question definitely calls for a positive word. That's the easy part; now we have to deal with a number of difficult words in the answer choices. Do the best you can with the words you know and leave the words you don't know alone. Starting with choice (A), it looks like we have a keeper. The prefix *bene-* is used in tons of positive words—*benefit, benefactor, benign, beneficent*. Choice (B) is a tough one, so let's leave it for now. The same goes for choice (C). Choice (D) isn't so bad. It has the root word *noble* in it, which is certainly a good word, but we've added the prefix *ig-* to the word. That's probably a bad thing. We should eliminate this choice. Similarly, choice (E) has the prefix *anti-*. That means against or opposite, which is also generally bad. So we should eliminate this choice as well.

So far, choice (A) is definitely in, while choices (D) and (E) are definitely out. Even without knowing either of the words in choices (B), (C), and (F), we would still have a one-in-three chance of guessing correctly—the answer is either (A) and (B), (A) and (C), or (A) and (F). Not too bad for only knowing four of the six words. If we want to take our POE a step further, we could probably even eliminate choice (B). The word has the prefix *pre-* in it, which means before. That doesn't really have much to do with good or bad, so we could probably eliminate it. That gives us a fifty-fifty chance of guessing correctly. The actual answer is choices (A) and (F). *Probity* means good behavior, while *parsimony* means stinginess.

Sentence Equivalence Practice Set

Work the following questions, using all the techniques you've learned for sentence equivalence. Check your answers in Part V when you're done.

1 of 5

Possessed of an insatiable sweet tooth, Jim enjoyed all kinds of candy, but he had a special _____ for gumdrops, his absolute favorite.

- ☐ container
- ☐ affinity
- ☐ odium
- ☐ nature
- ☐ disregard
- ☐ predilection

2 of 5

Although the Wright brothers first attempted flight in 1896 was a _____ and subsequent efforts similarly ended in failure, they persisted and ultimately made the first successful airplane flight in 1903.

- ☐ fiasco
- ☐ debacle
- ☐ hindrance
- ☐ feat
- ☐ triumph
- ☐ precedent

3 of 5

The fuel efficiency of most vehicles traveling speeds greater than 40 miles per hour _____ as the vehicle's speed increases, due to the additional demands placed on the vehicle.

- ☐ equalizes
- ☐ adapts
- ☐ stabilizes
- ☐ diminishes
- ☐ increases
- ☐ wanes

4 of 5

Robert's outwardly amiable disposition belied his _____ nature; he was more than willing to badmouth a colleague's work or spread gossip if he thought it would help him advance his career.

- ☐ innocuous
- ☐ malicious
- ☐ gregarious
- ☐ insipid
- ☐ affable
- ☐ churlish

5 of 5

The *kenjogo* or humble language used in Japanese to refer to oneself and the *sonkeigo* or honorific language used to describe the interlocutor are often toned down in English translation, as more accurate renderings might sound _____ to an ear accustomed to more egalitarian phrasings.

- ☐ servile
- ☐ garrulous
- ☐ obsequious
- ☐ circumspect
- ☐ querulous
- ☐ loquacious

Summary

○ The approach for sentence equivalence is the same as it is for text completions. Ignore the answer choices, look for clues and triggers, and fill your own words in for the blanks.

○ Use positive and negative associations to eliminate answers.

○ Try to group answers choices with their synonyms. Eliminate any choices that don't have a synonym.

○ Keep working on vocabulary every day!

Chapter 6
Reading Comprehension

Reading-comprehension questions on the GRE can be quite deceptive. On one hand, the answer to the question is somewhere in the passage. On the other hand, ETS is really good at crafting answers that seem right but are, in fact, wrong. This chapter will teach you the best way to approach the reading passages on the test and how to attack the questions. Furthermore, you'll learn how to use Process of Elimination to get rid of wrong answers and maximize your score.

Need more info? Check out the DVD.

WHAT YOU WILL SEE

On the GRE, you'll be presented with about eight reading passages, varying in length from a mere twelve lines to more than fifty lines. After each passage, you'll be asked to answer a number of questions. Your task is to choose the best answer to each question based on what is stated or implied in the passage. Translation: The correct answer to every question is somewhere in the passage. In fact, think of reading-comprehension questions as an open-book test. Your goal is simply to locate the answer within the passage.

Let's get started.

READING AND THE GRE

Although it might seem like reading-comprehension questions shouldn't be very hard, ETS makes these types of questions difficult by exploiting some common assumptions.

The reading skills you'll need to use for reading-comprehension questions on the GRE are quite different from the ones you use in your everyday life. The biggest challenge will probably be the limited time you have to answer the questions.

For one thing, ETS (intentionally) chooses reading passages that are complicated and are concerned with unfamiliar and, in some cases, intimidating topics, hoping that you'll have a tough time absorbing the entirety of the passage in the short amount of time they give you. In many cases, that is exactly what happens: Test takers spend too much time trying to understand what they've read and not enough time working on the questions.

ETS also hopes that you will overanalyze the text. This level of critical thinking is wholly appropriate for most types of academic reading, but on the GRE it only leads to trouble. The way to crack the reading portion of the GRE is to read less into the passages, not more.

Although it may sound counterintuitive, in some ways the passage itself is the least important part of reading-comprehension questions. This is for a simple reason—you don't get any points for reading the passage, and the only way to do well on the GRE is to amass as many points as possible.

Okay, you're ready to take a look at our approach to reading-comprehension questions.

READING COMPREHENSION: THE BASIC APPROACH

1. **Attack the Passage.** This step will vary slightly based on the length of the passage you're dealing with, but in each case, the goal is to read less, not more.
2. **Size Up the Questions.** Reading-comprehension questions on the GRE can ask you to do a variety of things. Make sure you know what the question's asking you to do.
3. **Find and Paraphrase the Answer.** This is the key. Always return to the passage to find your answer; never answer it from memory!
4. **Use Process of Elimination.** You can use a number of helpful POE guidelines on reading comprehension. We'll go over these in detail in a moment.

Let's start by looking at Step 1 in some more detail.

> The Directions
>
> These are the directions as they will appear on your GRE:
>
> Directions: Each passage in this group is followed by questions based on its content. After reading a passage, choose the best answer to each question. Answer all questions following a passage on the basis of what is stated or implied in that passage.
>
> Here are *our* directions:
>
> Directions: This is not really a test of reading, nor is it a test of comprehension. It's a treasure hunt! You can find all of the answers in the passage.

ATTACK THE PASSAGE

On the GRE, you should never read a passage just for the sake of reading it; that is, you should always have a goal in mind before you start reading. Most of the time you'll be reading with the goal of answering a particular question, but for your initial reading, you're concerned only with discovering the following:

1. **The Main Idea/Purpose.** What is the author writing about and why?
2. **The Structure.** How is the passage organized?
3. **The Tone.** How does the writer feel about the topic?

You don't have to read every single word of the passage in order to answer the questions.

Fortunately, you can often figure these things out with just a cursory initial reading. Additionally, because the GRE is a standardized test, you can also expect that you will see many passages types that are fairly similar in their tone and organization.

Reading Comprehension and the Computer

Reading comprehension is presented on a split screen. The passage is on the left side and stays there while you work on the questions; you may have to use the scroll button to read the whole passage. The questions are on the right side and they appear one at a time. It's very important to practice reading comprehension on the computer because you'll have to get used to not being able to circle or underline words, bracket text, write notes in the margin, and so on. Reading text on a computer is also more difficult than reading text on paper. Start practicing good habits right now. As you work through this chapter, and any time you practice reading comprehension, don't allow yourself to write on the passage. Anything you write must be written on scratch paper. In your preparation for the GRE, never give yourself a crutch you won't actually have when you take the real test.

Types of Passage

GRE passages cover topics in the sciences, social sciences, and humanities. But regardless of the topic, the passage itself will conform to the standards of "good" academic writing—meaning that the authors will generally write in a style that's characterized by clear organization, strong topic sentences and transitions, and summary information or concluding thoughts. You should expect to see the following types of passages on the GRE:

1. **Expository Passages**. In this passage type, the author's purpose is to inform or explain something, whether it be a new finding, a viewpoint, a trend, or an occurrence. In this type of passage, the tone is generally neutral.
2. **Argumentative Passages**. Here the author's purpose is to convince the reader of the validity of a certain belief or perspective. Argumentative passages usually have stronger tones and are structured around providing support for the author's conclusion.
3. **Evaluating Passages**. Some passages will present an idea or perspective, after which the author will evaluate or critique it. In this type of passage, the tone can be strong or neutral.

Of course, other types of passages may crop up on the GRE, but in general you should expect ones that fit into the categories above. Now let's look at some passages and practice finding their main idea, tone, and structure.

Understanding Structure in Writing

While the reading passages on the GRE may not represent some of the most engaging writing you've encountered, it is important to keep in mind the author's basic goal. Nonfiction writers want their writing to be understood; if you can't follow their arguments or their progression of ideas, they've failed in their jobs as writers. When you're reading or skimming a passage on the GRE, a good grasp of the structural elements in writing will aid your understanding.

First, pay attention to the structure of each paragraph. The most important information is probably going to be found at the beginning and end of the paragraph. If, while reading a passage, your eyes start to glaze over, rest assured you're not the only one. Good authors know this and make sure to put key points where they are likely to stand out. So, focus on the beginning and end of each paragraph.

Second, look for trigger words. Writers use these words as signposts to direct your reading. When you see same direction words such as *for example*, *in addition*, *and*, or *furthermore*, you know the author is going to be supporting an earlier statement. If you already understand the point of the paragraph, feel free to skim through these lines. However, opposite direction words like *although*, *but*, *yet*, and *however*, signify an important shift. Writers use words like this to direct the reader's attention to an important change or revelation in the progression of ideas.

Finally, the conclusion of the piece offers the author one last chance to get his or her point across. Always read the last paragraph. Does the piece wrap things up nicely or is there some doubt? Does the author suggest further avenues of inquiry? The way the passage ends can help you to understand what the author's main point or primary purpose in writing the passage was.

Paying attention to structural clues like the ones mentioned here can help you be a more effective reader. Following these principles in your own writing wouldn't hurt either.

Approaching Short Passages

Short passages on the GRE run about twelve to fifteen lines. Despite their brevity, they can still be difficult to follow and often a lot of information is packed into a small space. When you come across a short passage, read the entire passage quickly; pay close attention to the topic sentence, skim through the middle, and then read the last line carefully. This should be sufficient to figure out the main idea, structure, and tone.

Try reading the following passage and finding the main idea, tone, and structure:

> The constitutional concept of freedom of the press traces its origins to 1735 and the libel trial of John Peter Zenger. Zenger, born in Germany, emigrated to America in 1710 and established the *Weekly Journal* in 1733. The *Journal* starkly opposed the policies of New York governor William Cosby and while Zenger did not write the majority of the critical pieces, he was arrested on libel charges in 1734. In the ensuing trial, widely followed by the populace, Zenger was defended by Andrew Hamilton, a Pennsylvania lawyer who was brought in after Cosby disbarred all the New York lawyers who offered to defend Zenger. Hamilton's brilliant defense of Zenger was predicated on the argument that since Zenger's criticisms involved verifiable facts, they could not possibly be considered libel. The judge agreed and acquitted the publisher, establishing the basic concept of freedom of the press that was to be enshrined in the United States Constitution some 45 years later.

Remember to skim! Don't read every single word of the passage, even on short passages!

Main Idea/Purpose: _____

Structure: _____

Tone: _____

This is a typical expository passage. The first sentence is important; it tells us that the topic is "freedom of the press" and that there was a trial that helped establish it. The next few sentences provide the details. A quick skim should reveal that Zenger was arrested and tried. The final sentence states that Zenger's acquittal was one of the factors that lead to the First Amendment, which mandated that the press be free.

Your answers should look something like the following:

Main Idea/Purpose: Zenger's trial set a precedent that eventually led to the concept of freedom of the press and the First Amendment.

Structure: The passage states its main idea, provides some details on the trial, and ends with the implications of the situation.

Tone: Neutral. The author simply describes what happened.

Approaching Medium Passages

On medium-length passages, which run from sixteen to twenty lines, there's slightly more information to deal with. Once again, you want to avoid getting caught up in the text; read only enough of the passage to get the general idea. It's a good idea to read the first two lines of the passage, skim the middle portion, and then read the final line: This will give you a grasp of the meaning of the passage and its structure without burdening you with too much information. Now read the following passage and jot down the main idea, structure, and tone.

Do you need to read every single word to get the main idea?

What was it about Oscar Wilde's only novel, *The Picture of Dorian Gray*, that caused it to create such an uproar when it was published in 1891? While critics attacked the quality of Wilde's work, lambasting its plot as "incurably silly" and chiding the writer for using prose that was "clumsy" and "boring," these overt denunciations of the formal elements of Wilde's work merely masked the true concerns of many nineteenth-century critics. What these critics were actually railing against was the thematic content of Wilde's work, specifically his illustration of a lifestyle devoted to useless beauty. For many a nineteenth-century moralist, *The Picture of Dorian Gray* was nothing more than a primer for spiritual depravity. Wilde's ultimate sin was not his clunky plot or his sometimes cloying prose; it wasn't even his disregard for the time-honored tradition of English propriety. It was instead his leniency toward his protagonist. Wilde propagated the disdain of critics not simply because Dorian Gray was an unabashed hedonist, but because Wilde failed to punish his subject appropriately for his hedonism. To the critics, allowing an evil character to escape his just desserts was an unforgivable sin, and it was this transgression that resulted in such opprobrium for Wilde's work. In their mind, Wilde's work was corrupting the genteel reading public by failing to show the proper consequences of immoral behavior.

Main Idea/Purpose: _____

Structure: _____

Tone: _____

This is an Argumentative passage. The first two sentences tell us that there was some controversy when the book was released and that the author thinks that the critics had other reasons for attacking the book—besides its writing. A quick skim through the middle shows that the author thinks critics had a problem with the themes in the book. The final sentence gives more support to the argument, stating that the author believes that the critics thought Wilde was corrupting the public.

Main Idea/Purpose: To suggest that critics weren't responding only to the writing of the work, but also to its thematic content.

Structure: The author states a conclusion in the beginning and then provides details to support that conclusion.

Tone: Mostly neutral, although the author doesn't appear to support the critics' views.

Approaching Long Passages

What we consider long passages are about twice as long as medium-length passages; about forty to fifty lines long. When you come across a long passage, read the first line of each paragraph and then skim the rest of it, paying particular attention to any "trigger words" (the same types of words you encountered on text completions). When you get to the last paragraph, read the first line, skim the rest, and then read the last line of the entire passage.

You know the drill:

Make sure that you scroll down as far as you can, to guarantee that you see the entire passage.

> Scientists researching the aging process are increasingly investigating the role of telomeres, portions of DNA on the ends of chromosomes found in every cell. Unlike the rest of the chromosome, telomeres do not contain genes, the strands of DNA that code for particular enzymes and proteins. Telomeres primarily serve a protective role in cells, playing two key roles in maintaining healthy cells. First, telomeres prevent important genetic material from being lost during cell replication, functioning as a "cap" of sorts on the end of each chromosome. Second, telomeres serve as a biological marker that the chromosome is "complete"; without a telomere on the end of a chromosome, the body considers the

chromosome defective and takes steps against it. While the protective role of telomeres is fairly well understood, scientists are interested in another facet of telomeres. Telomeres contain between one to two thousand copies of a particular DNA sequence. Each time a cell divides, a minuscule bit of this DNA sequence is lopped off. When telomeres become too short, the cell becomes impaired, unable to divide, and prone to malfunction. Cells with critically short telomeres eventually die, leading many researchers to compare telomeres to biological clocks or fuses, counting down to the death of a cell.

Although the role of telomeres in cellular aging and malfunction is well documented, new research is focused on searching for a link between cellular aging and aging and disease in humans. One study has found that subjects with shorter telomeres are more likely to develop cancers of the lungs and kidneys than those with longer telomeres. Furthermore, the study noted that the participants with the shortest telomeres were at a higher risk of developing heart disease and also appeared more prone to infectious diseases. Another study posited a link between telomere link and life span. In that study, patients with shorter telomeres died about 4 or 5 years earlier than those with telomeres of greater length. Of course, many researchers are hesitant to conclude that shorter telomeres are a causative factor from this data, particularly because telomeres are susceptible to corruption from a number of factors besides cell division. For example, scientists have noted that telomeres are especially vulnerable to the byproducts of the body's oxidation process, by which oxygen is converted to energy. The byproducts of this process, called free radicals, can not only harm cells and DNA, but also artificially shorten telomeres. Further research is necessary to better establish what link, if any, exists between telomeres and aging. One promising avenue to consider is whether lengthening damaged telomeres has the opposite effect on subjects, making them healthier and conferring greater longevity. And while some scientists optimistically believe that a full understanding of telomeres will eventually bestow dominion over the very aging process itself, such a scenario is both unlikely and not technologically feasible at this juncture.

This passage contains a lot of details. Don't get bogged down in them!

Main Idea/Purpose: _____

Structure: _____

Tone: _____

A quick reading of this passage should reveal the following: First, from the first sentence of the first paragraph, we learn that scientists are interested in the role telomeres play in the processes of aging and disease. Skimming through the rest of the paragraph, we see a lot of technical details, which we of course don't want to concern ourselves with.

We might note that around lines five and six the author tells us the two primary functions of telomeres. Around line nine, we also might note the trigger word *while*, which shows that scientists are interested in properties other than the two primary ones we noted earlier. From the second paragraph, we see that new research is looking for a link between cellular aging and human aging. As we quickly skim through the rest of the paragraph we see trigger words like *furthermore, another, of course*. These words all indicate that the author is simply providing more details and examples. There's no need to try to understand exactly what the examples are at this point. Moving to the final sentence, we learn that while telomere research has potential, the author doesn't feel that it will result in a cure for all of our ills.

Main Idea/Purpose: To explain the role of telomeres in the aging process and the research the scientists are doing to better understand telomeres.

Structure: The first paragraph provides background information on telomeres; the second one details the research on them.

Tone: Mostly neutral, with some caution expressed about the potential results of telomere research.

> Don't get caught up in the details! Focus on the big picture.

Now that we've done some work on the passages, let's move onto the second important part of reading comprehension, the questions.

SIZE UP THE QUESTIONS

Reading-comprehension questions vary in both format and what they require you to do. Let's take a look at the different types of questions you'll see on test day, and then go through strategies for tackling each type.

Question Formats

The reading-comprehension questions on the GRE will appear in several different formats:

1. **Choose a Single Answer.** These are the standard, five-answer multiple-choice questions.
2. **Choose Multiple Answers.** These questions ask you to select more than one answer, kind of like how you answered sentence-equivalence questions.
3. **Text Selection.** These questions either refer you to a highlighted portion of the text or ask you to click on the portion of the text that contains a certain phrase or performs a certain function.

Question Types

While it might seem like there are tons of different reading comprehension tasks, there are really only two major types of questions on the GRE:

1. **"Fetch" Questions.** Some questions simply require you to go to the passage and "fetch" some information. The information you are asked to fetch might be a fact from the reading, the meaning of a word, the author's tone, or the main idea of the passage.
2. **Reasoning Questions.** Other questions require a little more work than just returning to the passage and figuring out what the author says. Reasoning questions can ask you why an author used a particular word or sentence, what inferences you can draw from the passage, or who the author's intended audience may be. Reasoning questions may also ask critical reasoning-style "argument" questions about conclusions, premises, and assumptions.

Each of these question types may show up in any of the question formats above. Let's look at some of these questions in more detail.

Fetch Questions

These questions ask, in one form or another, "What does the passage say?" They are the most straightforward of reading questions, and simply require you to return to the passage and retrieve information. To answer a retrieval question, follow these steps:

1. **Read the Question.** What kind of question are you dealing with?
2. **Make the Question Back into a Question.** Often the questions aren't questions at all; they're really incomplete sentences. To find an answer, you must first have a question. By putting the question into your own words, you interact qualitatively and actively with the question text. There is no possibility of your eyes glazing over or your brain going on autopilot (a real likelihood with a four-hour exam). To make the

> The best answer to a reading comprehension question has to be supported by the passage.

question into a question, simply start with a question word. Nine out of ten times *What* or *Why* will work, since most questions ask either *what* was said in the passage or *why* it was said.

3. **Find Proof.** This is the golden rule of reading comprehension. You will always be able to prove the correct answer with something in the passage. If you cannot put your finger on a specific word, phrase, or sentence that proves your answer choice, you can't pick it. To help find answers in the passage, use one or both of the following techniques:

   a. **Five Up/Five Down.** You can't trust ETS to put the correct answer exactly where they say it will be. If they highlight a portion of the passage, start reading five lines above and read until five lines below the highlighted passage. This way, you are always looking at things *in context*.

   b. **Lead Word.** A lead word is any word in the question that will be easy to skim for in the passage. Names, numbers, dates, large technical terms all make good lead words. Of course, once you find your lead word, read five lines up and five lines down (for a vocab-in-context question, you need to read only three lines up and three lines down).

4. **Answer the Question in Your Own Words.** The answer choices are designed to mislead you. If you know exactly what you're looking for, you can protect yourself from their feints and tricks.

5. **Use Process of Elimination.**

   a. **Extremes.** No matter what the passage says, ETS can phrase a correct answer any way they like. They want correct answers that are difficult to argue with. That means *wishy-washy* language (often, many, usually). *Extreme* language (is, all, every, always) is too easy to prove wrong, so it almost always is incorrect.

   b. **Scope.** If you can't put your finger on it in the passage, you cannot pick it. They are very good at slipping things into an answer choice that were never mentioned in the passage. Watch out for answer choices that expand the scope of the passage.

   c. **Half Right = All Wrong.** ETS likes to write answer choices that are half right; which also means they're half—and thus all—wrong. The first part of the answer choice will usually look good, but the second part will be incorrect. Make sure to read the entire choice carefully.

   d. **Garbled Information.** Some wrong answer choices just take parts of the passage and garble them. These answers usually contain information that's taken directly from the passage rather than paraphrasing it.

Correct answers are paraphrases of information stated in the passage.

Let's try a fetch question with the following passage, which you've seen before.

The constitutional concept of freedom of the press traces its origins to 1735 and the libel trial of John Peter Zenger. Zenger, born in Germany, emigrated to America in 1710 and established the *Weekly Journal* in 1733. The *Journal* starkly opposed the policies of New York governor William Cosby and while Zenger did not write the majority of the critical pieces, he was arrested on libel charges in 1734. In the ensuing trial, widely followed by the populace, Zenger was defended by Andrew Hamilton, a Pennsylvania lawyer who was brought in after Cosby disbarred all the New York lawyers who offered to defend Zenger. Hamilton's brilliant defense of Zenger was predicated on the argument that since Zenger's criticisms involved verifiable facts, they could not possibly be considered libel. The judge agreed and acquitted the publisher, establishing the basic concept of freedom of the press that was to be enshrined in the United States Constitution some 45 years later.

And here's the question:

The passage states that Zenger did all of the following EXCEPT

○ started his own newspaper

○ opposed the governor's administration

○ left his homeland to come to the United States

○ hired Andrew Hamilton to defend him

○ based his criticisms on factual issues

Always go back to the passage to verify your answer. Don't answer from memory.

Here's How to Crack It

Step 1: **Read the Question.** Essentially, "What did Zenger do?" This is a fetch question.

Step 2: **Make the Question Back into a Question.** What did Zenger do?

Step 3: **Find Proof.** "Zenger" will make a nice lead word. Find the first instance of it in the passage and read from five lines above to five lines below.

Step 4: **Answer the Question in Your Own Words.** In the passage, we are told that Zenger "emigrated to America," "established the *Weekly Journal*," and "opposed the policies of New York governor William Cosby."

Step 5: **Use Process of Elimination.** Use your scratch paper. Cross off answer choices (A), (B), and (C). Now we need more information, so go back to the passage and find more instances of the lead word *Zenger*. We are told that he "was defended by Andrew Hamilton" and that his "criticisms involved verifiable facts." Choice (D) says that Zenger "hired Andrew Hamilton to defend him." One might assume that since Hamilton defended him, Zenger must have hired Hamilton to do so. Be careful, and be literal. This is how they catch smart people. If you cannot prove your answer with something stated in the passage, you can't pick it. If the passage doesn't say Zenger hired Hamilton, we can't assume it. Assumptions always get you into trouble on reading comp. If you're not convinced, don't get hung up; just give (D) the *maybe,* and move on. Choice (E) says that he "based his criticisms on factual issues." We have proof for this one, so cross it off. Choice (D) is the only one left. That must be our answer.

Keep your hand moving. Don't get hung up on an answer choice in the first pass, and be incredibly literal. If the passage doesn't say it, you can't pick it.

Let's try another fetch question. Try the next question, again based on the passage we've already studied:

2 of 20

As used in the passage, the phrase "predicated on" most nearly means

○ derived from

○ extirpated on

○ conjectured on

○ covenanted on

○ relegated to

Remember to keep track of new vocabulary words as you work through this book!

Here's How to Crack It

Treat this type of question just like a text-completion problem. Go back to the passage and read the sentence that contains the highlighted phrase, imagining that the highlighted portion is missing: "Hamilton's brilliant defense of Zenger was _____ the argument that since Zenger's criticisms involved verifiable facts, they could not possibly be considered libel." Try to come up with your own word or phrase for the blank.

The clue is that the defense had something to do with the "argument that was...." A good phrase might be *based on* or *constructed on*. Now go to the answer choices and use POE. Does *derived from* mean based on? It's fairly close, so leave this choice. How about *extirpated*? Remember that if you're not sure of the meaning of this word, you can't eliminate it. Leave it for now. Answer choice (C) is not a match; *conjectured* means to guess or infer. A *covenant* is an agreement, so choice (D) doesn't make sense either. And *relegate* means to assign, so that's out too. If you're down to choices (A) and (B), go with the one you know works. Choice (A) definitely works, so that's our answer.

———————◯———————

By the way, to *extirpate* means to tear up by the roots or destroy completely. Remember to keep track of new vocabulary words as you work through this book!

Here's another fetch question, and another familiar passage to work with:

———————◯———————

Scientists researching the aging process are increasingly investigating the role of telomeres, portions of DNA on the ends of chromosomes found in every cell. Unlike the rest of the chromosome, telomeres do not contain genes, the strands of DNA that code for particular enzymes and proteins. Telomeres primarily serve a protective role in cells, playing two key roles in maintaining healthy cells. First, telomeres prevent important genetic material from being lost during cell replication, functioning as a "cap" of sorts on the end of each chromosome. Second, telomeres serve as a biological marker that the chromosome is "complete"; without a telomere on the end of a chromosome, the body considers the chromosome defective and takes steps against it. While the protective role of telomeres is fairly well understood, scientists are interested in another facet of telomeres. Telomeres contain between one to two thousand copies of a particular DNA sequence. Each time a cell divides, a minuscule bit of this DNA sequence is lopped off. When telomeres become too short, the cell becomes impaired, unable to divide, and prone to malfunction. Cells with critically short telomeres eventually die, leading many researchers to compare telomeres to biological clocks or fuses, counting down to the death of a cell.

Although the role of telomeres in cellular aging and malfunction is well documented, new research is focused on searching for a link between cellular aging and aging and diseases in humans. One study has found that subjects with shorter telomeres are more likely to develop cancers of the lungs and kidneys than those subjects with longer telomeres. Furthermore, the study noted that the participants with the shortest telomeres were at a higher risk of developing heart disease and also appeared more prone to infectious diseases. Another study posited a link between telomere link and life span. In that study, patients with shorter telomeres died about 4 or 5 years earlier than those with telomeres of greater length. Of course, many researchers are hesitant to conclude that shorter telomeres are a causative factor from this data, particularly because telomeres are susceptible to corruption from a number of factors besides cell division. For example, scientists have noted that telomeres are especially vulnerable to the byproducts of the body's oxidation process, by which oxygen is converted to energy. The byproducts of this process, called free radicals, can not only harm cells and DNA, but also artificially shorten telomeres. Further research is necessary to better establish what link, if any, exists between telomeres and aging. One promising avenue to consider is whether lengthening damaged telomeres has the opposite effect on subjects, making them healthier and conferring greater longevity. And while some scientists optimistically believe that a full understanding of telomeres will eventually bestow dominion over the very aging process itself, such a scenario is both unlikely and not technologically feasible at this juncture.

Can you prove
your answer?

The author's attitude toward a possible research project involving lengthening damaged telomeres is

○ hopeful that the research will shed light on the link between telomeres and the aging process

○ optimistic that researchers pursuing this project will prove whether shortening telomeres causes aging

○ indifferent to the possible outcomes of such a research project

○ skeptical that such research will conclusively prove that there is a link between telomeres and cell aging

○ uncertain that researchers pursuing such an avenue will be able to truly achieve dominion over the aging process

Here's How to Crack It

This question asks us what the author's attitude is. Our first step is, as always, to go back to the passage; here, look for the part that discusses the research project mentioned in the question. You'll find it toward the end, about 10 lines up from the bottom. Reading the lines around that portion of the passage, ask yourself what the tone is—is the author's tone positive, negative, or neutral? Once you've answered that, you've got to find evidence to support it.

One good piece of evidence is that the author uses the word *promising*, so the attitude must be somewhat positive. Going back to the answer choices, we can eliminate any choices that are negative. That would eliminate choice (D) and choice (E). Because *hopeful* is a pretty good match for *promising*, we should leave the first answer choice. Now let's use POE on the remaining options. Choice (B) involves a classic GRE trick: Notice that later in the passage, the author states that some scientists are *optimistic*. But there's no evidence that the author is optimistic about the research "proving" the link. The author only states that it's an avenue to consider. Answer choice (C) doesn't stand up to scrutiny either. The author certainly calls the research *promising*, which precludes a tone of *indifferent*. Thus, the best answer is (A).

Now that we've cracked the fetch questions, let's move onto the next major type: reasoning questions.

Reasoning Questions

Reasoning questions ask us to go a little bit beyond what the passage states. The best answer is still based on the passage, but we need to do a little more work to get it. Our steps for reasoning questions are pretty similar to those for fetch questions:

1. **Figure Out What the Question Wants.** Reasoning questions never ask for a simple fact from the passage. Instead, you'll need to figure out what type of information the question requires before you go back to the passage.

2. **Return to the Passage.** You'll still need to return to the passage to find the answer. In general, reasoning questions will require you to read more of the passage than simple fetch questions because often you'll need to know the context for a particular piece of information.

3. **Answer in Your Own Words If Possible.** You'll be able to complete this step for some reasoning questions, but not for others. If you can't answer in your words, go right to the answers and use POE.

POE Guidelines for Reasoning Questions

On many reasoning questions you'll have to make aggressive use of POE. Much of the guidelines you used for fetch questions still apply. However, on reasoning questions, look out for answer choices that do the following:

1. **Go Beyond the Information Given.** Often, wrong answers on these questions will go too far beyond the scope of the passage. Choose the answer that is closest to the information in the passage.

2. **Have the Wrong Tone.** Some reasoning questions, such as strengthen and weaken questions, can use extreme language while others, such as inference questions, generally should not. Make sure the tone of the answer choice is appropriate to the question task.

3. **Are Only Half Right.** Again, answers that are only half right are all wrong and you should eliminate them.

Here's a practice reasoning question:

What was it about Oscar Wilde's only novel, *The Picture of Dorian Gray*, that caused it to create such an uproar when it was published in 1891? While critics attacked the quality of Wilde's work, lambasting its plot as "incurably silly" and chiding the writer for using prose that was "clumsy" and "boring," these overt denunciations of the formal elements of Wilde's work merely masked the true concerns of many nineteenth-century critics. What these critics were actually railing against was the thematic content of Wilde's work, specifically his illustration of a lifestyle devoted to useless beauty. For many a nineteenth-century moralist, *The Picture of Dorian Gray* was nothing more than a primer for spiritual depravity. Wilde's ultimate sin was not his clunky plot or his sometimes cloying prose; it wasn't even his disregard for the time-honored tradition of English propriety. It was instead his leniency toward his protagonist. Wilde propagated the disdain of critics not simply because Dorian Gray was an unabashed hedonist, but because Wilde failed to punish his subject appropriately for his hedonism. To the critics, allowing an evil character to escape his just desserts was an unforgivable sin, and it was this transgression that resulted in such opprobrium for Wilde's work. In their mind, Wilde's work was corrupting the genteel reading public by failing to show the proper consequences of immoral behavior.

The author of the passage would probably consider which one of the following situations most analogous to the response of the critics in the highlighted sentence?

○ A college professor lowers a student's grade from an A to a B because the student is chronically late to class.

○ An accountant refuses to his help his clients cheat on their income tax returns.

○ A politician attacks the character of his opponent even though it is his opponent's positions that the politician disagrees with.

○ A district attorney indicts a person on a misdemeanor charge because he lacks the evidence to convict the person on a felony charge.

○ A reporter files a story despite not having been able to verify all her sources.

What sort of information do we need from the passage in order to answer this question?

Here's How to Crack It

This question wants us to figure out what the response of the critics is and then find a situation that is similar to it. First, return to the passage and read the high-lighted sentence. Next, state in your own words what that part of the passage says. Based on the sentence, it appears that the situation is that "the people attacked this thing for one reason, but there was really another reason they didn't like it."

Now you're ready to return to the answer choices and look for the best match. The situation in the first answer choice is not the same as what we've written; here the professor is penalizing the student for a transgression. Eliminate it. Choice (B) doesn't match—the accountant is refusing to do something illegal. The third choice seems like a good match; the politician attacks his opponent for one reason (his character), but there was another reason (his policies) for his dislike of the candidate.

Let's check the remaining choices to make sure our answer is the best answer. In choice (D), the district attorney indicts on a lesser charge because of a lack of evidence for a more serious charge. This is somewhat similar, in that there is an overt element (the misdemeanor charge) and also a second factor which is not overt (the felony charge). However, the part of the answer choice that mentions the lack of evidence makes this choice worse than (C). It goes beyond the informa-tion presented in the passage because the original situation in the passage doesn't mention a lack of evidence on behalf of the critics. Finally, choice (E) is not a match at all. This situation involves a reporter who puts forth something that has not been verified, which isn't the same as criticizing something for one reason when there is another, deeper reason. Thus, choice (C) is our answer.

Ready for another reasoning question? It's based on the passage we just used.

Consider each of the choices separately and select <u>all</u> that apply.

The author of the passage would probably agree with which of the following statements?

☐ Most critics of Oscar Wilde's novel objected primarily to the lifestyle of its author.

☐ If *The Picture of Dorian Gray* were written in the twentieth century, the critical reaction would be less severe.

☐ Some critics of Wilde's *The Picture of Dorian Gray* believed that an author of a book had a moral responsibility to the book's audience.

Here's How to Crack It

In order to answer this question we have to figure out which answer choice the author might agree with. How the heck are we supposed to know what the author might think? Well, all we know about what the author thinks is what's found in the passage. In many ways, "author-agree" questions are very similar to inference questions. In both types of questions, the best answer may not be explicitly stated in the passage, but there will be sufficient evidence in the passage to support the correct answer. The key here is to take each answer choice one by one and return to the passage to look for proof for it.

The first choice states that most critics objected to Wilde's lifestyle. Can you find any evidence of this in the passage? No. Nowhere does the passage mention his lifestyle. It says that the critics disagreed with the "thematic content," but we can't assume that Wilde based his work on his own lifestyle (and of course, you can't use any outside knowledge you may have of Wilde's licentious life). Remember, you have to stay inside the scope of the passage—don't go beyond the information given. Thus, choice (A) is no good.

Now look at the second choice. Is there any evidence about how the author would feel if the book were released today? Nope. Of course, you may assume that the author would agree with this choice, but again, on the GRE that isn't good enough. We need direct evidence from the passage and there is none for this choice. So, goodbye to choice (B). Let's go to the third and final answer. Return to the passage and look for the part about the book's audience. The last two lines make it clear that some critics saw Wilde's book as corrupting the public and for this they attacked it. This would support choice (C), so that's our best answer. Notice that in these multiple choice, multiple answer questions, there need not be two answers—sometimes there will just be one!

Select-in-Passage Questions

Think of these as regular fetch questions, but the answer choices are in the passage rather than part of the question. Most of the time you will find these questions on short passages, but should they occur on a long passage, ETS will limit the scope of the question to a single paragraph. Follow the same steps as you would on a fetch question. Put the question into your own words. Anticipate the answer; then select it from the five or six sentences in the paragraph or passage.

Here's a practice select-in-passage question:

Need more info? Check out the DVD.

The constitutional concept of freedom of the press traces its origins to 1735 and the libel trial of John Peter Zenger. Zenger, born in Germany, emigrated to America in 1710 and established the *Weekly Journal* in 1733. The *Journal* starkly opposed the policies of New York governor William Cosby and while Zenger did not write the majority of the critical pieces, he was arrested on libel charges in 1734. In the ensuing trial, widely followed by the populace, Zenger was defended by Andrew Hamilton, a Pennsylvania lawyer who was brought in after Cosby disbarred all the New York lawyers who offered to defend Zenger. Hamilton's brilliant defense of Zenger was predicated on the argument that since Zenger's criticisms involved verifiable facts, they could not possibly be considered libel. The judge agreed and acquitted the publisher, establishing the basic concept of freedom of the press that was to be enshrined in the United States Constitution some 45 years later.

Select the sentence in which the author offers an opinion.

Here's How to Crack it.

Select the sentence in which the author offers an opinion.

First, read the question and summarize it in your own words. The question is looking for an opinion, as opposed to a fact, and specifically, the author's opinion. Note that there are actually only six sentences in this passage, so you really have only six answer choices, just like a regular question. One of them must contain an opinion. The other four, therefore, must be factual. This is a great case for POE. Write A, B, C, D, and E on your scratch paper so you have something to eliminate.

Sentence 1—All dates and facts. Cross off (A)

Sentence 2—More facts. Cross off (B)

Sentence 3—More facts. Cross off (C)

Sentence 4—More facts. Cross off (D)

Sentence 5—The author describes Hamilton's defense as "brilliant." This is an opinion, not a fact. This is a possible answer. Give it a check.

Sentence 6—More facts. Cross off (F). The correct answer is sentence 5.

POE, REVISITED

As you've surely noticed by now, the answer to a reading-comprehension question is the one that is supported by evidence from the passage. Regardless of the question type or format, that rule is immutable. Here is a recap of other guidelines to use when using POE:

1. **Avoid Extreme Statements.** ETS prefers wishy-washy statements to extreme ones. When in doubt, pick the answer that has a weaker tone.
2. **Half Right = All Wrong.** ETS likes to write answer choices that are half right; which also means that they're half—and thus all—wrong. The first part of the answer choice will usually look good, but the second part will be incorrect. Make sure to read the entire choice carefully.
3. **Garbled Information.** Some wrong answer choices just take parts of the passage and garble them. These answers usually contain information that's taken directly from the passage rather than paraphrasing it. Eliminate them!
4. **Beyond the Information Given.** These answers go too far beyond what is written in the passage. If you can't point to a part of the passage that matches information in the answer choice, that choice is probably wrong.

Let's explore these guidelines in a little more detail.

> ETS constructs correct answer choices that cannot be disputed. The more extreme a choice is, the less likely it is to be the answer.

Avoid Extreme Statements

Extreme statements are answer choices that make absolute claims. There are very few absolutes in the world, so you shouldn't expect ETS reading passages (which are all excerpted or based on actual academic papers) to contain extreme statements.

Certain words make choices extreme and, therefore, easy to dispute. Here are a few of these words.

Extreme answers are bad!

- must
- the first
- each
- every
- all

- the best
- only
- totally
- always
- no

You shouldn't automatically eliminate a choice that contains one of these words, but you should turn your attention to it immediately and attack it vigorously. If you can find even one exception, you can eliminate that choice.

Other words make choices moderate, more mushy, and therefore hard to dispute. Here are a few of these words.

Moderate answers are good!

- may
- can
- some

- many
- sometimes
- often

For example, consider the following two answer choices:

○ There is assuredly life on other planets or moons in the solar system.

○ Scientists believe that there may be life on other planets or moons in the solar system.

Without even looking at a passage, you should pick the second answer choice because it's more wishy-washy; the first choice is too strong for ETS's liking.

Half Right = All Wrong

Careful reading of the answer choices is essential on reading comprehension. Remember that your job is to find flaws in answer choices and eliminate them. Many people focus on what they like about an answer, rather than what's wrong with it. ETS loves to write answer choices that start out fine, but then say something wrong. Don't be taken in by the part of the answer you like. Use a critical eye when applying POE; don't look for reasons to keep disputed answer choices, look for reasons to eliminate them. One word can make an answer choice wrong if that word isn't supported by the passage.

If an answer choice is half wrong, it's all wrong. Focus on flaws and on Process of Elimination.

Look at the following example for the next three example questions:

Within the atmosphere are small amounts of a number of important gases, popularly called "greenhouse gases," because they alter the flow of life- and heat-energy through the atmosphere, much as does the glass shell of a greenhouse. Their effect on incoming solar energy is minimal, but collectively they act as an insulating blanket around the planet. By absorbing and returning to the earth's surface much of its outgoing heat, these gases trap it within the lower atmosphere. A greenhouse effect is natural and essential to a livable climate on Earth.

The passage states which of the following about the effect of greenhouse gases on the environment?

○ Although their effect on incoming solar energy is minimal, the presence of artificial greenhouse gases is a danger to the planet.

○ The composite effect of the gases is necessary for maintaining a climate favorable to life on Earth.

In this case, the first answer starts out great—the passage does indeed state that the gases have a minimal effect on solar energy. But look at the rest of the passage. Does the passage ever talk about "artificial" greenhouse gases? Nope, so the first answer is half right, but all wrong. The second choice, however, is entirely supported by the passage. The second sentence states that "collectively they act…," while the final sentence says the greenhouse effect is "essential to a livable climate on Earth."

The Art of Paraphrasing

Because the right answer to every reading-comprehension question is literally right in front of you, ETS goes to great lengths to disguise the correct answer and to make the wrong answers more appealing. ETS does this by making the best answer a clever paraphrase of the words in the text, one that basically states the same idea but usually avoids repeating words verbatim from the text. By paraphrasing, ETS is able to create right answers that "fly under the radar"; they don't stand out and they're easy to dismiss in favor of the trap answers.

When tackling reading comprehension, your ability to paraphrase information is key. Try to take the dense and complicated ETS text and distill it to its simplest parts. For example, if the ETS text states "normative models of political behavior, despite being rife with questionable cultural assumptions that threaten to invalidate their claims of objectivity, still provide social scientists with useful ways of evaluating cultural practices," you might paraphrase this sentence as "this thing has problems but can still be useful." Sure, this paraphrase strips out all the important details, but on a multiple choice test, you don't always need the details. You just have to pick the best answer from among the available choices.

Successful paraphrases give you the essence of the idea without the complication of details. Practice paraphrasing to see your reading comprehension score rise.

Garbled Information

One of ETS's favorite tricks is to write answer choices that contain information from different parts of the passage than the one to which the question refers. If you aren't being careful you'll think, "I remember something like that from the passage" and pick the wrong answer choice. This is one reason it's so important to use lead words and line references to guide you to the right part of the passage. Never answer a question from memory.

ETS also likes to conflate different parts of a passage to create an answer that uses a lot of words from the passage, but doesn't say a whole lot. For example, use the passage from the previous section to answer the following question:

> The passage suggests which of the following about "greenhouse gases"?
>
> ○ They are a natural source of heat energy within the atmosphere.
>
> ○ They contribute to creating a habitable environment on Earth.

The first answer choice uses a lot of words from the passage, but says a whole lot of nothing. It garbles the information in the passage, which states that greenhouse gases "alter" heat energy. They are not a source of it. The second choice, which is the correct choice, is a nice paraphrase of the last sentence. It may not sound as "correct" the other choice, but close examination shows it to be the better answer.

Beyond the Information Given

ETS takes its reading passages from textbooks, collections of essays, works of scholarship, and other sources of serious reading matter. However, be careful not to answer questions based on the fact that you did your undergraduate thesis on the topic, or that you once read a newspaper article about the topic at hand. The answers are in the passage; don't use outside knowledge.

Remember: All of the answers you need are on the screen.

Often, these answers will make common sense, but unfortunately you can't use that as a criterion on the GRE. Which of the following answer choices is beyond the information in the passage from before?

> The author of the passage would probably agree with which of the following statements?
>
> ○ Without the presence of greenhouse gases, it is unlikely that the earth would be able to support life.
>
> ○ Air pollution may contribute to an increase in greenhouse gases, which will in turn lead to eventual warming of the earth.

Clearly, here the second choice is beyond the information given in the passage. It may be true and it makes common sense, but the passage never addresses it. Thus, it cannot be the correct answer on a GRE reading comprehension question.

CRACKING THE QUESTION

When it's time to attack a question, remember the following steps:

1. Read the question and determine the lead words; then make sure you understand what it's asking.

2. Go back to the passage, find the lead words, and read more in depth where you need to.

3. Paraphrase the answer in your own words.

4. Use POE on the answer choices.

Reading Comprehension Drill

Answers can be found in Part V.

Questions 1 through 4 are based on the following reading passage.

The term "revolution" has been reserved by most historians for social upheaval characterized by bloodshed, the use of force, and great technological change. Historian Robert Cornwall cogently argues that the term can be extended to apply to the massive agricultural transformation that took place in the mid- to late-eighteenth century.

Farming practices in the 1700s were largely unchanged from those in the preceding centuries: Hordes of peasants labored on the land for long hours with only meager crop yields to show for their hard work. The eighteenth century brought improved transportation, progress in animal breeding, new crops, and better farming techniques, all of which served to increase the overall crop yield. However, the greatest impact on English agricultural yields may well have come from the significant expansion of enclosure. Prior to the mid-eighteenth century, farming was a communal activity in which the entire village decided what, where, and when to plant. To combat soil exhaustion, farmers were required to leave a field fallow every third year, a practice which led to massive inefficiencies. The practice of enclosure allowed farmers to maintain a better balance between arable land and pasture. Land that was worn out could be converted to grazing land for cattle, thus enriching and restoring it.

To move beyond subsistence-level farming, new ways to transport excess crops to market had to be found. The development of canal systems as well as an expanded and improved roadway system facilitated transportation.

The passage suggests that which of the following needed to take place in order for the agricultural revolution to take hold?

○ large-scale social upheaval and bloodshed

○ an increase in the number of peasants free to work the fields

○ the infrastructure by which excess crops could be transported

○ a widespread understanding of the necessity of crop rotation

○ the lifting of legal restrictions preventing enclosure

The passage suggests that the author would be most likely to agree with which of the following?

○ In the past, historians have not generally considered large-scale changes in agriculture to be revolutionary.

○ Agricultural expansion in England would have occurred at a faster pace had it not been for the restriction of enclosure placed on farmers.

○ Communal farming had a disastrous effect on English agriculture.

○ Eighteenth century farming was hampered by insufficient numbers of peasants available to work the land.

○ Technological innovation did not play a role in the agricultural revolution.

Click on the sentence in the second paragraph that best illustrates the problems incurred by communal farmers.

The word cogently as it is used in this passage is closest in meaning to

○ persuasively

○ enigmatically

○ inadvertently

○ inconclusively

○ questioningly

Questions 5 through 6 are based on the following reading passage.

    Echinosorex gymnura, known colloquially as the moon rat or gymnure, is one of the many fascinating creatures that inhabit the jungles of Southeast Asia. A close relative of the hedgehog, the moon rat likewise belongs to the order *Insectivora* and the family *Erinaceidae.* However, the family then splits into the sub-family *Hylomyinae,* which contains three separate genera and eight distinct species. The appearance and habitat of the moon rat are actually far more similar to those of various members of the order *Rodentia,* though its eating habits are more in line with its fellow insectivores. Ultimately, the taxonomic classification of this animal is useful only when considered along with other information regarding the animal's ecological niche.

Consider each of the choices separately and select all that apply.

Which of the following scenarios demonstrates the idea put forth by the author of this passage regarding animal classification?

☐ While studying a population of bears, scientists rely solely on the traditional taxonomic designations to identify likely hunting grounds.

☐ A team of medical researchers closely monitors the actions of the animals involved in a study and compares its findings with prevailing beliefs about those animals.

☐ A zookeeper designs a habitat for a new acquisition disregards taxonomic classifications and instead focuses on observational data.

The author's tone could best be described as

○ exasperated

○ didactic

○ ambivalent

○ morose

○ laudatory

Click on the sentence that most directly exemplifies the rationale behind the author's conclusion.

Questions 8 through 10 are based on the following reading passage.

Chinua Achebe's masterpiece *Things Fall Apart* was borne out of Achebe's frustration at the manner in which African nations had, up until then, been portrayed in European novels. The book tells of Christian missionaries to Nigeria who disrupt traditional Igbo life, thereby driving the protagonist Oknokwo, a village elder, to suicide.

Achebe's book gained him instant recognition. Critics rightly praised the book's vivid accounts of tribal beliefs and culture, and commended Achebe's inclusion of Igbo proverbs. He was recognized not only as a historian, but also as a novelist whose work could be likened to that of a Greek tragedy.

However, not all critical views of Achebe's work were laudatory. Some critics felt that Achebe's novel placed undue blame on the colonialists. These critics argued that Achebe's portrayal did not show adequate gratitude for the introduction of Western culture and technology.

The word laudatory, as used in the passage, could most effectively be replaced with which of the following?

○ approbative

○ analytical

○ dispassionate

○ paradigmatic

○ unequivocal

Click on the sentence in the passage that best illustrates the author's opinion of Achebe's *Things Fall Apart*.

The primary purpose of the passage is to

○ explain the source of Achebe's desire to write his novel

○ present an overview of the critical context in which Achebe's work has been viewed

○ prove that Achebe's work is worthy of critical acclaim

○ analyze the historical background in which Achebe writes

○ explain how Achebe's novel fits within the context of Igbo literature

CRITICAL REASONING

Critical-reasoning questions are composed of short reading passages, typically just one paragraph long, followed by a series of questions about the author's argument. You should expect to see anywhere from 3 to 5 critical-reasoning questions within your two GRE Verbal sections.

Here's a sample critical-reasoning passage and question:

The answer to this question, by the way, is (D). Not sure why? Keep reading.

For over fifty years, many evolutionary biologists posited that early fish such as *Eusthenopteron* developed limbs as a result of the need to drag themselves across short distances when their watery habitats dried up during periods of drought. However, new fossil evidence suggests that this hypothesis is incorrect. Fossilized remains of *Acanthostega*, a primitive fish, reveal that even though the animal had rudimentary limbs, it could not walk on land. *Acanthostega* lacked ankles, which means that its limbs couldn't support its weight; furthermore, its ribs were too short to prevent the organism's chest cavity from collapsing once the animal left water.

Which of the following would most strengthen the author's argument?

○ The fossilized remains of the *Acanthostega* are the earliest known evidence of early fish.

○ The modern descendants of *Acanthostega* are not able to drag themselves across short distances on land.

○ Biologists have found that some aquatic species can successfully drag themselves across land even though these species do not possess ankles.

○ Any animal with a collapsed chest cavity is not able to survive long enough to travel even a short distance across land.

○ Some evolutionary biologists believe that the new fossils are not from *Acanthostega*.

What Exactly Is Critical Reasoning?

Critical reasoning is our term for a specific type of reading passage you'll encounter on the GRE. At first glance, critical-reasoning passages resemble the short reading-comprehension passages. However, what distinguishes critical reasoning from a regular reading passage is twofold:

1. The structure of the passage
2. The types of questions ETS will ask about it

We'll show you how to identify critical-reasoning passages and the most effective way of tackling these questions as well.

BREAKING AN ARGUMENT DOWN

The key to doing well on critical-reasoning questions is understanding how ETS authors construct an argument. All arguments contain two major parts—the conclusion, or the main point of the argument, and the premise—the facts that the author gives in support of his or her conclusion. Identifying these two parts is crucial to your success on these questions. Let's start our analysis of an author's argument in a critical-reasoning passage by learning how to identify the conclusion.

Identifying the Conclusion

The conclusion is the most important part of the argument; quite simply, it is the reason the argument exists. The conclusion of an argument is generally a statement of opinion—it's the author's belief or prediction about a situation. Let's look at the critical-reasoning passage we just saw, above:

> For over fifty years, many evolutionary biologists posited that early fish such as *Eusthenopteron* developed limbs as a result of the need to drag themselves across short distances when their watery habitats dried up during periods of drought. However, new fossil evidence suggests that this hypothesis is incorrect. Fossilized remains of *Acanthostega*, a primitive fish, reveal that even though the animal had rudimentary limbs, it could not walk on land. *Acanthostega* lacked ankles, which means that its limbs couldn't support its weight; furthermore, its ribs were too short to prevent the organism's chest cavity from collapsing once the animal left water.

You can identify the conclusion of the author's argument by asking yourself: What opinion does this author hold? Now underline the sentence that you think is the conclusion of the argument above.

The conclusion is the author's main point.

If you underlined "new fossil evidence suggests that this hypothesis is incorrect" you hit the nail on the head.

There are other ways of identifying conclusions in arguments. For example, often you can identify the conclusion by certain key words. Specifically, keep an eye out for the following:

> An argument's conclusion is often signaled by the words:
>
> *therefore*   *thus*   *consequently*   *and so*   *in conclusion*

You should also look for any words that indicate an opinion, such as the following:

> *suggest*   *believe*   *hope*   *indicate*   *argue*   *follow*

Remember, the conclusion is often the author's opinion about what *might* happen.

In addition, a conclusion is often a belief about what should or might happen. Look for the following:

> *should*   *would*   *must*   *will*

Practice: Identifying Conclusions

Underline the conclusions of the arguments in the following critical-reasoning passages. Answers can be found in Part V.

1 of 5

Despite the support of the president, it is unlikely that the new defense bill will pass. A bipartisan group of 15 senators has announced that it does not support the legislation.

2 of 5

The earliest known grass fossils date from approximately 55 million years ago. Dinosaurs most likely disappeared from the earth around 60 million years ago. Based on this evidence, as well as fossilized remains of dinosaur teeth that indicate the creatures were more suited to eating ferns and palms, scientists have concluded that grass was not a significant part of the dinosaur diet.

3 of 5

Automaker X has lost over 2 billion dollars this year due to rising costs, declining automobile sales, and new governmental regulations. Because of the company's poor financial situation, it has asked its employees to pay more for health care and to accept a pay cut. However, the workers at automaker X are threatening to go on strike. If that happens, automaker X will have no choice but to file for bankruptcy.

4 of 5

The rise of obesity among citizens of country Y has been linked to a variety of health problems. In response to this situation, the country's largest health organization has called for food manufacturers to help combat the problem. Since the leading members of the nation's food industry have agreed to provide healthier alternatives, reduce sugar and fat content, and reduce advertisements for unhealthy foods, it is likely that country Y will experience a decrease in obesity-related health problems.

5 of 5

Recent advances in technology have led to a new wave of "smart" appliances, including refrigerators that note when food supplies are low and place an order at the grocery store, washing machines that automatically adjust the wash cycle and temperature based upon the clothes in the machine, and doorknobs that can identify the house owner and automatically open the door. A technology expert predicts that, due to these new innovations, machines will soon outnumber humans as the number-one users of the Internet.

Some critical-reasoning questions ask you to find the conclusion of the argument. Here's an example:

Mutation breeding is a method of crop development that requires breeders to first find plants that randomly display the traits researchers are looking for, and then breed those plants with other plants displaying similar traits. In order to bring about the required mutations, researchers bombard plants with thermal neutrons, x-rays, and known carcinogenic chemicals in order to damage the plant's DNA. Today, almost all varieties of wheat grown commercially are products of mutation breeding. Ironically, when scientists discovered how to splice desirable genes directly into the plants, thus avoiding the use of harmful chemicals and radiation, critics derided the new process as potentially dangerous despite the lack of any supporting evidence, resulting in boycotts and bans on genetically modified foods.

The argument as a whole is structured to lead to which of the following conclusions?

○ Genetically modified food may have been unfairly stigmatized by its critics.

○ Mutation breeding produces safer food than does genetic modification.

○ Foods produced by genetic modification are healthier than foods produced by mutation breeding.

○ Researchers should stop using mutation breeding in order to modify foods.

○ Genetic modification of plants is more cost effective than mutation breeding of plants.

Here's How to Crack It

The conclusion, as you'll recall, is the author's opinion or belief. As you read the argument, look for indicators of the author's opinion. The first three sentences of the argument do not state opinions; the author is simply describing the method of mutation breeding. However, in the fourth sentence, the author uses the word *ironically*. This is an indicator of how the author feels. The author believes it is ironic that genetically modified foods are banned, despite "any supporting evidence" that they are dangerous, while foods created with mutation breeding, which use "harmful chemicals and radiation" account for "almost all varieties of wheat..."

Now we just need to find an answer choice that matches this opinion. Answer choice (A) looks pretty close, so let's hang on to it. Choice (B) is the opposite of what the author argues; the argument implies that genetic modification is safer. Choice (C) is close, but the argument doesn't really discuss which foods are "healthier," just that one type is banned and the other type isn't. Choice (D) also isn't discussed. The author thinks it's ironic that genetically modified foods are banned, but never states that mutation breeding should be stopped. Finally, choice (E) doesn't work because the argument doesn't express any opinion about cost effectiveness. Thus, choice (A) is the best answer.

Finding the Premise

After you identify the conclusion of an argument, your next task is to find the argument's premise. The premise (or premises—there can be more than one) is the evidence that the author gives in support of the conclusion.

You can find the premise of an argument in two ways. First, look for statements of fact. Critical-reasoning passages are usually based on statistics, surveys, polls, or reports and all of these things are premises—in fact, these are the most common types of premises. Second, you can use a strategy we call the "Why?" Test. Once you've found the conclusion, ask yourself "Why" you should accept it; the answer or answers to that question will be the premise(s). Let's look again at the passage from the beginning of the chapter:

> For over fifty years, many evolutionary biologists posited that early fish such as *Eusthenopteron* developed limbs as a result of the need to drag themselves across short distances when their watery habitats dried up during periods of drought. However, new fossil evidence suggests that this hypothesis is incorrect. Fossilized remains of *Acanthostega*, a primitive fish, reveal that even though the animal had rudimentary limbs, it could not walk on land. *Acanthostega* lacked ankles, which means that its limbs couldn't support its weight; furthermore, its ribs were too short to prevent the organism's chest cavity from collapsing once the animal left water.

Why should you believe this conclusion?

What facts does the author give in support of the conclusion? In this argument, the author provides the following facts: (1) *Acanthostega* lacked ankles, and (2) the creature's ribs were too short to prevent its chest cavity from collapsing. These facts are the premises of the argument.

Is the statement a fact, something that you could verify or prove? Then it's a premise.

Finally, just like conclusions, premises have certain indicator words. The following words will probably tell you that you're looking at a premise:

An argument's premise is often signaled by the words:

because   *due to*   *since*   *based on*

Practice: Finding the Premise

For each of the following arguments, identify the premise or premises that support the conclusion. Answers can be found in Part V.

1 of 5

Despite the support of the president, it is unlikely that the new defense bill will pass. A bipartisan group of 15 senators has announced that it does not support the legislation.

Conclusion: _____

Why?

Premise: _____

2 of 5

The earliest known grass fossils date from approximately 55 million years ago. Dinosaurs most likely disappeared from the earth around 60 million years ago. Based on this evidence, as well as fossilized remains of dinosaur teeth that indicate the creatures were more suited to eating ferns and palms, scientists have concluded that grass was not a significant part of the dinosaur diet.

Conclusion: _____

Why?

Premise: _____

3 of 5

Automaker X has lost over 2 billion dollars this year due to rising costs, declining automobile sales, and new governmental regulations. Because of the company's poor financial situation, it has asked its employees to pay more for health care and to accept a pay cut. However, the workers at automaker X are threatening to go on strike. If that happens, automaker X will have no choice but to file for bankruptcy.

Conclusion: _____

Why?

Premise: _____

4 of 5

The rise of obesity among citizens of country Y has been linked to a variety of health problems. In response to this situation, the country's largest health organization has called for food manufacturers to help combat the problem. Since the leading members of the nation's food industry have agreed to provide healthier alternatives, reduce sugar and fat content, and reduce advertisements for unhealthy foods, it is likely that country Y will experience a decrease in obesity-related health problems.

Conclusion: _____

Why?

Premise: _____

5 of 5

Recent advances in technology have led to a new wave of "smart" appliances, including refrigerators that note when food supplies are low and place an order at the grocery store, washing machines that automatically adjust the wash cycle and temperature based upon the clothes in the machine, and doorknobs that can identify the house owner and automatically open the door. A technology expert predicts that, due to these new innovations, machines will soon outnumber humans as the number-one users of the Internet.

Conclusion: _____

Why?

Premise: _____

Okay. So you know how to identify the conclusion and premise(s) of an argument. Are you ready to try a critical-reasoning question? Here's one way in which ETS will test your knowledge of the parts of an argument.

20 of 20

A common myth is that animals can sense an impending earthquake. And while most geophysicists dispute this assertion and claim that there is no way to predict an earthquake, a new hypothesis for predicting earthquakes is generating interest in the scientific community. This hypothesis is based on a well-known principle: **subjecting rocks to extreme pressures causes the rocks to produce electrical currents**. Now, a leading physicist has proposed that this principle may help predict earthquakes. For example, an earthquake along the San Andreas Fault in California could produce hundreds of thousands of amperes (units of electrical current) that would disrupt the ionosphere surrounding the Earth. **By monitoring the ionosphere for electrical fluctuations, scientists may be able to predict earthquakes.**

In the argument above, the two boldfaced statements play which of the following roles?

○ The first statement expresses the conclusion of the argument while the second statement provides support for that conclusion.

○ The first statement expresses the conclusion of the argument as a whole; the second statement provides a possible consequence of the conclusion.

○ The first statement presents support for the conclusion of the argument as a whole; the second statement states the conclusion of the argument.

○ The first statement expresses an intermediary conclusion of the argument while the second statement presents a possible objection to the intermediary conclusion.

○ The first statement provides support for a conclusion that the argument opposes; the second statement expresses the conclusion that the argument as a whole opposes.

Here's How to Crack It

The key to cracking this question is using the "Why?" test. Let's try using the "Why?" test on the two boldfaced statements and see which one works best. If we make the first statement the conclusion, we'd end up with something like this:

Conclusion: Subjecting rocks to extreme pressures causes the rocks to produce electrical currents.

Why?

Premise: By monitoring the ionosphere for electrical fluctuations, scientists may be able to predict earthquakes.

Does that make sense? Nope, so let's eliminate any answers that say that the first sentence is the argument's conclusion. That allows us to eliminate choices (A), (B), and (D). Now let's see what happens if we flip the statements around:

Conclusion: By monitoring the ionosphere for electrical fluctuations, scientists may be able to predict earthquakes.

Why?

Premise: Subjecting rocks to extreme pressures causes the rocks to produce electrical currents.

That makes much more sense. Answer choice (E) states that the argument opposes the conclusion, which it doesn't, so we can eliminate that choice. Answer choice (C) is the best answer.

The "Why?" test helps to identify premises and conclusions.

Locating Assumptions

Although ETS frequently asks critical-reasoning questions about the premise or the conclusion of an argument, there are a number of other question types that require you to work with one final part of an argument. The final part of an argument is the assumption. The assumption is never explicitly stated in the passage, which means that it can sometimes be tricky to find. Basically, the assumption is the missing link that connects the conclusion of an argument to its premise.

Let's look back at one of the arguments you've already worked on.

Conclusion: It is unlikely that the new defense bill will pass.

Why?

Premise: A bipartisan group of 15 senators has announced that it does not support the legislation.

In order for this argument to be convincing, the reader has to make an assumption that because 15 senators do not support the bill, the bill will probably not pass. If you don't assume that the opposition of 15 senators means that the bill is unlikely to pass, the argument fails. Thus, assumptions are necessary to a successful argument.

To find the assumption or assumptions in an argument, you need to look for a "gap" in the reasoning of the argument. You can often accomplish this by asking yourself the following question:

>	*Just because (**premise**) is true, does it really mean (**conclusion**) is true?*

For example, let's return to another of the arguments you've already tackled.

Conclusion: Country *Y* will experience a decrease in obesity-related health problems.

Why?

Premise: The leading members of the nation's food industry have agreed to provide healthier alternatives, reduce sugar and fat content, and reduce advertisements for unhealthy foods.

Now, let's ask ourselves the question: Just because it's true that the food industry has agreed to provide healthier alternatives, reduce sugar and fat content, and reduce advertisements for unhealthy foods, does it really mean that obesity-related health problems will decrease?

If you accept this argument, you must assume that the food industry's actions will lead to a decrease in obesity-related health problems. That's the missing link—or the assumption—required by the argument.

Practice: Locating Assumptions

For each of the following critical-reasoning questions, identify the conclusion and the premise. Then note what assumption is required to make the argument work. Answers can be found in Part V.

City University recently announced the retirement of Professor Jones. Professor Jones is a leading biologist and widely published author and her presence was a major factor in many students' decisions to attend City University. The University predicts no decline in enrollment, however, because it plans to hire two highly credentialed biology professors to replace Professor Jones.

Conclusion: _____

Premise: _____

Assumption: _____

It makes no sense to charge more to customers under 25 years of age who rent cars. After all, most states allow people as young as 16 to have a driver's license and all states allow 18-year-olds the right to vote.

Conclusion: _____

Premise: _____

Assumption: _____

It is easy to demonstrate that extraterrestrial life exists by simply looking at our own solar system. In our solar system, there are eight planets and at least one of them obviously has life on it. Thus, roughly 12.5% of planets in the universe should have life on them.

Conclusion: _____

Premise: _____

Assumption: _____

State A is facing a serious budget shortfall for the upcoming year. Recent polls indicate that 58% of voters in Township B approve of a proposed 2-cent gasoline tax in order to make up the deficit. It is clear, therefore, that the leaders of State A should institute the gas tax.

Conclusion: _____

Premise: _____

Assumption: _____

QUESTION TYPES

Now that you've familiarized yourself with the basics of an argument, let's look at the types of argument questions you'll encounter on the GRE. Each of the following types of questions will require you to first identify the argument's premise and conclusion; after that, your task will vary depending on the type.

Reasoning Questions

You can identify Reasoning questions because they will have the following question stems:

> In the argument given, the boldfaced statements play which of the following roles?

> Which of the following best describes the function of the boldfaced statements in the argument above?

> The argument above is structured to lead to which of the following conclusions?

For Reasoning questions, you must isolate the premise and conclusion, but you don't need to find the assumption.

Assumption Questions

Assumption questions are usually phrased in the following ways:

> The argument above assumes which of the following?

> The argument above relies on which of the following?

> The author's argument presupposes which of the following?

On assumption questions, you need to first locate the premise and conclusion. After that, look for the gap as described in the "Locating Assumptions" section above.

Strengthen Questions

Strengthen questions will ask you to make the argument stronger. You'll be asked to do this by identifying answer choices that will support the assumption. Strengthen questions are often phrased as:

> Which one of the following, if true, would most strengthen the argument?

> Which of the following, if true, would most support the author's argument?

Supporters of the argument would most likely cite
which of following pieces of additional evidence?

To strengthen an argument, find the premise, the conclusion, and the assumption. The correct answer will be a premise that supports the assumption.

Weaken Questions

As we've learned, the assumption is what makes an argument work. It follows, then, that if you attack the assumption, you will weaken the argument. You can identify Weaken questions by looking for the following:

> Which one of the following, if true, would most
> weaken the argument?
>
> Which one of the following, if true, casts the most
> doubt on the argument above?
>
> Which one of the following, if true, would most
> undermine the author's argument?

On weaken questions, once again you'll need to find the premise, conclusion, and assumption. The right answer will attack the assumption, breaking the link between the premise and the conclusion.

CRACKING CRITICAL-REASONING QUESTIONS

Ready to tackle some critical-reasoning questions? Let's go through steps you take when you run into one of these questions on the test.

The Basic Approach

When you identify a question as being a critical-reasoning question on the exam, go through the following steps:

1. **Read the Question Carefully.** Don't dive into the passage without being aware of exactly what you're dealing with—start by making sure that it really is critical reasoning and not a plain old reading comprehension passage.
2. **Analyze the Argument.** Identify the premise, conclusion, and assumption of the argument.
3. **Predict the Answer.** Before even looking at the answer choices, try to answer the question in your own words.

4. **Use Process of Elimination**. Process of Elimination (POE) is a valuable tool. If you're not sure what the correct answer is, look for the wrong answers instead; eliminate them, and even if you still can't identify the correct answer, you have a much greater chance of guessing the correct answer.

Try going through these steps on the following question.

———————○———————

After examining the bodies of a dozen beached whales and finding evidence of bleeding around the animals' eyes and brains as well as lesions on their kidneys and livers, environmental groups fear that the Navy's use of sonar is causing serious harm to marine animals. A leading marine biologist reports that sonar induces whales to panic and surface too quickly, which causes nitrogen bubbles to form in their blood.

1 of 20

The argument above relies on which of the following assumptions?

○ Marine biologists have documented that other marine animals, including dolphins and sea turtles, have exhibited kidney and liver lesions.

○ No studies have been conducted on the possible detrimental effects of sonar on marine animals.

○ Whales in captivity panic only when exposed to man-made, rather than natural, sound waves.

○ The presence of nitrogen bubbles in the blood has been demonstrated to cause damage to various internal organs.

○ It is unlikely that the symptoms found in the beached whales could be caused by any known disease.

What type of question is this?

Here's How to Crack It

First, read the question. This is an Assumption question—we know this because it asks you to determine what the argument relies on. Next, analyze the argument, precisely identifying the conclusion and premise. You should come up with the following:

Conclusion: The Navy's use of sonar is causing serious harm to marine animals.

Why?

Premise: Surfacing too quickly causes nitrogen bubbles to form in the whale's blood.

For Step 2, we need to locate the assumption. Remember to use the question we introduced earlier—here it would be phrased as follows:

"Just because the whales have nitrogen bubbles in their blood, does that really mean that sonar is causing them serious harm?"

In Step 3, we need to try to predict the answer before looking at the answer choices. Remember that arguments require an assumption in order to succeed. In this case, the right answer should say something along the lines of "nitrogen bubbles do cause serious harm." Okay, on to Step 4—process of elimination. Check out the grey box for some POE tips on "assumption" questions.

Eliminate answers that aren't relevant to the argument!

Now, returning to the answer choices, let's see which one is best. Answer choice (A) is wrong; this choice doesn't connect the premise to the conclusion. Even though it states that other animals have exhibited similar symptoms, we need the answer choice to connect the symptoms—in whales—to the use of sonar. Choice (B) is wrong as well. (B) brings in information that isn't part of the original argument: it's irrelevant whether or not the Navy has conducted studies on the harmful effects of sonar. Answer choice (C) doesn't help much either; the argument is not concerned with the situations under which whales panic. Answer (D) looks pretty good. It connects the nitrogen bubbles found in the premise to the serious harm mentioned in the conclusion, so hold on to this choice. Remember that since we're looking for the BEST answer, we still need to check the final answer; however, answer choice (E) is no good. Like choice (B), this choice brings in information that isn't relevant to the argument. The fact that the symptoms are unlikely to be caused by any known disease does not make the link between the sonar and the harm to the animals. Thus, choice (D) is the best answer.

POE for Assumption Questions

When you're using POE on Assumption questions, always eliminate answer choices that do the following:

1. **Give New Information.** The assumption must link the premise and the conclusion. Any answer choices that discuss information that is not part of the original argument are wrong.
2. **Have the Wrong Tone.** The tone of the answer choice should match the tone of the argument. Arguments that have very strong conclusions require very strongly worded answer choices, and arguments that have milder tones require milder answer choices.
3. **Weaken the Argument.** The assumption is necessary to the argument. Eliminate any answer choice that would weaken or hurt the argument—unless of course you're dealing with a "weaken the argument" question!

Strengthen Questions

Here's another critical-reasoning question:

Remember to identify the question type first.

The Japan Aerospace Exploration Agency has announced plans for a new unmanned space probe. The probe, named Hayabusa, will rendezvous with an asteroid some 290 million kilometers away from Earth and attempt to land on the asteroid. After the landing, Hayabusa will release a robotic rover which will photograph the surface of the asteroid and also collect rock and dust samples. The probe will then return to Earth with the samples. Scientists believe that the mission, if successful, will provide important clues about the composition of the early solar system.

Which of the following, if true, most strongly supports the scientists' conclusion about the Hayabusa mission?

○ Once the Hayabusa probe reaches the asteroid, researchers calculate that it will have a 60% chance of successfully landing on the asteroid.

○ The asteroid targeted by the Hayabusa mission is known to have been formed at the inception of the solar system.

○ The Japan Aerospace Exploration Agency has yet to experience a mechanical failure with one of its unmanned space probes.

○ Some astronomers believe that many asteroids originate outside the solar system and are captured by the gravitational pull of the sun and planets.

○ The Hayabusa probe is the first ever to attempt a landing on an asteroid.

Here's How to Crack It

Following the four steps, you would first identify the question. It's a Strengthen question; we know this because the word "strengthen" is actually used in the question! Second, find the premise, conclusion, and assumption.

Here's what you should end up with:

Conclusion: The mission, if successful, will provide important clues about the composition of the early solar system.

Why?

Premise: Hayabusa will release a robotic rover which will photograph the surface of the asteroid and also collect rock and dust samples.

Assumption: Rock and dust samples from an asteroid will provide scientists with information about the early solar system.

Always check all five answer choices.

Next, let's predict what the right answer should do. For a strengthen question, we're looking for an answer that supports the assumption. In this case, the right answer should provide some information that confirms the idea that dust and rock samples will aid scientists in understanding the early solar system.

Check out the grey box on this page for some POE guidelines on "strengthen" questions.

Looking back at the answer choices, we see that answer choice (A) is not the best answer. This answer is only half good, indicating that the probe has a better-than-even chance of landing successfully. However, it doesn't address whether the probe's mission will help scientists understand the early solar system. Eliminate this choice. Choice (B) seems to be right on the money. The answer we're looking for should support the assumption that rock and dust samples from an asteroid will provide clues about the early solar system. Choice (B) states that the asteroid in question is, in fact, from the early solar system. Keep looking through—remember that you're looking for the best choice.

Like answer choice (A), choice (C) is half right. However, while it might be helpful to know that it's unlikely that the probe will suffer a mechanical failure, you still have to assume that the mission itself will aid scientists in their attempts to understand the early solar system. That's just too much of a leap. Answer choice (D) actually weakens the argument. If asteroids come from outside the solar system, studying dust from them probably won't help researchers understand much from the solar system. Finally, choice (E) does nothing for the argument. The fact

POE for Strengthen Questions
When you're using POE on Strengthen questions, always eliminate answer choices that:

1. **Are Only Half Good.** Some answers will be on the right track, but they won't strengthen the argument enough. Again remember, you're looking for the best answer, not an answer that might be good enough. You shouldn't have to make any assumptions about the answer choice in order for it to strengthen the argument.

2. **Weaken the Argument.** Typically, one of the answer choices will weaken the argument. Unless your task is to weaken the argument, you can easily eliminate it.

3. **Do Nothing.** Some answer choices do nothing to the argument; they neither strengthen nor weaken it. Get rid of these, they're decoys.

On Strengthen questions, note that answer choices that offer new information are okay, provided of course that they help strengthen the argument. Also note that answers that have strong tones are often correct for Strengthen questions.

that the probe is the first of its kind says nothing about its scientific value. It looks like choice (B) is best; choose it and move on.

Weaken Questions

Try one last critical-reasoning question:

Psychologists have just completed an extensive study of recently divorced parents in order to determine which factors contributed most to the dissolution of the marriage. The researchers found that in a great majority of the cases of failed marriages, the couples ate, on average, fewer than ten meals per week with each other. From this data, the psychologists have determined that a failure to spend time together during meal times is a major factor leading to divorce.

3 of 20

Which of the following, if true, would cast the most doubt on the researchers' hypothesis?

○ Many couples who have long and successful marriages eat together fewer than ten times per week.

○ Most of the couples in the study who were unable to share meals with each other worked outside of the home.

○ People who lack a regular dining schedule tend to have more disorders and illnesses of the digestive system.

○ Couples in the study who reported that they ate together more than ten times per week also indicated that they tended to perceive their relationships with their spouses as healthy.

○ In many cases, people in unhappy marriages tend to express their displeasure by avoiding contact with their partners when possible.

Do you recognize what type of argument this is?

Here's How to Crack It

This is a Weaken question. Once again, we'll break the argument down into its premise, conclusion, and assumption:

Conclusion: A failure to spend time together during meal times is a major factor leading to divorce.

Why?

Premise: In a great majority of the cases of failed marriages, the couples ate, on average, less than ten meals per week with each other.

Assumption: A lack of time spent eating meals together causes marital problems; there is no other cause.

As you can see, this is a causal argument. The assumptions are, first, that there is no other cause, and second, that the cause and effect are not reversed. Since we want to weaken this argument, we can predict that the best answer will provide some other cause for the divorces, or show that the psychologists have the cause and effect backwards.

Check out the grey box for POE guidelines on "weaken" questions.

Looking through the answer choices, you can probably see right away that answer choice (A) is not the correct answer. The argument is not about what successful couples do; it is only concerned with divorced couples. Move on. Choice (B) doesn't really do anything to the argument; it's unclear how this information would affect the causal link assumed in the argument. The same goes for choice (C): All this choice indicates is that there may be other problems linked to eating—it doesn't address the connection between dining and marriage success.

Choice (D) seems like it might strengthen the argument. These couples are reporting a link between eating together more and perceiving their marriages as healthy. Eliminate this choice. Choice (E) is the best answer. This answer choice shows that the researchers have reversed the cause and effect. It is not that a failure to dine together causes marital strife; rather, couples that are already unhappy express it by not eating together. This weakens the argument, and (E) is correct.

> ### POE for Weaken Questions
> The guidelines for Weaken questions are basically the same as those for strengthen. Eliminate any answer choices that:
>
> 1. **Are Half Good.** Make sure the answer attacks the assumption thoroughly.
> 2. **Strengthen the Argument.** Once again, one answer usually does the opposite of the question task—eliminate the odd man out.
> 3. **Do Nothing.** Some answer choices neither strengthen nor weaken the argument: eliminate them.
>
> As is the case with Strengthen questions, new information and extreme tones in Weaken questions need not be eliminated.

OTHER CRITICAL-REASONING QUESTION TYPES

The GRE also contains inference and resolve/explain questions, and these types of questions will require you to use different approaches from those you use for weaken and strengthen questions. Let's go through how to crack inference and resolve/explain questions now.

> Inference and resolve/explain questions do not require you to find the premise and conclusion.

Inference Questions

An inference is a conclusion that's based on a set of given facts. You can identify inference questions because they'll look a lot like the following:

> If the statements above are true, which of the following must also be true?
>
> Which of the following statements can be properly inferred from the information above?
>
> Based on the information above, which of the following can logically be concluded?

Here's an example:

11 of 20

The Mayville Fire Department always fills its employment vacancies "in-house"—when a firefighter retires or leaves the force, his or her position is filled by interviewing all qualified members of the Mayville Department who are interested in the position. Only if this process fails to produce a qualified candidate does the department begin interviewing potential employees from outside the department. This year, the Mayville Fire Department has hired three new firefighters from outside the department.

On inference questions, you don't have to find the premise and conclusion.

If the statements above are true, which of the following must also be true?

○ For the coming year, the Mayville Fire Department will be understaffed unless it hires three additional firefighters.

○ Firefighters hired from outside the Mayville Fire Department take longer to properly train for the job.

○ At the time of the vacancies in the Mayville Fire Department, either there were no qualified in-house candidates or no qualified in-house candidates were interested in the open positions.

○ The three firefighters who left the department had jobs for which no other members of the Mayville Fire Department were qualified to fill.

○ The three new firefighters are the first new employees hired by the Mayville Fire Department.

Here's How to Crack It

Inference questions are often associated with critical-reasoning passages that are not structured like the clear-cut arguments we've seen thus far. Often these wacky arguments don't even have conclusions and premises; instead, they might simply resemble a set of facts.

Our strategy for approaching these types of questions, of course, begins with identifying them as inference questions. However, for Step 2, don't attempt to identify a conclusion or premise, simply read the argument. If the argument is complex or hard to follow, don't spend too much time trying to untangle it. Most of the work on inference questions should be done when you get to the answer choices.

For inference questions, don't even do Step 3 (predict the answer). There's no way to predict what sort of inference you'll be asked to make, so proceed directly to Step 4, using POE.

Check out the POE guidelines for inference questions in the grey box.

Let's start with answer choice (A). This choice says that the department will be "understaffed." Is there any part of the argument that indicates that this is true? Nope, so eliminate this choice. Answer choice (B) states that firefighters from outside the department take longer to train, but the argument says nothing at all about training. Eliminate this choice. Choice (C) states that either there were no qualified candidates in house or there were no qualified candidates interested in the jobs. Returning to the argument, we see that the hiring policy is that a vacant

Can you prove your answer choice? If not, eliminate it.

On inference questions, eliminate answer choices that

1. **Go beyond the Information**. Stick to the facts on inference questions. Avoid answers that are overly broad or general.
2. *Could* **Be True**. The correct answer on an inference *must* be true. Answers that might be true or could be true are no good.
3. **Use Extreme Language**. Be suspicious of strong language. The presence of words such as *all, none, always, never,* or *impossible* often means that an answer choice wrong.

The key to inference questions is using Process of Elimination: Take each answer choice and return to the argument to see if you can prove that it's true. If you can't point to the part of the argument that supports the answer choice, the answer is wrong.

"position is filled by interviewing all qualified members of the Mayville Department who are interested in the position." If this process fails, the department goes outside the department for candidates. Thus, since Mayville hired three new fire fighters from outside the department, answer choice (C) must be true.

Let's go through the remaining answers. Choice (D) is tempting, but on inference questions, we need to make sure that every part of the answer choice holds up to scrutiny. This answer states that no other members of the department were qualified to take the open positions. This could be true; however, based on the facts presented, it could also be true that there were qualified members who simply weren't interested in applying for the position. Thus, choice (D) isn't the best choice—it isn't better than (C). Finally, choice (E) goes beyond the information presented. There is no way of knowing whether these new firefighters were the first new employees. Answer choice (C) is still the best.

Resolve/Explain

Some critical-reasoning questions will present you with a paradox; a set of facts that seem to contradict each other. On these questions, your task is to find the answer choice that best explains the contradiction. You can recognize these questions because they often contain the following phrases:

Which of the following choices would best explain the situation presented above?

Which of the following, if true, would best resolve the discrepancy above?

Which of the following, if true, best reconciles the seeming paradox above?

Take a look at the following example:

Over the past ten years, the emergence of digital file sharing technology has threatened the traditional market for compact discs. Internet users are now able to share songs from their favorite artists with little or no loss of quality in the music, acquiring the songs they desire without having to purchase the entire compact disc. Music industry leaders contend that this practice violates their copyright and causes untold financial losses. However, consumer groups report that there has been an increase in the sales of compact discs.

Which of the following, if true, would best explain the situation above?

○ Some consumers who have downloaded songs from the Internet have been sued by major record companies.

○ Research indicates that persons who engage in file sharing or song downloading are usually only casual music fans.

○ The music industry is developing new technology to help prevent users from downloading songs.

○ Music artists tend to release more material, on average, today than they did ten years ago.

○ Compact discs released now often include bonus features that are appealing to fans, such as interviews with the band and music videos, that are not available for download.

Here's How to Crack It

Like inference questions, resolve/explain questions require a slightly different approach. Step 1 remains the same—read the question and identify the question type. Once you've identified the question as a resolve/explain question, read the critical-reasoning passage. However, instead of looking for a premise and conclusion, for Step 2 you're going to look for two facts that are in conflict. The basic pattern for a resolve/explain argument is as follows:

Fact I:
But
Fact II:

For the above argument, the two facts that are in conflict are:

Fact I: Internet users are able to download individual songs instead of purchasing compact discs.

But

Fact II: There has been an increase in compact disc sales.

For resolve/explain questions, as for inference questions, you can skip Step 3. You might be able to predict a possible explanation for the discrepancy, but there's no guarantee that your explanation will be similar to the credited response. Proceed to Step 4, use POE, and as you read each answer choice, ask yourself the following question:

How can both (Fact I) and (Fact II) be true?

Check out the POE guidelines for resolve/explain questions in the grey box.

> ## POE for Resolve/Explain Questions
>
> On resolve/explain questions, you should eliminate answer choices that:
>
> 1. **Do Nothing.** Many wrong answers simply do nothing to the paradox.
> 2. **Are Only Half Right.** Some answers will only deal with half of the conflict. Make sure the answer you select addresses both facts.
> 3. **Worsen the Situation.** Eliminate choices that appear to make the situation worse.

Let's use Process of Elimination on the answer choices in our example. The first answer choice doesn't resolve the conflict. It might explain why fewer users download music, but it doesn't explain why compact disc sales have increased. Eliminate choice (A). Answer choice (B) does nothing to the paradox. The fact that the people who download music are casual fans doesn't really explain anything. Like answer choice (A), choice (C) is partly correct; however, it doesn't explain the increase in sales. Also, the answer choice states that the industry is "developing" technology; it doesn't state that the technology has been implemented yet. So this couldn't affect the current situation. Choice (D) doesn't help much either. You might assume that more material on the market means that sales could increase even with downloading, but that line of thought requires you to fill in too many missing pieces. The correct answer should do all the work. Look at answer choice (E). This choice states that compact discs feature bonus material that can't be downloaded. This could explain both the fact that people are downloading music and that compact disc sales are increasing. Since choice (E) is a more complete explanation, it's the best answer.

WON'T ALL THIS TAKE TOO MUCH TIME?

While it may seem at first like you will need a lot of time to break down the arguments and apply the strategies, you'll get faster at doing this with practice. It's better to take your time and truly understand how the questions work than to rush through the problems, only to get them wrong.

Working more slowly increases your accuracy, which increases your GRE score!

Critical Reasoning Practice Set

In this practice set follow the steps exactly as we've presented them. Answers can be found in Part V.

A large manufacturer of electronic equipment expects to refurbish 1,800 units next year. Yet it is unlikely that a sufficient number of replacement parts will be available because the number of factory returns has been consistently decreasing over the past five years.

The argument above assumes that

○ factory returns provide a significant portion of the replacement parts used by the manufacturer to refurbish electronics equipment

○ during the next two years, factory returns will increase in number

○ in the coming year, no more than 1,800 people will try to purchase refurbished units from the manufacturer

○ in previous years, the manufacturer's predictions as to the number of refurbished units needed have been very inaccurate

⊙ every factory return produces a needed replacement part for the manufacturer

From 1983 to 1993, millions of gallons of liquid waste from commercial manufacturing plants were dumped into inland waterways. There is increasing apprehension that the liquid waste will leak contaminants into local water supplies. That apprehension is unwarranted, as tests of the local water supplies of regions near commercial manufacturers who practiced such dumping during the 1960s showed little or no evidence of such contaminants.

Which of the following, if true, most seriously undermines the argument above?

○ Commercial manufacturing plants in the 1960s leaked significantly fewer gallons of liquid waste into local water supplies than did plants from 1983 to 1993.

○ In the 1960s, liquid waste dumped by commercial manufacturing plants contained a greater concentration of harmful agents.

○ In the 1960s, solid waste pollution of inland waterways constituted a greater hazard to local water supplies than did liquid waste during the period from 1983 to 1993.

○ In recent years, environmentalists have made serious attempts to curb liquid waste pollution by commercial manufacturers.

○ During the period from 1983 to 1993, commercial manufacturing plants were less likely to dump liquid waste than were plants during the 1960s.

The greater the number of autonomous departments in a government, the more essential is a high level of cooperation. Increased numbers of autonomous departments demand a larger number of specialized policy makers, which leads to a greater burden on administrators and, possibly, to a greater number of difficulties in setting a general policy

There are always greater numbers of autonomous departments in democratic governments than there are in centralized governments.

Which of the following statements must be true if all of the statements above are true?

○ Difficulties in setting general policy occur more often in centralized governments than they do in democratic governments.

○ There are more specialized policy makers in centralized governments than there are in democratic governments.

○ A high level of cooperation is more essential in democratic governments than it is in centralized governments.

○ An administrator's job is easier in a democratic government than it is in a centralized government.

○ Autonomous departments operate with greater efficiency in democratic governments than they do in centralized governments.

Statement I. From 1983 to 1991, the yearly level of ultraviolet rays, or UVRs, to which the average person was exposed went down considerably.

Statement II. From 1983 to 1991, the occurrence of retinal irritations caused by UVR exposure went up twofold from previous levels, which were already high. This was true for those people whose exposure was average for each year during the eight-year period.

Which of the following, if true, would reconcile the apparent inconsistency between Statement I and Statement II?

○ The retinal irritations caused by UVR are only temporary.

○ Atmospheric elements fail to weaken UVRs.

○ From 1975 to 1983, the average level of exposure to UVRs also decreased.

○ Since 1991, the average level of exposure to UVRs has gone back up to pre-1983 levels.

○ The period of time between exposure to UVRs and the incidence of retinal irritations caused by such exposure is usually longer than 8 years.

Since running an automobile engine requires fuel, many drivers turn off the engines in their cars when they make a short stop. Yet, scientific studies demonstrate that, in those cases, the cars actually consume more fuel than they would have if the drivers had left the engines running.

Which one of the following, if true, most contributes to an explanation of the apparently paradoxical results of the studies?

○ Starting an automotive engine consumes more fuel than does running the engine for a short time.

○ The more often a car engine is started, the less fuel is consumed in bringing the motor up to its running temperature.

○ Continual stopping and starting of an automotive engine can decrease the output of the engine.

○ Continually running an automotive engine prevents the release of dangerous gases into the atmosphere.

○ Many people use their cars for commuting to and from their work places without making any short stops.

The average length of time that a patient lived after being diagnosed with stomach cancer in a certain state increased steadily beginning in 1982. The reason for this increase is that more people experienced a complete remission of their disease than previously. Improved surgical techniques that increased the effectiveness of removing cancerous growths at an advanced stage of development were responsible for the increase in longevity of people diagnosed with stomach cancer.

Which of the following, if true, would most likely be used as evidence to show that improved surgical techniques used on cancer patients diagnosed with stomach cancer were responsible for increasing the longevity of stomach cancer patients?

○ After 1982, patients whose cancer was diagnosed at an earlier state underwent more surgery than did those who were diagnosed at a more advanced stage.

○ The percentage of people diagnosed with stomach cancer whose cancerous growths were at an advanced stage of development was the same before 1982 as after 1982.

○ A greater percentage of the population was diagnosed with stomach cancer from 1982 to 1992 than was prior to 1982.

○ Stomach surgery was performed on the same percentage of the general population before 1982 as after 1982.

○ Other improvements in health care, including earlier detection and nonsurgical treatments, were instituted at major hospitals throughout the state beginning in 1982.

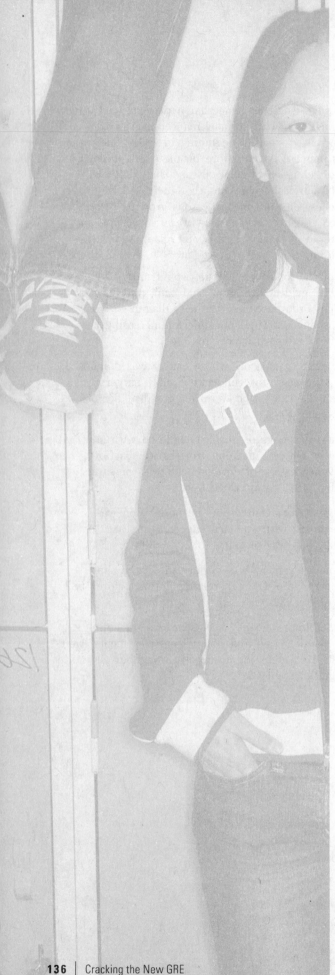

Summary

o Before answering the questions, attack the passage. Read the passages looking for the main idea, structure, and tone.

o For short passages, read the entire passage. For medium passages, focus on the beginning and end. For longer passages, read the first few lines of each paragraph and the final lines of the entire passage.

o Take a moment to understand the question task. Fetch questions ask you to retrieve information from the passage. Reasoning questions ask you to do something more than simply figure out what the author is saying.

o Return to the passage to find the answer to the question. Don't answer from memory! Go back to the text and find the answer.

o Try to come up with an answer in your own words before looking at the answer choices ETS provides. Remember to look for paraphrases of the text, not direct quotes.

o Eliminate answers that contain extreme language, go beyond the information provided, garble the meaning of the text, or otherwise have information that you can't support from the text.

o Most critical-reasoning questions require you break down an argument. The conclusion is the main point of an argument. The premise is the fact cited in support of the conclusion.

o The assumption is used to link the premise and the conclusion with each other. Without an assumption, an argument breaks down.

o The GRE uses many standard argument patterns. These include causal, analogy, and sampling arguments.

o To crack a critical-reasoning question, read the question first so you understand the task. Some questions require you to identify the conclusion and the premise of an argument. Others ask you to find the assumption or to strengthen or weaken the argument.

o After reading the question, break down the argument into its premise and conclusion and, if necessary, the assumption.

o Try to predict in your own words what the correct answer needs to do in order to answer the question.

o Use Process of Elimination to get rid of bad answers.

o Inference and resolve/explain questions do not require you to find the premise and the conclusion.

Chapter 7
Vocabulary
for the GRE

Words, words, words. That's what you'll find in this chapter. The following pages contain the Hit Parade, a list of some of the most common words that appear on the GRE. There are also some handy tips on studying and learning new vocabulary words and exercises to test your progress. Be advised, though, that the words in the chapter ahead are just a starting point. As you prepare for your GRE, keep your eyes open for words you don't know and look them up!

VOCAB, VOCAB, VOCAB

As much as ETS would like to claim that the new GRE doesn't rely as much on vocabulary as the old one did, the simple fact remains that many of the questions, answer choices, and reading passages contain some difficult vocabulary. You can't improve your score substantially without increasing your vocabulary. You might think that studying vocabulary is the most boring part of preparing for the GRE, but it's one of the most important, and it's also the one part of GRE preparation that's actually useful to you beyond the confines of the test itself. And the more words that you recognize (and know the meaning of) on the test, the easier it will be. So there's no avoiding the importance of vocabulary to your success on the GRE. Unfortunately, it is virtually impossible to fairly test someone's vocabulary on a standardized test. If you memorize 1,000 words and on test day none of those words appear, does that mean you have a bad vocabulary? Of course not—it just means that you've been victimized by the limitations of standardized testing.

This doesn't mean that you should take a defeatist attitude toward learning vocabulary! Even if you only have a few weeks before your test, you can still expand your vocabulary and increase your prospects of doing better on the GRE. One thing you have working in your favor is the fact that ETS loves to do the same things over and over. The words we've collected for you in this chapter are the words that appear most frequently on the GRE. So let's get started learning some new words!

Improving your vocabulary is the single most important thing you can do to improve your Verbal score.

LEARN TO LOVE THE DICTIONARY

Get used to looking up words. ETS uses words that they believe the average college-educated adult should know. These words show up in newspaper and magazine articles, in books, and in textbooks. If you see a word you don't know while studying for the GRE or elsewhere, it's probably a good GRE word. Look it up and make a flash card. Dictionaries will give you the pronunciation, while digital apps can provide quick, handy look-ups for new words. Looking up words is a habit. You may have to force yourself to do it in the beginning, but it becomes more natural over time. Many of the techniques in this book will help you on the GRE but don't have much relevance in day-to-day life, but a great vocabulary and good vocabulary habits will add a tremendous amount of value to your graduate school career and beyond.

Learning New Words

How will you remember all the new words you should learn for the test? By developing a routine for learning new words. Here are some tips:

- To learn words that you find on your own, get in the habit of reading good books, magazines, and newspapers. Start paying attention to words you come across for which you don't know the definition. You might be tempted to just skip these, as usual, but train yourself to write them down and look them up.
- When you look up the word, say it out loud, being careful to pronounce it correctly. This will help you remember it.
- When you look up a word in the dictionary, don't assume that the first definition is the only one you need to know. The first definition may be an archaic one, or one that applies only in a particular context, so scan through all the definitions.
- Now that you've learned the dictionary's definition of a new word, restate it in your own words. You'll find it much easier to remember a word's meaning if you make it your own.
- Mnemonics—Use your imagination to create a mental image to fix the new word in your mind. For example, if you're trying to remember the word *voracious*, which means having an insatiable appetite for an activity or pursuit, picture an incredibly hungry boar, eating huge piles of food. The voracious boar will help you to recall the meaning of the word. The crazier the image, the better.
- Keep a vocabulary notebook, or make a file with a list of new vocabulary words and put it on your desktop. Simply having a notebook with you will remind you to be on the lookout for new words, and using it will help you to remember the ones you encounter. Writing something down also makes it easier to memorize. Jot down the word when you find it, note its pronunciation and definition (in your own words) when you look it up, and jot down your mnemonic or mental image. You might also copy the sentence in which you originally found the word, to remind yourself of how the word looks in context.
- Do the same thing with flashcards. Write the word on one side and the pronunciation, the meaning, and perhaps a mental image on the other. Stick five or six of your flashcards in your pocket every morning and use them when you can.
- Use your new word every chance you get. Make it part of your life. Insert it into your speech at every opportunity. Developing a powerful vocabulary requires lots of exercise.
- Learn word roots. Many words share similar origins. By learning these common roots, you'll be better able to work with words you've never seen before. A good dictionary should list the origin and roots of the words in it.

Learn new words little by little; don't try to learn a ton at once!

THE HIT PARADE

You should start your vocabulary work by studying the Hit Parade, which is a list we've compiled of some of the most frequently tested words on the GRE. We put together this list by analyzing released GREs and keeping tabs on the test to make sure that these words are still popular with ETS. At the very least, answer choices that contain Hit Parade words make very good guesses on questions for which you don't know the answer. Each word on the Hit Parade is followed by the part of speech and a brief definition for the word. Some of the words on this list may have other definitions as well, but the definitions we have given are the ones most likely to appear on the GRE.

We've broken the Hit Parade down into four groups of about 75 words each. Don't try to learn all four groups of words at once—work with one list at a time. Write the words and their definitions down in a notebook or on flashcards. It is very important to write them down yourself, because this will help you remember them. Just glancing through the lists printed in this book won't be nearly as effective: Before doing the exercises for each group, spend some time studying and learning the words first, then use the exercises as a way to test yourself. Answers for the matching exercises appear in Part V of this book.

Hit Parade Group 1

Abscond (verb)	to depart clandestinely; to steal off and hide
Aberrant (adj.)	deviating from the norm (noun form: *aberration*)
Alacrity (noun)	eager and enthusiastic willingness
Anomaly (noun)	deviation from the normal order, form, or rule; abnormality (adj. form: *anomalous*)
Approbation (noun)	an expression of approval or praise
Arduous (adj.)	strenuous, taxing; requiring significant effort
Assuage (verb)	to ease or lessen; to appease or pacify
Audacious (adj.)	daring and fearless; recklessly bold (noun form: *audacity*)
Austere (adj.)	without adornment; bare; severely simple; ascetic (noun form: *austerity*)
Axiomatic (adj.)	taken as a given; possessing self-evident truth (noun form: *axiom*)
Canonical (adj.)	following or in agreement with accepted, traditional standards (noun form: *canon*)
Capricious (adj.)	inclined to change one's mind impulsively; erratic, unpredictable

Censure (verb)	to criticize severely; to officially rebuke
Chicanery (noun)	trickery or subterfuge
Connoisseur (noun)	an informed and astute judge in matters of taste; expert
Convoluted (adj.)	complex or complicated
Disabuse (verb)	to undeceive; to set right
Discordant (adj.)	conflicting; dissonant or harsh in sound
Disparate (adj.)	fundamentally distinct or dissimilar
Effrontery (noun)	extreme boldness; presumptuousness
Eloquent (adj.)	well-spoken, expressive, articulate (noun form: *eloquence*)
Enervate (verb)	to weaken; to reduce in vitality
Ennui (noun)	dissatisfaction and restlessness resulting from boredom or apathy
Equivocate (verb)	to use ambiguous language with a deceptive intent (adj. form: *equivocal*)
Erudite (adj.)	very learned; scholarly (noun form: *erudition*)
Exculpate (verb)	exonerate; to clear of blame
Exigent (adj.)	urgent, pressing; requiring immediate action or attention
Extemporaneous (adj.)	improvised; done without preparation
Filibuster (noun)	intentional obstruction, esp. using prolonged speechmaking to delay legislative action
Fulminate (verb)	to loudly attack or denounce
Ingenuous (adj.)	artless; frank and candid; lacking in sophistication
Inured (adj.)	accustomed to accepting something undesirable
Irascible (adj.)	easily angered; prone to temperamental outbursts
Laud (verb)	to praise highly (adj. form: *laudatory*)
Lucid (adj.)	clear; easily understood
Magnanimity (noun)	the quality of being generously noble in mind and heart, esp. in forgiving (adj. form: *magnanimous*)
Martial (adj.)	associated with war and the armed forces
Mundane (adj.)	of the world; typical of or concerned with the ordinary

Nascent (adj.)	coming into being; in early developmental stages
Nebulous (adj.)	vague; cloudy; lacking clearly defined form
Neologism (noun)	a new word, expression, or usage; the creation or use of new words or senses
Noxious (adj.)	harmful, injurious
Obtuse (adj.)	lacking sharpness of intellect; not clear or precise in thought or expression
Obviate (verb)	to anticipate and make unnecessary
Onerous (adj.)	troubling; burdensome
Paean (noun)	a song or hymn of praise and thanksgiving
Parody (noun)	a humorous imitation intended for ridicule or comic effect, esp. in literature and art
Perennial (adj.)	recurrent through the year or many years; happening repeatedly
Perfidy (noun)	intentional breach of faith; treachery (adj. form: *perfidious*)
Perfunctory (adj.)	cursory; done without care or interest
Perspicacious (adj.)	acutely perceptive; having keen discernment (noun form: *perspicacity*)
Prattle (verb)	to babble meaninglessly; to talk in an empty and idle manner
Precipitate (adj.)	acting with excessive haste or impulse
Precipitate (verb)	to cause or happen before anticipated or required
Predilection (noun)	a disposition in favor of something; preference
Prescience (noun)	foreknowledge of events; knowing of events prior to their occurring (adj. form: *prescient*)
Prevaricate (verb)	to deliberately avoid the truth; to mislead
Qualms (noun)	misgivings; reservations; causes for hesitancy
Recant (verb)	to retract, esp. a previously held belief
Refute (verb)	to disprove; to successfully argue against
Relegate (verb)	to forcibly assign, esp. to a lower place or position
Reticent (adj.)	quiet; reserved; reluctant to express thoughts and feelings
Solicitous (adj.)	concerned and attentive; eager
Sordid (adj.)	characterized by filth, grime, or squalor; foul

Sporadic (adj.)	occurring only occasionally, or in scattered instances
Squander (verb)	to waste by spending or using irresponsibly
Static (adj.)	not moving, active, or in motion; at rest
Stupefy (verb)	to stun, baffle, or amaze
Stymie (verb)	to block; to thwart
Synthesis (noun)	the combination of parts to make a whole (verb form: *synthesize*)
Torque (noun)	a force that causes rotation
Tortuous (adj.)	winding, twisting; excessively complicated
Truculent (adj.)	fierce and cruel; eager to fight
Veracity (noun)	truthfulness, honesty
Virulent (adj.)	extremely harmful or poisonous; bitterly hostile or antagonistic
Voracious (adj.)	having an insatiable appetite for an activity or pursuit; ravenous
Waver (verb)	to move to and fro; to sway; to be unsettled in opinion

Group 1 Exercises

Match the following words to their definitions. Answers can be found in Part V.

1.	Improvised; without preparation	A.	Veracity
2.	A newly coined word or expression	B.	Recant
3.	A song of joy and praise	C.	Extemporaneous
4.	To praise highly	D.	Stymie
5.	Truthfulness; honesty	E.	Paean
6.	Frank and candid	F.	Lucid
7.	Associated with war and the military	G.	Laud
8.	To retract a belief or statement	H.	Onerous
9.	Cursory; done without care or interest	I.	Tortuous
10.	Troubling; burdensome	J.	Neologism
11.	To criticize; to officially rebuke	K.	Martial
12.	Winding; twisting; complicated	L.	Ingenuous
13.	To block; to thwart	M.	Censure
14.	Clear; easily understood	N.	Perfunctory

Hit Parade Group 2

Abate (verb)	to lessen in intensity or degree
Accolade (noun)	an expression of praise
Adulation (noun)	excessive praise; intense adoration
Aesthetic (adj.)	dealing with, appreciative of, or responsive to art or the beautiful
Ameliorate (verb)	to make better or more tolerable
Ascetic (noun)	one who practices rigid self-denial, esp. as an act of religious devotion
Avarice (noun)	greed, esp. for wealth (adj. form: *avaricious*)
Axiom (noun)	a universally recognized principle (adj. form: *axiomatic*)
Burgeon (verb)	to grow rapidly or flourish
Bucolic (adj.)	rustic and pastoral; characteristic of rural areas and their inhabitants
Cacophony (noun)	harsh, jarring, discordant sound; dissonance (adj. form: *cacophonous*)
Canon (noun)	an established set of principles or code of laws, often religious in nature (adj. form: *canonical*)
Castigation (noun)	severe criticism or punishment (verb form: *castigate*)
Catalyst (noun)	a substance that accelerates the rate of a chemical reaction without itself changing; a person or thing that causes change
Caustic (adj.)	burning or stinging; causing corrosion
Chary (adj.)	wary; cautious; sparing
Cogent (adj.)	appealing forcibly to the mind or reason; convincing
Complaisance (noun)	the willingness to comply with the wishes of others (adj. form: *complaisant*)
Contentious (adj.)	argumentative; quarrelsome; causing controversy or disagreement
Contrite (adj.)	regretful; penitent; seeking forgiveness (noun form: *contrition*)
Culpable (adj.)	deserving blame (noun form: *culpability*)
Dearth (noun)	smallness of quantity or number; scarcity; a lack
Demur (verb)	to question or oppose
Didactic (adj.)	intended to teach or instruct
Discretion (noun)	cautious reserve in speech; ability to make responsible decisions (adj. form: *discrete*)
Disinterested (adj.)	free of bias or self-interest; impartial

Dogmatic (adj.)	expressing a rigid opinion based on unproved or improvable principles (noun form: *dogma*)
Ebullience (noun)	the quality of lively or enthusiastic expression of thoughts and feelings (adj. form: *ebullient*)
Eclectic (adj.)	composed of elements drawn from various sources
Elegy (noun)	a mournful poem, esp. one lamenting the dead (adj. form: *elegiac*)
Emollient (adj.)/ (noun)	soothing, esp. to the skin; making less harsh; mollifying; an agent that softens or smoothes the skin
Empirical (adj.)	based on observation or experiment
Enigmatic (adj.)	mysterious; obscure; difficult to understand (noun form: *enigma*)
Ephemeral (adj.)	brief; fleeting
Esoteric (adj.)	intended for or understood by a small, specific group
Eulogy (noun)	a speech honoring the dead (verb form: *eulogize*)
Exonerate (verb)	to remove blame
Facetious (adj.)	playful; humorous
Fallacy (noun)	an invalid or incorrect notion; a mistaken belief (adj. form: *fallacious*)
Furtive (adj.)	marked by stealth; covert; surreptitious
Gregarious (adj.)	sociable; outgoing; enjoying the company of other people
Harangue (verb)/ (noun)	to deliver a pompous speech or tirade; a long, pompous speech
Heretical (adj.)	violating accepted dogma or convention (noun form: *heresy*)
Hyperbole (noun)	an exaggerated statement, often used as a figure of speech (adj. form: *hyperbolic*)
Impecunious (adj.)	lacking funds; without money
Incipient (adj.)	beginning to come into being or to become apparent
Inert (adj.)	unmoving; lethargic; sluggish
Innocuous (adj.)	harmless; causing no damage
Intransigent (adj.)	refusing to compromise (noun form: *intransigence*)
Inveigle (verb)	to obtain by deception or flattery
Morose (adj.)	sad; sullen; melancholy
Odious (adj.)	evoking intense aversion or dislike
Opaque (adj.)	impenetrable by light; not reflecting light
Oscillation (noun)	the act or state of swinging back and forth with a steady, uninterrupted rhythm (verb form: *oscillate*)
Penurious (adj.)	penny-pinching; excessively thrifty; ungenerous

Pernicious (adj.)	extremely harmful; potentially causing death
Peruse (verb)	to examine with great care (noun form: *perusal*)
Pious (adj.)	extremely reverent or devout; showing strong religious devotion (noun form: *piety*)
Precursor (noun)	one that precedes and indicates or announces another
Preen (verb)	to dress up; to primp; to groom oneself with elaborate care
Prodigious (adj.)	abundant in size, force, or extent; extraordinary
Prolific (adj.)	producing large volumes or amounts; productive
Putrefy (verb)	to rot; to decay and give off a foul odor (adj. form: *putrid*)
Quaff (verb)	to drink deeply
Quiescence (noun)	stillness; motionlessness; quality of being at rest (adj. form: *quiescent*)
Redoubtable (adj.)	awe-inspiring; worthy of honor
Sanction (noun)/(verb)	authoritative permission or approval; a penalty intended to enforce compliance; to give permission or authority to
Satire (noun)	a literary work that ridicules or criticizes a human vice through humor or derision (adj. form: *satirical*)
Squalid (adj.)	sordid; wretched and dirty as from neglect (noun form: *squalor*)
Stoic (adj.)	indifferent to or unaffected by pleasure or pain; steadfast (noun form: *stoicism*)
Supplant (verb)	to take the place of; to supersede
Torpid (adj.)	lethargic; sluggish; dormant (noun form: *torpor*)
Ubiquitous (adj.)	existing everywhere at the same time; constantly encountered; widespread
Urbane (adj.)	sophisticated; refined; elegant (noun form: *urbanity*)
Vilify (verb)	to defame; to characterize harshly
Viscous (adj.)	thick; sticky (noun form: *viscosity*)

Group 2 Exercises

Match the following words to their definitions. Answers can be found in Part V.

1.	Brief; fleeting	A.	Pernicious
2.	A long, pompous speech	B.	Ephemeral
3.	Arousing strong dislike or aversion	C.	Avarice
4.	To free from blame or responsibility	D.	Quaff
5.	Arousing fear or awe; worthy of honor; formidable	E.	Caustic
6.	Very harmful; deadly	F.	Odious
7.	To drink deeply	G.	Dearth
8.	Stinging; corrosive; sarcastic; biting	H.	Inert
9.	Impressively great in size, force, or extent; enormous	I.	Disinterested
10.	Greed; hunger for money	J.	Exonerate
11.	Unmoving; lethargic	K.	Inveigle
12.	Impartial; unbiased	L.	Prodigious
13.	Lack; scarcity	M.	Harangue
14.	To win over by deception, coaxing or flattery	N.	Redoubtable

Hit Parade Group 3

Acumen (noun)	keen, accurate judgment or insight
Adulterate (verb)	to reduce purity by combining with inferior ingredients
Amalgamate (verb)	to combine several elements into a whole (noun form: *amalgamation*)
Archaic (adj.)	outdated; associated with an earlier, perhaps more primitive, time
Aver (verb)	to state as a fact; to declare or assert
Bolster (verb)	to provide support or reinforcement
Bombastic (adj.)	pompous; grandiloquent (noun form: *bombast*)
Diatribe (noun)	a harsh denunciation
Dissemble (verb)	to disguise or conceal; to mislead
Eccentric (adj.)	departing from norms or conventions
Endemic (adj.)	characteristic of or often found in a particular locality, region, or people
Evanescent (adj.)	tending to disappear like vapor; vanishing
Exacerbate (verb)	to make worse or more severe
Fervent (adj.)	greatly emotional or zealous (noun form: *fervor*)
Fortuitous (adj.)	happening by accident or chance

Germane (adj.)	relevant to the subject at hand; appropriate in subject matter
Grandiloquence (noun)	pompous speech or expression (adj. form: *grandiloquent*)
Hackneyed (adj.)	rendered trite or commonplace by frequent usage
Halcyon (adj.)	calm and peaceful
Hedonism (noun)	devotion to pleasurable pursuits, esp. to the pleasures of the senses (a *hedonist* is someone who pursues pleasure)
Hegemony (noun)	the consistent dominance of one state or ideology over others
Iconoclast (noun)	one who attacks or undermines traditional conventions or institutions
Idolatrous (adj.)	given to intense or excessive devotion to something (noun form: *idolatry*)
Impassive (adj.)	revealing no emotion
Imperturbable (adj.)	marked by extreme calm, impassivity, and steadiness
Implacable (adj.)	not capable of being appeased or significantly changed
Impunity (noun)	immunity from punishment or penalty
Inchoate (adj.)	in an initial stage; not fully formed
Infelicitous (adj.)	unfortunate; inappropriate
Insipid (adj.)	without taste or flavor; lacking in spirit; bland
Loquacious (adj.)	extremely talkative (noun form: *loquacity*)
Luminous (adj.)	characterized by brightness and the emission of light
Malevolent (adj.)	having or showing often vicious ill will, spite, or hatred (noun form: *malevolence*)
Malleable (adj.)	capable of being shaped or formed; tractable; pliable
Mendacity (noun)	the condition of being untruthful; dishonesty (adj. form: *mendacious*)
Meticulous (adj.)	characterized by extreme care and precision; attentive to detail
Misanthrope (noun)	one who hates all other humans (adj. form: *misanthropic*)
Mitigate (verb)	to make or become less severe or intense; to moderate
Obdurate (adj.)	unyielding; hardhearted; intractable
Obsequious (adj.)	exhibiting a fawning attentiveness
Occlude (verb)	to obstruct or block
Opprobrium (noun)	disgrace; contempt; scorn
Pedagogy (noun)	the profession or principles of teaching, or instructing

Pedantic (adj.)	overly concerned with the trivial details of learning or education; show-offish about one's knowledge
Penury (noun)	poverty; destitution
Pervasive (adj.)	having the tendency to permeate or spread throughout
Pine (verb)	to yearn intensely; to languish; to lose vigor
Pirate (verb)	to illegally use or reproduce
Pith (noun)	the essential or central part
Pithy (adj.)	precise and brief
Placate (verb)	to appease; to calm by making concessions
Platitude (noun)	a superficial remark, esp. one offered as meaningful
Plummet (verb)	to plunge or drop straight down
Polemical (adj.)	controversial; argumentative
Prodigal (adj.)	recklessly wasteful; extravagant; profuse; lavish
Profuse (adj.)	given or coming forth abundantly; extravagant
Proliferate (verb)	to grow or increase swiftly and abundantly
Queries (noun)	questions; inquiries; doubts in the mind; reservations
Querulous (adj.)	prone to complaining or grumbling; peevish
Rancorous (adj.)	characterized by bitter, long-lasting resentment (noun form: *rancor*)
Recalcitrant (adj.)	obstinately defiant of authority; difficult to manage
Repudiate (verb)	to refuse to have anything to do with; to disown
Rescind (verb)	to invalidate; to repeal; to retract
Reverent (adj.)	marked by, feeling, or expressing a feeling of profound awe and respect (noun form: *reverence*)
Rhetoric (noun)	the art or study of effective use of language for communication and persuasion
Salubrious (adj.)	promoting health or well-being
Solvent (adj.)	able to meet financial obligations; able to dissolve another substance
Specious (adj.)	seeming true, but actually being fallacious; misleadingly attractive; plausible but false
Spurious (adj.)	lacking authenticity or validity; false; counterfeit
Subpoena (noun)	a court order requiring appearance and/or testimony
Succinct (adj.)	brief; concise
Superfluous (adj.)	exceeding what is sufficient or necessary
Surfeit (verb)	an overabundant supply; excess; to feed or supply to excess
Tenacity (noun)	the quality of adherence or persistence to something valued; persistent determination (adj. form: *tenacious*)

Tenuous (adj.)	having little substance or strength; flimsy; weak
Tirade (noun)	a long and extremely critical speech; a harsh denunciation
Transient (adj.)	fleeting; passing quickly; brief
Zealous (adj.)	fervent; ardent; impassioned, devoted to a cause (a *zealot* is a zealous person)

Group 3 Exercises

Match the following words to their definitions. Answers can be found in Part V.

1.	Brief; concise; tersely cogent	A.	Hegemony
2.	Prone to complaining; whining	B.	Aver
3.	Fawning; ingratiating	C.	Insipid
4.	Marked by bitter, deep-seated resentment	D.	Pithy
5.	Controversial; argumentative	E.	Placate
6.	Dominance of one state or ideology	F.	Prodigal over others
7.	Uninteresting; tasteless; flat; dull	G.	Querulous
8.	Thin; flimsy; of little substance	H.	Surfeit
9.	Excess; overindulgence	I.	Rancorous
10.	Wasteful; recklessly extravagant	J.	Bombastic
11.	To appease; to pacify with concessions	K.	Obsequious
12.	To assert; to declare; to allege; to state as fact	L.	Evanescent
13.	Pompous; grandiloquent	M.	Polemical
14.	Tending to vanish like vapor	N.	Tenuous

Hit Parade Group 4

Acerbic (adj.)	having a sour or bitter taste or character; sharp; biting
Aggrandize (verb)	to increase in intensity, power, influence, or prestige
Alchemy (noun)	a medieval science aimed at the transmutation of metals, esp. base metals into gold (an *alchemist* is one who practices alchemy)
Amenable (adj.)	agreeable; responsive to suggestion
Anachronism (noun)	something or someone out of place in terms of historical or chronological context
Astringent (adj.)	having a tightening effect on living tissue; harsh; severe; something with a tightening effect on tissue
Contiguous (adj.)	sharing a border; touching; adjacent
Convention (noun)	a generally agreed-upon practice or attitude
Credulous (adj.)	tending to believe too readily; gullible (noun form: *credulity*)

Cynicism (noun)	an attitude or quality of belief that all people are motivated by selfishness (adj. form: *cynical*)
Decorum (noun)	polite or appropriate conduct or behavior (adj. form: *decorous*)
Derision (noun)	scorn, ridicule, contemptuous treatment (adj. form: *derisive*; verb form: *deride*)
Desiccate (verb)	to dry out or dehydrate; to make dry or dull
Dilettante (noun)	one with an amateurish or superficial interest in the arts or a branch of knowledge
Disparage (verb)	to slight or belittle
Divulge (verb)	to disclose something secret
Fawn (verb)	to flatter or praise excessively
Flout (verb)	to show contempt for, as in a rule or convention
Garrulous (adj.)	pointlessly talkative; talking too much
Glib (adj.)	marked by ease or informality; nonchalant; lacking in depth; superficial
Hubris (noun)	overbearing presumption or pride; arrogance
Imminent (adj.)	about to happen; impending
Immutable (adj.)	not capable of change
Impetuous (adj.)	hastily or rashly energetic; impulsive and vehement
Indifferent (adj.)	having no interest or concern; showing no bias or prejudice
Inimical (adj.)	damaging; harmful; injurious
Intractable (adj.)	not easily managed or directed; stubborn; obstinate
Intrepid (adj.)	steadfast and courageous
Laconic (adj.)	using few words; terse
Maverick (noun)	an independent individual who does not go along with a group or party
Mercurial (adj.)	characterized by rapid and unpredictable change in mood
Mollify (verb)	to calm or soothe; to reduce in emotional intensity
Neophyte (noun)	a recent convert; a beginner; novice
Obfuscate (verb)	to deliberately obscure; to make confusing
Obstinate (adj.)	stubborn; hard-headed; uncompromising
Ostentatious (adj.)	characterized by or given to pretentious display; showy
Pervade (verb)	to permeate throughout (adj. form: *pervasive*)
Phlegmatic (adj.)	calm; sluggish; unemotional
Plethora (noun)	an overabundance; a surplus
Pragmatic (adj.)	practical rather than idealistic

Presumptuous (adj.)	overstepping due bounds (as of propriety or courtesy); taking liberties
Pristine (adj.)	pure; uncorrupted; clean
Probity (noun)	adherence to highest principles; complete and confirmed integrity; uprightness
Proclivity (noun)	a natural predisposition or inclination
Profligate (adj.)	excessively wasteful; recklessly extravagant (noun form: *profligacy*)
Propensity (noun)	a natural inclination or tendency; penchant
Prosaic (adj.)	dull; lacking in spirit or imagination
Pungent (adj.)	characterized by a strong, sharp smell or taste
Quixotic (adj.)	foolishly impractical; marked by lofty romantic ideals
Quotidian (adj.)	occurring or recurring daily; commonplace
Rarefy (verb)	to make or become thin, less dense; to refine
Recondite (adj.)	hidden; concealed; difficult to understand; obscure
Refulgent (adj.)	radiant; shiny; brilliant
Renege (verb)	to fail to honor a commitment; to go back on a promise
Sedulous (adj.)	diligent; persistent; hard-working
Shard (noun)	a piece of broken pottery or glass
Soporific (adj.)	causing drowsiness; tending to induce sleep
Sparse (adj.)	thin; not dense; arranged at widely spaced intervals
Spendthrift (noun)	one who spends money wastefully
Subtle (adj.)	not obvious; elusive; difficult to discern
Tacit (adj.)	implied; not explicitly stated
Terse (adj.)	brief and concise in wording
Tout (verb)	to publicly praise or promote
Trenchant (adj.)	sharply perceptive; keen; penetrating
Unfeigned (adj.)	genuine; not false or hypocritical
Untenable (adj.)	indefensible; not viable; uninhabitable
Vacillate (verb)	to waver indecisively between one course of action or opinion and another
Variegated (adj.)	multicolored; characterized by a variety of patches of different color
Vexation (noun)	annoyance; irritation (noun form: *vex*)
Vigilant (adj.)	alertly watchful (noun form: *vigilance*)
Vituperate (verb)	to use harsh condemnatory language; to abuse or censure severely or abusively; to berate
Volatile (adj.)	readily changing to a vapor; changeable; fickle; explosive (noun form: *volatility*)

Group 4 Exercises

Match the following words to their definitions. Answers can be found in Part V.

1.	Acid or biting; bitter in taste or tone	A.	Anachronism
2.	Sleep-inducing; causing drowsiness	B.	Contiguous
3.	A surplus; an overabundance	C.	Dilettante
4.	One with superficial interest in a subject	D.	Intractable
5.	Arrogance; overbearing pride	E.	Prosaic
6.	Sharing a border; touching; adjacent	F.	Quixotic
7.	Talking too much; rambling	G.	Recondite
8.	Something out of place in history or chronology	H.	Vituperate
9.	Difficult to understand; obscure; hidden	I.	Acerbic
10.	Dull; unimaginative; ordinary	J.	Garrulous
11.	Unemotional; calm	K.	Hubris
12.	Stubborn; obstinate; difficult to manage or govern	L.	Soporific
13.	Condemn with harsh, abusive words;	M.	Phlegmatic berate
14.	Foolishly impractical; marked by lofty ideals	N.	Plethora

BEYOND THE HIT PARADE

So you've finished the Hit Parade and you're now the master of many more words than you were before. What to do next? Why, go *beyond the Hit Parade* of course! The Hit Parade was just the beginning. To maximize your score on the GRE you must be relentless in increasing your vocabulary. Don't let up. Keep learning words until the day you sit down for the exam. The three following lists of extra words don't have exercises, so just keep working with your notebook or flashcards and get your friends to quiz you. You are a vocabulary machine!

Beyond the Hit Parade Group 1

The following list contains some of those simple-sounding words with less common secondary meanings that ETS likes to test on the GRE.

Alloy (verb)	to commingle; to debase by mixing with something inferior; *unalloyed* means pure
Appropriate (verb)	to take for one's own use; to confiscate
Arrest, arresting (verb)/(adj.)	to suspend; to engage; holding one's attention: as in arrested adolescence, an arresting portrait
August (adj.)	majestic, venerable
Bent (noun)	leaning, inclination, proclivity, tendency

Broach (verb)	to bring up; to announce; to begin to talk about
Brook (verb)	to tolerate; to endure; to countenance
Cardinal (adj.)	major, as in cardinal sin
Chauvinist (noun)	a blindly devoted patriot
Color (verb)	to change as if by dyeing, i.e., to distort, gloss, or affect (usually the first)
Consequential (adj.)	pompous, self-important (primary definitions are: logically following; important)
Damp (verb)	to diminish the intensity or check the vibration of a sound
Die (noun)	a tool used for shaping, as in a tool-and-die shop
Essay (verb)	to test or try; to attempt; to experiment
Exact (verb)	to demand; to call for; to require; to take
Fell (verb)	to cause to fall by striking
Fell (adj.)	inhumanly cruel
Flag (verb)	to sag or droop; to become spiritless; to decline
Flip (adj.)	sarcastic, impertinent, as in flippant: a flip remark
Ford (verb)	to wade across the shallow part of a river or stream
Grouse (verb)	to complain or grumble
Guy (noun)	a rope, cord, or cable attached to something as a brace or guide; to steady or reinforce using a guy: Think *guide*.
Intimate (verb)	to imply, suggest, or insinuate
List (verb)	to tilt or lean to one side
Lumber (verb)	to move heavily and clumsily
Meet (adj.)	fitting, proper
Milk (verb)	to exploit; to squeeze every last ounce of
Mince (verb)	to pronounce or speak affectedly; to euphemize to speak too carefully. Also, to take tiny steps; to tiptoe
Nice (adj.)	exacting, fastidious, extremely precise
Obtain (adj.)	to be established, accepted, or customary
Occult (adj.)	hidden, concealed, beyond comprehension
Pedestrian (adj.)	commonplace, trite, unremarkable, quotidian
Pied (adj.)	multicolored, usually in blotches
Pine (verb)	to lose vigor (as through grief); to yearn
Plastic (adj.)	moldable, pliable, not rigid
Pluck (noun)	courage, spunk, fortitude
Prize (verb)	to pry, to press or force with a lever; something taken by force, spoils
Rail (verb)	to complain about bitterly

Rent (verb)	torn (past tense of *rend*); an opening or tear caused by such
Quail (verb)	to lose courage; to turn frightened
Qualify (verb)	to limit
Sap (verb)	to enervate or weaken the vitality of
Sap (noun)	a fool or nitwit
Scurvy (adj.)	contemptible, despicable
Singular (adj.)	exceptional, unusual, odd
Stand (noun)	a group of trees
Steep (verb)	to saturate or completely soak, as in to let a tea bag steep
Strut (noun)	the supporting structural cross-part of a wing
Table (verb)	to remove (as a parliamentary motion) from consideration
Tender (verb)	to proffer or offer
Waffle (verb)	to equivocate; to change one's position
Wag (noun)	wit, joker

Beyond the Hit Parade Group 2

Abjure (verb)	to renounce or reject solemnly; to recant; to avoid
Adumbrate (verb)	to foreshadow vaguely or intimate; to suggest or outline sketchily; to obscure or overshadow
Anathema (noun)	a solemn or ecclesiastical (religious) curse; accursed or thoroughly loathed person or thing
Anodyne (adj.)/(noun)	soothing; something that assuages or allays pain or comforts
Apogee (noun)	farthest or highest point; culmination; zenith
Apostate (noun)	one who abandons long-held religious or political convictions
Apotheosis (noun)	deification; glorification to godliness; an exalted example; a model of excellence or perfection
Asperity (noun)	severity, rigor; roughness, harshness; acrimony, irritability
Asseverate (verb)	to aver, allege, or assert
Assiduous (adj.)	diligent, hard-working, sedulous
Augury (noun)	omen, portent
Bellicose (adj.)	belligerent, pugnacious, warlike

Calumniate (verb)	to slander, to make a false accusation; *calumny* means slander, aspersion
Captious (adj.)	disposed to point out trivial faults; calculated to confuse or entrap in argument
Cavil (verb)	to find fault without good reason
Celerity (noun)	speed, alacrity; think *accelerate*
Chimera (noun)	an illusion; originally, an imaginary fire-breathing she-monster
Contumacious (adj.)	insubordinate, rebellious; *contumely* means insult, scorn, aspersion
Debacle (noun)	rout, fiasco, complete failure
Denouement (noun)	an outcome or solution; the unraveling of a plot
Descry (verb)	to discriminate or discern
Desuetude (noun)	disuse
Desultory (adj.)	random; aimless; marked by a lack of plan or purpose
Diaphanous (adj.)	transparent, gauzy
Diffident (adj.)	reserved, shy, unassuming; lacking in self-confidence
Dirge (noun)	a song of grief or lamentation
Encomium (noun)	glowing and enthusiastic praise; panegyric, tribute, eulogy
Eschew (verb)	to shun or avoid
Excoriate (verb)	to censure scathingly, to upbraid
Execrate (verb)	to denounce, to feel loathing for, to curse, to declare to be evil
Exegesis (noun)	critical examination, explication
Expiate (verb)	to atone or make amends for
Extirpate (verb)	to destroy, to exterminate, to cut out, to exscind
Fatuous (adj.)	silly, inanely foolish
Fractious (adj.)	quarrelsome, rebellious, unruly, refractory, irritable
Gainsay (verb)	to deny, to dispute, to contradict, to oppose
Heterodox (adj.)	unorthodox, heretical, iconoclastic
Imbroglio (noun)	difficult or embarrassing situation
Indefatigable (adj.)	not easily exhaustible; tireless, dogged
Ineluctable (adj.)	certain, inevitable
Inimitable (adj.)	one of a kind, peerless

Insouciant (adj.)	unconcerned, carefree, heedless
Inveterate (adj.)	deep rooted, ingrained, habitual
Jejune (adj.)	vapid, uninteresting, nugatory; childish, immature, puerile
Lubricious (adj.)	lewd, wanton, greasy, slippery
Mendicant (noun)	a beggar, supplicant
Meretricious (adj.)	cheap, gaudy, tawdry, flashy, showy; attracting by false show
Minatory (adj.)	menacing, threatening (reminds you of the Minotaur, a threatening creature indeed)
Nadir (noun)	low point, perigee
Nonplussed (adj.)	baffled, bewildered, at a loss for what to do or think
Obstreperous (adj.)	noisily and stubbornly defiant, aggressively boisterous
Ossified (adj.)	tending to become more rigid, conventional, sterile, and reactionary with age; literally, turned into bone
Palliate (verb)	to make something seem less serious, to gloss over, to make less severe or intense
Panegyric (noun)	formal praise, eulogy, encomium; *panegyrical* means expressing elaborate praise
Parsimonious (adj.)	cheap, miserly
Pellucid (adj.)	transparent, easy to understand, limpid
Peroration (noun)	the concluding part of a speech; flowery, rhetorical speech
Plangent (adj.)	pounding, thundering, resounding
Prolix (adj.)	long-winded, verbose; *prolixity* means verbosity
Propitiate (verb)	to appease; to conciliate; *propitious* means auspicious, favorable
Puerile (adj.)	childish, immature, jejune, nugatory
Puissance (noun)	power, strength; *puissant* means powerful, strong
Pusillanimous (adj.)	cowardly, craven
Remonstrate (verb)	to protest, to object
Sagacious (adj.)	having sound judgment; perceptive, wise; like a sage
Salacious (adj.)	lustful, lascivious, bawdy
Salutary (adj.)	remedial, wholesome, causing improvement
Sanguine (adj.)	cheerful, confident, optimistic
Saturnine (adj.)	gloomy, dark, sullen, morose

Sententious (adj.)	aphoristic or moralistic; epigrammatic; tending to moralize excessively
Stentorian (adj.)	extremely loud and powerful
Stygian (adj.)	gloomy, dark
Sycophant (noun)	toady, servile, self-seeking flatterer; parasite
Tendentious (adj.)	biased; showing marked tendencies
Timorous (adj.)	timid, fearful, diffident
Tyro (noun)	novice, greenhorn, rank amateur
Vitiate (verb)	to corrupt, to debase, to spoil, to make ineffective
Voluble (adj.)	fluent, verbal, having easy use of spoken language

Part III
How to Crack the Math Section

Chapter 8
The Geography of the Math Section

This chapter contains an overview of the content and structure you'll see on the Math sections of the GRE. It provides valuable information on pacing strategies and the various question formats you'll encounter on the GRE. It also goes over how to use basic test-taking techniques such as Process of Elimination and Ballparking as they relate to math questions. After finishing this chapter, you'll have a good idea of what the Math section of the GRE looks like and some basic approaches to help you navigate it.

WHAT'S IN THE MATH SECTION

The GRE Math section primarily tests math concepts you learned in the seventh through tenth grade, including arithmetic, algebra, and geometry. ETS alleges that the Math sections on the new version of the exam better test the reasoning skills that you'll use in graduate school, but what the Math section primarily tests is your comfort level with some basic math topics and your ability to take a test with strange-looking questions under timed conditions.

The Math section of the exam consists of two 35-minute sections, each of which will consist of 20 questions. The first seven or eight questions of each section will be *quantitative comparisons* (quant comp, for short). The remainder will consist of multiple-choice or numeric-entry questions.

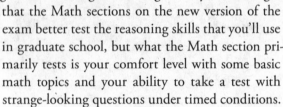

Junior High School?

The Math section of the GRE mostly tests how much you remember from the math courses you took in seventh, eighth, ninth, and tenth grade. But here's some good news: GRE math is easier than SAT math. Why? Because many people study little or no math in college. If the GRE tested college-level math, everyone but math majors would bomb the test.

If you're willing to do a little work, this is good news for you. By brushing up on the modest amount of math you need to know for the test, you can significantly increase your GRE Math score. All you have to do is shake off the dust.

Predictable Triggers

The beauty of a standardized test is that it is, well, standardized. Standardized means predictable. We know exactly what ETS is going to test and how they're going to test it. The math side of the test consists of a series of utterly predictable triggers, to which we have designed a series of highly scripted responses. ETS wants you to see each problem as a new challenge to solve. What you will find, however, is that there are only about 20 math concepts that are being tested. All of the questions you will see are just different ways of asking about these different concepts. Most of these concepts you already know. Once you recognize what's being tested, even the trickiest questions become familiar and easy to solve.

Need more info? Check out the DVD.

It's Really a Reading Test

In constructing the Math section, ETS is limited to the math that nearly everyone has studied: arithmetic, basic algebra, basic geometry, and elementary statistics. There's no calculus (or even precalculus), no trigonometry, and no major-league algebra or geometry. Because of these limitations, ETS has to resort to traps in order to create hard problems. Even the most commonly missed GRE math problems are typically based on relatively simple principles. What makes the problems difficult is that these simple principles are disguised.

Many test takers have no problem doing the actual calculations involved in the math questions on the GRE; in fact, you'll even be allowed to use a calculator (more on that soon). However, on this test your ability to carefully read the problems and figure out how to set them up is more important than your ability to make calculations.

As you work through this section, don't worry about how quickly you're doing the problems. Instead, take the time to really understand what the questions are asking; pay close attention to the wording of the problems. Most math errors are the result of careless mistakes caused by not reading the problem carefully enough!

Read and Copy Carefully

You can do all the calculations right and still get a question wrong. How? What if you solve for x but the question asked for the value of $x + 4$? Ugh. Always reread the question before you choose an answer. Take your time and don't be careless. The problem will stay on the screen as long as you want it to, so reread the question and double-check your work before answering it.

Or how about this? The radius of the circle was 5, but when you copied the picture onto your scratch paper, you accidentally made it 6. Ugh! If you make a mistake copying down information from the screen, you'll get the question wrong no matter how perfect your calculations are. You have to be extra careful when copying down information.

THE CALCULATOR

As we mentioned above, on this new GRE you'll be given an on-screen calculator. The calculator program on the GRE is a rudimentary one that gives you the five basic operations: add, subtract, multiply, divide, and square root, plus a decimal function and a positive/negative feature. It also follows the order of operations, or PEMDAS (more on this topic in Chapter 9). The calculator also has the ability to transfer the answer you've calculated directly into the answer box for certain questions. The on-screen calculator can be a huge advantage—if it's used correctly!

As you might have realized by this point, ETS is not exactly looking out for your best interests. Giving you a calculator might seem like an altruistic act, but rest assured that ETS knows that there are certain ways in which calculator use can be exploited. Keep in mind the following:

1. **Calculators Can't Think**. Calculators are good for one thing and one thing only: calculation. You still have to figure out how to set up the problem correctly. If you're not sure what to calculate, then a calculator isn't helpful. For example, if you do a percent calculation on your calculator and then hit "Transfer Display," you will have to remember to move the decimal point accordingly, depending on whether the question asks for a percent or a decimal.

2. **The Calculator as a Liability**. ETS will give you questions that you can solve with a calculator, but the calculator can actually be a liability. You will be tempted to use it. For example, students who are uncomfortable adding, subtracting, multiplying, or dividing fractions may be tempted to convert all fractions to decimals using the calculator. Don't do it. You are better off mastering fractions than avoiding

them. Working with exponents and square roots is another place where the calculator will be tempting but may yield really big and awkward numbers or long decimals. You are much better off learning the rules of manipulating exponents and square roots (there are only five rules). Most of these problems will be faster and cleaner to solve with rules than with a calculator. The questions may also use numbers that are too big for the calculator. Time spent trying to get an answer out of a calculator for problems involving really big numbers will be time wasted. Find another way around.

3. **A Calculator Won't Make You Faster.** Having a calculator should make you more accurate, but not necessarily faster. You still need to take time to read each problem carefully and set it up. Don't expect to blast through problems just because you have a calculator.

4. **The Calculator Is No Excuse for Not Using Scratch Paper.** Scratch paper is where good technique happens. Working problems by hand on scratch paper will help to avoid careless errors or skipped steps. Just because you can do multiple functions in a row on your calculator does not mean that you should be solving problems on your calculator. Use the calculator to do simple calculations that would otherwise take you time to solve. Make sure you are still writing steps out on your scratch paper, labeling results, and using set-ups. Accuracy is more important than speed!

Of course, you should not fear the calculator; by all means, use it and be grateful for it. Having a calculator should help you eliminate all those careless math mistakes.

You will score higher if you spend your time working carefully. Double-check your work before you hit confirm.

GEOGRAPHY OF A MATH SECTION

Math sections contain 20 questions each. Test takers are allowed 35 minutes per section. The first 7 or 8 questions of each math section are quantitative comparisons, while the remainder are a mixed bag of problem solving, all that apply, numeric entry, and charts and graphs. Each section covers a mixture of algebra, arithmetic, quantitative reasoning, geometry, and real-world math.

QUESTION FORMATS

Much like the Verbal section, the Math section on the GRE contains a variety of different question formats. Let's go through each question format and discuss how to crack it.

Standard Multiple Choice

These questions are the basic five-answer multiple-choice questions. These are great candidates for POE (Process of Elimination) strategies we will discuss later in this chapter.

Multiple Choice, Multiple Answer

These questions appear similar to the standard multiple-choice questions; however, on these you will have the opportunity to pick more than one answer. There may be anywhere from three to eight answer choices. Here's an example of what these will look like:

11 of 20

If $\dfrac{1}{12} < x < \dfrac{1}{6}$, then x could equal which of the following?

Indicate **_all_** *possible answers.*

☐ $\dfrac{2}{9}$

☐ $\dfrac{1}{5}$

☐ $\dfrac{1}{10}$

☐ $\dfrac{2}{15}$

☐ $\dfrac{2}{25}$

Your approach on these questions won't be radically different from the approach you use on standard multiple-choice questions. But obviously, you'll have to consider all of the answers—make sure you read each question carefully and remember that more than one answer can be correct. For example, for this question, you'd click on choices (C), (D), and (E). You must select *every* correct choice to get credit for the problem.

Quantitative Comparison Questions

Quantitative comparison questions, hereafter affectionately known as "quant comp" questions, ask you to compare some Quantity A to some Quantity B. These questions will have four answer choices instead of five, and all quant comp answer choices are the same. Here they are:

- ○ Quantity A is greater.
- ○ Quantity B is greater.
- ○ The two quantities are equal.
- ○ The relationship cannot be determined from the information given.

Your job is to compare the two quantities and choose one of these answers.

Quant comp problems test the same basic arithmetic, algebra, and geometry concepts as do the other GRE math problems. So, to solve these problems, you'll apply the same techniques you use on the other GRE math questions. But quant comps also have a few special rules you need to remember.

There Is No "E"

Because there are only four choices on quant comp questions, after you use POE to eliminate all of the answer choices you can, your odds of guessing correctly are even better. Think about it this way: Eliminating even one answer on a quant comp question will give you a one-in-three chance of guessing correctly.

If a Quant Comp Question Contains Only Numbers, the Answer Can't Be (D)

Any quant comp problem that contains only numbers and no variables must have a single solution. Therefore, on these problems, you can eliminate choice (D) immediately because the larger quantity can be determined. For example, if you're asked to compare $\frac{3}{2}$ and $\frac{3}{4}$, you can determine which fraction is larger, so the answer cannot be (D).

Compare, Don't Calculate

Do only as much work as you need to.

You don't always have to calculate the exact value of each quantity before you compare them. After all, your mission is simply to compare the two quantities. It's often helpful to treat the two quantities as if they were two sides of an equation. Anything you can do to both sides of an equation, you can also do to both quantities. You can add the same number to both sides; you can multiply both sides by the same positive number; and you can simplify a single side by multiplying it by one.

If you can simplify the terms of a quant comp, you should always do so.

Here's a quick example:

───────────────○───────────────

Quantity A	Quantity B
$\frac{1}{16}+\frac{1}{7}+\frac{1}{4}$	$\frac{1}{4}+\frac{1}{16}+\frac{1}{6}$

○ Quantity A is greater.

○ Quantity B is greater.

○ The two quantities are equal.

○ The relationship cannot be determined from the information given.

Here's How to Crack It

Don't do any calculating! Remember: Do only as much work as you need to in order to answer the question! The first thing you should do is eliminate (D). After all, there are only numbers here. After that, get rid of numbers that are common to both columns (think of this as simplifying). Both columns contain a $\frac{1}{16}$ and a $\frac{1}{4}$, so because we're talking about addition, they can't make a difference to the outcome. With them gone, you're merely comparing the $\frac{1}{7}$ in Column A to the $\frac{1}{6}$ in Column B. Now we can eliminate (C) as well—after all, there is no way that $\frac{1}{7}$ is equal to $\frac{1}{6}$. So, we're down to two choices, (A) and (B). If you don't remember how to compare fractions, don't worry—it's covered in Chapter 10 (Real World Math). The answer to this question is (B).

───────────────○───────────────

Okay, let's talk about another wacky question type you'll see in the Math section.

Enter a Number

Some questions on the GRE won't even have answer choices, and you'll have to generate your own answer. For example:

14 of 20

> Renaldo earns a monthly commission of 10.5% of his total sales for the month, plus a flat salary of $2,500. If Renaldo earns $3,025 in a certain month, what were his total sales? Disregard the $ sign when entering your answer.

Click on the box, then type in a number.

On this type of question, POE is not going to help you! That means if you're not sure how to do one of these questions, you should immediately move on. Leave it blank and come back to it in your second pass through the test.

To answer this question, you'd enter 5,000 into the box. Alternately, you could transfer your work directly from the on-screen calculator to the text box.

MAXIMIZE YOUR SCORE

As you're probably aware by now, doing well on the Math section will involve more than just knowing some math. It will also require the use of some good strategies. Let's go through some good strategies now; make sure you read this section carefully; it will be important for you to keep these techniques in mind as you work through the content chapters that follow this one!

Need more info? Check out the DVD.

The Two Roles of Techniques

The techniques are there to ensure that the questions that you should get right, you do get right. A couple of careless error on easy questions will kill your score. The techniques are not just tools; they are proven standard approaches that save time and effort and guarantee points. Use these techniques on every question. Turn them into a habitual approach that you use every time.

Take the Easy Test First

The new GRE offers the opportunity to mark a question and return to it. Since all questions count equally toward your score, why not do the easy ones first? Getting questions right is far more important than getting to every question, so start with the low hanging fruit. There is no law that says you have to take the test in the order in which it is given. If you see a question you don't like, keep moving. Play to your strengths and get all of the questions that you're good at in the bank, before you start spending time on the hard ones. It makes no sense to spend valuable minutes wrestling with hard questions while there are still easy ones on the table. It makes even less sense if you end up having to rush some easy ones (making mistakes in the process), as a result. Free yourself from numerical hegemony! Take the easy test first!

Bend, Don't Push

Eighty percent of the errors on the math side of the test are really reading errors. It is a four-hour test and at some point during these four hours your brain is going to get tired. When this happens you will read, see, or understand questions incorrectly. Once you see a problem wrong, it is nearly impossible to un-see it and see it correctly. When this happens, even simple problems can become extremely frustrating. If you solve a problem and your answer is not one of the choices, this is what has happened. When you would swear that a problem can't be solved, this is what has happened. When you have absolutely no idea how to solve a problem, this is what has happened. If you find yourself with half a page full of calculations and are no closer to the answer, this is what has happened. You are in La La Land. Once you are in La La Land, you can continue to push on that problem all day and you won't get any closer.

There is a good chance that you are already familiar with this frustration. The first step is to learn to recognize it when it is happening. Here are some keys to recognizing when you are off track.

You know you are in La La Land when…

- You have spent more than three minutes on a single problem.
- Your hand is not moving.
- You don't know what to do next.
- Your answer is not one of the choices.
- You're spending lots of time with the calculator and working with some ugly numbers.

Once you recognize that you are in La La Land, get out. Continuing to push on a problem, at this point, is a waste of your time. You could easily spend three or four precious minutes on this problem and be no closer to the answer. Spend those three or four minutes on other questions. That time should be yielding you points, not frustration.

After you have done two or three other questions, return to the one that was giving you trouble. Most likely, the reason it was giving you trouble is that you missed something or misread something the first time around. If the problem is still difficult, walk away again.

This is called Bend, Don't Push. The minute you encounter any resistance on the test, walk away. Bend. There are plenty of other easier points for you to get with that time. Then return to the problem a few questions later. It's OK to take two or three runs at a tough problem. If you run out of time before returning to the question, so be it. Your time is better spent on easier problems anyway, since all problems count the same.

Forcing yourself to walk away can be difficult, especially when you have already invested time in a question. You will have to train yourself to recognize resistance when it occurs, to walk away, and then to remember to come back. Employ this technique anytime you are practicing for the GRE. It will take some time to master. Be patient and give it a chance to work. With this technique, there are no questions that are out of your reach on the GRE.

POE: Ballparking and Trap Answers

Need more info? Check out the DVD.

Use Process of Elimination whenever you can on questions that are in standard multiple-choice format. Always read the answer choices before you start to solve a math problem because often they will help guide you—you might even be able to eliminate a couple of answer choices before you begin to calculate the answer.

Two effective POE tools are Ballparking and Trap Answers.

You Know More Than You Think

Say you were asked to find 30 percent of 50. Wait—don't do any math yet. Let's say that you glance at the answer choices and you see these:

- ○　　5
- ○　　15
- ○　　30
- ○　　80
- ○　　150

Think about it. Whatever 30 percent of 50 is, it must be less than 50, right? So any answer choice that's greater than 50 can't be right. That means you should eliminate both (D) and (E) before you even do any calculations! Thirty percent is less than half, so we can get rid of anything greater than 25, which means that choice (C) is gone too. What is 10% of 50? Eliminate choice (A). You're done. The only answer left is (B). This process is known as Ballparking. Remember that the answers are part of the question. There are more than four times the number of wrong answers on the GRE as there are right ones. If it were easy to find the right ones, you wouldn't need this book. It is almost always easier to identify and eliminate the wrong answers than it is to calculate the right one. Just make sure that you are using your scratch paper to eliminate answer choices instead of keeping track in your head.

Ballparking helps you eliminate answer choices and increases your odds of zeroing in on the correct answer. The key is to eliminate any answer choice that is "out of the ballpark."

Let's look at another problem:

A 100-foot rope is cut so that the shorter piece is $\frac{2}{3}$ the length of the longer piece. How many feet long is the shorter piece?

- ○ 75
- ○ $66\frac{2}{3}$
- ○ 50
- ○ 40
- ○ $33\frac{1}{3}$

Here's How to Crack It

Now, before we dive into the calculations, let's use a little common sense. The rope is 100 feet long. If we cut the rope in half, each part would be 50 feet. However, we didn't cut the rope in half; we cut it so that there's a longer part and a shorter part. What has to be true of the shorter piece then? It has to be smaller than 50 feet. If it weren't, it wouldn't be shorter than the other piece. So looking at our answers, we can eliminate (A), (B), and (C) without doing any real math. That's Ballparking. By the way, the answer is (D) and you'll learn how to tackle this type of problem when you get to Chapter 9.

Trap Answers

ETS likes to include "trap answers" in the answer choices to their math problems. Trap answers are answer choices that appear correct upon first glance. Often these answers will look so tempting that you'll choose them without actually bothering to complete the necessary calculations. Watch out for this! If a problem seems way too easy, be careful and double-check your work.

What are the trap answers in the problem about the rope?

Look at the next problem:

---

17 of 20

The price of a jacket was reduced by 10%. During a special sale, the price was discounted another 10%. What was the total percentage discount from the original price of the jacket?

- ○ 15%
- ○ 19%
- ○ 20%
- ○ 21%
- ○ 25%

Here's How to Crack It

The answer might seem like it should be 20 percent. But wait a minute: Does it seem likely that the GRE is going to give you a problem that you can solve just by adding 10 + 10? Probably not. Choice (C) is a trap answer.

To solve this problem, imagine that the original price of the jacket was $100. After a 10 percent discount the new price is $90. But now when we take another 10 percent discount, we're taking it from $90, not $100. 10 percent of 90 is 9, so we take off another $9 from the price and our final price is $81. That represents a 19 percent total discount because we started with a $100 jacket. The correct answer is (B).

HOW TO STUDY

Make sure you learn the content of each of the following chapters before you go on to the next one. Don't try to cram everything in all at once. It's much better to do a small amount of studying each day over a longer period; you will master both the math concepts and the techniques if you focus on the material a little bit at a time.

Need more info? Check out the DVD.

Practice, Practice, Practice

Practice may not make "perfect," but it sure will help. Use everyday math calculations as practice opportunities. Balance your checkbook without a calculator! Make sure your check has been added correctly at a restaurant, and figure out the exact percentage you want to leave for a tip. The more you practice simple adding, subtracting, multiplying, and dividing on a day-to-day basis, the more your arithmetic skills will improve for the GRE.

After you work through this book, be sure to practice doing questions on our online tests and on real GREs. There are always sample questions at **ets.org**, and practice will rapidly sharpen your test-taking skills.

Finally, unless you trust our techniques, you may be reluctant to use them fully and automatically on the real GRE. The best way to develop that trust is to practice before you get to the real test.

Summary

o The GRE contains two 35-minute Math sections. Each section has 20 questions.

o The GRE tests math concepts up to about the tenth grade level of difficulty.

o You will be allowed to use a calculator on the GRE. The calculator is part of the on-screen display.

o The Math section employs a number of different question formats, including multiple choice, fill in the blank, and quantitative comparison questions.

o Use the Two-Pass system on the Math section. Find the easier questions and do them first. Use your remaining time to work some of the more difficult questions.

o When you get stuck on a problem, walk away. Do a few other problems to distract your brain, and then return to the question that was giving you problems.

o Ballpark or estimate the answers to math questions and eliminate answers that don't make sense.

o Watch out for trap answers. If an answer seems too easy or obvious, it's probably a trap.

o Always do your work on your scratch paper, not in your head. Even when you are Ballparking, make sure that you are eliminating answer choices on your scratch paper. If your hand isn't moving, you're stuck and you need to walk away, or you're doing work in your head, which leads to errors.

Chapter 9
Numbers and Equations

Numbers and equations form the basis of all the math questions on the GRE. Simply put, the more comfortable you are working with numbers and equations, the easier the math portion of the exam will be. This chapter gives you a review of all the basic mathematical concepts including properties of numbers; factors and multiples; exponents and square roots; and lessons on manipulating and solving equations. This chapter also introduces you to one of The Princeton Review's key mathematical strategies: Plugging In.

IN THE BEGINNING...

...there were numbers. If you wish to do well on the GRE Math section, you'll have to be comfortable working with numbers. The concepts tested on the GRE are not exceptionally difficult, but if you are even the least bit skittish about numbers you'll have a harder time working the problems.

This chapter will familiarize you with all the basics you need to know about numbers and how to work with them. If you're a mathphobe or haven't used math in a while, take it slowly and make sure you're comfortable with this chapter before moving onto the succeeding ones.

You may be a little rusty when it comes to working with numbers but you'll be surprised at how quickly you'll become comfortable again.

GRE MATH VOCABULARY

Quick—what's an integer? Is 0 even or odd? How many even prime numbers are there?

Before we go through our techniques for specific types of math problems, we'll acquaint ourselves with some basic vocabulary and properties of numbers. The GRE loves to test your knowledge of integers, fractions, decimals, and all those other concepts you probably learned years ago. Make sure you're comfortable with the topics in this chapter before moving on. Even if you feel fairly at ease with number concepts, you should still work through this chapter. ETS is very good at coming up with questions that require you to know ideas forwards and backwards.

Learn your vocabulary!

The math terms we will review in this section are very simple, but that doesn't mean they're not important. Every GRE math question uses simple terms, rules, and definitions. You absolutely need to know this math "vocabulary." Don't worry; we will cover only the math terms that you *must* know for the GRE.

Digits

Digit refers to the numbers that make up other numbers. There are 10 digits: 0, 1, 2, 3, 4, 5, 6, 7, 8, 9, and every number is made up of a collection of digits. For example, the number 10,897 has five digits: 1, 0, 8, 9, and 7. Each of the digits in a number has its own name, which is designated by a place value. In the number 10,897:

- 7 is the ones or units digit.
- 9 is the tens digit.
- 8 is the hundreds digit.
- 0 is the thousands digit.
- 1 is the ten-thousands digit.

Numbers

A **number** is simply a digit or a collection of digits. There are, of course, an infinite number of numbers. Basically, any combination of digits you can imagine is a number, which includes 0, negative numbers, fractions and decimals, and even weird numbers such as $\sqrt{2}$.

GRE problems like to try to trip you up on the difference between a number and an integer.

Integers

The **integers** are the counting numbers, such as –6, –5, –4, –3, –2, –1, 0, 1, 2, 3, 4, 5, 6, and so on.

Notice that fractions, such as $\frac{1}{2}$, are not integers.

Remember that the number zero is an integer! Positive integers get bigger as they move away from 0 (6 is bigger than 5); negative integers get smaller as they move away from zero (–6 is smaller than –5).

Remember: Fractions are NOT integers.

PROPERTIES OF NUMBERS AND INTEGERS

Now that you've learned the proper names for various types of numbers, let's look at properties of numbers and integers.

Positive or Negative

Numbers can be positive or negative. Negative numbers are less than zero, while positive numbers are greater than zero. Zero, itself, is neither positive nor negative—all other numbers are one or the other.

Even or Odd

Only integers possess the property of being even or odd. Fractions, decimals, and other non-integers can never be even or odd. Integers that are even are those that are divisible by 2; odd integers are those integers that are not divisible by 2.

- Here are some even integers: –4, –2, 0, 2, 4, 6, 8, 10.
- Here are some odd integers: –3, –1, 1, 3, 5, 7, 9, 11.

Zero

Zero is a special little number. It is an integer, but it is neither positive nor negative. However:

- 0 is even.
- 0 plus any other number is equal to that other number.
- 0 multiplied by any other number is equal to 0.
- You cannot divide by 0.

Keep in Mind

- Fractions are neither even nor odd.
- Any integer is even if its units digit is even; any integer is odd if its units digit is odd.
- The results of adding and multiplying odd and even integers are as follows:
  - even + even = even
  - odd + odd = even
  - even + odd = odd
  - even × even = even
  - odd × odd = odd
  - even × odd = even

If you have trouble remembering some of these rules for odd and even, don't worry. As long as you remember that there are rules, you can always figure them out by plugging in numbers. Let's say you forget what happens when an odd number is multiplied by an odd number. Just pick two odd numbers, say 3 and 5, and multiply them. 3 × 5 = 15. Now you know: odd × odd = odd.

Consecutive Integers

Consecutive integers are integers listed in order of increasing value without any integers missing in between them. Here are some examples:

- 0, 1, 2, 3, 4, 5
- −6, −5, −4, −3, −2, −1, 0
- −3, −2, −1, 0, 1, 2, 3

By the way, fractions and decimals cannot be consecutive, only integers can be consecutive. However, you can have different types of consecutive integers. For example consecutive even numbers could be 2, 4, 6, 8, 10. Consecutive multiples of four could be 4, 8, 12, 16.

Absolute Value

The absolute value of a number is equal to its distance away from 0 on the number line, which means that the absolute value of any number is always positive, whether the number itself is positive or negative. The symbol for absolute value is a set of double lines: | |. Thus |−5| = 5, and |5| = 5.

Zero has a number of special properties that are tested frequently on the GRE. Technically, zero is a multiple of every number, but this fact is rarely tested on the GRE.

Be careful: Don't confuse odd and even with positive and negative!

FACTORS, MULTIPLES, AND DIVISIBILITY

Now let's look at some ways that integers are related to each other.

Factors

A factor of a particular number is a number that will divide evenly into the number in question. For example, 1, 2, 3, 4, 6, and 12 are all factors of 12 because each number divides evenly into 12. In order to find all the factors of a particular number, write down the factors systematically in pairs of numbers that, when multiplied together, make 12, starting with 1 and the number itself:

- 1 and 12
- 2 and 6
- 3 and 4

If you always start with 1 and the number itself and work your way up, you'll make sure you got them all.

Multiples

A multiple of a number is one that the number itself is a factor of. For example, the multiples of 8 are all the numbers of which 8 is a factor: 8, 16, 24, 32, 40 and so on and so on. Note that there are an infinite number of multiples for any given number. Also, zero is a multiple of every number, although this concept is rarely tested on the GRE.

There are only a few factors of any number; there are many multiples of any number.

Prime Numbers

A prime number is an integer that only has two factors; itself and one. Thus, 37 is prime because the only integers that divide evenly into it are 1 and 37, while 10 is not prime because its factors are 1, 2, 5, and 10.

Here is a list of all the prime numbers that are less than 30: 2, 3, 5, 7, 11, 13, 17, 19, 23, 29.

- 0 is not a prime number.
- 1 is not a prime number.
- 2 is the only even prime number.
- Prime numbers are positive integers. There's no such thing as a negative prime number or a prime fraction.

1 is not prime!

DIVISIBILITY

A number is always divisible by its factors. If you're not sure if one number is divisible by another, a surefire way to find out is to use the calculator. However, there are also certain rules you can use to determine whether one number is a factor of another.

- An integer is divisible by 2 if its units digit is divisible by 2. For example, we know just by glancing at it that 598,447,896 is divisible by 2, because the units digit, 6, is divisible by 2.
- An integer is divisible by 3 if the sum of its digits is divisible by 3. For example, we know that 2,145 is divisible by 3 because 2 + 1 + 4 + 5 = 12, and 12 is divisible by 3.
- An integer is divisible by 4 if its last two digits form a number that's divisible by 4. For example, 712 is divisible by 4 because 12 is divisible by 4.
- An integer is divisible by 5 if its units digit is either 0 or 5.
- An integer is divisible by 6 if it's divisible by both 2 and 3.
- An integer is divisible by 8 if its last three digits form a number that's divisible by 8. For example, 11,640 is divisible by 8 because 640 is divisible by 8.
- An integer is divisible by 9 if the sum of its digits is divisible by 9.
- An integer is divisible by 10 if its units digit is 0.

Remainders

If one number is not divisible by another—meaning that the second number is not a factor of the first number—you'll have a number left over when you divide. This left-over number is called a remainder; you probably remember working with remainders in grade school.

If a question asks about a remainder, don't use the calculator. Use long division.

For example, when 4 is divided by 2, there's nothing left over so there's no remainder. In other words, 4 is divisible by 2. You could also say that the remainder is 0.

Five divided by 2 is 2, with 1 left over; 1 is the remainder. Thirteen divided by 8 is 1, with 5 left over as the remainder.

MORE MATH VOCABULARY

In a way, the Math section is almost as much of a vocabulary test as the Verbal section. Below, you'll find some more standard terms that you should commit to memory before you do any practice problems.

Term	Meaning
sum	the result of addition
difference	the result of subtraction
product	the result of multiplication
quotient	the result of division
divisor	the number you divide by
numerator	the top number in a fraction
denominator	the bottom number in a fraction
consecutive	in order from least to greatest
term	the numbers used in an equation

BASIC OPERATIONS WITH NUMBERS

Now that you've learned about numbers and their properties, you're ready to begin working with them. As we mentioned above, there are four basic operations you can perform on a number: addition, subtraction, multiplication, and division.

Order of Operations

Unfortunately, when you work with numbers you can't just perform the four operations in any way you please. Instead, math has some very specific rules to follow, which are commonly referred to as the order of operations.

It is absolutely necessary that you perform these operations in exactly the right order. In many cases, the correct order will be apparent from the way the problem is written. In cases where the correct order is not apparent, you need to remember the following mnemonic.

Please Excuse My Dear Aunt Sally, or **PEMDAS**.

What does PEMDAS stand for?

$$P \mid E \mid MD \mid AS$$
$$\rightarrow \quad \rightarrow$$

P stands for "parentheses." Solve anything in parentheses first.

E stands for "exponents." Solve exponents next. (We'll review exponents soon.)

M stands for "multiplication" and **D** stands for "division." The arrow indicates that you do all your multiplication and division together in the same step, going from left to right.

A stands for "addition" and **S** stands for "subtraction." Again, the arrow indicates that you do all your addition and subtraction together in one step, from left to right.

Let's look at an example:

$$12 + 4(2 + 1)^2 \div 6 - 7 =$$

Here's How to Crack It

Start by doing all the math inside the parentheses. $2 + 1 = 3$. Now the problem looks like this:

$$12 + 4(3)^2 \div 6 - 7 =$$

Next we have to apply the exponent. $3^2 = 9$. Now this is what we have:

$$12 + 4(9) \div 6 - 7 =$$

Now we do multiplication and division from left to right. $4 \times 9 = 36$, and $36 \div 6 = 6$, which gives us

$$12 + 6 - 7 =$$

Finally, we do the addition and subtraction from left to right. $12 + 6 = 18$, and $18 - 7 = 11$. Therefore,

$$12 + 4(2 + 1)^2 \div 6 - 7 = 11$$

Multiplication and Division

When multiplying or dividing, keep the following rules in mind:

- positive × positive = positive $2 \times 2 = 4$
- negative × negative = positive $-2 \times -2 = 4$
- positive × negative = negative $2 \times -2 = -4$
- positive ÷ positive = positive $8 \div 2 = 4$
- negative ÷ negative = positive $-8 \div -2 = 4$
- positive ÷ negative = negative $8 \div -2 = -4$

Before taking the GRE, you should have your times tables memorized from 1 through 15. It will be a tremendous advantage if you can quickly and confidently figure out, for example, what 7×12 is (it's 84).

It seems like a small thing, but memorizing your times tables will really help you on test day.

A FEW LAWS

These two basic laws are not necessary for success on the GRE, so if you have trouble with them, don't worry too much. However, ETS likes to use these laws to make certain math problems more difficult to work with. If you're comfortable with these two laws, you'll be able to simplify problems using them, so it's definitely worth it to use them.

Associative Laws

There are two associative laws—one for addition and one for multiplication. For the sake of simplicity, we've lumped them together.

Here's what you need to know:

> When you are adding or multiplying a series of numbers, you can regroup the numbers in any way you'd like.

Write everything down on scratch paper! Don't do anything in your head!

Here are some examples:

$$4 + (5 + 8) = (4 + 5) + 8 = (4 + 8) + 5$$
$$(a + b) + (c + d) = a + (b + c + d)$$
$$4 \times (5 \times 8) = (4 \times 5) \times 8 = (4 \times 8) \times 5$$
$$(ab)(cd) = a(bcd)$$

Distributive Law

This is often tested on the GRE. Here's what it looks like:

$$a(b + c) = ab + ac$$
$$a(b - c) = ab - ac$$

For example:

$$12(66) + 12(24) = ?$$

Here's How to Crack It

This is in the same form as $ab + ac$. Using the distributive law, this must equal $12(66 + 24)$, or $12(90) = 1,080$.

EXPONENTS AND SQUARE ROOTS

Exponents and square roots are a popular topic on the GRE. Here's the information you need to know in order to work with them.

What Are Exponents?

Exponents are a sort of mathematical shorthand for repeated multiplication. Instead of writing (2)(2)(2)(2), you can use an exponent and write 2^4. The little 4 is the **exponent** and the 2 is called the **base**. If you're stuck on an exponent problem, it's often helpful to write out the repeated multiplication: When in doubt, expand it out!

There are only five rules for exponents:

1. $a^2 = a \cdot a$

2. $a^2 \cdot a^3 = (a \cdot a)(a \cdot a \cdot a) = a^{2+3} = a^5$

3. $(a^2)^3 = (a \cdot a)(a \cdot a)(a \cdot a) = a^{2 \cdot 3} = a^6$

4. $\dfrac{a^2}{a^3} = \dfrac{a \cdot a}{a \cdot a \cdot a} = \dfrac{1}{a} = a^{2-3} = a^{-1}$

5. $15^{12} - 15^{11} = 15^{11}(15 - 1) = 15^{11}(14)$

Multiplication with Exponents

It's simple to multiply two or more numbers that are raised to exponents, as long as they have the same base. In this situation, all you have to do is add up the exponents. For example:

$$2^2 \times 2^4 =$$
$$2^{2+4} = 2^6$$

You can see that this is true when you expand it out, which is just as good a way to solve the problem:

$$2^2 \times 2^4 =$$
$$2 \times 2 \times 2 \times 2 \times 2 \times 2 = 2^6$$

Be careful, though. This rule does not apply to addition. $2^2 + 2^4$ does not equal 2^6. There's no quick and easy method for adding numbers with exponents.

Division with Exponents

Dividing two or more numbers with the same base that are raised to exponents is simple, too. All you have to do is subtract the exponents. For example:

$$2^6 \div 2^2 = 2^{6-2} = 2^4$$

You can see that this is true when you expand it out:

$$2^6 \div 2^2 = (2 \times 2 \times 2 \times 2 \times 2 \times 2) \div (2 \times 2) = 2 \times 2 \times 2 \times 2 = 2^4$$

Once again, don't assume this same shortcut applies to subtraction of numbers with exponents. It doesn't.

Another time you might need to divide with exponents is when you see a negative exponent. In this situation, you just put 1 over it (in other words, take its reciprocal) and get rid of the negative. For example:

$$3^{-2}$$

should be rewritten as

$$\frac{1}{3^2}$$

and this gives us:

$$\frac{1}{9}$$

Exponents and Parentheses

When there are exponents inside and outside the parentheses, you simply multiply them:

$$(4^5)^2 =$$
$$4^{5 \times 2} =$$
$$4^{10}$$

This is what the shorthand notation is really telling us to do:

$$(4^5)^2 =$$
$$(4 \times 4 \times 4 \times 4 \times 4)(4 \times 4 \times 4 \times 4 \times 4) = 4^{10}$$

If You Expand It Out, You'll Never Be in Doubt

When solving problems that involve exponents, it's extremely important to pay careful attention to terms within parentheses. When an exponent appears on the outside of a parenthetical expression, expanding it out is the best way to ensure that you don't make a careless mistake. For example, $(3x)^2 = (3x)(3x) = 9x^2$, not $3x^2$.

The same is true of fractions within parentheses: $\left(\dfrac{3}{2}\right)^2 = \left(\dfrac{3}{2}\right)\left(\dfrac{3}{2}\right) = \dfrac{9}{4}$.

The Peculiar Behavior of Exponents

- Raising a number greater than 1 to a power greater than 1 results in a bigger number. For example, $2^2 = 4$.

- Raising a fraction that's between 0 and 1 to a power greater than 1 results in a smaller number. For example, $\left(\dfrac{1}{2}\right)^2 = \dfrac{1}{4}$.

- A negative number raised to an even power becomes positive. For example, $(-2)^2 = 4$, because $(-2)(-2) = 4$.

- A negative number raised to an odd power remains negative. For example, $(-2)^3 = -8$, because $(-2)(-2)(-2) = -8$.

- A number raised to a negative power is equal to 1 over the number raised to the positive power. For example, $2^{-2} = \dfrac{1}{2^2} = \dfrac{1}{4}$.

- A number raised to the 0 power is 1, no matter what the number is. For example, $1,000^0 = 1$. Note, however, that 0 to the 0 power is undefined.

- A number raised to the first power is ALWAYS the number itself. For example, $1,000^1 = 1,000$.

Here's an example of a question you might see on the GRE:

If $a \neq 0$, then $\dfrac{(a^6)^2}{a \cdot a^2} =$

○ a^5

○ a^6

○ a^7

○ a^8

○ a^9

Here's How to Crack It

In the numerator, we have $(a^6)^2$, which is a^{12}. In the denominator, we have $a \cdot a^2$, which is a^3. So, $a^{12} \div a^3 = a^9$. That's choice (E).

Let's try another—this time, a quant comp:

Quantity A	**Quantity B**
27^4	9^6

○ Quantity A is greater.

○ Quantity B is greater.

○ The two quantities are equal.

○ The relationship cannot be determined from the information given.

Always cross off wrong answer choices on your scratch paper.

ALWAYS write down A, B, C, D for quant comps.

Here's How to Crack It

Looks scary, huh? But remember what you learned about quant comp problems in the math introduction. Your job is to compare the two quantities, not calculate their values. First of all, eliminate (D)—when just numbers are being compared, the answer can always be determined. Now, as they're written, we can't compare these exponents—they don't have the same base. But we can fix that. Both 27 and 9 are powers of 3: 27 is $3 \times 3 \times 3$, so 27^4 is $(3 \times 3 \times 3)^4$. This equals $(3 \times 3 \times 3)$ $(3 \times 3 \times 3)(3 \times 3 \times 3)(3 \times 3 \times 3)$, also known as 3^{12}. That takes care of Column A. In Column B, 9 is 3×3, so 9^6 is $(3 \times 3)^6$. This equals $(3 \times 3)(3 \times 3)(3 \times 3)(3 \times 3)$ $(3 \times 3)(3 \times 3)$, also known as 3^{12}. So, we have 3^{12} in Column A and 3^{12} in Column B. They're equal, and the answer is (C).

What Is a Square Root?

The sign $\sqrt{}$ indicates the square root of a number. For example, $\sqrt{2}$ means that some value, squared, equals 2.

If $x^2 = 16$, then $x = \pm 4$. You must be especially careful to remember this on quantitative comparison questions. But when ETS asks you for the value of $\sqrt{16}$, or the square root of any number, it is asking you for the positive root only. Although squaring –5 will result in 25, just as squaring 5 will, when ETS asks for $\sqrt{25}$, the only answer it's looking for is 5.

Playing with Square Roots

You can multiply and divide any square roots, but you can add or subtract roots only when they are the same.

You multiply and divide square roots just like you would any other number.

$$\sqrt{3} \times \sqrt{12} = \sqrt{36} = 6$$

$$\sqrt{\frac{16}{4}} = \frac{\sqrt{16}}{\sqrt{4}} = \frac{4}{2} = 2$$

However, you can't add or subtract square roots unless the roots are the same.

So, $\sqrt{2} + \sqrt{2} = 2\sqrt{2}$. (Just pretend there's an invisible 1 in front of the root sign.) But $\sqrt{2} + \sqrt{3}$ does **not** equal $\sqrt{5}$. In order to add different roots, you need to estimate their values first and then add them. We'll cover how to estimate roots in the pages to come.

Here's an example:

---

3 of 20

$$z^2 = 144$$

Quantity A   **Quantity B**

z $\sqrt{144}$

○ Quantity A is greater.

○ Quantity B is greater.

○ The two quantities are equal.

○ The relationship cannot be determined from the information given.

Here's How to Crack It

You want to pick choice (C), don't you? After all, if z^2 is 144, then the square root of 144 must be z, right? Not so fast. If $z^2 = 144$, then z could be either 12 or –12. But when the radical sign ($\sqrt{}$) is used, only the positive root is being referred to. Therefore, Column A is equal to 12 or –12, but Column B is 12. And that gives us (D) as the answer.

Estimating and Simplifying Roots

When you have a perfect square, such as 25 or 36, finding the square root is easy. $\sqrt{25} = 5$ and $\sqrt{36} = 6$. But what about finding $\sqrt{32}$? You could use your calculator, although that may be too time-consuming. Since 32 is between 25 and 36, you can estimate that $\sqrt{32}$ must be between $\sqrt{25}$ and $\sqrt{36}$. So $\sqrt{32}$ is somewhere between 5 and 6. You also know that 32 is closer to 36 than it is to 25, so $\sqrt{32}$ will be closer to 6 than it is to 5, and will probably be about 5.6 or 5.7 (it's actually 5.66). This process of estimating roots for numbers that aren't perfect squares can be extremely helpful in eliminating answer choices through Ballparking.

The other thing you might be able to do with a root is simplify it. As we've seen, 32 isn't a perfect square, but one of its factors is a perfect square. 32 can be split into 16 × 2, which means that $\sqrt{32}$ is the same thing as $\sqrt{16 \times 2}$. We can get the square root of 16 and move that outside the square root symbol, giving us $4\sqrt{2}$.

$4\sqrt{2}$ has exactly the same value as $\sqrt{32}$, it's just written in simpler form. Since, on the GRE, answer choices will nearly always be in simplest terms, it's important to know how to do this.

Try the following problem:

$$\frac{\sqrt{75}}{\sqrt{27}} =$$

○ $\dfrac{5}{3}$

○ $\dfrac{25}{9}$

○ 3

○ $3\sqrt{3}$

○ $3\sqrt{5}$

Here's How to Crack It

First, let's try to simplify each of these roots. $\sqrt{75}$ has a factor that is a perfect square—25, so it can be rewritten as $\sqrt{25 \times 3}$ and simplified to $5\sqrt{3}$. $\sqrt{27}$ has the perfect square 9 as a factor, so it can be written as $\sqrt{9 \times 3}$ and then simplified to $3\sqrt{3}$. This means that $\dfrac{\sqrt{75}}{\sqrt{27}}$ is equal to $\dfrac{5\sqrt{3}}{3\sqrt{3}}$; the $\sqrt{3}$ in the top and bottom will cancel, leaving you with $\dfrac{5}{3}$. The answer is (A).

Learn These Four Values

To make calculations of square roots easier, you should memorize the following values. You should be able to recite them without hesitation.

$$\sqrt{1} = 1$$

$$\sqrt{2} = 1.4$$

$$\sqrt{3} = 1.7$$

$$\sqrt{4} = 2$$

You'll see them again when we discuss geometry, in Chapter 11.

ALGEBRA: OPERATIONS WITH LETTERS

Algebra is simply a way of performing operations without numbers; in algebraic expressions, a variable stands in for the missing number or numbers. While the GRE Math section is not by and large an algebra test, you should be comfortable with the basics of working with equations.

Dealing with Variables

Now that you've familiarized yourself with number concepts, it's time to put your knowledge to work. The math topics found in this chapter—together with the information in the next chapter—form the crux of the GRE Math section. Master these and you'll score well on test day. Expect to see a number of problems dealing with fractions, percents, rates, averages, and equations, so pay particular attention to these topics, which we discuss in Chapter 10.

So far, we've been showing you how to manipulate numbers, but many GRE math problems involve variables (such as n, x, or y). It's time to learn how to deal with those.

Manipulating Equations

When working with equations, you can do pretty much anything you want to them as long as you follow the golden rule:

> Whatever you do on one side of the equals sign you must also do on the other side.

Solving for One Variable

Don't assume you'll always need to solve for the variable on the GRE; sometimes you'll simply have to manipulate the equation to get the answer.

You can solve equations that have just one variable. In these cases, you start by isolating the variable on one side of the equation and the numbers on the other side. You can do this by adding, subtracting, multiplying, or dividing both sides of the equation by the same number. Just remember that anything you do to one side of an equation, you must do to the other side. Be sure to write down every step. Let's look at a simple example:

$$3x - 4 = 5$$

Here's How to Crack It

In this case, you can collect all the constants on the right side of the equation by adding 4 to both sides of the equation. (If for some reason you wanted to move the 5 to the left side of the equation, you would have to subtract 5 from both sides. That's just how it works.) In general, you can eliminate negative numbers by adding them to both sides of the equation, just as you can eliminate positives by subtracting them from both sides of the equation.

$$\begin{array}{r} 3x - 4 = 5 \\ + 4 = + 4 \\ \hline 3x = 9 \end{array}$$

The above rule also applies to numbers in the equation that are divided or multiplied. So in this case, in order to get rid of the 3 that's multiplied by the variable, x, we would need to divide both sides of the equation by 3 to solve for x.

$$\frac{3x}{3} = \frac{9}{3}$$

$$x = 3$$

Let's try another one:

$$5x - 13 = 12 - 20x$$

Here's How to Crack It
Again, we want to get all the x values on the same side of the equation:

$$
\begin{array}{r}
5x - 13 = 12 - 20x \\
+ 20x \qquad\qquad + 20x \\
\hline
25x - 13 = 12
\end{array}
$$

Now let's get rid of that negative 13:

$$
\begin{array}{r}
25x - 13 = 12 \\
+ 13 + 13 \\
\hline
25x = 25
\end{array}
$$

It might be pretty obvious that x is 1, but let's just finish it:

$$25x = 25$$
$$\frac{25x}{25} = \frac{25}{25}$$
$$x = 1$$

Let's try another one:

$$5x + \frac{3}{2} = 7x$$

Here's How to Crack It
First multiply both sides by 2 to get rid of the fraction. Remember to multiply all of the members of the equation!

$$10x + 3 = 14x$$

Always write A, B, C, D, E on your scratch paper to represent the answer choices (or A, B, C, D if it's quant comp).

You must always do the same thing to both sides of an equation.

Now collect the x's on the same side:

$$
\begin{array}{r}
10x + 3 = 14x \\
-10x \quad\ \ -10x \\
\hline
3 = 4x
\end{array}
$$

Now finish it up:

$$3 = 4x$$
$$\frac{3}{4} = \frac{4x}{4}$$
$$\frac{3}{4} = x$$

INEQUALITIES

In an equation, one side is always equal to another. In an inequality, one side of the equation does *not* equal the other. Equations contain equal signs, while inequalities contain one of the following symbols:

$\neq$	is not equal to
$>$	is greater than
$<$	is less than
$\geq$	is greater than or equal to
$\leq$	is less than or equal to

The point of the inequality sign always points to the smaller value.

You can manipulate any inequality in the same way you can an equation, with one important difference. When you multiply or divide both sides of an inequality by a negative number, the direction of the inequality symbol must change. That is, if $x > y$, then $-x < -y$.

To see what we mean, take a look at this simple inequality:

$$12 - 6x > 0$$

Here's How to Crack It

You could manipulate this inequality without ever multiplying or dividing by a negative number by just adding $6x$ to both sides. The sign stays the same. Then divide both sides by positive 6. Again, the sign stays the same.

$$12 - 6x > 0$$
$$\underline{+\ 6x > +\ 6x}$$
$$12 > 6x$$

$$\frac{12}{6} > \frac{6x}{6}$$

$$2 > x$$

But suppose you subtract 12 from both sides at first:

$$12 - 6x > 0$$
$$\underline{-12 > -12}$$
$$-6x > -12$$

$$\frac{-6x}{-6} < \frac{-12}{-6}$$

$$x < 2$$

Flip the sign! When you multiply or divide both sides of an inequality by a negative number, the greater than/less than sign points the opposite way.

Notice that the sign flipped because you divided both sides by a negative number. But the answer means the same thing: the first answer says that the number 2 is greater than x, and the second says that x is less than the number 2!

———————○———————

Sometimes, ETS will give you a range for two variables and then combine them in some way. It looks something like this:

> If $0 < x < 10$, and $-10 < y < -1$, then what is the range for $x - y$?

Here's How to Crack It.

First, treat the inequality sign like an equal sign. You need all possible combinations of $x - y$, which means that you need the biggest x minus the biggest y, the biggest x minus the smallest y, the smallest x minus the biggest y, and the smallest x minus the smallest y. There is a simple set-up to do this.

On your scratch paper write:

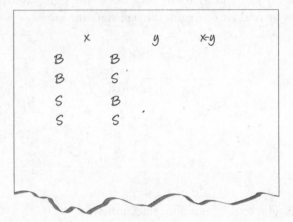

Now just solve for $x - y$. When you're done, the biggest and smallest numbers are your answers.

	x		y	x-y
B	10	B	-1	11
B	10	S	-10	20
S	0	B	-1	1
S	0	S	-10	10

The range for $x - y$, therefore is $1 < x - y < 20$. Check your answer choices and eliminate.

WORKING WITH TWO VARIABLES

So far we've only dealt with simple equations that involving one variable. But on the GRE you'll sometimes have to deal with equations with two variables. Here's an example:

$$3x + 10y = 64$$

Here's How to Crack It

The important thing to note about this situation is that we cannot solve this equation. Why, you ask? The problem is that since there are two variables, there are many possible solutions to this equation and we have no way of knowing which solutions are correct. For example, the values $x = 8$ and $y = 4$ satisfy the equation. But so do the values $x = 10$ and $y = 3.4$. Which solutions are correct? We just don't know. In order to solve equations with two variables, we need two equations. Having two equations allows us to find definitive values for our variables.

$$3x + 10y = 64$$
$$6x - 10y = 8$$

When we're given two equations, we can combine them by adding or subtracting them. We do this so that we can cancel out one of the variables, leaving us with a simple equation with one variable. In this case, it's easier to add the two equations together:

$$
\begin{array}{r}
3x + 10y = 64 \\
\underline{6x - 10y = 8} \\
9x \quad\quad = 72
\end{array}
$$

When we add these two equations we get $9x = 72$. This is a simple equation which we can solve to find $x = 8$. Once we've done that, we plug that value back into one of the equations and solve for the other variable. Substituting $x = 8$ into either equation gives us $y = 4$.

———————————○———————————

Try this one:

———————————○———————————

$$4x + 7y = 41$$
$$2x + 3y = 19$$

Here's How to Crack It

You might notice that if we add or subtract the two equations, we won't be left with one variable: Adding the two yields $6x + 10y = 60$. That doesn't help. Subtracting the equations leaves $2x + 4y = 22$. No help there, either. In cases like this one, you'll have to manipulate one of the equations so that subtracting or adding gets rid of one of the variables. In this case, let's multiply the second equation by 2:

$$2(2x + 3y) = 2(19)$$

This gives us the following:

$$4x + 6y = 38$$

You can't solve an equation with two variables unless you have a second equation.

Now we can subtract this equation from the first equation, yielding $y = 3$. If we substitute $y = 3$ into either of the equations we find that $x = 5$.

Quadratic Equations

Quadratic equations are special types of equations that involve, as the name suggests, four terms. Here is an example of a quadratic:

$$(x + 4)(x - 7)$$

In order to work with quadratics on the GRE, you must be familiar with two concepts: FOIL and factoring.

FOIL

When you see two sets of parentheses, all you have to do is remember to multiply every term in the first set of parentheses by every term in the second set of parentheses. Use FOIL to remember this method. FOIL stands for *first, outer, inner, last*—the four steps of multiplication. For example, if you see $(x + 4)(x + 3)$, you would multiply the first terms $(x \times x)$, the outer terms $(x \times 3)$, the inner terms $(4 \times x)$, and the last terms (4×3), as follows:

$$(x \times x) + (x \times 3) + (4 \times x) + (4 \times 3)$$
$$x^2 + 3x + 4x + 12$$
$$x^2 + 7x + 12$$

This also works in the opposite direction. For example, if you were given $x^2 + 7x + 12 = 0$, you could solve it by breaking it down as follows:

$$(x +)(x +) = 0$$

We know to use plus signs inside the parentheses because both the 7 and the 12 are positive. Now we have to think of two numbers that, when added together, give us 7, and when multiplied together, give us 12. Yep, they're 4 and 3:

$$(x + 4)(x + 3) = 0$$

Note that there are two solutions for x. So x can either be -4 or -3.

Quadratic Equations

There are three expressions of quadratic equations that can appear on the GRE. You should know them cold, in both their factored and unfactored forms. Here they are:

1. Factored form: $x^2 - y^2$ (the difference between two squares)
   Unfactored form: $(x + y)(x - y)$

2. Factored form: $(x + y)^2$
   Unfactored form: $x^2 + 2xy + y^2$

3. Factored form: $(x - y)^2$
   Unfactored form: $x^2 - 2xy + y^2$

Let's see how this could be used on the GRE:

> If x and y are positive integers, and if
> $x^2 + 2xy + y^2 = 25$, then $(x + y)^3 =$
>
> ○ 5
>
> ○ 15
>
> ○ 50
>
> ○ 75
>
> ○ 125

Here's How to Crack It

Problems like this one are the reason you have to memorize those quadratic equations. The equation in this question is Expression 2 from the previous page: $x^2 + 2xy + y^2 = (x + y)^2$. The question tells us that $x^2 + 2xy + y^2$ is equal to 25, which means that $(x + y)^2$ is also equal to 25. Think of $x + y$ as one unit that, when squared, is equal to 25. Since this question specifies that x and y are positive integers, what positive integer squared equals 25? Right, 5. So $x + y = 5$. The question is asking for $(x + y)^3$. In other words, what's 5 cubed, or $5 \times 5 \times 5$? It's 125. Choice (E).

Here's another one:

Quantity A	Quantity B
$(4 + \sqrt{6})(4 - \sqrt{6})$	10

○ Quantity A is greater.

○ Quantity B is greater.

○ The two quantities are equal.

○ The relationship cannot be determined from the information given.

Here's How to Crack It

First, eliminate choice (D)—we only have numbers here, so the answer can be determined. Now, Quantity A looks like a job for FOIL! Multiply the first terms, and you get 16. Multiply the outer terms and you get $-4\sqrt{6}$. Multiply the inner terms and you get $4\sqrt{6}$. Multiply the last terms and you get -6. So, we have $16 - 4\sqrt{6} + 4\sqrt{6} - 6$. Those two inner terms cancel each other out, and we're left with $16 - 6$, or 10. What do you know? That's what we have in Quantity B, too! So, the answer is (C). You might also notice that Quantity A is common quadratic Expression 1 from the previous page: $(x + y)(x - y) = x^2 - y^2$. Therefore, $(4 + \sqrt{6})(4 - \sqrt{6}) = 4^2 - \sqrt{6}^2 = 16 - 6 = 10$.

Factoring

The process of factoring "undoes" the FOIL process. Here is a quadratic in its unfactored, or expanded, form:

$$x^2 - 10x + 24$$

From this point, we can factor a quadratic by taking the following steps:

1. Separate the x^2 into $(x\ \ )(x\ \ )$.
2. Find the factors of the third term that, when added or subtracted, yield the second term.
3. Figure out the signs (+/−) for the terms. The signs have to yield the middle number when added and the last term when multiplied.

If we apply these steps to the expression above, we first set up the problem by splitting x^2 into

$$(x\ \ )(x\ \ )$$

Next, write down the factors of the third term, 24. The factors are: 1 and 24, 2 and 12, 3 and 8, and 4 and 6. Of these pairs of factors, which contains two numbers that we can add or subtract to get the second term, 10? 4 and 6 are the only two that work. That gives us

$$(x\ \ 4)(x\ \ 6)$$

The final step is to figure out the signs. We need to end up with a negative 10 and a positive 24. If we add −6 and −4, we'll get −10. Similarly, if we multiply −6 and −4, we'll end up with 24. So the answer is

$$(x - 4)(x - 6)$$

Solving Quadratic Equations

ETS likes to use quadratic equations because they have an interesting quirk; often when you solve a quadratic equation, you get not one answer, but two. This property makes quadratic equations perfect ways for ETS to try to trick you.

Here's an example:

6 of 20

$$x^2 + 2x - 15 = 0$$

Quantity A	Quantity B
2	x

○ Quantity A is greater.

○ Quantity B is greater.

○ The two quantities are equal.

○ The relationship cannot be determined from the information given.

Quadratic equations often have two solutions.

Here's How to Crack It

In order to solve a quadratic equation, the equation must be set equal to zero. Normally, this will already be the case on the GRE, as it is in this example. But if you encounter a quadratic equation that isn't set equal to zero, you must first manipulate the equation so that it is. Next you must factor the equation; otherwise you cannot solve it. So let's factor the quadratic equation in this example. We need to figure out the factors of 15 that we can add or subtract to give us 2. The only possible factors are 3 and 5. In order to get a negative 15 and a positive 2, we need to use 5 and –3. So that leaves us

$$(x - 3)(x + 5) = 0$$

Next, we're going to solve each of the two expressions within parentheses separately:

$$x - 3 = 0 \text{ and } x + 5 = 0$$

Thus, $x = 3$ and $x = -5$. This means that in this particular problem, the answer must be (D). If $x = 3$, then Quantity B is greater, but if $x = -5$ then Quantity A is greater.

Let's try another one:

If $x^2 + 8x + 16 = 0$, then $x =$

[ ]

Type your answer in the box.

Here's How to Crack It

Let's factor the equation. Start with $(x \quad) (x \quad)$. Next, find the factors of 16 that add or subtract to 8. The factors of 16 are 1 and 16, 2 and 8, and 4 and 4. Of these pairs, only 4 and 4 work. Since we have a positive 8 and a positive 16, the signs for both numbers must be positive. Thus, we end up with: $(x + 4) (x + 4) = 0$. Now, we need to solve the equation. If $x + 4 = 0$, then $x = -4$. This is the number we'd enter into the text box on the GRE.

Simultaneous Equations

ETS will sometimes give you two equations and ask you to use them to find the value of a given expression. Don't worry, you won't need any math-class algebra; in most cases, all you will have to do to find ETS's answer is to add or subtract the two equations.

Here's an example:

If $5x + 4y = 6$ and $4x + 3y = 5$, then what does $x + y$ equal?

Here's How to Crack It

All you have to do is add together or subtract one from the other. Here's what we get when we add them:

$$\begin{array}{r} 5x + 4y = 6 \\ + \ 4x + 3y = 5 \\ \hline 9x + 7y = 11 \end{array}$$

A dead end. So let's try subtracting them:

$$
\begin{array}{r}
5x + 4y = 6 \\
-\ 4x + 3y = 5 \\
\hline
x + \ y = 1
\end{array}
$$

Bingo. The value of the expression $(x + y)$ is exactly what we're looking for. On the GRE, you may see the two equations written horizontally. Just re-write the two equations, putting one on top of the other, then simply add or subtract them.

PLUGGING IN

Some of the hardest questions you might encounter on the GRE involve algebra. Algebra questions are generally difficult for two reasons. First, they are often complicated, multistep problems. Second, the answer choices often involve "distractor" choices. These are answer choices that look right, but they are actually wrong. They're designed to tempt you or to influence how you think about a problem.

If you don't like algebra, you're in luck. You don't have to do it. Plugging In will take even the hardest, messiest GRE problem and turn it into a simple arithmetic problem. It will never let you down, and it will never take more than a minute per problem.

Here are the steps:

Step 1:   **Recognize the opportunity.** You can Plug In on any problem that has variables in the answer choices. The minute you see variables in the answers, even before you have read the problem, you know you can Plug In.

Why Plug In?

Plugging In is a powerful tool that can greatly enhance your math score, but you may be wondering why you should plug in when algebra works just fine. Here's why:

Plugging In converts algebra problems into arithmetic problems. No matter how good you are at algebra, you're better at arithmetic. Why? Because you use arithmetic every day, every time you go to a store, balance your checkbook, or tip a waiter. Chances are you rarely use algebra in your day to day activities.

Plugging In is more accurate than algebra. By Plugging In real numbers, you make the problems concrete rather than abstract. Once you're working with real numbers, it's easier to notice when and where you've messed up a calculation. It's much harder to see where you went wrong (or to even know you've done something wrong) when you're staring at a bunch of x's and y's.

The GRE allows the use of a calculator. A calculator can do arithmetic but it can't do algebra, so Plugging In allows you to take advantage of the calculator function.

ETS expects its students to attack the problems algebraically and many of the tricks and the traps built into the problem are designed to catch students who do the problems with algebra. By Plugging In, you'll avoid these pitfalls.

As you can see, there are a number of excellent reasons for Plugging In. Mastering this technique can have a significant impact on your score.

Step 2: **Engage the Hand.** You cannot solve Plugging In problems in your head. Even if it seems like an easy question of translating a word problem into an algebraic equation, remember that there are trap answer choices. When a question pops up, the minute you see variables, list your answer choices, A–E on your scratch paper.

Step 3: **Plug In.** If the question asks for "x apples," come up with a number for x. The goal here is to make your life easier, so Plug In something simple and happy, but avoid 1 or 0. If you Plug In a number and the math starts getting creepy (anything involving fractions or negative numbers is creepy), don't be afraid to just change the number you Plug In. Always label each variable on your scratch paper.

Step 4: **ID Target Number.** The Target Number is the value the problem asks you to solve for. Once you you've arrived at a Target Number, write it down on your scratch paper and circle it.

Step 5: **Check All Answer Choices.** Anywhere you see a variable, Plug In the number you have written down for that variable. Do any required math. The correct answer is the one that matches your target number. If more than one answer matches your target number, just Plug In a different number for your variables and test the remaining answer choices.

Can I Just Plug In Anything?

Plug In numbers that will make the math EASY.

You can Plug In any numbers you like, as long as they're consistent with any restrictions stated in the problem, but it's faster if you use easy numbers. What makes a number easy? That depends on the problem. In most cases, smaller numbers are easier to work with than larger numbers. Usually, it's best to start small, with 2, for example. Avoid 0 and 1; both 0 and 1 have special properties, which you'll hear more about later. You want to avoid these numbers because they will often make more than one answer choice appear correct. For example, if we Plug In 0 for a variable, then the answers $2x$, $3x$, and $5x$ would all equal 0. If you avoid these bad number choices, you should also avoid these bad situations. Also, do not Plug In any numbers that show up a lot in the question or answer choices.

Try this one. Read through the whole question before you start to Plug In numbers:

The price of a certain stock increased 8 points, then decreased 13 points, and then increased 9 points. If the stock price before the changes was x points, which of the following was the stock price, in points, after the changes?

- ○ $x - 5$
- ○ $x - 4$
- ○ $x + 4$
- ○ $x + 5$
- ○ $x + 8$

Here's How to Crack It

Let's use an easy number like 10 for the variable (write down "$x = 10$" on your scratch paper!). If the original price was 10, and then it increased 8 points, that's 18. Then it decreased 13 points, so now it's 5 (do everything out on the scratch paper—don't even add or subtract in your head). Then it increased 9 points, so now it's 14. So, it started at 10 and ended at 14. Circle 14 (our target answer) and Plug In 10 for every x in the answer choices. Which one gives you 14?

- (A) $10 - 5 = 5$—Nope.
- (B) $10 - 4 = 6$—Nope.
- (C) $10 + 4 = 14$—Bingo!
- (D) $10 + 5 = 15$—Nope.
- (E) $10 + 8 = 18$—Nope.

Pretty easy, huh?

Good Numbers Make Life Easier

Small numbers aren't always the best choices for Plugging In, though. In a problem involving percentages, for example, 10 and 100 are good numbers to use. In a problem involving minutes or seconds, 30 or 120 are often good choices. (Avoid 60, however; it tends to cause problems.) You should look for clues in the problem itself to help you choose good numbers.

Don't skip steps! Use your scratch paper.

Always Plug In when you see variables in the answer choices!

Let's work through the following problem, using the steps above:

Mara has six more than twice as many apples as does Robert and half as many apples as does Sheila. If Robert has x apples, then, in terms of x, how many apples do Mara, Robert, and Sheila have?

- ○ $2x + 6$
- ○ $2x + 9$
- ○ $3x + 12$
- ○ $4x + 9$
- ○ $7x + 18$

On the GRE, Plugging In is often safer, and easier, than doing the algebra.

What's your target number?

Here's How to Crack It

Step 1: **Identify the Opportunity.** You're sitting in your cubical at the Thompson Prometric Center and this question pops up. What do you see? The variable, x, is in both the question and the answer choices. Good, so what do you do?

Step 2: **Engage the Hand.** On the upper left-hand corner of your scratch paper, list answer choices (A) through (E). The answers aren't actually labeled (A) through (E), but this will help you to identify each one.

Step 3: **Plug In.** The problem tells us that Robert has x apples, so Plug In a number for x. Make it something nice and happy. Try 4. On your scratch paper, write $x = 4$.

Step 4: **ID Target Number.** The problem tells us that "Mara has six more than twice as many apples as does Robert." If Robert has 4 apples, then Mara must have 14. On your scratch paper, write $m = 14$. We are also told that Mara has "half as many apples as does Shelia." Ignoring the weird diction, that means that Shelia must have 28 apples. Write down $s = 28$. Now, what does the question ask you to find? It asks for the number of apples that Mara, Robert, and Shelia have. That's no problem; add the three up to come up with 46 apples. This is your target number. Write it down and circle it.

Step 5: **Check All Answer Choices.** You are allowed to perform only one mathematical function in your head at a time. Anything more than that leads to trouble. For the first answer choice, therefore, you can do $2x$ in your head; that's 8, but write down 8 + 6. You don't need to go any farther than that because this clearly will not add up to 46. Cross off choice (A). Choice (B) gives you 8 + 9. Cross that off. Choice (C) is 12 + 12. This is also too small, so cross it off. Choice (D) gives you 16 + 9. That gets you to 25, which is not your target number, so cross it off. Choice (E) is 28 + 18. Do this on your scratch paper or with the calculator. Do NOT do it in your head. It equals 46, which is your target number. Choice (E) is the correct answer.

(A) $2(4) + 6 = 14$ This is not 46, so eliminate it.

(B) $2(4) + 9 = 17$ No good either.

(C) $3(4) + 12 = 24$ Still not 46.

(D) $4(4) + 9 = 25$ This isn't 46 either.

(E) $7(4) + 18 = 46$ Bingo! This is your answer.

On the GRE, you can Plug In any time the question has variables in the answer choices. You can usually Plug In any number you wish, although you should always pick numbers that will be easy to work with. Some numbers can end up causing more trouble than they're worth.

When a problem has variables in the answer choices, PLUG IN!

When Plugging In, follow these rules:

1. Don't Plug In 0 or 1. These numbers, while easy to work with, have special properties.
2. Don't Plug In numbers that are already in the problem; this might confuse you as you work through it.
3. Don't Plug In the same number for multiple variables. For example, if a problem has x, y, and z in it, pick three different numbers to Plug In for the three variables.

Finally, Plugging In can be a powerful tool, but you must remember to always check all five answer choices when you plug in. In certain cases, two answer choices can yield the same target number. This doesn't necessarily mean you did anything wrong; you just hit some bad luck. Plug In some new numbers, get a new target and recheck the answers that worked the first time.

PLUGGING IN THE ANSWERS (PITA)

Some questions may not have variables in them but will try to tempt you into applying algebra to solve them. We call these Plugging In The Answers, or PITA for short. These are almost always difficult problems. Once you recognize the opportunity, however, they turn into simple arithmetic questions. In fact, the hardest part of these problems is often identifying them as opportunities for PITA. The beauty of these questions is that they take advantage of one of the inherent limitations of a multiple-choice test. ETS has actually given you the answers, and one of them must be correct. In fact, only one can work. The essence of this technique is to systematically Plug In The Answers into the question to see which answer choice works.

Here are the steps:

Step 1:   **Recognize the Opportunity.** There are three ways to do this. The first triggers are the phrases "how much…," "how many…," or "what is the value of…." When you see one of these phrases in a question, you can Plug In The Answers. The second tip-off is specific numbers in the answer choices in ascending or descending order. The last tip-off is your own inclination. If you find yourself tempted to write your own algebraic formulas and to invent your own variables to solve the problem, it's a sure bet that you can just Plug In The Answer choices.

Step 2:   **Engage the Hand.** The minute you recognize the opportunity, list the numbers in the answer choices in a column in the upper left-hand corner of your scratch paper.

Step 3:   **Label the First Column.** What do these numbers represent? The question asks you to find a specific number. The answer choices are this number. At the top of the column, write down what these numbers represent.

Step 4:   **Assume (C) to be Correct.** Choice (C) will always be the number in the middle. This the most efficient place to start because it will allow you to eliminate as many as three answer choices if it is wrong.

Step 5:   **Create Your Spreadsheet.** Assuming the number in choice (C) is correct; use this number to work through the problem. It is always easier to understand the problem using a specific number. Work through the problem in bite-size pieces, and every time you have to do something with the number, make a new column. You can't have too many columns. Each column is a step in solving the problem.

Step 6: **Rinse and Repeat.** On single-answer multiple-choice questions, only one answer choice can work. If choice (C) is correct, you are done. If it is not correct, you may be able to identify if it is too big or too small. If it is too big, you can eliminate it and every answer choice that is bigger. This very quickly get's you down to a 50/50 shot. It also gives you a little spreadsheet specifically designed to calculate the correct answer. When you need to check the remaining answer choices, let the spreadsheet do the thinking for you. All you need to do is to fill in the cells. As soon as you find an answer choice that works, you're done.

The following is an example of a PITA problem:

———————○———————

9 of 20

An office supply store charged $13.10 for the purchase of 85 paper clips. If some of the clips were 16 cents each and the remainder were 14 cents each, how many of the paper clips were 14-cent clips?

○ 16

○ 25

○ 30

○ 35

○ 65

Are you tempted to do algebra? Are there numbers in the answer choices? Plug In The Answers.

Here's How to Crack It

Step 1: **Recognize the Opportunity.** The question asks "how many of the paper clips…." That's your first sign. Additionally, you have specific numbers in the answer choices in ascending order.

Step 2: **Engage the Hand.** The minute you recognize this as a PITA question, list your answer choices in a column on your scratch paper.

Step 3: **Label the First Column.** What do those answer choices represent? They are the number of 14-cent clips, so label this column 14¢.

Step 4: **Assume (C) to be Correct.** Start with choice (C) and assume that 30 of the clips were 14 cents each.

Step 5: **Create Your Spreadsheet.** If 30 of the clips were 14 cents each, then the purchaser would have spent $4.20 on 14-cent clips. Label this column "amount spent." Now you know that there were 85 clips total, so if 30 of the clips were 14 cents each, there must have been 55 clips that were 16 cents each. Write down a 55 and label this column 16¢. The purchaser then spent $8.80 on 16-cent clips. Write this down and label this column "amount spent." You can now calculate the total spent. 4.20 + 8.80 = 13.00. Write this down and label this column "total."

Step 6: **Rinse and Repeat.** You know that the purchaser spent $13.10 on paper clips. If answer choice C were correct, then the purchaser would have spent only $13.00 on paper clips. Since you know this is wrong, choice (C) cannot be correct. Cross it off. You also know that your total is too small. You need a greater portion of your clips to be the more expensive ones to get a higher total, so cross off choices (D) and (E). Now try choice (B). If 25 of the clips cost 14 cents each, the purchaser would have spent $3.50. There must have been 60 clips that cost 16 cents each (85 − 25 = 60). Then, the purchaser would have spent $9.60 on them. The total spent on clips, therefore, comes to $13.10, and you're done.

Make sure to keep your hand moving, to write down all steps, and to use your calculator for simple arithmetic steps like multiplying and adding complex numbers. Here's what your scratch paper should look like after this problem:

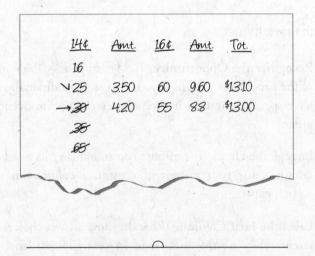

On PITA questions, you can stop once you've found the correct answer; you don't have to check all five answer choices. Just make sure you write EVERYTHING down when doing these questions (and, indeed, all math questions).

PLUGGING IN ON QUANTITATIVE COMPARISON QUESTIONS

These questions often test your knowledge of the properties of fractions, zero, one, negatives, and other odd numbers.

Quantitative Comparison questions with variables can be extremely tricky because the obvious answer is often wrong, whereas the correct answer may be a scenario most people would never think of. On the other hand, there is a simple set-up and approach that you can use that ensures that you get these questions right without taking too much time. As always, whenever you see variables, replace them with real numbers. On quant comp questions, however, it is crucial that you Plug In more than once and specifically that you Plug In all of the weird and obscure numbers that you would never use elsewhere. Always keep the nature of the answer choices in mind. Picking choice (A) means that you believe that the quantity in column A will *always* be bigger—*no matter what you Plug In*. Choice (B) means the column B will *always* be bigger—*no matter what you Plug In,* and so forth. To prove that one of these statements is true you have to Plug In every possible number that could change the outcome. Don't worry. We have a simple process to help figure out what to Plug In and how to track your progress as you do.

Here are the steps:

Step 1: **Recognize the Opportunity.** The first six, seven, or eight questions of any math section will be quant comp. When a quant comp question pops up and you see variables, make your set up.

Step 2: **Engage the Hand**. The minute you see quant comp and variables make your set up in the upper left hand of your scratch paper. Your set-up looks like this:

$$\underline{A} \quad a\,b\,c\,d \quad \underline{B}$$
$$y =$$
$$y =$$
$$y =$$

Step 3: **Plug In and Eliminate.** Start with something nice and happy. Paying close attention to the rules the question gives you for what you are allowed to Plug In, and start with a simple, happy number. With a number for the variable, calculate the value in Quantity A and write it down. Then calculate the value in Quantity B and write it down. If Quantity A is bigger, eliminate choices (B) and (C). If Quantity B is bigger, eliminate (A) and (C). If they are both the same, eliminate choices (A) and (B). Note that you are already down to a 50/50 shot.

Step 4: **Rinse and Repeat**—There are still two answer choices left, so you're not done yet. The second time you Plug In, you want to try to get a different result. What can you Plug In the second time that messes with the problem? If you're not sure, use this simple check list: ZONE F. This stands for Zero, One, Negative, Extremely Big or Small, and Fractions. You won't always be allowed to Plug In all of these and rarely will you have to. Your goal is to eliminate choices (A), (B), and (C). If you Plug In everything on the checklist and (A), (B), or (C) is still standing, that's your answer.

The easiest way to solve most quant comp questions that involve variables is to Plug In, just as you would on word problems. But because answer choice (D) is always an option, you always have to make sure it isn't the answer. So...

Always Plug In at Least Twice in Quant Comp Questions

Plugging In on quant comp questions is just like Plugging In on "must be" problems. The reason for this is (D). On quant comp questions, it's not enough to determine whether one quantity is sometimes greater than, less than, or equal to the other; you have to determine whether it *always* is. If different numbers lead to different answers, then the correct answer is (D). To figure out if one quantity is always bigger, you have to Plug In weird numbers to account for all possible situations.

What makes certain numbers weird? They behave in unexpected ways when added, multiplied, or raised to powers. Here are some examples:

- 0 times any number is 0.
- 0^2 is 0.
- 1^2 is 1.

- $\left(\dfrac{1}{2}\right)^2$ is less than $\dfrac{1}{2}$.

- $(-2)(-2)$ is 4.
- A negative number squared is positive.
- Really big numbers (100, 1,000) can make a really big difference in your answer.

On quant comp, Plug In "normal" numbers, and eliminate two choices. Then Plug In "weird" numbers (zero, one, negatives, fractions, or big numbers) to try to disprove your first answer. If different numbers give you different answers, you've proved that the answer is (D).

Here's how it works:

$\bigcirc$

---

5 of 20

Quantity A	**Quantity B**
$2x^3$	$4x^2$

○ Quantity A is greater.

○ Quantity B is greater.

○ The two quantities are equal.

○ The relationship cannot be determined from the information given.

Here's How to Crack It

Step 1: **Recognize the Opportunity.** First you see quant comp. Second, you see variables. It takes all of three seconds to recognize a quant comp Plug In. You don't even have to understand the problem at this point. Just recognize the opportunity.

Step 2: **Engage the Hand.** The minute you recognize this as a quant comp Plug In, make your set-up on your scratch paper. List "$x =$" three times down the middle.

Step 3: **Plug In.** Let's start with something nice and happy, like 2. Write down 2 next to your first x. When $x = 2$, the quantity in column A is 16 ($2 \cdot 2^3$), and the quantity in column B is also 16 ($4 \cdot 2^2$). Since you have followed the rules and both columns are the same, neither (A) nor (B) can be the answer. Cross them off. Note that you haven't worked very hard yet, haven't spent much time at all, and you are already down to a 50/50 shot.

Step 4: **Rinse and Repeat.** Now try something different for x. What if $x = 1$? The quantity in column A will be 2, and the quantity in column B will be 4. In this case, they are not the same, so choice (C) cannot be the correct answer. Cross it off. Only choice (D) is left, so you're done.

Here is what your scratch paper should look like:

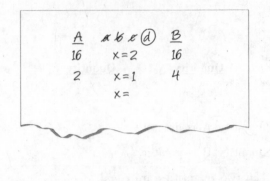

You might also have noticed that Plugging In $x = 0$ would also yield different results. On quant comp questions, ETS hopes you'll forget to consider what happens when you use numbers such as 0, 1, fractions, and negatives. Therefore, when Plugging In, make sure to use the following numbers whenever possible:

> **Zero**
> **One**
> **Negatives**
> **Extreme Values**
> **Fractions**

We call these weird numbers the ZONE-F numbers. Make sure you use them aggressively on quant comp problems because they can radically affect the relationship between the two quantities.

Phew. Now we've covered the basics of mathematical operations; hopefully a lot of this material came back to you as we went through it, but if not don't worry! You'll have plenty of opportunities to refresh your memory of this material as you read through the next two chapters and work the problems you see in the drills.

In the next chapter we'll look at some everyday math topics that are tested on the GRE, so practice the techniques in the drill that follows, and move on!

Numbers and Equations Drill

Ready to try out your new skills? Give this drill a shot and then check your answers in Part V.

Which of the following is equal to 10 ?

*Indicate **all** possible values.*

☐ $\frac{2}{3} \times 33 - 12$

☐ $\frac{2}{3} \times 51 - 24$

☐ $33 - 22 \times 1\frac{1}{2}$

☐ $51 \div (17 \times 3) + 9$

☐ $(51 \div 17) \times 3 + 9$

Click on your choice(s).

$$a + 7 = 23$$
$$b - a = -10$$

Quantity A	**Quantity B**
b	4

○ Quantity A is greater.

○ Quantity B is greater.

○ The two quantities are equal.

○ The relationship cannot be determined from the information given.

If $3^3 \times 9^{12} = 3^x$, what is the value of x ?

Click on the answer box, then type in a number. Backspace to erase.

If $x - y > 6$ and $2x + y > 30$, then which one represents all possible values of x ?

○ $x > 6$

○ $6 < x < 18$

○ $x > 12$

○ $12 < x < 36$

○ $x > 36$

A merchant sells three different sizes of canned tomatoes. A large can costs as much as 5 medium cans or 7 small cans. If a customer buys an equal number of small and large cans of tomatoes for the exact amount of money that would buy 200 medium cans, how many small cans will she buy?

○ 35

○ 45

○ 72

○ 199

○ 208

If $(x + y)^2 = 16$ and $(x - y)^2 = 9$, what is one possible value of $(x^2 - y^2)$?

Click on the answer box, then type in a number. Backspace to erase.

When the integer a is multiplied by 3, the result is 4 less than 6 times the integer b. Therefore, $a - 2b$ is

○ -12

○ $-\dfrac{4}{3}$

○ $-\dfrac{3}{4}$

○ $\dfrac{4}{3}$

○ 12

Quantity A	Quantity B
$\dfrac{\sqrt{12}}{\sqrt{5}-\sqrt{2}}$	$\dfrac{\sqrt{2}+\sqrt{5}}{\sqrt{27}}$

○ Quantity A is greater.

○ Quantity B is greater.

○ The two quantities are equal.

○ The relationship cannot be determined from the information given.

$$\dfrac{a + \dfrac{b}{c}}{\dfrac{d}{e}}$$

If the value of the expression above is to be halved by doubling exactly one of the five numbers a, b, c, d, or e, which should be doubled?

○ a

○ b

○ c

○ d

○ e

If $x = 3a$ and $y = 9b$, then all of the following are equal to $2(x + y)$ EXCEPT

☐ $2(3a) + 9b$

☐ $12a + 9b$

☐ $6a + 18b$

☐ $6(a + 3b)$

☐ $6a + 21b$

Summary

- Digits are the numbers that make up other numbers. Numbers include whole numbers, fractions, negative numbers, and weird values like the square root of 2. Integers are numbers with no decimal or fractional part.

- Positive numbers are greater than zero and negative numbers less than zero. The number zero is neither positive nor negative.

- Even numbers are divisible by 2; odd numbers aren't. Only integers can be even or odd.

- A factor divides evenly into a number. A multiple is a number that a certain number is a factor of. Every number is a factor and a multiple of itself.

- The order of operations is PEMDAS.

- An exponent is shorthand for repeated multiplication. When in doubt on exponent problems, expand them out.

- The Golden Rule of Equations: Whatever you do to one side of the equation, you must do to the other.

- With inequalities you have to flip the sign when multiplying or dividing by a negative number.

- In order to solve an equation with two variables you need two equations. Stack them up and add or subtract to cancel out one of the variables.

- Use the FOIL process to expand quadratics. To solve a quadratic equation, set it equal to zero and factor.

- Plugging In converts algebra problems to arithmetic problems. Plug In by replacing variables in the question with real numbers or by working backwards from the answer choices provided.

- Use the ZONE-F numbers on tricky quant comp questions with variables.

Chapter 10
Real World Math

Real world math is our title for the grab bag of math topics that will be heavily tested on the GRE. This chapter details a number of important math concepts, many of which you've probably used at one point or another in your daily adventures, even if you didn't recognize that you were. After completing this chapter you'll have brushed up on important topics such as fractions, percents, ratios, proportions, and average. You'll also learn some important Princeton Review methods for organizing your work and efficiently and accurately answering questions on these topics.

EVERYDAY MATH

As we've mentioned, when ETS reconfigured the GRE, one of its goals was to make the Math section reflect more of the kind of math that a typical graduate school student would use. Another of their goals was to test more of what it calls "real-life" scenarios. You can therefore expect the math questions on the GRE to heavily test things such as fractions, percents, proportions, averages, and ratios—mathematical concepts that are theoretically part of your everyday life. Regardless of whether that's true of your daily life or not, you'll have to master these concepts in order to do well on the GRE Math section.

FRACTIONS, DECIMALS, AND PERCENTS

In the previous chapter we spent most of our time working with integers. Now we'll expand our discussion to include concepts like fractions, decimals, and percents—all of which will appear frequently on the GRE.

Fractions

A fraction expresses a specific piece of information; namely the number of parts out of a whole. In the fraction $\frac{2}{3}$, for instance, the top part, or numerator, tells us that we have 2 parts, while the bottom part of the fraction, the denominator, indicates that the whole, or total, consists of 3 parts. We use fractions whenever we're dealing with a quantity that's less than one.

Notice that the fraction bar is simply another way of expressing division. Thus, the fraction $\frac{2}{3}$ is just expressing the idea of "2 divided by 3."

Reducing and Expanding Fractions

Fractions express a relationship between numbers, not actual amounts. For example, saying that you did $\frac{1}{2}$ of your homework expresses the same idea whether you had 10 pages of homework to do and you've done 5, or you had 50 pages to do and you've done 25 pages. This concept is important because on the GRE you'll frequently have to reduce or expand fractions.

To reduce a fraction, simply express the numerator and denominator as the products of their factors. Then cross out, or "cancel," factors that are common to both the numerator and denominator. Here's an example:

$$\frac{16}{20} = \frac{2 \times 2 \times 2 \times 2}{2 \times 2 \times 5} = \frac{\cancel{2} \times \cancel{2} \times 2 \times 2}{\cancel{2} \times \cancel{2} \times 5} = \frac{2 \times 2}{5} = \frac{4}{5}$$

You can achieve the same result by dividing the numerator and denominator by the factors that are common to both. In the example you just saw, you might realize that 4 is a factor of both the numerator and the denominator. That is, both the numerator and the denominator can be divided evenly (without remainder) by 4. Doing this yields the much more manageable fraction $\frac{4}{5}$.

When you confront GRE math problems that involve big fractions, always reduce them before doing anything else.

> Remember: You can only reduce across a multiplication sign.

Look at each of the following fractions:

$$\frac{1}{4} \qquad \frac{2}{8} \qquad \frac{6}{24} \qquad \frac{18}{72} \qquad \frac{90}{360} \qquad \frac{236}{944}$$

What do you notice about each of these fractions? They all express the same information! Each of these fractions expresses the relationship of "1 part out of 4 total parts."

Adding and Subtracting Fractions

Adding and subtracting fractions that have a common denominator is easy—you just add the numerators and put the sum over the common denominator. Here's an example:

$$\frac{1}{10} + \frac{2}{10} + \frac{4}{10} =$$

$$\frac{1+2+4}{10} = \frac{7}{10}$$

Why Bother?

You may be wondering why, if the GRE allows the use of a calculator, you should bother learning how to add or subtract fractions or to reduce them or even know any of the topics covered in the next few pages. While it's true that you can use a calculator for these tasks, for many problems it's actually slower to do the math with the calculator than without. Scoring well on the GRE Math section requires a fairly strong grasp of the basic relationships among numbers, fractions, percents, and so on, so it's in your best interest to really understand these concepts rather than to rely on your calculator to get you through the day. In fact, if you put in the work now, you'll be surprised at how easy some of the problems become, especially when you don't have to refer constantly to the calculator to perform basic operations.

In order to add or subtract fractions that have different denominators, you need to start by finding a common denominator. You may remember your teachers from grade school imploring you to find the "lowest common denominator." Actually, any common denominator will do, so find whichever one you find most comfortable working with.

$$\frac{7}{8} - \frac{5}{12} = \frac{21}{24} - \frac{10}{24} = \frac{11}{24}$$

Here, we expanded the fraction $\frac{7}{8}$ into the equivalent fraction $\frac{21}{24}$ by multiplying both the numerator and denominator by 3. Similarly, we converted $\frac{5}{12}$ to $\frac{10}{24}$ by multiplying both denominator and numerator by 2. This left us with two fractions that had the same denominator, which meant that we could simply subtract their numerators.

When adding and subtracting fractions, you can also use a technique we call the Bowtie. The Bowtie method accomplishes exactly what we just did in one fell swoop. To use the Bowtie, first multiply the denominators of each fraction. This gives us a common denominator. Then multiply the denominator of each fraction by the numerator of the other fraction. Take these numbers and add or subtract them—depending on what the question asks you to do—to get the numerator of the answer. Then reduce if necessary.

$$\frac{2}{3} + \frac{3}{4} =$$

$$\frac{2}{3} \times \frac{3}{4} = \frac{8}{12} + \frac{9}{12} = \frac{17}{12}$$

and

$$\frac{2}{3} - \frac{3}{4} =$$

$$\frac{2}{3} \times \frac{3}{4} = \frac{8}{12} - \frac{9}{12} = -\frac{1}{12}$$

Multiplying Fractions

There's nothing tricky about multiplying fractions: All you do is multiply straight across—multiply the first numerator by the second numerator and the first denominator by the second denominator. Here's an example:

$$\frac{4}{5} \times \frac{10}{12} = \frac{40}{60}$$

At this point, we'd probably want to reduce our fraction. When multiplying fractions, we can make our lives easier by reducing before we multiply. We do this once again by dividing out common factors.

$$\frac{4}{5} \times \frac{10}{12} = \frac{4}{5} \times \frac{5}{6}$$

Also remember that when we're multiplying fractions, we can even reduce diagonally; as long as we're working with a numerator and a denominator of opposite fractions; they don't have to be in the same fraction. So we end up with

$$\frac{4}{5} \times \frac{5}{6} = \frac{2}{1} \times \frac{1}{3} = \frac{2}{3}$$

Of course, you get the same answer either way, so attack fractions in whatever fashion you find easiest.

Dividing Fractions

Dividing fractions is just like multiplying fractions, with one crucial difference: Before you multiply, you have to turn the second fraction upside down (that is, put its denominator over its numerator, or to use fancy math lingo, find its reciprocal). In some cases, you can also reduce before you multiply. Here's an example:

$$\frac{2}{3} \div \frac{4}{5} = \frac{2}{3} \times \frac{5}{4} = \frac{1}{3} \times \frac{5}{2} = \frac{5}{6}$$

Multiplying fractions is a snap: just multiply straight across, numerator times numerator and denominator times denominator.

ETS sometimes gives you problems that involve fractions whose numerators or denominators are themselves fractions. These problems might look intimidating, but if you're careful, you won't have any trouble with them. All you have to do is remember what we said about a fraction being shorthand for division. Always rewrite the expression horizontally. Here's an example:

$$\frac{7}{\frac{1}{4}} = 7 \div \frac{1}{4} = \frac{7}{1} \times \frac{4}{1} = \frac{28}{1} = 28$$

Comparing Fractions

The GRE might also present you with math problems that require that you to compare two fractions and decide which is larger, especially on quant comp questions. There are a couple of ways to accomplish this. One is to find equivalent fractions that have a common denominator. This works with simpler fractions, but on some problems the common denominator might be hard to find or hard to work with.

As an alternative, you can use a variant of the Bowtie technique. In this variant, you don't have to multiply the denominators, just the denominators and the numerators. The fraction with the larger product in its numerator is the bigger fraction. Let's say we had to compare the following fractions:

$$\frac{3}{7} \qquad \frac{7}{12}$$

$$\overset{36}{\underset{}{\frac{3}{7}}} \times \overset{49}{\underset{}{\frac{7}{12}}}$$

You can also use the calculator feature to change the fractions into decimals.

Multiplying the first denominator by the second numerator gives us 49. This means the numerator of the second fraction $\left(\frac{7}{12}\right)$ will be 49. Multiplying the second denominator by the first numerator gives us 36, which means the first fraction will have a numerator of 36. If 49 is bigger than 36, $\frac{7}{12}$ is bigger than $\frac{3}{7}$. Remember that when you use this method, it's the numerators that matter.

Comparing More Than Two Fractions

You may also be asked to compare more than two fractions. On these types of problems, don't waste time trying to find a common denominator for all of them. Simply use the Bowtie to compare two of the fractions at a time.

Here's an example:

Which of the following statements is true?

○ $\dfrac{3}{8} < \dfrac{2}{9} < \dfrac{4}{11}$

○ $\dfrac{2}{5} < \dfrac{3}{7} < \dfrac{4}{13}$

○ $\dfrac{4}{13} < \dfrac{2}{5} < \dfrac{3}{7}$

○ $\dfrac{3}{7} < \dfrac{3}{8} < \dfrac{2}{5}$

○ $\dfrac{2}{9} < \dfrac{3}{7} < \dfrac{3}{8}$

Here's How to Crack It

As you can see, it would be a nightmare to try to find common denominators for all these funky fractions, so instead we'll use the Bowtie method. Simply multiply the denominators and numerators of a pair of fractions and note the results. For example, to check answer choice (A), we first multiply 8 and 2, which gives us a numerator of 16 for the fraction $\dfrac{2}{9}$. But multiplying 9 and 3 gives us a numerator of 27 for the first fraction. This means that $\dfrac{3}{8}$ is bigger than $\dfrac{2}{9}$, and we can eliminate choice (A), because the first part of it is wrong. Here's how the rest of the choices shape up:

○ $\dfrac{2}{5} < \dfrac{3}{7} < \dfrac{4}{13}$ Compare $\dfrac{3}{7}$ and $\dfrac{4}{13}$; $\dfrac{3}{7}$ is larger.

○ $\dfrac{4}{13} < \dfrac{2}{5} < \dfrac{3}{7}$ These fractions are in order.

○ $\dfrac{3}{7} < \dfrac{3}{8} < \dfrac{2}{5}$ $\dfrac{3}{7}$ is larger than $\dfrac{3}{8}$.

○ $\dfrac{2}{9} < \dfrac{3}{7} < \dfrac{3}{8}$ $\dfrac{3}{7}$ is larger than $\dfrac{3}{8}$.

Make sure you are doing all of this work in an organized fashion on your scratch paper.

Converting Mixed Numbers into Fractions

A **mixed number** is a number that is represented as an integer and a fraction, such as $2\frac{2}{3}$. In most cases on the GRE, you should get rid of mixed fractions by converting them to fractions. How do you do this? By multiplying the denominator of the fraction by the integer, then adding that number to the numerator, and then putting the whole thing over the denominator. In other words, for the fraction above we would get $\frac{3 \times 2 + 2}{3}$ or $\frac{8}{3}$.

The result, $\frac{8}{3}$, is equivalent to $2\frac{2}{3}$. The only difference is that $\frac{8}{3}$ is easier to work with in math problems. Also, answer choices are usually not in the form of mixed numbers.

Decimals

Decimals are just fractions in disguise. Basically, decimals and fractions are two different ways of expressing the same thing. Every decimal can be written as a fraction, and every fraction can be written as a decimal. For example, the decimal .35 can be written as the fraction $\frac{35}{100}$: These two expressions, .35 and $\frac{35}{100}$, have the same value.

To turn a fraction into its decimal equivalent, all you have to do is divide the numerator by the denominator. Here, for example, is how you would find the decimal equivalent of $\frac{3}{4}$:

$$\frac{3}{4} = 3 \div 4 = 4\overline{)3.00}^{\,0.75}$$

Try this problem:

$$7 < x < 8$$
$$y = 9$$

Quantity A   **Quantity B**

$\dfrac{x}{y}$ .85

○ Quantity A is greater.

○ Quantity B is greater.

○ The two quantities are equal.

○ The relationship cannot be determined
from the information given.

Here's How to Crack It

So, you're sitting at your cubical at the Thompson Prometric Center and this problem pops up. What do you see? Before we even talk about fractions, the first thing
you should note is that this is a quant comp with variables. With your hand, on
your scratch paper, make your set-up. It should look like this:

```
 A    a b c d    B
  x =        y =
  x =        y =
  x =        y =
```

Now they've told us that *x* is going to be seven point something. Try Plugging In
the smallest value you can think of for *x*. Write down *x* = 7.1 and *y* = 9. The value
in Quantity A is .78. The value in Quantity B is .85. Quantity B is bigger, so eliminate choices (A) and (C). Now try making *x* as big as you can make it. Write down
x = 7.9 and *y* = 9. The value in column A is .87 and the value in Quantity B is .85.
Quantity A is bigger so eliminate choice B, and you're done. The answer is (D).

Your scratch paper should look like this:

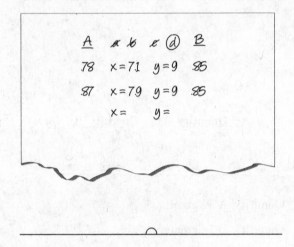

Comparing Decimals

Which is larger: 0.00099 or 0.001? ETS loves this sort of problem. You'll never go wrong, though, if you follow these easy steps.

- Line up the numbers by their decimal points.
- Fill in the missing zeros.

Here's how to answer the question we just asked. First, line up the two numbers by their decimal points.

$$0.00099$$
$$0.001$$

Now fill in the missing zeros.

$$0.00099$$
$$0.00100$$

Can you tell which number is larger? Of course you can. 0.00100 is larger than 0.00099, because 100 is larger than 99.

Digits and Decimals

Remember our discussion about digits, earlier? Well, sometimes the GRE will ask you questions about digits that fall after the decimal point as well. Suppose you have the number 0.584.

- 0 is the units digit.
- 5 is the tenths digit.
- 8 is the hundredths digit.
- 4 is the thousandths digit.

Percentages

The final member of our numbers family is percents. A percent is just a special type of fraction, one that always has 100 as the denominator. Percent literally means "per 100" or "out of 100" or "divided by 100." If your best friend finds a dollar and gives you 50¢, your friend has given you 50¢ out of 100, or $\frac{50}{100}$ of a dollar, or 50 percent of the dollar. To convert fractions to percents, just expand the fraction so it has a denominator of 100. For example:

$$\frac{3}{5} = \frac{60}{100} = 60\%$$

For the GRE, you should memorize the following percentage-decimal-fraction equivalents. Use these friendly fractions and percentages to eliminate answer choices that are way out of the ballpark.

$$0.01 = \frac{1}{100} = 1\% \qquad\qquad 0.1 = \frac{1}{10} = 10\%$$

$$0.2 = \frac{1}{5} = 20\% \qquad\qquad 0.25 = \frac{1}{4} = 25\%$$

$$0.333... = \frac{1}{3} = 33\frac{1}{3}\% \qquad\qquad 0.4 = \frac{2}{5} = 40\%$$

$$0.5 = \frac{1}{2} = 50\% \qquad\qquad 0.6 = \frac{3}{5} = 60\%$$

Percents are another very common topic on the GRE.

$$0.666\ldots = \frac{2}{3} = 66\frac{2}{3}\% \qquad\qquad 0.75 = \frac{3}{4} = 75\%$$

$$0.8 = \frac{4}{5} = 80\% \qquad\qquad 1.0 = \frac{1}{1} = 100\%$$

$$2.0 = \frac{2}{1} = 200\%$$

Converting Decimals to Percentages

In order to convert decimals to percents, just move the decimal point two places to the right. This turns 0.8 into 80 percent, 0.25 into 25 percent, 0.5 into 50 percent, and 1 into 100 percent.

Translation

One of the best tricks for handling percentages in word problems is knowing how to translate them into an equation that you can manipulate. Use the following table to help you translate percentage word problems into equations you can work with.

These translations apply to any word problem, not just percent problems.

Word	Equivalent Symbol
percent	/100
is	=
of, times, product	×
what (or any unknown value)	any variable *(x, k, b)*

Here's an example:

---

15 of 20

56 is what percent of 80 ?

○ 66%

○ 70%

○ 75%

○ 80%

○ 142%

Here's How to Crack It

To solve this problem, let's translate the question and then solve for the variable. So, "56 is what percent of 80," in math speak, is equal to

$$56 = \frac{x}{100}(80)$$

$$56 = \frac{80x}{100}$$

Don't forget to reduce: $56 = \frac{5}{4}x$

Now multiply both sides of the equation by $\frac{5}{4}$.

$$\left(\frac{5}{4}\right)\left(\frac{56}{1}\right) = \left(\frac{5}{4}\right)\left(\frac{4x}{5}\right)$$
$$(5)(14) = x$$
$$70 = x$$

That's answer choice (B). Did you notice choice (E)? Because 56 is less than 80, the answer would have to be less than 100 percent, so 142 percent is way too big, and you could have eliminated it from the get-go by Ballparking.

———————○———————

Let's try a quant comp example.

———————○———————

5 of 20

5 is r percent of 25

s is 25 percent of 60

Quantity A	Quantity B
r	s

○ Quantity A is greater.

○ Quantity B is greater.

○ The two quantities are equal.

○ The relationship cannot be determined from the information given.

Here's How to Crack It
First translate the first statement.

$$5 = \frac{r}{100}(25)$$

$$5 = \frac{25r}{100}$$

$$5 = \frac{r}{4}$$

$$(4)(5) = \left(\frac{r}{4}\right)(4)$$

$$20 = r$$

That takes care of Quantity A. Now translate the second statement.

$$s = \frac{25}{100}(60)$$

$$s = \frac{1}{4}(60)$$

$$s = 15$$

That takes care of Quantity B. The answer is (A).

———————◯———————

Percentage Increase/Decrease
To find the percentage by which something has increased or decreased, use the following formula.

On percent increase problems, the original is always the smaller number. On percent decrease problems, the original is the larger number.

$$\text{Percent Change} = \frac{\text{Difference}}{\text{Original}} \times 100$$

The "difference" is simply what you get when you subtract the smaller number from the larger number. The "original" is whichever number you started with. If the question asks you to find a percent increase, then the original number will be the smaller number. If the question asks you to find a percent decrease, then the original number will be the larger number.

Here's an example.

───────────────○───────────────

19 of 20

Vandelay Industries reported a $6,000 profit over the three-month period from March to May of the current year. If, over the previous three-month period, Vandelay Industries realized a $3,500 profit, by approximately what percent did its profit increase?

○   25%

○   32%

○   42%

○   55%

○   70%

What number goes on the bottom of the fraction?

Here's How to Crack It

Let's use the percent change formula we just learned. The first step is to find the difference between the two numbers. The initial profit was $3,500 and the final profit is $6,000. The difference between these two numbers is: 6,000 − 3,500 = 2,500. Next, we need to divide this number by the original, or starting, value.

One way to help you figure out what value to use as the original value is to check to see whether you're dealing with a percent increase or a percent decrease question. Remember that on a percent increase question, you should always use the smaller of the two numbers as the denominator and that on percent decrease you need to use the larger of the two numbers as the denominator. Because here we want to find the percent increase, the number we want to use for our denominator is 3,500. So our percent increase fraction looks like this: $\frac{2,500}{3,500}$. We can reduce this down to $\frac{25}{35}$ by dividing by 100, and reduce even further by dividing by 5. This leaves us with $\frac{5}{7}$, which is approximately 70% (remember, the fraction bar means divide, so if you divide 5 by 7, you'll get .71). Thus, choice (E) is the answer.

───────────────○───────────────

Here's another question.

Model	Original Price	Sale Price
A	$12,000	$9,500
B	$16,000	$13,000
C	$10,000	$7,500
D	$17,500	$13,000
E	$20,000	$15,500
F	$22,000	$16,000

The table above shows the original price and the sale price of six different models of cars. Which models of car would a consumer have to buy to get at least a 25% discount? Select all that apply.

☐ A

☐ B

☐ C

☐ D

☐ E

☐ F

Here's How to Crack It

First list A, B, C, D, E, and F in a column in the upper left corner of your scratch paper. You are asked to identify a 25% change or greater between the two numbers. You know the formula for this. It is diff/original × 100. Using your calculator, subtract 9,500 from 12,000. You should get 2,500. This is the difference. Divide it by the original, 12,000, to get 0.2. You don't even need to multiply by 100. You know that this is 20%, which is less than 25%, so cross it off on your scratch paper. Try the next one. 16,000 − 13,000 = 3,000. Divide by 16,000. Too small. Cross it off. Repeat this process for each of the answer choices. Choices (C), (D), and (F) all work.

PLUGGING IN ON FRACTION AND PERCENT PROBLEMS

Now that you've become familiar with fractions and percents, we'll show you a neat trick. When you come to regular multiple-choice questions, or multiple choice, multiple answers, that involve fractions or percents, you can simply Plug In a number and work through the problem using that number. This approach works even when the problem doesn't have variables in it. Why? Because, as you know, fractions and percents only express a relationship between numbers—the actual numbers don't matter. For example, look at the following problem:

17 of 20

A recent survey of registered voters in City x found that $\frac{1}{3}$ of the respondents support the mayor's property tax plan. Of those who did not support the mayor's plan, $\frac{1}{8}$ indicated they would not vote to reelect the mayor if the plan was implemented. Of all the respondents, what fraction indicated that it would not vote for the mayor if the plan is enacted?

- $\bigcirc \quad \dfrac{1}{16}$
- $\bigcirc \quad \dfrac{1}{12}$
- $\bigcirc \quad \dfrac{1}{6}$
- $\bigcirc \quad \dfrac{1}{3}$
- $\bigcirc \quad \dfrac{2}{3}$

Here's How to Crack It

Even though there are no variables in this problem, we can still Plug In. On fraction and percent problems, ETS will often leave out one key piece of information: the total. Plugging In for that missing value will make your life much easier. What crucial information did ETS leave out of this problem? The total number of respondents. So let's Plug In a value for it. Let's say that there were 24 respondents to the survey. 24 is a good number to use because we'll have to work with $\frac{1}{3}$ and

Plugging In on fraction and percent problems is a great way to make your life easier.

What important information is missing from the problem?

$\dfrac{1}{8}$, so we want a number that's divisible by both those fractions. Working through the problem with our number, we see that $\dfrac{1}{3}$ of the respondents support the plan. $\dfrac{1}{3}$ of 24 is 8, so that means 16 people do not support the plan. Next, the problem says that $\dfrac{1}{8}$ of those who do not support the plan will not vote for the mayor. $\dfrac{1}{8}$ of 16 is 2, so 2 people won't vote for the mayor. Now we just have to answer the question: of all respondents, how many will not vote for the mayor? Well, there were 24 total respondents and we figured out that 2 aren't voting. So that's $\dfrac{2}{24}$ or $\dfrac{1}{12}$. Answer choice (B) is the one we want.

RATIOS AND PROPORTIONS

If you're comfortable working with fractions and percents, you'll be comfortable working with ratios and proportions, because ratios and proportions are simply special types of fractions. Don't let them make you nervous. Let's look at ratios first and then deal with proportions.

What Is a Ratio?

A ratio is just another type of fraction.

Recall that a fraction expresses the relationship of a part to the whole. A ratio expresses a different relationship: part to part. Imagine yourself at a party with 8 women and 10 men in attendance. What fraction of the partygoers are female? $\dfrac{8}{18}$, or 8 women out of a total of 18 people at the party. But what's the ratio of women to men? $\dfrac{8}{10}$, or, as ratios are more commonly expressed, 8 : 10. You can reduce this ratio to 4 : 5, just like you would a fraction.

On the GRE, you may see ratios expressed in several different ways:

Ratios can be expressed in these ways.

- $x : y$
- the ratio of x to y
- x is to y

In each case, the ratio is telling us the relationship between parts of a whole.

Every Fraction Can Be a Ratio, and Vice Versa

Every ratio can be expressed as a fraction. A ratio of 1 : 2 means that there's either a total of three things or a multiple of three, and the fraction $\frac{1}{2}$ means "1 out of 2."

On the GRE, you may see ratios expressed in several different ways:

$x : y$

the ratio of x to y

x is to y

Treat a Ratio Like a Fraction

Anything you can do to a fraction you can also do to a ratio. You can cross-multiply, find common denominators, reduce, and so on.

Find the Total

The key to dealing with ratio questions is to find the whole, or the total. Remember, a ratio only tells us about the parts, not the total. In order to find the total, add up the numbers in the ratio. A ratio of 2 : 1 means that there are three total parts. A ratio of 2 : 5 means that we're talking about a total of 7 parts. And a ratio of 2 : 5 : 7 means there are 14 total parts. Once you have a total you can start to do some fun things with ratios.

For example, let's say you have a handful of pennies and nickels. If you have 30 total coins and the pennies and nickels are in a 2 :1 ratio, how many pennies do you have? The total for our ratio is 3, meaning that out of every 3 coins, there are 2 pennies and 1 nickel. So if there are 30 total coins, there must be 20 pennies and 10 nickels. Notice that $\frac{20}{10}$ is the same as $\frac{2}{1}$, is the same as 2 : 1!

When working with ratios, there's an easy way not only to keep track of the numbers in the problem but also to quickly figure out the values in the problem. It's called the Ratio Box. Let's try the same question, but with some different numbers; if you have 24 coins in your pocket and the ratio of pennies to nickels is 2 : 1, how many pennies and nickels are there? The Ratio Box for this question is below, with all of the information we're given already filled in.

	Pennies	Nickels	Total
ratio	2	1	3
multiply by			
real			24

Like a fraction, a ratio expresses a relationship between numbers.

The minute you see the word "ratio," draw your box on your scratch paper.

Remember that ratios are relationships between numbers, not real numbers, so the real total is 24; meaning we have 24 actual coins in our pocket. The ratio total (the number you get when you add up the number of parts in the ratio) is 3.

The middle row of the table is for our multiplier. How do you get from 3 to 24? You multiply by 8. Remember when we talked about finding equivalent fractions? All we did was multiply the numerator and denominator by the same value. That's exactly what we're going to do with ratios. This is what the ratio box would look like now:

	Pennies	Nickels	Total
ratio	2	1	3
multiply by	8	8	8
real			24

Now let's finish filling in the box by multiplying out everything else.

	Pennies	Nickels	Total
ratio	2	1	3
multiply by	8	8	8
real	16	8	24

Let's try a GRE example.

---

8 of 20

Flour, eggs, yeast, and salt are mixed by weight in the ratio of 11 : 9 : 3 : 2, respectively. How many pounds of yeast are there in 20 pounds of the mixture?

○ $1\frac{3}{5}$

○ $1\frac{4}{5}$

○ 2

○ $2\frac{2}{5}$

○ $8\frac{4}{5}$

Here's How to Crack It

The minute you see the word "ratio," draw your box on your scratch paper and fill in what you know.

	Flour	Eggs	Yeast	Salt	Total
ratio	11	9	3	2	
multiply by					
real					20

First, add up all of the numbers in the ratio to get the ratio total.

	Flour	Eggs	Yeast	Salt	Total
ratio	11	9	3	2	25
multiply by					
real					20

Now, what do we multiply 25 by to get 20?

$$25x = 20$$

$$\frac{25x}{25} = \frac{20}{25}$$

$$x = \frac{20}{25}$$

$$x = \frac{4}{5}$$

So $\frac{4}{5}$ is our "multiply by" number. Let's fill it in.

	Flour	Eggs	Yeast	Salt	Total
ratio	11	9	3	2	25
multiply by	$\frac{4}{5}$	$\frac{4}{5}$	$\frac{4}{5}$	$\frac{4}{5}$	$\frac{4}{5}$
real					20

The question asks for the amount of yeast, so we don't have to worry about the other ingredients, just look at the yeast column. All we have to do is multiply 3 by $\frac{4}{5}$ and we have our answer: $3 \times \frac{4}{5} = \frac{12}{5}$, or $3 \times \frac{4}{5} = \frac{12}{5}$, which is answer choice (D).

What Is a Proportion?

So you know that a fraction is a relationship between part and whole, and that a ratio is a relationship between part and part. A proportion is an equivalent relationship between two fractions or ratios. Thus, $\frac{1}{2}$ and $\frac{4}{8}$ are proportionate because they are equivalent fractions. But $\frac{1}{2}$ and $\frac{2}{3}$ are not in proportion because they are not equal ratios.

The GRE often contains problems in which you are given two proportional, or equal, ratios from which one piece of information is missing. These questions take a relationship or ratio, and project it onto a larger or smaller scale. Proportion problems are recognizable because they always give you three values and ask for a fourth value. Here's an example:

10 of 20

If the cost of a one-hour telephone call is $7.20, what would be the cost in dollars of a ten-minute telephone call at the same rate?

The key to proportions is setting them up correctly.

☐ dollars

Enter your answer in the box provided.

Here's How to Crack It

It's very important to set up proportion problems correctly. That means using your hand and parking your information on your scratch paper. Be essentially careful to label *everything*. It takes only an extra two or three seconds, but doing this will help you catch lots of errors.

For this question, let's express the ratios as dollars over minutes, because we're being asked to find the cost of a ten-minute call. That means that we have to convert 1 hour to 60 minutes (otherwise it wouldn't be a proportion).

$$\frac{\$}{\min} = \frac{\$7.20}{60} = \frac{x}{10}$$

Now cross-multiply.

$$60x = (7.2)(10)$$
$$60x = 72$$
$$\frac{60x}{60} = \frac{72}{60}$$
$$x = \frac{6}{5}$$

Now we can enter 1.20 into the box.

> ### Relationship Review
>
> You may have noticed a trend in the preceding pages. Each of the major topics covered—fractions, percents, ratios, and proportions—described a particular relationship between numbers. To review:
>
> - A fraction expresses the relationship between a part and the whole.
> - A percent is a special type of fraction, one that expresses the relationship of part to whole as a fraction with the number 100 in the denominator.
> - A ratio expresses the relationship between part and part. Adding up the parts of a ratio give you the whole.
> - A proportion expresses the relationship between equal fractions, percents, or ratios.
> - Each of these relationships shares all the characteristics of a fraction. You can reduce them, expand them, multiply them, and divide them using the exact same rules you used for working with fractions.

AVERAGES

The average (arithmetic mean) of a set of numbers is the sum, or total value, of all the numbers in the set divided by the number of numbers in the set. The average of the set {1, 2, 3, 4, 5} is equal to the total of the numbers (1 + 2 + 3 + 4 + 5, or 15) divided by the number of numbers in the set (which is 5). Dividing 15 by 5 gives us 3, so 3 is the average of the set.

ETS always refers to an average as an "average (arithmetic mean)." This confusing parenthetical remark is meant to keep you from being confused by other kinds of averages, such as medians and modes. You'll be less confused if you simply

GRE average problems always give you two of the three numbers needed.

ignore the parenthetical remark and know that average means total of the elements divided by the number of elements. We'll tell you about medians and modes later.

Think Total

Don't try to solve average problems all at once. Do them piece by piece. The key formula to keep in mind when doing problems that involve averages is:

$$\text{Average} = \frac{\text{Total}}{\text{\# of things}}$$

Drawing an Average Pie will help you organize your information.

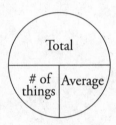

Here's how the Average Pie works. The *total* is the sum of the numbers being averaged. The *number of things* is the number of different elements that you are averaging. And the *average* is, naturally, the average.

Say you wanted to find the average of 4, 7, and 13. You would add those numbers to get the total and divide that total by three.

$$4 + 7 + 13 = 24$$
$$\frac{24}{3} = 8$$

Mathematically, the Average Pie works like this:

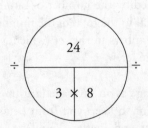

The horizontal bar is a division bar. If you divide the *total* by the *number of things*, you get the *average*. If you divide the total by the *average*, you get the *number of things*. If you have the *number of things* and the *average*, you can simply multiply them together to find the *total*. This is one of the most important things you need to be able to do to solve GRE average problems.

Using the Average Pie has several benefits. First, it's an easy way to organize information. Furthermore, the Average Pie makes it clear that if you have two of the three pieces, you can always find the third. This makes it easier to figure out how to approach the problem. If you fill in the number of things, for example, and the question wants to know the average, the Average Pie shows you that the key to unlocking that problem is finding the total.

Try this one.

The average of seven numbers is 9. The average of three of these numbers is 5. What is the average of the other four numbers?

- ○ 4
- ○ 5
- ○ 7
- ○ 10
- ○ 12

If you see the word "average" twice in a problem, draw two pies. If you see it three times, then draw three pies.

Here's How to Crack It

Let's take the first sentence. You have the word "average," so draw your pie and fill in what you know. We have seven numbers with an average of 9, so plug those values into your Average Pie and multiply to find the total.

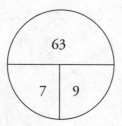

Now we also know that three of the numbers have an average of 5, so draw another Average Pie, plug those values into their places, and multiply to find the total of those three numbers.

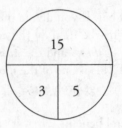

The question is asking for the average of the four remaining numbers. Draw one more Average Pie and Plug In 4 for the number of things.

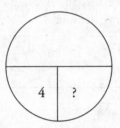

In order to solve for the average, we need to know the total of those four numbers. How do we find this? From our first Average Pie we know that the total of all seven numbers is 63. The second Average Pie tells us that the total of three of those numbers was 15. Thus, the total of the remaining four has to be 63 − 15, which is 48. Plug 48 into the last Average Pie, and divide by 4 to get the average of the four numbers.

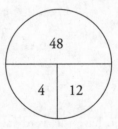

The average is 12, which is answer choice (E).

Let's try one more.

———————————————○———————————————

The average (arithmetic mean) of a set of 6 numbers is 28. If a certain number, y, is removed from the set, the average of the remaining numbers in the set is 24.

Quantity A	**Quantity B**
y	48

○ Quantity A is greater.

○ Quantity B is greater.

○ The two quantities are equal.

○ The relationship cannot be determined from the information given.

Here's How to Crack It

All right, let's attack this one. The problem says that the "average" of a set of six numbers is 28, so let's immediately draw an average pie and calculate the total.

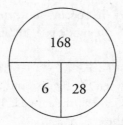

If a certain number, y, is removed from the set, there are now five numbers left. We already know that the new average is 24, so draw another Average Pie.

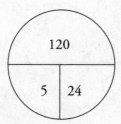

The difference between the totals must be equal to y. 168 – 120 = 48. Thus, the two quantities are equal, and the answer is (C).

———————————————○———————————————

Up and Down

Averages are very predictable. You should make sure you automatically know what happens to them in certain situations. For example, suppose you take three tests and earn an average score of 90. Now you take a fourth test. What do you know?

If your average goes up as a result of the fourth score, then you know that your fourth score was higher than 90. If your average stays the same as a result of the fourth score, then you know that your fourth score was exactly 90. If your average goes down as a result of the fourth score, then you know that your fourth score was less than 90.

MEDIAN, MODE, AND RANGE

Don't confuse median and mode!

The **median** is the middle value in a set of numbers; above and below the median lie an equal number of values. For example, in the set {1, 2, 3, 4, 5, 6, 7} the median is 4, because it's the middle number (and there are an odd number of numbers in the set). If the set contained an even number of integers {1, 2, 3, 4, 5, 6}, the median would be the average of 3 and 4, or 3.5. When looking for the median, sometimes you have to put the numbers in order yourself. What is the median of the set {13, 5, 6, 3, 19, 14, 8}? First, put the numbers in order from least to greatest, {3, 5, 6, 8, 13, 14, 19}. Then take the middle number. The median is 8. Just think *median = middle* and always make sure the numbers are in order.

The minute you see the word "median" in a question, find a bunch of numbers and put them in order.

The **mode** is the number in a set that occurs most frequently. For example, in the set {2, 3, 4, 5, 3, 8, 6, 9, 3, 9, 3} the mode is 3, because 3 shows up the most. Just think *mode = most*.

The **range** is the difference between the biggest and the smallest numbers in your set. So, in the set {2, 6, 13, 3, 15, 4, 9}, the range is 15 (the highest number in the set) − 2 (the lowest number in the set), or 13.

Here's an example:

$$F = \{4, 2, 7, 11, 8, 9\}$$

Quantity A	Quantity B
The range of Set F	The median of Set F

○ Quantity A is greater.

○ Quantity B is greater.

○ The two quantities are equal.

○ The relationship cannot be determined from the information given.

What do we need to do to the numbers in this list?

Here's How to Crack It

Let's put the numbers in order first, so it'll be easier to see what we have: {2, 4, 7, 8, 9, 11}. First let's look at Quantity A: The range is the largest number, or 11, minus the smallest number, or 2. That's 9. Now let's look at Quantity B: The minute you see the word "median," find a bunch of numbers and put them in order. The median is the middle number of the set, but because there are two middle numbers, 7 and 8, we have to find the average. Or do we? Isn't the average of 7 and 8 clearly going to be smaller than the number in Quantity A, which is 9? Yes (remember, in quant comp questions, we compare, not calculate). The answer is (A).

STANDARD DEVIATION

Standard deviation is one of those phrases that math people like to throw around to scare non-math people, but it's really not that scary. The GRE might ask you questions about standard deviation, but you'll never have to actually calculate it; instead, you'll just need a basic understanding of what standard deviation is. In order to understand standard deviation, we must first look at something all standardized testers should be familiar with, the bell curve.

You'll never have to calculate the standard deviation on the GRE.

Your Friend the Bell Curve

The first thing to know about a bell curve is that the number in the middle is the mean, the median, and the mode.

> The minute you see the phrase "standard deviation" or "normal distribution," draw your curve and fill in your percentages.

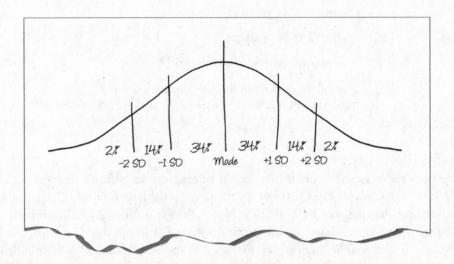

Imagine that 100 students take a test and the results follow a normal distribution. The minute you see the phrase, "normal distribution," draw your curve. Let's say that the average score on this test is an 80. That means that the median and the mode must also be 80. Put 80 in the middle of your curve. You know, however, that a few of those students were extremely well prepared and got a really high score, let's say that 2% of them got a 96 or higher. Put a 96 above the right 2% line on your curve.

Standard deviation measures how much a score differs from the norm (the average) in even increments. The curve tells us that a score earned by only 2% of the students is two standard deviations from the norm. If the norm is 80 and 96 is two standard deviations away; then one standard deviation on this test is 8 points. Two standard deviations above the norm is 96 while two standard deviations below the norm is 64. One standard deviation above the norm is 88, and one standard deviation below the norm is 72. Fill these in on your bell curve.

Now you know quite a bit about the distribution of scores on this test. Sixty-eight percent of the students received a score between 72 and 88. Ninety-eight percent scored above a 64. That's all there is to know about standard deviations. The percentages don't change, so memorize those. When you see the phrase, just make your curve and fill in what you know. Here's what the curve would look like for this test:

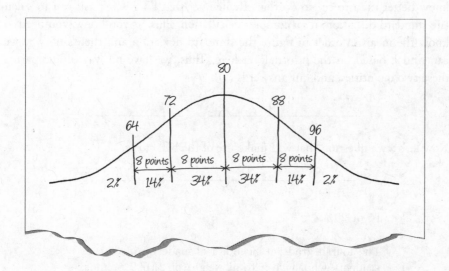

When it comes to standard deviation, the percentages don't change, so memorize those: 2, 14, and 34.

Here's an example of how ETS might test standard deviation:

———————————○———————————

5 of 20

Quantity A	**Quantity B**
The standard deviation of a set of data consisting of 10 integers ranging from –20 to –5	The standard deviation of a set of data consisting of 10 integers ranging from 5 to 20

○ Quantity A is greater.

○ Quantity B is greater.

○ The two quantities are equal.

○ The relationship cannot be determined from the information given.

Here's How to Crack It

ETS is hoping you'll make a couple of wrong turns on this problem. The first trap they set is that one set of numbers contains negative integers while the other doesn't—but this doesn't mean that one set will have a negative standard deviation. Standard deviation is defined as the distance a point is from the mean, so it can never be negative. The second trap is that ETS hopes you'll waste a lot of time trying to calculate standard deviation based on the information given. But you know better than to try to do that. Remember that ETS won't ask you to calculate standard deviation; it's a complex calculation. Plus, as you know, you need to know the mean in order to figure the standard deviation and there's no way we can find it based on the information here. Thus, we have no way of comparing these two quantities, and our answer is (D).

———————○———————

Now let's try a question that will make use of the bell curve.

———————○———————

The fourth grade at School x is made up of 300 students who have a total weight of 21,600 pounds. If the weight of these fourth graders has a normal distribution and the standard deviation equals 12 pounds, approximately what percentage of the fourth graders weighs more than 84 pounds?

○ 12%

○ 16%

○ 36%

○ 48%

○ 60%

Here's How to Crack It

This one's a little tougher than the earlier standard deviation questions. The first step is to determine the average weight of the students, which is $\dfrac{21{,}600}{300} = 72$ pounds. If the standard deviation is 12 pounds, then 84 pounds places us exactly one standard deviation above the mean, or at the 84th percentile (remember the bell curve?). Because 16 percent of all students weigh more than 84 pounds, the answer is (B).

———————○———————

RATE

Rate problems are similar to average problems. A rate problem might ask for an average speed, distance, or the length of a trip, or how long a trip (or a job) takes. To solve rate problems, use the Rate Pie.

A rate problem is really just an average problem.

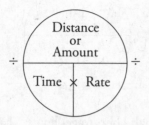

The Rate Pie works exactly the same way as the Average Pie. If you divide the *distance* or *amount* by the *rate,* you get the *time*. If you divide the *distance* or *amount* by the *time,* you get the *rate*. If you multiply the *rate* by the *time,* you get the *distance* or *amount*.

Let's take a look.

———————————○———————————

16 of 20

It takes Carla three hours to drive to her brother's house at an average speed of 50 miles per hour. If she takes the same route home, but her average speed is 60 miles per hour, how long does it take her to get home?

○ 2 hours

○ 2 hours and 14 minutes

○ 2 hours and 30 minutes

○ 2 hours and 45 minutes

○ 3 hours

Here's How to Crack It

The trip to her brother's house takes three hours, and the rate is 50 miles per hour. Plug those numbers into a Rate Pie and multiply to find the distance.

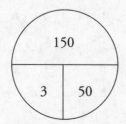

So the distance is 150 miles. On her trip home, Carla travels at a rate of 60 miles per hour. Draw another Rate Pie and Plug In 150 and 60. Then all you have to do is divide 150 by 60 to find the time.

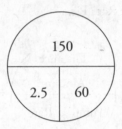

So it takes Carla two and a half hours to get home. That's answer choice (C).

Try another one.

A machine can stamp 20 envelopes in 4 minutes. How many of these machines, working simultaneously, are needed to stamp 60 envelopes per minute?

○ 5

○ 10

○ 12

○ 20

○ 24

Here's How to Crack It

First we have to find the rate per minute of one machine. Plug 20 and 4 into a Rate Pie and divide to find the rate.

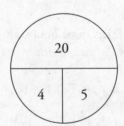

The rate is 5. If one machine can stamp 5 envelopes per minute, how many machines do you need to stamp 60 per minute? $60 \div 5 = 12$, or answer choice (C).

—————————————○—————————————

CHARTS

Every GRE Math section has a few questions that are based on a chart or graph (or on a group of charts or graphs). But don't worry; the most important thing that chart questions test is your ability to remember the difference between real-life charts and ETS charts.

In real life, charts are often provided in order to display information in a way that's easier to understand. Conversely, ETS constructs charts to hide information you need to know and to make that information harder to understand.

Chart questions frequently test percents, percent change, ratios, proportions, and averages.

Chart Questions

There are usually two or three questions per chart or per set of charts. Like the reading comprehension questions, chart questions appear on split screens. Be sure to click on the scroll bar and scroll down as far as you can; there may be additional charts underneath the top one, and you want to make sure you've seen all of them.

Chart problems just recycle the basic arithmetic concepts we've already covered: fractions, percentages, and so on. This means you can use the techniques we've discussed for each type of question, but there are two additional techniques that are especially important to use when doing chart questions.

On charts, look for the information ETS is trying to hide.

Don't Start with the Questions: Start with the Charts

Take a minute to note the following key bits of information from any chart you see.

- **Information in titles:** Make sure you know what each chart is telling you.
- **Asterisks, footnotes, parentheses, and small print:** Often there will be crucial information hidden away at the bottom of the chart. Don't miss it!
- **Funny units:** Pay special attention when a title says "in thousands" or "in millions." You can usually ignore the units as you do the calculations, but you have to use them to get the right answer.

Approximate, Estimate, and Ballpark

Like some of our other techniques, you have to train yourself to estimate when looking at charts and graphs. You should estimate, not calculate exactly:

- Whenever you see the word *approximately* in a question
- Whenever the question has answer choices and when the answer choices are far apart in value
- Whenever you start to answer a question and you justifiably say to yourself, "This is going to take a lot of calculation!"

Review those "friendly" percentages and their fractions from earlier in the chapter. Try estimating this question:

What is approximately 9.6 percent of 21.4?

Here's How to Crack It

Use 10 percent as a friendlier percentage and 20 as a friendlier number. One-tenth of 20 is 2 (it says "approximately"—who are you to argue?). That's all you need to do to answer most chart questions.

Chart Problems

Make sure you've read everything on the chart carefully before you try the first question.

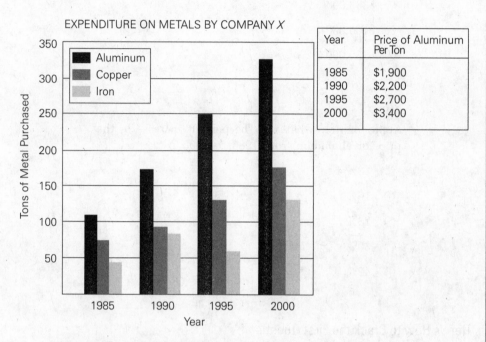

EXPENDITURE ON METALS BY COMPANY X

Year	Price of Aluminum Per Ton
1985	$1,900
1990	$2,200
1995	$2,700
2000	$3,400

Note: Graphs drawn to scale.

Approximately how many tons of aluminum and copper combined were purchased in 1995 ?

- ○ 125
- ○ 255
- ○ 325
- ○ 375
- ○ 515

How much did Company *X* spend on aluminum in 1990 ?

- ○ $675,000
- ○ $385,000
- ○ $333,000
- ○ $165,000
- ○ $139,000

Approximately what was the percent increase in the price of aluminum from 1985 to 1995 ?

- ○ 8%
- ○ 16%
- ○ 23%
- ○ 30%
- ○ 42%

Here's How to Crack the First Question

As you can see from the graph on the previous page, in 1995, the black bar (which indicates aluminum) is at 250, and the dark grey bar (which indicates copper) is at approximately 125. Add those up and you get the number of tons of aluminum and copper combined that were purchased in 1995: 250 + 125 = 375. That's choice (D). Notice that the question says "approximately." Also notice that the numbers in the answer choices are pretty far apart.

Here's How to Crack the Second Question

We need to use the chart and the graph to answer this question, because we need to find the number of tons of aluminum purchased in 1990 and multiply it by the price per ton of aluminum in 1990 in order to figure out how much was spent on aluminum in 1990. The bar graph tells us that 175 tons of aluminum was purchased in 1990, and the little chart tells us that aluminum was $2,200 per ton in 1990. 175 × $2,200 = $385,000. That's choice (B).

Here's How to Crack the Third Question

Remember that percent increase formula from earlier in this chapter?

$$\text{Percent change} = \frac{\text{Difference}}{\text{Original}} \times 100$$

We'll need to use the little chart for this one. In 1985, the price of aluminum was $1,900 per ton. In 1995, the price of aluminum was $2,700 per ton. Now let's use the formula. $2{,}700 - 1{,}900 = 800$, so that's the difference. This is a percent increase problem, so the original number is the smaller one. Thus, the original is 1,900, and our formula looks like this: Percent change $= \frac{800}{1{,}900} \times 100$. By canceling the 0's in the fraction you get $\frac{8}{19} \times 100$, and multiplying gives you $\frac{800}{19}$. At this point you could divide 800 by 19 to get the exact answer, but because they're looking for an approximation, let's round 19 to 20. What's $800 \div 20$? That's 40, and answer choice (E) is the only one that's close.

Real World Math Drill

Now it's time to try out what you've learned on some practice questions. Try the following problems and then check your answers in Part V.

If $3(r + s) = 7$, then, in terms of r, $s =$

○ $\dfrac{7}{3} - r$

○ $\dfrac{7}{3} + r$

○ $7 - 3r$

○ $\dfrac{7}{3} - \dfrac{r}{3}$

○ $\dfrac{7}{3} + \dfrac{r}{3}$

Sadie distributes her collection of paintings, giving one-third of the paintings to friends and selling half of the paintings. If she keeps the remaining paintings, what fraction of her collection does Sadie keep?

$$\boxed{}$$

Click on the answer box, then type in a number. Backspace to erase.

During a sale, a store decreases prices on all its scarves by 25 to 50 percent. If all of the scarves in the store originally cost $20, which of the following could be the sale price of a scarf?

Indicate all possible values.

☐ $8

☐ $10

☐ $12

☐ $14

☐ $16

Click on your choice(s).

Quantity A	**Quantity B**
12 percent of 35	35 percent of 12

○ Quantity A is greater.

○ Quantity B is greater.

○ The two quantities are equal.

○ The relationship cannot be determined from the information given.

Quantity A	Quantity B
$\dfrac{2.6}{0.259}$	10

○ Quantity A is greater.

○ Quantity B is greater.

○ The two quantities are equal.

○ The relationship cannot be determined from the information given.

Questions 6 through 9 refer to the following graph.

PERCENT OF POPULATION IN NEW ENGLAND
BY STATE IN YEAR X AND YEAR Y

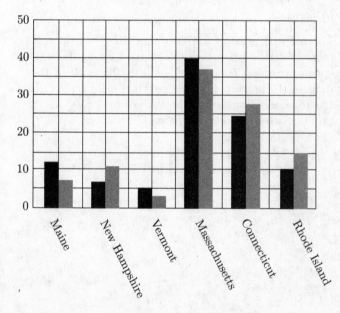

Note: Drawn to scale

■ Year X: Total New England population= 15 million

▨ Year Y: Total New England population= 25 million

The six New England states are ranked by population in Year X and in Year Y. How many states had a different ranking from Year X to Year Y?

○ None

○ One

○ Two

○ Three

○ Four

In Year Y, the population of Massachusetts was approximately what percent of the population of Vermont?

○ 50%

○ 120%

○ 300%

○ 400%

○ 1,200%

By approximately how much did the population of Rhode Island increase from Year X to Year Y?

○ 750,000

○ 1,250,000

○ 1,500,000

○ 2,250,000

○ 3,375,000

Approximately what is the difference between the percent change of Connecticut's percent of total New England population from Year X to Year Y and the percent change of Massachusetts percent of total New England population from Year X to Year Y ?

○ –12.5

○ 5

○ 12.5

○ 25

○ 50

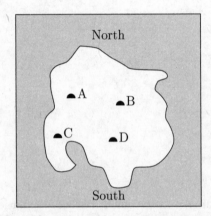

Towns A, B, C, and D are located on the map as shown. Towns A and B have 3,000 people each who support referendum R, and the referendum has an average of 3,500 supporters in towns B and D.

Quantity A	**Quantity B**
The average number of supporters of referendum R in the two southern-most towns	2,500

○ Quantity A is greater.

○ Quantity B is greater.

○ The two quantities are equal.

○ The relationship cannot be determined from the information given.

A company paid $500,000 in merit raises to employees whose performances were rated A, B, or C. Each employee rated A received twice the amount of the raise that was paid to each employee rated C; each employee rated B received one-and-a-half times the amount of the raise that was paid to each employee rated C. If 50 workers were rated A, 100 were rated B, and 150 were rated C, how much was the raise paid to each employee rated A ?

○ $370

○ $625

○ $740

○ $1,250

○ $2,500

The original price of an item at a store is 40 percent more than the price the retailer paid for it. To encourage sales, the retailer reduces the price of the item by 15 percent from the original selling price. If the retailer sells the item at the reduced cost, his profit is what percent of his cost?

 percent

Click on the answer box, then type in a number. Backspace to erase.

Questions 13 through 15 refer to the following graphs.

NUMBER OF STUDENTS IN GRADES 9
THROUGH 12 FOR SCHOOL DISTRICT
X IN 1975 AND 1993

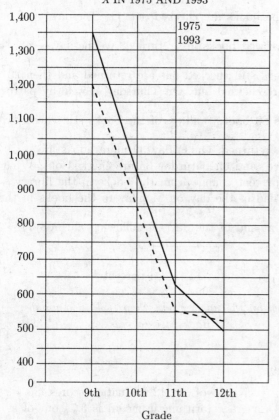

Grade

DISTRIBUTION OF READING TEST
SCORES* FOR SCHOOL DISTRICT *X*
STUDENTS IN 1993
(*Reading Test scores can range from
0–100 points)

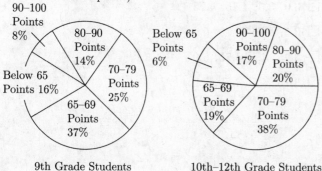

9th Grade Students   10th–12th Grade Students

Note: Drawn to scale.

In 1993, the median reading test score for ninth grade students was in which score range?

○ Below 65 points

○ 65–69 points

○ 70–79 points

○ 80–89 points

○ 90–100 points

If the number of students in grades 9 through 12 comprised 35 percent of the number of students in School District *X* in 1975, then approximately how many students were in School District *X* in 1975 ?

○ 9,700

○ 8,700

○ 3,400

○ 3,000

○ 1,200

Assume that all students in School District *X* took the reading test each year. In 1993, approximately how many more ninth grade students had reading test scores in the 70–79 point range than in the 80–89 point range?

○ 470

○ 300

○ 240

○ 170

○ 130

Quantity A	**Quantity B**
$2 - \dfrac{27}{25}$	$\dfrac{3}{5} + \dfrac{12}{125}$

○ Quantity A is greater.

○ Quantity B is greater.

○ The two quantities are equal.

○ The relationship cannot be determined from the information given.

Solution X contains only ingredients a and b in a ratio of 2 : 3. Solution Y contains only ingredients a and b in a ratio of 1 : 2. If Solution Z is created by mixing solutions X and Y in a ratio of 3 : 11, then 630 ounces of Solution Z contains how many ounces of a ?

○ 68

○ 73

○ 89

○ 219

○ 236

On Sunday, Belmond Public Library has 160 books, none of which have been checked out. On Monday, 40 of the books are checked out. On Tuesday, $\frac{1}{2}$ of the borrowed books are returned. Wednesday, $\frac{1}{2}$ of the books still checked out are returned and then 20 more are checked out. On Thursday, a wealthy patron donates 80 books, and $\frac{1}{6}$ of the books still checked out are returned. On Friday 30 more books are borrowed, and on Saturday 35 are checked out. What is the percent change from the books in the library at the end of the day on Monday to the books in the library at end of the day the following Saturday?

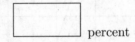 percent

Click on the answer box, then type in a number. Backspace to erase.

Jill has received 8 of her 12 evaluation scores. So far, Jill's average (arithmetic mean) is 3.75 out of a possible 5. If Jill needs an average of 4.0 points to get a promotion, which set of scores will allow Jill to receive her promotion?

*Indicate **all** possible answers.*

☐ 3.0, 3.5, 4.75, 4.75

☐ 3.5, 4.75, 4.75, 5.0

☐ 3.25, 4.5, 4.75, 5.0

☐ 3.75, 4.5, 4.75, 5.0

Click on your choice(s).

Summary

o Fractions, decimals, and percents are all ways of expressing parts of integers.

o Translation is a useful tool for converting fraction and percent problems into mathematical equations.

o Percent change is expressed as the difference between two numbers divided by the original number.

o Plug In on questions that ask about percents or fractions of an unknown amount.

o A ratio expresses a part to part relationship. The key to ratio problems is finding the total. Use the ratio box to organize ratio questions.

o A proportion expresses the relationship between equal fractions, percents, or ratios. A proportion problem always provides you with three pieces of information and asks you for a fourth.

o Use the Average Pie to organize and crack average problems.

o The median is the middle number in a set of values. The mode is the value that appears most frequently in a set. The range of a set is the difference between the largest and smallest value in the set.

o You will never have to calculate standard deviation on the GRE.

o Standard deviation problems are really average and percent problems. Make sure you know the percentages associated with the bell curve: 34%–14%–2%.

o Use the Rate Pie for rate questions.

o On chart questions, make sure you take a moment to understand what information the chart is providing. Estimate answers to chart questions whenever possible.

Chapter 11
Geometry

Chances are you probably haven't used the Pythagorean theorem recently or had to find the area of a circle
in quite a while. However, you'll be expected to know
geometry concepts such as these on the new GRE.
This chapter reviews all the important rules and formulas you'll need to crack the geometry problems on the
GRE. It also provides examples of how such concepts
will be tested on the GRE Math section.

WHY GEOMETRY?

Good question. If you're going to graduate school for political science or linguistics or history or practically anything that doesn't involve math, you might be wondering why the heck you have to know the area of a circle or the Pythagorean theorem for this exam. While we may not be able to give you a satisfactory answer to that question, we can help you do well on the geometry questions on the GRE.

Expect to see a handful of basic geometry problems on each of your Math sections.

WHAT YOU NEED TO KNOW

The good news is that you don't need to know much about actual geometry to do well on the GRE; we've boiled down geometry to the handful of bits and pieces that ETS actually tests.

Before we begin, consider yourself warned: Since you'll be taking your test on a computer screen, you'll have to be sure to transcribe all the figures onto your scrap paper accurately. All it takes is one mistaken angle or line and you're sure to get the problem wrong. So make ample use of your scratch paper and always double-check your figures. Start practicing now, by using scratch paper with this book.

Another important thing to know is that you cannot necessarily trust the diagrams ETS gives you. Sometimes they are very deceptive and are intended to confuse you. Always go by what you read, not what you see.

Problem-solving questions will be drawn to scale unless they clearly tell you otherwise. Quant comp questions, on the other hand, may *not* be drawn to scale, so be on your guard!

DEGREES, LINES, AND ANGLES

For the GRE, you will need to know that

1. A line is a 180-degree angle. In other words, a line is a perfectly flat angle.
2. When two lines intersect, four angles are formed; the sum of these angles is 360 degrees.
3. When two lines are perpendicular to each other, their intersection forms four 90-degree angles. Here is the symbol ETS uses to indicate a perpendicular angle: $\perp$.

4. Ninety-degree angles are also called *right angles*. A right angle on the GRE is identified by a little box at the intersection of the angle's arms:

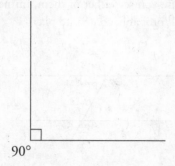

90°

5. The three angles inside a triangle add up to 180 degrees.
6. The four angles inside any four-sided figure add up to 360 degrees.
7. A circle contains 360 degrees.
8. Any line that extends from the center of the circle to the edge of the circle is called a *radius* (plural is *radii*).

Vertical Angles

Vertical angles are the angles that are across from each other when two lines intersect. Vertical angles are always equal. In the drawing below, angle *x* is equal to angle *y* (they are vertical angles) and angle *a* is equal to angle *b* (they are also vertical angles).

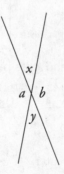

Parallel Lines

Parallel lines are lines that never intersect. When a pair of parallel lines is intersected by a third, two types of angles are formed: big angles and small angles. Any big angle is equal to any big angle, and any small angle is equal to any small angle. The sum of any big angle and any small angle will always equal 180. When ETS

On the GRE, the measure of only one of the vertical angles is typically shown. But usually you'll need to use the other angle to solve the problem.

tells you that two lines are parallel, this is what is being tested. The symbol for parallel lines and the word "parallel" are both clues that tell you what to look for in the problem. The minute you see either of them, immediately identify your big and small angles; they will probably come into play.

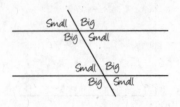

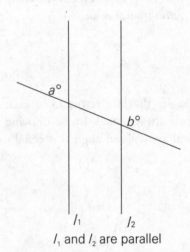

l_1 and l_2 are parallel

Quantity A	Quantity B
$a + b$	180

○ Quantity A is greater.

○ Quantity B is greater.

○ The two quantities are equal.

○ The relationship cannot be determined
from the information given.

Here's How to Crack It

Notice that you're told that these lines are parallel. Here's one very important point: You need to be told that. You can't assume that they are parallel just because they look like they are.

Okay, so as you just learned, only two angles are formed when two parallel lines are intersected by a third line: a big angle (greater than 90 degrees) and a small one (smaller than 90 degrees). Look at angle *a*. It looks smaller than 90, right? Now look at angle *b*. It looks bigger than 90, right? You also know that *a* + *b* must add up to 180. The answer is (C).

TRIANGLES

Triangles are perhaps ETS's favorite geometrical shape. Triangles have many properties, which make them great candidates for standardized test questions. Make sure you familiarize yourself with the following triangle facts.

Triangles are frequently tested on the GRE.

Angles in a Triangle

Every triangle contains three angles that add up to 180 degrees. You must know this fact cold for the exam. This rule applies to every triangle, no matter what it looks like. Here are some examples:

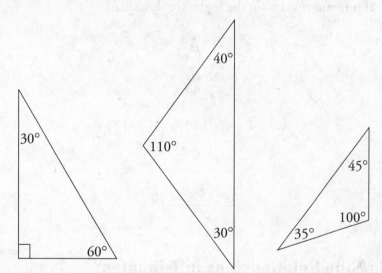

Equilateral Triangles

An equilateral triangle is a triangle in which all three sides are equal in length. Because all of the sides are equal in these triangles, all of the angles are equal. Each angle is 60 degrees because 180 divided by 3 is 60.

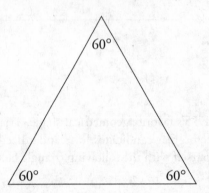

Isosceles Triangles

An isosceles triangle is a triangle in which two of the three sides are equal in length. This means that two of the angles are also equal.

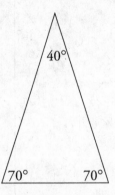

Angle/Side Relationships in Triangles

In any triangle, the longest side is opposite the largest interior angle; the shortest side is opposite the smallest interior angle. That's why the hypotenuse of a right triangle is its longest side—there couldn't be another angle in the triangle bigger than 90 degrees. Furthermore, equal sides are opposite equal angles.

Perimeter of a Triangle

The perimeter of a triangle is simply a measure of the distance around it. All you have to do to find the perimeter of a triangle is add up the lengths of the sides.

The Third Side Rule

Why is it impossible for the following triangle to exist? (Hint: It's not drawn to scale.)

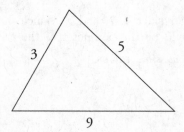

This triangle could not exist because the length of any one side of a triangle is limited by the lengths of the other two sides. This can be summarized by the **Third Side rule**:

> The length of any one side of a triangle must be less than the sum of the other two sides and greater than the difference between the other two sides.

This rule is not tested frequently on the GRE, but when it is, it's usually the key to solving the problem. Here's what the rule means in application: Take the lengths of any two sides of a triangle. Add them together, then subtract one from the other. The length of the third side must lie between those two numbers.

Take the sides 3 and 5 from the triangle above. What's the longest the third side could measure? Just add and subtract. It could not be as long as 8 (5 + 3) and it could not be as short as 2 (5 − 3).

Therefore, the third side must lie between 2 and 8. It's important to remember that the third side cannot be equal to either 2 or 8. It must be greater than 2 and less than 8.

Try the following question:

A triangle has sides 4, 7, and x. Which of the following could be the perimeter of the triangle?

*Indicate **all** possible values.*

- ☐ 13
- ☐ 16
- ☐ 17
- ☐ 20
- ☐ 22

Here's How to Crack It

The perimeter of a triangle is equal to the sum of its three sides. So far, we have sides of 4 and 7, so our partial perimeter is 4 + 7 = 11. What about the third side, x? The third-side rule tells us that the side could not be longer than 7 + 4 = 11 or shorter than 7 − 4 = 3. The third side must be greater than 3 and less than 11. Next we add the partial perimeter, 11, to both of these numbers to find the range of the perimeter. 11 + 3 = 14 and 11 + 11 = 22, so the perimeter must be greater than 14 and less than 22. Only choices (A) and (E) fall outside this range. For this question, we have to click on all of the answers that work, so the best answer is (B), (C), and (D).

Any time you see the word "area" or any other word that indicates that a formula is to be used, write the formula on your scratch paper and park the information you're given directly underneath.

Area of a Triangle

The area of any triangle is equal to its height (or "altitude") multiplied by its base, divided by 2, so

$$A = \frac{1}{2}bh$$

The height of a triangle is defined as the length of a perpendicular line drawn from the point of the triangle to its base.

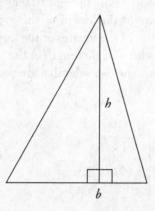

This area formula works on any triangle.

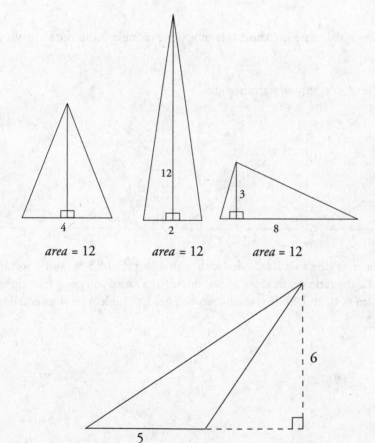

area = 12   *area* = 12   *area* = 12

area = 15

The Pythagorean Theorem

The Pythagorean theorem applies only to right triangles. This theorem states that in a right triangle, the square of the length of the hypotenuse (the longest side, remember?) is equal to the sum of the squares of the lengths of the two other sides. In other words, $c^2 = a^2 + b^2$, where c is the length of the hypotenuse and a and b are the lengths of the other sides. (The two sides that are not the hypotenuse are called the legs.)

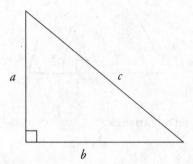

You can always calculate the third side of a right triangle using the Pythagorean theorem.

Here are the most common right triangles:

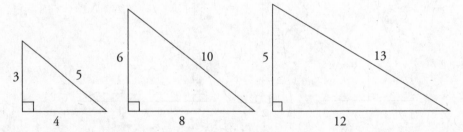

Note that a triangle could have sides with actual lengths of 3, 4, and 5, or 3:4:5 could just be the ratio of the sides. If you double the ratio, you get a triangle with sides equal to 6, 8, and 10. If you triple it, you get a triangle with sides equal to 9, 12, and 15.

Let's try an example.

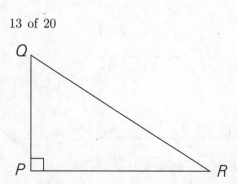

In the figure above, if the distance from point P to point Q is 6 miles and the distance from point Q to point R is 10 miles, what is the distance from point P to point R?

○ 4

○ 5

○ 6

○ 7

○ 8

Write everything down on scratch paper! Don't do anything in your head.

Here's How to Crack It

Once you've sensitized yourself to the standard right triangles, this problem couldn't be easier. When you see a right triangle, be suspicious. One leg is 6. The hypotenuse is 10. The triangle has a ratio of 3:4:5. Therefore, the third side (the other leg) must be 8.

The Pythagorean theorem will sometimes help you solve problems that involve squares or rectangles. For example, every rectangle or square can be divided into two right triangles. This means that if you know the length and width of any rectangle or square, you also know the length of the diagonal—it's the shared hypotenuse of the hidden right triangles.

Here's an example:

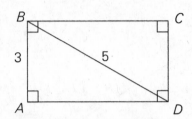

In the rectangle above, what is the area of triangle *ABD* ?

Enter your answer in the box above.

Here's How to Crack It

We were told that this is a rectangle (remember that you can never assume!), which means that triangle *ABD* is a right triangle. Not only that, but it's a 3-4-5 right triangle (with a side of 3 and a hypotenuse of 5, it must be), with side *AD* = 4. So, the area of triangle *ABD* is $\frac{1}{2}$ the base (3) times the height (4). That's $\frac{1}{2}$ of 12, otherwise known as 6. You could enter that value into the box.

Right Isosceles Triangles

If you take a square and cut it in half along its diagonal, you will create a right isosceles triangle. The two sides of the square stay the same. The 90-degree angle will stay the same, and the other two angles that were 90 degrees each get cut in half and are now 45 degrees. The ratio of sides in a right isosceles triangle is $x : x : x\sqrt{2}$. This is significant for two reasons. First, if you see a problem with a right triangle and there is a $\sqrt{2}$ anywhere in the problem, you know what to look for. Second, you always know the length of the diagonal of a square because it is one side times the square root of two.

You always know the length of the diagonal of a square because it is one side of the square times $\sqrt{2}$.

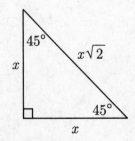

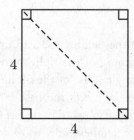 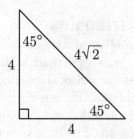

Let's try an example involving a special right triangle.

───────────○───────────

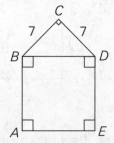

In the figure above, what is the area of square *ABDE* ?

○ $28\sqrt{2}$

○ 49

○ $49\sqrt{2}$

○ 98

○ $98\sqrt{2}$

Here's How to Crack It

In order to figure out the area of square *ABDE*, we need to know the length of one of its sides. We can get the length of *BD* by using the isosceles right triangle attached to it. *BD* is the hypotenuse, which means its length is $7\sqrt{2}$. To get the area of the square we have to square the length of the side we know, or $\left(7\sqrt{2}\right)\left(7\sqrt{2}\right) =$ (49)(2) = 98. That's choice (D).

───────────○───────────

30 : 60 : 90 Triangles

If you take an equilateral triangle and draw in the height, you end up cutting it in half and creating a right triangle. The hypotenuse of the right triangle has not changed; it's just one side of the equilateral triangle. One of the 60 degree angles stays the same as well. The angle where the height meets the base is 90 degrees, naturally, and the side that was the base of the equilateral triangle has been cut in half. The smallest angle, at the top, opposite the smallest side, is 30 degrees. The ratio of sides on a 30°-60°-90° triangle is $x : x\sqrt{3} : 2x$. Here's what it looks like:

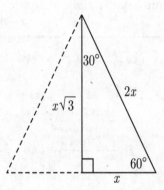

This is significant for two reasons. The first is that if you see a problem with a right triangle and one side is double the other or there is a $\sqrt{3}$ anywhere in the problem, you know what to look for. The second is that you always know the area of an equilateral triangle because you always know the height. It is one half of one side times the square root of three.

Here's one more:

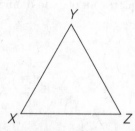

Triangle XYZ in the figure above is an equilateral triangle. If the perimeter of the triangle is 12, what is its area?

○ $2\sqrt{3}$

○ $4\sqrt{3}$

○   8

○   12

○ $8\sqrt{3}$

If you see $\sqrt{2}$ or $\sqrt{3}$ in the answer choices of the problem it's a tip-off that the problem is testing special right triangles.

Here's How to Crack It

Here we have an equilateral triangle with a perimeter of 12, which means that each side has a length of 4 and each angle is 60 degrees. Remember that in order to find the area of a triangle, we use the triangle area formula: $A = \dfrac{1}{2} bh$, but first we need to know the base and the height of the triangle. The base is 4, which now gives us $A = \dfrac{1}{2} 4h$, and now the only thing we need is the height. Remember: The height always has to be perpendicular to the base. Draw a vertical line that splits the equilateral triangle in half. The top angle is also split in half, so now we have this:

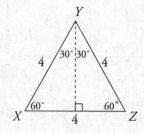

What we've done is create two 30°-60°-90° right triangles, and we're going to use one of these right triangles to find the height. Let's use the one on the right. We know that the hypotenuse in a 30°-60°-90° right triangle is always twice the length of the short side. Here we have a hypotenuse (*YZ*) of 4, so our short side has to be 2. The long side of a 30°-60°-90° right triangle is always equal to the short side multiplied by the square root of 3. So if our short side is 2, then our long side must be $2\sqrt{3}$. That's the height.

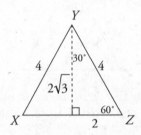

Finally, we return to our area formula. Now we have $A = \dfrac{1}{2} \times 4 \times 2\sqrt{3}$. Multiply it out and you get $A = 4\sqrt{3}$. The answer is (B).

FOUR-SIDED FIGURES

The four angles inside any figure that has four sides add up to 360 degrees. That includes rectangles, squares, and parallelograms. Parallelograms are four-sided figures made out of two sets of parallel lines whose area can be found with the formula $A = bh$, where *h* is the height of a line drawn perpendicular to the base.

Perimeter of a Rectangle

The perimeter of a rectangle is just the sum of the lengths of its four sides.

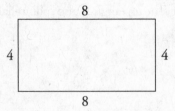

$$perimeter = 4 + 8 + 4 + 8$$

The area of a rectangle is equal to its length times its width. For example, the area of the rectangle above is 32 (or 8 × 4).

Area of a Rectangle

The area of a rectangle is equal to its length times its width. For example, the area of the rectangle above is 32 (or 8 × 4).

Squares

A square has four equal sides. The perimeter of a square is, therefore, 4 times the length of any side. The area of a square is equal to the length of any side times itself, or in other words, the length of any side, squared. The diagonal of a square splits it into two 45°-45°-90°, or isosceles, right triangles.

CIRCLES

Circles are a popular test topic for ETS. They have a few properties that the GRE likes to test over and over again and problems with circles also always seem to use that funny little symbol π. Here's all you need to know about circles.

Radius and Diameter

The **radius** of a circle is any line that extends from the center of the circle to the edge of the circle. If the line extends from one edge of a circle to the other and goes through the circle's center, it's the circle's **diameter**. Therefore, the diameter of a circle is twice as long as its radius.

The radius is always the key to circle problems.

Circumference of a Circle

The **circumference** of a circle is like the perimeter of a triangle: It's the distance around the outside. The formula for finding the circumference of a circle is 2 times π times the radius, or π times the diameter.

$$\text{circumference} = 2\pi r \text{ or } \pi d$$

Circumference is just a fancy way of saying perimeter.

If the diameter of a circle is 4, then its circumference is 4π, or roughly 12+. If the diameter of a circle is 10, then its circumference is 10π, or a little more than 30.

An **arc** is a section of the outside, or circumference, of a circle. An angle formed by two radii is called a **central angle** (it comes out to the edge from the center of the circle). There are 360 degrees in a circle, so if there is an arc formed by, say, a 60-degree central angle, and 60 is $\frac{1}{6}$ of 360, then the arc formed by this 60-degree central angle will be $\frac{1}{6}$ of the circumference of the circle.

AREA OF A CIRCLE

The area of a circle is equal to π times the square of its radius.

$$\text{area} = \pi r^2$$

Let's try an example of a circle question.

13 of 20

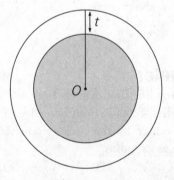

Note: Figure not drawn to scale.

In the wheel above, with center O, the area of the entire wheel is 169π. If the area of the shaded hubcap is 144π, then $t =$

Enter your answer in the box above.

Here's How to Crack It

We have to figure out what t is, and it's going to be the length of the radius of the entire wheel minus the length of the radius of the hubcap. If the area of the entire wheel is 169π, the radius is $\sqrt{169}$, or 13. If the area of the hubcap is 144π, the radius is $\sqrt{144}$, or 12. $13 - 12 = 1$. Enter this value into the box.

Let's try another one.

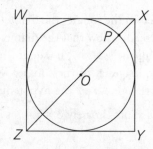

In the figure above, a circle with the center O is inscribed in square $WXYZ$. If the circle has radius 3, then $PZ =$

○ 6

○ $3\sqrt{2}$

○ $6 + \sqrt{2}$

○ $3 + \sqrt{3}$

○ $3\sqrt{2} + 3$

Ballparking answers will help you eliminate choices.

Here's How to Crack It

Inscribed means that the edges of the shapes are touching. The radius of the circle is 3, which means that PO is 3. If Z were at the other end of the diameter from P, this problem would be easy and the answer would be 6, right? But Z is beyond the edge of the circle, which means that PZ is a little more than 6. Let's stop there for a minute and glance at the answer choices. We can eliminate anything that's "out of the ballpark"—in other words, any answer choice that's less than 6, equal to 6 itself, or a lot more than 6. Remember when we told you to memorize a few of those square roots?

Let's use them:

(A) Exactly 6? Nope.

(B) That's 1.4 × 3, which is 4.2. Too small.

(C) That's 6 + 1.4, or 7.4. Not bad. Let's leave that one in.

(D) That's 3 + 1.7, or 4.7. Too small.

(E) That's (3 × 1.4) + 3, which is 4.2 + 3, or 7.2. Not bad. Let's leave that one in, too.

So we eliminated three choices with Ballparking. We're left with (C) and (E). You could take a guess here if you had to, but let's do a little more geometry to find the correct answer.

Because this circle is inscribed in the square, the diameter of the circle is the same as a side of the square. We already know that the diameter of the circle is 6, so that means that ZY, and indeed all the sides of the square, are also 6. Now, if ZY is 6, and XY is 6, what's XZ, the diagonal of the square? Well, XZ is also the hypotenuse of the isosceles right triangle XYZ. The hypotenuse of a right triangle with two sides of 6 is $6\sqrt{2}$. That's approximately 6 × 1.4, or 8.4.

The question is asking for PZ, which is a little less than XZ. It's somewhere between 6 and 8.4. The pieces that aren't part of the diameter of the circle are equal to 8.4 − 6, or 2.4. Divide that in half to get 1.2, which is the distance from the edge of the circle to Z. That means that PZ is 6 + 1.2, or 7.2. Check your remaining answers: Choice (C) is 7.4, and choice (E) is 7.2. Bingo! The answer is (E).

THE COORDINATE SYSTEM

On a coordinate system, the horizontal line is called the **x-axis** and the vertical line is called the **y-axis**. The four areas formed by the intersection of these axes are called **quadrants**. The point where the axes intersect is called the **origin**. This is what it looks like:

Coordinate geometry questions often test basic shapes such as triangles and squares.

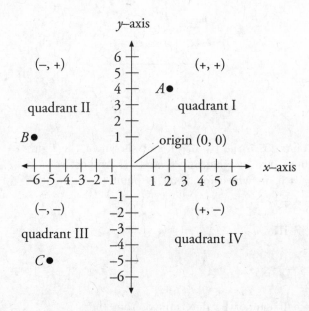

To express any point in the coordinate system, you first give the horizontal value, then the vertical value, or (*x*, *y*). In the diagram above, point *A* can be described by the coordinates (2, 4). That is, the point is two spaces to the right of the origin and four spaces above the origin. Point *B* can be described by the coordinates (–6, 1). That is, it is six spaces to the left and one space above the origin. What are the coordinates of point *C*? Right, it's (–5, –5).

Here's a GRE example:

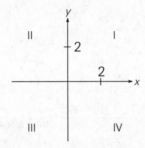

Points $(x, 5)$ and $(-6, y)$, not shown in the figure above, are in quadrants I and III, respectively. If $xy \neq 0$, in which quadrant is point (x, y) ?

○ IV

○ III

○ II

○ I

○ It cannot be determined from the information given.

Here's How to Crack It

If point $(x, 5)$ is in quadrant I, that means x is positive. If point y is in quadrant III, then y is negative. The quadrant that would contain coordinate points with a positive x and a negative y is quadrant IV. That's answer choice (A).

Slope

Trickier questions involving the coordinate system might give you the equation for a line on the grid, which will involve something called the slope of the line. The equation of a line is

$$y = mx + b$$

In this equation x and y are both points on the line, b stands for the y-intercept, or the point at which the line crosses the y-axis, and m is the slope of the line.

Slope is defined as the vertical change divided by the horizontal change, often called "the rise over the run" or the "change in *y* over the change in *x*."

$$\text{Slope} = \frac{\text{rise}}{\text{run}}$$

Sometimes on the GRE, *m* is written instead as *a*, as in *y = ax + b*. You'll see all this in action in a moment.

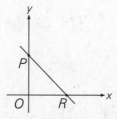

The line $y = -\frac{8}{7}x + 1$ is graphed on the rectangular coordinate axes.

Quantity A	**Quantity B**
OR	*OP*

○ Quantity A is greater.

○ Quantity B is greater.

○ The two quantities are equal.

○ The relationship cannot be determined from the information given.

Here's How to Crack It

The *y*-intercept, or *b*, in this case is 1. That means the line crosses the *y*-axis at 1. So the coordinates of point *P* are (0, 1). Now we have to figure out what the coordinates of point *R* are. We know the *y*-coordinate is 0, so let's stick that into the equation (the slope and the *y*-intercept are constant; they don't change).

$$y = mx + b$$

$$0 = -\frac{8}{7}x + 1$$

Now let's solve for *x*.

$$0 = -\frac{8}{7}x + 1$$

$$0 - 1 = -\frac{8}{7}x + 1 - 1$$

$$-1 = -\frac{8}{7}x$$

$$\left(-\frac{7}{8}\right)(-1) = \left(-\frac{7}{8}\right)\left(-\frac{8}{7}\right)x$$

$$\frac{7}{8} = x$$

So the coordinates of point *R* are ($\frac{7}{8}$, 0). That means *OR*, in Quantity A, is equal to $\frac{7}{8}$, and *OP*, in Quantity B, is equal to 1. The answer is (B).

Another approach to this question would be to focus on the meaning of slope. Because the slope is $-\frac{8}{7}$, that means the vertical change is 8 and the horizontal change is 7. In other words, you count up 8 and over 7. Clearly the "up" is more than the "over," thus *OP* is more than *OR*.

Incidentally, if you're curious about the difference between a positive and negative slope, any line that rises from left to right has a positive slope. Any line that falls from left to right has a negative slope. (A horizontal line has a slope of 0, and a vertical line is said to have "no slope.")

VOLUME

You can find the volume of a three-dimensional figure by multiplying the area of a two-dimensional figure by its height (or depth). For example, to find the volume of a rectangular solid, you would take the area of a rectangle and multiply it by the depth. The formula is *lwh* (length × width × height). To find the volume of a circular cylinder, take the area of a circle and multiply by the height. The formula is πr^2 times the height (or $\pi r^2 h$).

DIAGONALS IN THREE DIMENSIONS

There's a special formula that you can use if you are ever asked to find the length of a diagonal (the longest distance between any two corners) inside a three-dimensional rectangular box. It is $a^2 + b^2 + c^2 = d^2$, where *a*, *b*, and *c* are the dimensions of the figure (kind of looks like the Pythagorean theorem, huh?).

Questions that ask about diagonals are really about the Pythagorean theorem.

Take a look:

What is the length of the longest distance between any two corners in a rectangular box with dimensions 3 inches by 4 inches by 5 inches?

- ○ 5
- ○ 12
- ○ $5\sqrt{2}$
- ○ $12\sqrt{2}$
- ○ 50

Here's How to Crack It

Let's use our formula, $a^2 + b^2 + c^2 = d^2$. The dimensions of the box are 3, 4, and 5.

$$3^2 + 4^2 + 5^2 = d^2$$
$$9 + 16 + 25 = d^2$$
$$50 = d^2$$
$$\sqrt{50} = d$$
$$\sqrt{25 \times 2} = d$$
$$\sqrt{25} \times \sqrt{2} = d$$
$$5\sqrt{2} = d$$

That's choice (C).

SURFACE AREA

Don't confuse surface area with volume.

The surface area of a rectangular box is equal to the sum of the areas of all of its sides. In other words, if you had a box whose dimensions were 2 × 3 × 4, there would be two sides that are 2 by 3 (this surface would have an area of 6), two sides that are 3 by 4 (area of 12), and two sides that are 2 by 4 (area of 8). So, the total surface area would be 6 + 6 + 12 + 12 + 8 + 8, which is 52.

Key Formulas and Rules

Here is a review of the key rules and formulas to know for the GRE Math section.

Lines and angles
- All straight lines have 180 degrees.
- A right angle measures 90 degrees.
- Vertical angles are equal.
- Parallel lines cut by a third lines have two angles, big angles and small angles. All of the big angles are equal and all of the small angles are equal. The sum of a big angle and a small angle is 180 degrees.

Triangles
- All triangles have 180 degrees.
- The angles and sides of a triangle are in proportion—the largest angle is opposite the largest side and the smallest side is opposite the smallest angle.
- The Pythagorean theorem is $c^2 = a^2 + b^2$ where c is the length of the hypotenuse.
- The area formula for a triangle is
$A = \dfrac{bh}{2}$.

Quadrilaterals
- All quadrilaterals have 360 degrees.
- The area formula for a squares and rectangles is bh.

Circles
- All circles have 360 degrees.
- The radius is the distance from the center of the circle to any point on the edge.
- The area of a circle is πr^2.
- The perimeter of a circle is $2\pi r$.

PLUGGING IN ON GEOMETRY PROBLEMS

Remember, whenever you have a question that has answer choices, like a regular multiple choice or a multiple choice, multiple answer question that has variables in the answer choices, Plug In. On geometry problems, you can plug in values for angles or lengths as long as the values you plug in don't contradict either the wording of the problem or the laws of geometry (you can't have the interior angles of a triangle add up to anything but 180, for instance).

Here's an example:

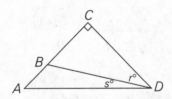

In the drawing above, if $AC = CD$, then $r =$

- ○ 45 − s
- ○ 90 − s
- ○ s
- ○ 45 + s
- ○ 60 + s

Here's How to Crack It

See the variables in the answer choices? Let's Plug In. First of all, we're told that *AC* and *CD* are equal, which means that *ACD* is an isosceles right triangle. So angles *A* and *D* both have to be 45 degrees. Now it's Plugging In time. The smaller angles, *r* and *s*, must add up to 45 degrees, so let's make *r* = 40 degrees and *s* = 5 degrees. The question asks for the value of *r*, which is 40, so that's our target answer. Now eliminate answer choices by plugging in 5 for *s* .

> (A) 45 – 5 = 40. Bingo! Check the other choices to
>   be sure.
>
> (B) 90 – 5 = 85. Nope.
>
> (C) 5. Nope.
>
> (D) 45 + 5 = 50. Eliminate it.
>
> (E) 60 + 5 = 65. No way.

By the way, we knew that the correct answer couldn't be greater than 45 degrees, because that's the measure of the entire angle *D*, so you could have eliminated (D) and (E) right away.

Don't forget to Plug In on geometry questions. Just pick numbers according to the rules of geometry.

───────────────○───────────────

DRAW IT YOURSELF

When ETS doesn't include a drawing with a geometry problem, it usually means that the drawing, if supplied, would make ETS's answer obvious. In cases like this, you should just draw it yourself. Here's an example:

───────────────○───────────────

7 of 20

Quantity A	**Quantity B**
The diameter of a circle with area 49π	14

○ Quantity A is greater.

○ Quantity B is greater.

○ The two quantities are equal.

○ The relationship cannot be determined
   from the information given.

Here's How to Crack It

Visualizing the figure, if the area is 49π, what's the radius? Right: 7. And if the radius is 7, what's the diameter? Right: 14. The answer is (C).

Redraw

On tricky quant comp questions, you may need to draw the figure once, eliminate two answer choices, and then draw it another way to try to disprove your first answer; in order to see if the answer is (D). Here's an example of a problem that might require you to do this:

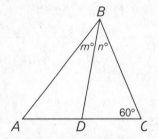

D is the midpoint of AC.

Quantity A	Quantity B
m	n

○ Quantity A is greater.

○ Quantity B is greater.

○ The two quantities are equal.

○ The relationship cannot be determined from the information given.

Here's How to Crack It

Are you sure that the triangle looks exactly like this? Nope. We only know what it tells us—that the lengths of AD and DC are equal; from this figure, it looks like angles m and n are also equal. Because this means that it's possible for them to be, we can eliminate choices (A) and (B). But let's redraw the figure to try to disprove our first answer.

For quant comp geometry questions, draw, eliminate, and REDRAW; it's like Plugging In twice.

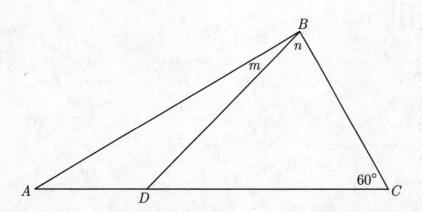

Try drawing the triangle as stretched out as possible. Notice that *n* is now clearly greater than *m,* so you can eliminate (C), and the answer is (D).

———————○———————

Geometry Drill

Think you've mastered these concepts? Try your hand at the following problems and check your work after you've finished. You can find the answers in Part V.

Which of the following could be the degree measures of two angles in a right triangle?

*Indicate **all** possible values.*

☐ 20° and 70°

☐ 30° and 60°

☐ 45° and 45°

☐ 55° and 55°

☐ 75° and 75°

Click on your choice(s).

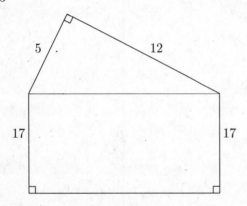

What is the perimeter of the figure above?

○ 51

○ 64

○ 68

○ 77

○ 91

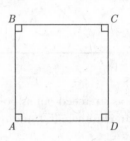 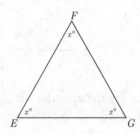

$$AB = BC = EG$$
$$FG = 8$$

Quantity A	**Quantity B**
The area of square $ABCD$	32

○ Quantity A is greater.

○ Quantity B is greater.

○ The two quantities are equal.

○ The relationship cannot be determined from the information given.

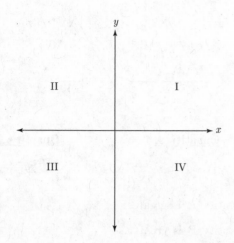

$(a, 6)$ is a point (not shown) in Region I.

$(-6, b)$ is a point (not shown) in Region II.

Quantity A	**Quantity B**
a	b

○ Quantity A is greater.

○ Quantity B is greater.

○ The two quantities are equal.

○ The relationship cannot be determined from the information given.

A piece of twine of length t is cut into two pieces. The length of the longer piece is 2 yards greater than 3 times the length of the shorter piece. Which of the following is the length, in yards, of the longer piece?

○ $\dfrac{t + 3}{3}$

○ $\dfrac{3t + 2}{3}$

○ $\dfrac{t - 2}{4}$

○ $\dfrac{3t + 4}{4}$

○ $\dfrac{3t + 2}{4}$

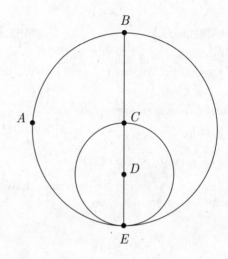

A circle with center D is drawn inside in a circle with center C, as shown. If $CD = 3$, what is the area of semicircle EAB ?

○ $\dfrac{9}{2}\pi$

○ 9π

○ 12π

○ 18π

○ 36π

For the final exam in a scuba diving certification course, Karl has to navigate underwater from one point in a lake to another. Karl began the test at the boat and swam due south for 7 meters. He then turned due east and swam for x meters. When he surfaced, he was 25 meters from the boat. What is the value of x ?

[   ] meters

Click on the answer box, then type in a number. Backspace to erase.

Quantity A	Quantity B
The circumference of a circular region with radius r	The perimeter of a square with side r

○ Quantity A is greater.

○ Quantity B is greater.

○ The two quantities are equal.

○ The relationship cannot be determined from the information given.

Triangle ABC is contained within a circle with center C. Points A and B lie on the circle. If the area of circle C is 25π, and the measure of angle C is 60°, which of the following are possible lengths for the legs of triangle ABC ?

*Indicate **all** possible values.*

☐ 3

☐ 4

☐ 5

☐ 6

☐ 7

Click on your choice(s).

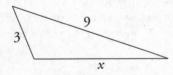

Quantity A	Quantity B
x	5.9

○ Quantity A is greater.

○ Quantity B is greater.

○ The two quantities are equal.

○ The relationship cannot be determined from the information given.

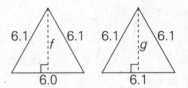

Quantity A	Quantity B
f	g

○ Quantity A is greater.

○ Quantity B is greater.

○ The two quantities are equal.

○ The relationship cannot be determined from the information given.

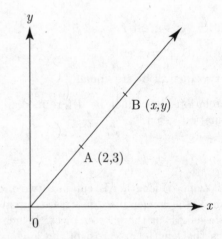

Given points $A(2, 3)$ and $B(x, y)$ in the rectangular coordinate system above, if $y = 4.2$, then $x =$

○ 2.6

○ 2.8

○ 2.9

○ 3.0

○ 3.2

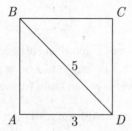

In rectangle *ABCD* above, which of the following is the area of the triangle *ABD* ?

○   6

○   7.5

○   10

○   12

○   15

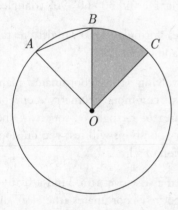

The circle above has a center *O*.
$$\angle AOB = \angle BOC$$

Quantity A   **Quantity B**

The area of triangle *AOB*   The area of the shaded region

○ Quantity A is greater.

○ Quantity B is greater.

○ The two quantities are equal.

○ The relationship cannot be determined from the information given.

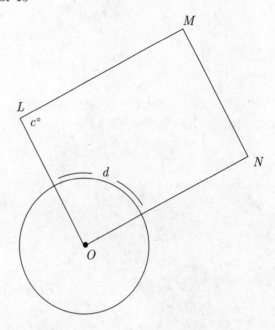

The circumference of the circle with center *O* is 15π. *LMNO* is a parallelogram and $c = 108$. What is the value of *d* ?

○ 15π

○ 9π

○ 3π

○ 2π

○ It cannot be determined from the information given.

Summary

o There may only be a handful of geometry questions on the GRE, but you'll be expected to know a fair amount of rules and formulas.

o Line and angle problems typically test your knowledge of vertical angles, parallel lines, right angles, and straight angles.

o Triangles are a popular geometry topic on the GRE. Make sure you know your triangle basics, including the total degrees of a triangle, the relationship between the angles and sides of a triangle, and the third side rule.

o Right triangle problems frequently test the Pythagorean theorem.

o Be aware of the two special right triangles that ETS likes to torture test takers with: the 45°-45°-90° triangle and 30°-60°-90° triangle.

o Know the area formulas for triangles, rectangles, squares, and circles.

o Problems involving the coordinate plane frequently test common geometry concepts such as the area of triangle or square. Other plane geometry questions will test you on slope and the equation of a line.

o Slope is defined as rise over run. Find it by finding the change in y-coordinates (the rise) and the change in x-coordinates (the run).

o The equation of a line is $y = mx + b$, where x and y are the coordinates of any point on the line, m is the slope and b is the y-intercept, the point at which the line crosses the y-axis.

o Don't forget to Plug In on geometry problems!

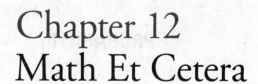

Chapter 12
Math Et Cetera

There are a few more math topics that may appear on the GRE that don't fit nicely into the preceding chapters. This chapter looks at some of these leftover topics, including probability, permutations and combinations, and factorials. The topics in this chapter are not essential to your GRE Math score, because these areas are not tested as frequently as the topics detailed earlier. However, if you feel confident with the previous math topics, and you're looking to maximize your GRE Math score, this chapter will show you all you need to know to tackle these more obscure GRE problems.

These topics show up rarely on the GRE, but if you're going for a very high score, they are useful to know.

OTHER MATH TOPICS

The bulk of the GRE Math section tests your knowledge of fundamentals, basic algebra, and geometry. However, there are a few other topics that may appear. These "et cetera" concepts usually show up only once or twice per test (although at higher scoring levels they may appear more frequently) and often cause anxiety among test takers. Many test takers worry excessively about probability problems, for example, even though knowledge of more familiar topics such as fractions and percents will be far more important in determining your GRE math score. So tackle these problems only after you've mastered the rest. If you find these concepts more difficult, don't worry—they won't make or break your GRE score.

PROBABILITY

If you flip a coin, what's the probability that it will land heads up? The probability is equal to one out of two, or $\frac{1}{2}$. What is the probability that it won't land heads up? Again, one out of two, or $\frac{1}{2}$. If you flip a coin nine times, what's the probability that the coin will land on "heads" on the tenth flip? Still 1 out of 2, or $\frac{1}{2}$. Previous flips do not affect the outcome of the current coin flip.

There's no need to be intimidated by probability questions. If you can work with fractions, you can work with probability questions!

You can think of probability as just another type of fraction. Probabilities express a special relationship, namely the chance of a certain outcome occurring. In a probability fraction, the denominator is the total number of possible outcomes that may occur, while the numerator is the number of outcomes that would satisfy the criteria. For example, if you have 10 shirts and 3 of them are black, the probability of selecting a black shirt from your closet without looking is $\frac{3}{10}$.

Think of probability in terms of fractions:

- If it is impossible for something to happen—if no outcomes satisfy the criteria—then the numerator of the probability fraction is 0 and the probability is equal to 0.
- If something is certain to happen—if all possible outcomes satisfy the criteria—then the numerator and denominator of the fraction are equal and the probability is equal to 1.
- If it is possible for something to occur, but it will not definitely occur, then the probability of it occurring is between 0 and 1.

$$\text{probablity} = \frac{\text{number of possible outcomes that satisfy the condition}}{\text{number of total possible outcomes}}$$

Let's see how it works.

At a meeting of 375 members of a neighborhood association, $\frac{1}{5}$ of the participants have lived in the community for less than 5 years and $\frac{2}{3}$ of the attendees have lived in the neighborhood for over 10 years. If a member of the meeting is selected at random, what is the probability that the person has lived in the neighborhood for more than 5 years but less than 10 years?

○ $\frac{2}{15}$

○ $\frac{3}{10}$

○ $\frac{4}{15}$

○ $\frac{1}{2}$

○ $\frac{8}{15}$

Here's How to Crack It

In order to solve this problem, we need to put together our probability fraction. The denominator of our fraction is going to be 375; the total number of people from which we are selecting. Next we need to figure out how many attendees satisfy the criteria of having lived in the neighborhood for more than 5 years but fewer than 10 years.

What number goes on the bottom of the probability fraction?

First, we know that $\frac{1}{5}$ of the participants have lived in the neighborhood for less than 5 years. $\frac{1}{5}$ of 375 is 75 people, so we can take them out of the running. Also, $\frac{2}{3}$ of the attendees have lived in the neighborhood for over 10 years. $\frac{2}{3}$ of 375 (be careful not to use 300 as the total!) is 250, so we can also remove them from consideration. Thus, if 75 people have lived in the neighborhood for less than 5 years and 250 have lived for more than 10, the remaining people are the ones we want. 250 + 75 is 325, so that leaves us with 50 people who satisfy the criteria. We need to make 50 the numerator of our fraction, which gives us $\frac{50}{375}$. This reduces to $\frac{2}{15}$, and answer choice (A) is the best answer.

Two Important Laws of Probability

> Probability of A and B
> = Probability of A
> × Probability of B

When you want to find the probability of a series of events in a row, you multiply the probabilities of the individual events. What is the probability of getting two heads in a row if you flip a coin twice? The probability of getting a head on the first flip is $\frac{1}{2}$. The probability is also $\frac{1}{2}$ that you'll get a head on the second flip, so the combined probability of two heads is $\frac{1}{2} \times \frac{1}{2}$, which equals $\frac{1}{4}$. Another way to look at it is that there are four possible outcomes: HH, TT, HT, TH. Only one of those outcomes consists of two heads in a row. Thus, $\frac{1}{4}$ of the outcomes consist of two heads in a row. Sometimes the number of outcomes is small enough that you can list them out and calculate the probability that way.

> Probability of A or B
> = Probability of A
> + Probability of B

Occasionally, instead of finding the probability of one event AND another event happening, you'll be asked to find the probability of either one event OR another event happening. In this situation, instead of multiplying the probabilities, you add them. Let's say you have a normal deck of 52 cards. If you select a card at random, what's the probability that you select a 7 or a 4? The probability of selecting a 7 is $\frac{4}{52}$, which reduces to $\frac{1}{13}$. The probability of selecting a 4 is the same; $\frac{1}{13}$. Therefore the probability of selecting a 7 or a 4 is $\frac{1}{13} + \frac{1}{13} = \frac{2}{13}$.

Let's look at a problem:

> Julie is going to roll a pair of six-sided dice, one at a time. What is the probability that she rolls a 3 and then a 4, OR a 5 and then a prime number?

$$\boxed{}$$

Click on the answer box, then type in a number. Backspace to erase.

Here's How to Crack It

Let's start with the first possibility. The probability of rolling a 3 is $\frac{1}{6}$, and the probability of rolling a 4 is $\frac{1}{6}$. So the probability of rolling a 3 and then a 4 is $\frac{1}{6} \times \frac{1}{6} = \frac{1}{36}$. Now let's look at the second possibility. The probability of rolling a 5 is $\frac{1}{6}$ and the probability of rolling a prime number is $\frac{1}{2}$. (There are six outcomes when you roll a die and three of them are prime: 2, 3, and 5. So the probability of rolling a prime number is $\frac{3}{6}$, which reduces to $\frac{1}{2}$.) Therefore, the probability of rolling a 5 and then a prime number is $\frac{1}{6} \times \frac{1}{2} = \frac{1}{12}$. So now we know the probability of rolling a 3 and then a 4 is $\frac{1}{36}$, and we know the probability of rolling a 5 and a prime number is $\frac{1}{12}$. To find the probability of one of these things OR the other happening, we add the individual probabilities. So $\frac{1}{12} + \frac{1}{36} = \frac{4}{36}$ which reduces to $\frac{1}{9}$.

One last important thing you should know about probabilities is that the probability of an event happening and the probability of an event not happening must add up to 1. For example, if the probability of snow falling on one night is $\frac{2}{3}$, then the probability of no snow falling must be $\frac{1}{3}$. If the probability that it will rain is 80%, then the probability that it won't rain must be 20%. The reason this is useful is that, on some GRE probability problems, it will be easier to find the probability that an event doesn't occur; once you have that, just subtract from 1 to find the answer.

Let's look at the following example.

Dipak has a 25% chance of winning each hand of blackjack he plays. If he has $150 and bets $50 a hand, what is the probability that he will still have money after the third hand?

- ○ $\dfrac{1}{64}$
- ○ $\dfrac{3}{16}$
- ○ $\dfrac{27}{64}$
- ○ $\dfrac{37}{64}$
- ○ $\dfrac{3}{4}$

Here's How to Crack It

If Dipak still has money after the third hand, then he must have won at least one of the hands, and possibly more than one. However, directly calculating the probability that he wins at least one hand is tricky because there are so many ways it could happen (for example, he could lose-lose-win, or W-W-L or W-L-W or L-W-L, etc.). So think about it this way: The question asks for the probability that he will win at least one hand. What if he doesn't? That would mean that he doesn't win any hands at all. If we calculate the probability that he loses every hand, we can then subtract that from 1 and find the corresponding probability that he wins at least one hand. Since Dipak has a 25% chance of winning each hand, this means that he has a 75% chance of losing it, or $\dfrac{3}{4}$ (the answers are in fractions, so it's best to work with fractions). To find the probability that he loses all three hands, simply multiply the probabilities of his losing each individual hand. $\dfrac{3}{4} \times \dfrac{3}{4} \times \dfrac{3}{4} = \dfrac{27}{64}$ so there is a $\dfrac{27}{64}$ probability that he will lose all three hands. Subtracting this from 1 gives you the answer you're looking for. $1 - \dfrac{27}{64} = \dfrac{37}{64}$. The answer is (D).

Given events A and B, the probability of:
- A and B = (Probability of A) × (Probability of B)
- A or B = Probability of A + Probability of B

Given event A:
- A + *not* A = 1

FACTORIALS

The factorial of a number is equal to that number times every positive whole number smaller than that number, down to 1. For example, the factorial of 6 is equal to $6 \times 5 \times 4 \times 3 \times 2 \times 1$, which equals 720. The symbol for a factorial is ! so 4! doesn't mean we're really excited about the number 4, it means $4 \times 3 \times 2 \times 1$, which is equal to 24. (0! is equal to 1, by the way.) When factorials show up in GRE problems, always look for a shortcut like canceling or factoring. The point of a factorial problem is not to make you do a lot of multiplication. Let's try one.

8 of 20

Quantity A	Quantity B
$\dfrac{12!}{11!}$	$\dfrac{4!}{2!}$

○ Quantity A is greater.

○ Quantity B is greater.

○ The two quantities are equal.

○ The relationship cannot be determined from the information given.

Here's How to Crack It

Let's tackle Quantity A. We definitely don't want to multiply out the factorials since that would be pretty time-consuming: 12! and 11! are both huge numbers. Instead let's look at what they have in common. What we're really talking about here is $\dfrac{12 \times 11 \times 10 \times 9 \times 8 \times 7 \times 6 \times 5 \times 4 \times 3 \times 2 \times 1}{11 \times 10 \times 9 \times 8 \times 7 \times 6 \times 5 \times 4 \times 3 \times 2 \times 1}$. Now it's clear that both factorials share everything from 11 on down to 1. The entire bottom of the fraction will cancel and the only thing left on top will be 12, so the value of Quantity A is 12. For Quantity B, we can also write out the factorials and get $\dfrac{4 \times 3 \times 2 \times 1}{2 \times 1}$.

The 2 and the 1 in the bottom cancel, and the only thing left on top will be 4 × 3, which is equal to 12. The two quantities are equal and the answer is (C).

PERMUTATIONS AND COMBINATIONS

The basic definition of a **permutation** is an arrangement of things in a particular order. Suppose you were asked to figure out how many different ways you could arrange five statues on a shelf. All you have to do is multiply 5 × 4 × 3 × 2 × 1, or 120. (Yes, this is another application of factorials.) You have five possible statues that could fill the first slot on the shelf, then, once the first slot is filled, there are four remaining statues that could fill the second slot, three that could fill the third slot, and so on, down to one.

Now suppose that there are five people running in a race. The winner of the race will get a gold medal, the person who comes in second will get a silver medal, and the person who comes in third will get a bronze medal. You're asked to figure out how many different orders of gold-silver-bronze winners there can be. (Notice that this is a permutation because the order definitely matters.)

First, ask yourself how many of these runners can come in first? Five. Once one of them comes in first, she's out of the picture, so how many can then come in second? Four. Once one of them comes in second, she's out of the picture, so how many of them can come in third? Three. And now you're done because all three slots have been filled. The answer is 5 × 4 × 3, which is 60.

> To solve a permutation
> - Figure out how many slots you have.
> - Write down the number of options for each slot.
> - Multiply them.

Permutation problems often ask for arrangements, orders, schedules, or lists.

The difference between a permutation and a combination is that in a combination, the order is irrelevant. A **combination** is just a group, and the order of elements within the group doesn't matter. For example, suppose you were asked to go to the store and bring home three different types of ice cream. Now suppose that when you got to the store, there were five flavors in the freezer—chocolate, vanilla, strawberry, butter pecan, and mocha. How many combinations of three ice cream flavors could you bring home? Notice that the order doesn't matter, because bringing home chocolate, strawberry, and vanilla is the same thing as bringing home strawberry, vanilla, and chocolate. One way to solve this is the brute force method; in other words, write out every combination.

Combination problems usually ask for groups, teams, or committees.

VCS VCB VCM VSB VSM VBM CSB CSM CBM SBM

Does the order matter?

That's 10 combinations, but there's a quicker way to do it. Start by filling in the three slots as you would with a permutation (there are three slots because you're supposed to bring home three different types of ice cream). Five flavors could be in the first slot, four could be in the second, and three could be in the third. So far, that's $5 \times 4 \times 3$. But remember, this takes into account all the different orders that three flavors can be arranged in. We don't want that, because the order doesn't matter in a combination. So we have to divide $5 \times 4 \times 3$ by the number of ways of arranging three things. In how many ways can three things be arranged? That's 3!, $3 \times 2 \times 1$, which is 6. Thus we end up with $\dfrac{5 \times 4 \times 3}{3 \times 2 \times 1}$, which is equal to $\dfrac{60}{6}$, or 10. Bingo.

To solve a combination

- Figure out how many slots you have.
- Fill in the slots as you would a permutation.
- Divide by the factorial of the number of slots.

The denominator of the fraction will always cancel out completely, so you can cancel first before you multiply.

Always cross off wrong
answer choices on your
scratch paper.

Here's an example:

———————————○———————————

15 of 20

Brooke wants to hang three paintings in a row on
her wall. She has six paintings to choose from. How
many arrangements of paintings on the wall can she
create?

○   6

○   30

○   90

○   120

○   720

Here's How to Crack It

The first thing you need to do is determine whether the order matters. In this case
it does, because we're arranging the paintings on the wall. Putting the Monet on
the left and the Van Gogh in the middle isn't the same arrangement as putting the
Van Gogh on the left and the Monet in the middle. This is a permutation question. We have three slots to fill because we're arranging three paintings. There are
6 paintings that could fill the first slot, 5 paintings that could fill the second slot,
and 4 paintings that could fill the third slot. So we have 6 × 5 × 4, which equals
120. Thus, the correct answer is (D).

———————————○———————————

Here's another example:

A pizza may be ordered with any of eight possible toppings.

Quantity A	Quantity B
The number of different ways to order a pizza with three different toppings	The number of different ways to order a pizza with five different toppings

○ Quantity A is greater.

○ Quantity B is greater.

○ The two quantities are equal.

○ The relationship cannot be determined from the information given.

Here's How to Crack It

First, note that for both quantities we're dealing with a combination, because the order of toppings doesn't matter. A pizza with mushrooms and pepperoni is the same thing as a pizza with pepperoni and mushrooms. Let's figure out Quantity A first.

We have eight toppings and we're picking three of them. That means we have three slots to fill. There are 8 toppings that could fill the first slot, 7 that could fill the second slot, and 6 that could fill the third, so we have $8 \times 7 \times 6$. Since this is a combination, we have to divide by the factorial of the number of slots. In this case we have three slots, so we have to divide by 3!, or $3 \times 2 \times 1$. So our problem looks like this: $\frac{8 \times 7 \times 6}{3 \times 2 \times 1}$. To make the multiplication easier, let's cancel first. The 6 on top will cancel with the 3×2 on the bottom, leaving us with $\frac{8 \times 7}{1}$, which is 56. Thus, there are 56 ways to order a three-topping pizza with eight toppings to choose from. Now let's look at Quantity B.

We still have eight toppings, but this time we're picking five of them so we have five slots to fill. There are 8 toppings that could fill the first slot, 7 that could fill the second slot, 6 that could fill the third, 5 that could fill the fourth, and 4 that could fill the fifth. That's $8 \times 7 \times 6 \times 5 \times 4$, but we still have to divide by the factorial of the number of slots. We have five slots, so that means we need to divide by 5!, or $5 \times 4 \times 3 \times 2 \times 1$. Thus we have $\frac{8 \times 7 \times 6 \times 5 \times 4}{5 \times 4 \times 3 \times 2 \times 1}$. We definitely want to cancel first here, rather than doing all that multiplication. The 5 on top will cancel with the 5 on the bottom. Likewise, the 4 on top will cancel with the 4 on the bottom. The 6 on top will cancel with the 3 × 2 on the bottom, leaving us again with $\frac{8 \times 7}{1}$, which is 56. Therefore, there are also 56 ways to order a five-topping pizza with eight toppings to choose from. The two quantities are equal, and the answer is (C).

Let's try one more:

Nicole needs to form a committee of 3 from a group of 8 research attorneys to study possible changes to the Superior Court. If two of the attorneys are too inexperienced to serve together on the committee, how many different arrangements of committees can Nicole form?

○   20

○   30

○   50

○   56

○   336

Here's How to Crack It

This problem is a little more complicated than an ordinary combination problem, because an extra condition has been placed on the committee. Without that condition, this would be a fairly ordinary combination problem, and we'd simply calculate how many groups of three can be created with eight people to choose from.

There's more than one way to approach this problem. First, you should realize that there are two ways that we could form this committee. We could have three experienced attorneys, or we could have two experienced attorneys and one inexperienced attorney. If we find the number of ways to create each of those two possibilities, we can add them together and have our answer. It's fairly straightforward to calculate the number of ways to have three experienced attorneys on a committee: There are three slots to fill, and we have 6 options for the first slot, 5 for the second, and 4 for the third. Here the order doesn't matter, so we divide by 3! to get $\frac{6 \times 5 \times 4}{3 \times 2 \times 1} = 20$. Thus there are 20 ways to create the committee using three experienced attorneys. What about creating a committee that has two experienced attorneys and one inexperienced attorney? We have 6 options for the first experienced attorney and 5 options for the second. Order doesn't matter so we divide by 2!. So far we have $\frac{6 \times 5}{2 \times 1}$. Next we have 2 options for the inexperienced attorney, so now we have to multiply by 2, and our calculation is $\frac{6 \times 5}{2 \times 1} \times \frac{2}{1} = 30$. As you can see, there are 30 ways to create the committee using two experienced attorneys and one inexperienced attorney. Adding 20 and 30 gives us 50 total committees, and the answer is (C).

Here's another way that you could solve the problem. If there were no conditions placed on the committee, we could just calculate $\frac{8 \times 7 \times 6}{3 \times 2 \times 1}$, which would give us 56 committees. But we know some of those committees are not allowed; any committee that has the two inexperienced attorneys on it isn't allowed. How many of these types of committees are there? Let's call the inexperienced attorneys A and B. An illegal committee would be A B __, in which the last slot could be filled by any of the experienced attorneys. Since there are 6 experienced attorneys, there are 6 illegal committees. Subtracting them from 56 gives us 50 legal committees. Hey, the answer's still (C)!

FUNCTIONS AND FUNNY-LOOKING SYMBOLS

The GRE contains "function" problems, but they aren't like the functions that you may have learned in high school. GRE functions use funny-looking symbols, such as @, *, and #. Each symbol represents an arithmetic operation or a series of arithmetic operations. All you have to do is follow directions in the problem. Here's an example:

With funny-looking symbols, simply follow the directions.

---

5 of 20

For any non-negative integer x, let $x^* = x - 1$

Quantity A	Quantity B
$\dfrac{15^*}{3^*}$	$\left(\dfrac{15}{3}\right)^*$

○ Quantity A is greater.

○ Quantity B is greater.

○ The two quantities are equal.

○ The relationship cannot be determined from the information given.

Here's How to Crack It

Just follow the directions—15* = 15 − 1, or 14, and 3* = 3 − 1, or 2. So we get $\frac{14}{2}$, or 7, in Quantity A. Don't forget PEMDAS for Quantity B. First, $\frac{15}{3}$ is 5. Then, 5* = 5 − 1, or 4. So because Quantity A is 7 and Quantity B is 4, the answer is (A). Function questions aren't scary if you follow the directions. Be sure to write everything down on your scratch paper. By the way, these funny-looking symbols don't necessarily indicate exponents, but you'll always be told what they mean.

GROUPS

Group problems, although not too common on the GRE, can be troublesome if you don't know how to set them up. When confronted by a group problem, use the group equation

$$T = G_1 + G_2 - B + N$$

In the equation, T represents the Total, G_1 is one group, G_2 is the second group, B is for the members in both groups and N is for the members in neither group. Here's an example of a typical group problem.

You might see one group problem on the GRE.

A biologist studying breeding groups noted that of 225 birds tagged for the study, 85 birds made nests in pine trees, 175 made nests in oak trees, and 40 birds did not build nests in either type of tree. How many birds built nests in both types of trees?

○   45

○   60

○   75

○   80

○   125

Here's How to Crack It

Let's use the group equation. The total is 225, one group consists of 85 birds, the other group has 175 birds in it, and we know that 40 birds built nests in neither type of tree. Our equation would look like this:

$$225 = 85 + 175 - B + 40$$

All we have to do is solve for B. Simplifying the equation gives us $225 = 300 - B$, so B must equal 75. Choice (C) is our answer.

Et Cetera Drill

Here are some math questions to practice on. Remember to check your answers when you finish. You can find the answers in Part V.

15 marbles are placed in a bowl; some are red, and some are blue. If the number of red marbles is 1 more than the number of blue marbles, what is the probability that a marble taken from the bowl is blue?

○ $\dfrac{1}{15}$

○ $\dfrac{2}{15}$

○ $\dfrac{7}{15}$

○ $\dfrac{1}{2}$

○ $\dfrac{8}{15}$

If $¥(x) = 10x - 1$, what is $¥(5) - ¥(3)$?

○ 15

○ 18

○ 19

○ 20

○ 46

Quantity A	**Quantity B**
The largest odd factor of 78	The largest prime factor of 78

○ Quantity A is greater.

○ Quantity B is greater.

○ The two quantities are equal.

○ The relationship cannot be determined from the information given.

At a recent dog show, there were 5 finalists. One of the finalists was awarded "Best in Show" and another finalist was awarded "Honorable Mention." In how many ways could the two awards be given out?

[ ]

Click on the answer box, then type in a number. Backspace to erase.

Company X spends $40,000 per year on advertising for product A and $30,000 per year on advertising for product B. The company spends $15,000 on advertisements that advertise both product A and B as a system. The company spends $90,000 total on advertising for all of its products.

Quantity A	**Quantity B**
The total amount the company spends advertising products other than products A and B.	$20,000

○ Quantity A is greater.

○ Quantity B is greater.

○ The two quantities are equal.

○ The relationship cannot be determined from the information given.

Lee randomly selects a 2-digit prime number less than 50. What is the probability that the tens digit is greater than the units digit?

- ○ $\dfrac{3}{14}$
- ○ $\dfrac{3}{11}$
- ○ $\dfrac{3}{8}$
- ○ $\dfrac{1}{2}$
- ○ $\dfrac{8}{11}$

An elected official wants to take five members of his staff to an undisclosed secure location. What is the minimum number of staff members the elected official must have in order to have at least 20 different groups from which to choose?

- ○ 7
- ○ 8
- ○ 9
- ○ 10
- ○ 11

For all real numbers x and y, if $x \# y = x(x - y)$, then $x \# (x \# y) =$

- ○ $x^2 - xy$
- ○ $x^2 - 2xy$
- ○ $x^3 - x^2 - xy$
- ○ $x^3 - (xy)^2$
- ○ $x^2 - x^3 + x^2 y$

A jar contains 12 marbles. Each is either yellow or green and there are twice as many yellow marbles as green marbles. If two marbles are to be selected from the jar at random, what is the probability that exactly one of each color is selected?

- ○ $\dfrac{8}{33}$
- ○ $\dfrac{16}{33}$
- ○ $\dfrac{1}{2}$
- ○ $\dfrac{17}{33}$
- ○ $\dfrac{25}{33}$

A set of 10 points lie in a plane such that no three points are collinear.

Quantity A	**Quantity B**
The number of distinct triangles that can be created from the set	The number of distinct quadrilaterals that can be created from the set

- ○ Quantity A is greater.
- ○ Quantity B is greater.
- ○ The two quantities are equal.
- ○ The relationship cannot be determined from the information given.

Comprehensive Math Drill

Let's do a drill involving all of the math topics we've covered throughout the book. Remember to check your answers when you finish. You can find the answers in Part V.

$$\frac{0.05}{0.6} = \frac{x}{.18}$$

Quantity A	Quantity B
x	.015

○ Quantity A is greater.

○ Quantity B is greater.

○ The two quantities are equal.

○ The relationship cannot be determined from the information given.

$$x \neq 0$$

Quantity A	Quantity B
$\dfrac{x}{10}$	$\dfrac{\left(\dfrac{x}{5}\right)}{2}$

○ Quantity A is greater.

○ Quantity B is greater.

○ The two quantities are equal.

○ The relationship cannot be determined from the information given.

The test scores for a class have a normal distribution, a mean of 50, and a standard deviation of 4.

Quantity A	Quantity B
Percentage of scores at or above 58	Percentage of scores at or below 42

○ Quantity A is greater.

○ Quantity B is greater.

○ The two quantities are equal.

○ The relationship cannot be determined from the information given.

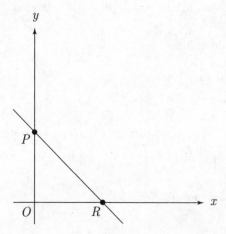

The line $y = -\dfrac{5}{6}x + 1$ is graphed on the rectangular coordinate axes.

Quantity A	Quantity B
OR	OP

○ Quantity A is greater.

○ Quantity B is greater.

○ The two quantities are equal.

○ The relationship cannot be determined from the information given.

At a dog show, there are 20 judges and 10 dogs in the final round.

Quantity A	Quantity B
The number of distinct pairs of judges	The number of possible rankings of dogs from first to third place

○ Quantity A is greater.

○ Quantity B is greater.

○ The two quantities are equal.

○ The relationship cannot be determined from the information given.

$$k > 0$$
$$l > 1$$

Quantity A	Quantity B
$\dfrac{1}{\dfrac{1}{k} + \dfrac{1}{l}}$	$\dfrac{kl}{\dfrac{1}{k} + \dfrac{1}{l}}$

○ Quantity A is greater.

○ Quantity B is greater.

○ The two quantities are equal.

○ The relationship cannot be determined from the information given.

Quantity A	Quantity B
$\sqrt{3} + \sqrt{4}$	$\sqrt{7}$

○ Quantity A is greater.

○ Quantity B is greater.

○ The two quantities are equal.

○ The relationship cannot be determined from the information given.

Joe has $200. If he buys a CD player for $150, what is the greatest number of CDs he can buy with the remaining money if CDs cost $12 each?

Click on the answer box, then type in a number. Backspace to erase.

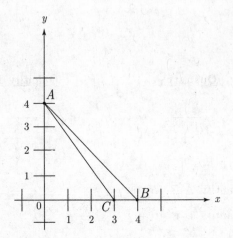

What is the area of triangle ABC in the figure above?

○ 2

○ 4

○ $4\sqrt{2}$

○ 7

○ 8

Which of the following could equal $10(3^2 - 2)$ divided by a positive integer?

Indicate **all** possible values.

☐ 140

☐ 70

☐ 35

☐ 10

☐ 0

Click on your choice(s).

Roberta drove 50 miles in 2 hours. Her rate in miles per hour is equivalent to which of the following proportions?

Indicate **all** possible values.

☐ 5 to 20

☐ 100 to 4

☐ 400 to 16

☐ 20 to 500

Click on your choice(s).

TEMPERATURES OF U.S. CITIES IN YEARS X AND Y

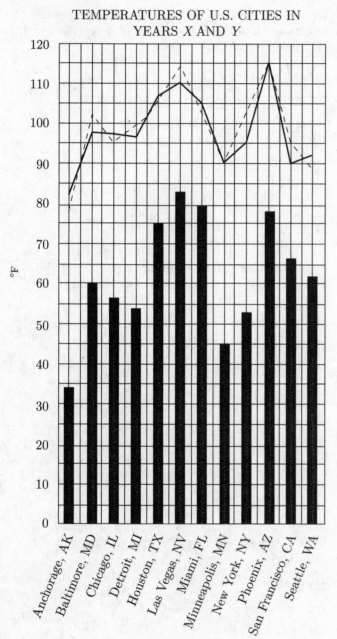

◼ Average Temperature for Years X and Y

- - - - High for Year Y

——— High for Year X

For how many of the cities shown was the highest temperature in Year Y greater than or equal to the highest temperature in Year X ?

○   4

○   5

○   7

○   8

○   12

What is the approximate percent increase from the lowest average temperature for Years X and Y to the highest average temperature?

○   60%

○   82%

○   140%

○   188%

○   213%

If the average temperature for Years X and Y in Baltimore is equal to the average of that city's high and low temperatures for each of those years, then what is the average of the low temperatures for Baltimore in Years X and Y ?

○ –9° F

○ 11° F

○ 20° F

○ 44° F

○ It cannot be determined from the information given.

If $|2x - 3| + 2 > 7$, which of the following could be the value of x ?

Indicate **all** possible values.

☐ –4

☐ –3

☐ –2

☐ –1

☐ 0

☐ 1

☐ 2

☐ 3

Click on your choice(s).

If x, y, and z are consecutive odd integers where $x < y < z$ and $x + y + z < z$, then whch of the following could be the value of x ?

Indicate **all** possible values.

☐ –3

☐ –1

☐ 0

☐ 1

☐ 3

Click on your choice(s).

If $4^x = 1024$, then $(4^{x+1})(5^{x-1}) =$

○ 10^6

○ $(5^4)(10^5)$

○ $(4^4)(10^5)$

○ $(5^4)(10^4)$

○ $(4^4)(10^4)$

What is the greatest distance between two vertices of a rectangular solid with a height of 5, a length of 12, and a volume of 780?

○ 12

○ $12\sqrt{2}$

○ 13

○ $13\sqrt{2}$

○ $13\sqrt{3}$

Six children, three boys and three girls, sit in a row on a park bench. How many arrangements of children are possible if no boy can sit on either end of the bench?

Indicate **all** possible values.

☐ 46,656

☐ 38,880

☐ 1,256

☐ 144

☐ 38

Click on your choice(s).

If 16 is the average of p, 24, and q, what is $16(p + q)$?

○ 180

○ 192

○ 384

○ 524

○ 768

Summary

- Topics such as probability, permutations and combinations, factorials, and functions represent only a small percentage of the math topics tested on the GRE. Make sure you've mastered all the more important topics before attempting these.

- Probability is expressed as a fraction. The denominator of the fraction represents the total number of possible outcomes, while the numerator stands for the desired outcomes.

- If a probability question asks for the chance of event A or event B, find the probability of each event and add them together. If the question asks for the probability of event A and event B, multiply the individual probabilities.

- The key to factorial problems is to look for ways to cancel or factor out terms.

- Permutations and combinations are related concepts. A permutation tells you how many arrangements or orderings of things are possible. A combination tells you how many groupings of things are possible.

- Function problems use funny looking symbols as shorthand for the operations to perform on a certain number.

- The group equation is: Total = Group I + Group II – Members of Both Groups + Members of Neither Group.

Part IV
How to Crack the Critical Thinking and Analytical Writing Section

Chapter 13
The Geography of the Critical Thinking and Analytical Writing Section

This chapter clues you in on everything you've ever wanted to know about the Critical Thinking and Analytical Writing sections of the GRE. It contains important information on how the essays are used by graduate schools, the scoring system ETS graders use to evaluate your essays, and the crucial distinctions between the issue essay and the argument essay. This chapter also looks at the basic word-processing program used by ETS.

ESSAYS AND THE GRE

The Critical Thinking and Analytical Writing section of the GRE requires you to write two essays—one will be an analysis of an issue and the other will be an analysis of an argument. You will have 30 minutes each for both the Issue and Argument essay.

In the past, ETS has had problems with test takers relying on preplanned essays. The essay questions have been reformulated to reduce the possibility of testers preparing their essays in advance. However, while you may not be able to plan your entire essay in advance, you can still go into your test session having a good idea of what type of essay you're going to write.

How Do Schools Use the Writing Assessment?

First, the essays are probably more important for international students and those for whom English is not a first language. If you are not a native English speaker, expect your essay score and the essays you wrote to receive more attention. (ETS also makes the essays available to schools, which may choose to read them or not.) Second, and not surprisingly, the essays will probably be weighted more heavily by programs for which writing is a frequent and necessary task. A master's program in applied mathematics might not care so much about your 30-minute written opinion about whether or not it's necessary for a person to read imaginative literature, but a program in creative writing probably would.

Ultimately, though, the most honest answer to this question is: It depends. Some schools will not care at all about the Critical Thinking and Analytical Writing score, while others will say that they only want applicants who scored a 5 or higher on this section. Call the schools you're interested in and talk to people in the department. By finding out how important your target schools consider the Analytical Writing section, you'll be able to determine the appropriate amount of effort to devote to it.

> Even if your program doesn't care much for the essay, a poor score might still raise a red flag.

Regardless of your target score on this section, you should at least read through these chapters to get a better sense of what ETS is looking for. You'll have to write these essays, so no matter what, you want to do a decent job. You'll find that writing high-scoring essays is not as hard as it may seem once you've been shown how to do it.

How Will the Essays Be Scored?

Your essays will be read by two graders, and each will assign a score from 1 to 6, based on how well you do the following:

> What you write—the content—will be weighted more than how you write.

- follow the instructions of the prompt
- consider the complexities of the issue or argument
- effectively organize and develop your ideas

- support your position with relevant examples
- control the elements of written English

The grades you receive for each essay will be totaled and averaged. For example, if you receive a 4 and a 5 on your issue essay and a 3 and a 4 on your argument essay, your Analytical Writing score will be a 4.0; 16 total points divided by 4 scores. If the graders' scores for your essays differ by more than one point, a third person will be brought in to read the essay. The graders use a "holistic" grading system; they're trained to look at the big picture, not to focus on minor details. Your essay is not expected to be perfect, so the graders will overlook minor errors in spelling, punctuation, and grammar. However, pervasive or egregious errors will affect your score.

Here are ETS's descriptions of the scoring levels:

Issue Essay		Argument Essay	
6	An essay that scores a 6 presents a cogent, well-articulated critique of the issue and conveys meaning skillfully.	6	An essay that scores a 6 presents a cogent, well-articulated critique of the argument and conveys meaning skillfully.
5	An essay that scores a 5 presents a generally thoughtful, well-developed analysis of the complexities of the issue and conveys meaning clearly.	5	An essay that scores a 5 presents a generally thoughtful, well-developed critique of the argument and conveys meaning clearly.
4	An essay that scores a 4 presents a competent analysis of the issue and conveys meaning adequately.	4	An essay that scores a 4 presents a competent critique of the argument and conveys meaning adequately.
3	An essay that scores a 3 demonstrates some competence in its analysis of the issue and in conveying meaning but is obviously flawed.	3	An essay that scores a 3 demonstrates some competence in its critique of the argument and in conveying meaning but is obviously flawed.
2	An essay that scores a 2 demonstrates serious weaknesses in analytical writing.	2	An essay that scores a 2 demonstrates serious weaknesses in analytical writing.
1	An essay that scores a 1 demonstrates fundamental deficiencies in analytical writing skills.	1	An essay that scores a 1 demonstrates fundamental deficiencies in both analysis and writing.

An essay written on a topic other than the one provided will receive a score of 0.

Who Are These Readers Anyway?

We'll put this in the form of a multiple-choice question:

Your essays will initially be read by

(A)   captains of industry

(B)   leading professors

(C)   college TAs working part time

If you guessed (C), you're correct. Each essay will be read by part-time employees of ETS, mostly culled from graduate school programs.

How Much Time Do They Devote to Each Essay?

The short answer is: not much. It is unusual for a grader to spend more than two minutes grading an essay, and some essays are graded in less than a minute. The graders are reading many, many GRE essays and they aren't going to spend time admiring that clever turn of phrase you came up with. So don't sweat the small stuff—it probably won't even be noticed. Focus on the big picture—that's what the graders will be focusing on.

So How Do You Score High on the Analytical Writing Essays?

On the face of it, you might think it would be pretty difficult to impress these jaded readers, but it turns out that there are some very specific ways to persuade them of your superior writing skills.

What ETS Doesn't Want You to Know

In a recent analysis of a group of essays written by actual test takers, and the grades that those essays received, ETS researchers noticed that the most successful essays had one thing in common. Which of the following characteristics do you think it was?

- Good organization
- Proper diction
- Noteworthy ideas
- Good vocabulary
- Sentence variety
- Length

What Your Essay Needs in Order to Look Like a Successful Essay

The ETS researchers discovered that the essays that received the highest grades from ETS essay graders had one single factor in common: length.

To ace the Analytical Writing section, you need to take one simple step: Write as much as you possibly can. Each essay should include *at least* four indented paragraphs. Your Issue essay should be 400 to 750 words in length, and your Argument essay should be 350 to 600 words.

So All I Have to Do Is Type "I Hate the GRE" Over and Over Again?

Well, no. The length issue isn't that easy. The ETS researchers also noted that, not surprisingly, the high-scoring essays all made reasonably good points addressing the topic. So you have to actually write something that covers the essay topic. And in your quest for length, it's more important that you add depth than breadth. What this means is that it's better to have a few good examples that are thoroughly and deeply explored than it is to add length by tacking more and more examples and paragraphs onto your essay until it starts to feel like a superficial list of bulleted points rather than a thoughtful piece of writing.

Read the Directions Every Time

You should read the directions for each essay prompt. The instructions we provide here for each essay task are not necessarily the ones you will see on the GRE. Directions can vary in focus, so you shouldn't memorize any particular set of instructions. Visit the ETS website at **www.ets.org/gre** for a complete list of all the potential essay topics and direction variants. (Yes, you really get to see this information in advance of the test!) Practice responding to the different instructions, combined with a variety of issue and argument prompts. Be sure to mix it up; the prompt/directions pairings you see on the ETS website are not necessarily the duos you will see on the real test. Practicing with a variety of these essays will prepare you for whatever comes your way on test day.

Oh, Yes, You Can Plan Your Essays in Advance

In fact, there are some very specific ways to prepare for the essays that go beyond length and good typing skills. So how can you prepare ahead of time?

Creating a Template

When a builder builds a house, the first thing he does is construct a frame. The frame supports the entire house. After the frame is completed, he can nail the walls and windows to the frame. We're going to show you how to build the frame for the perfect GRE essay. Of course, you won't know the exact topic of the essay until you get there (just as the builder may not know what color his client is going to paint the living room), but you will have an all-purpose frame on which to construct a great essay no matter what the topic is. We call this frame the template.

Preconstruction

Just as a builder can construct the windows of a house in his workshop weeks before he arrives to install them, so can you pre-build certain elements of your essay. We call this "preconstruction."

In the next two chapters we'll show you how to prepare ahead of time to write essays on two topics that you won't see until they appear on your screen.

ISSUE VERSUS ARGUMENT ESSAY

It is worth noting at this time that the essay section gives you two very distinct writing tasks, and that a failure to appropriately address the question tasks will severely reduce your score.

The Issue Essay

The Issue essay asks for your opinion; you're expected to present your viewpoint on a particular topic and support that viewpoint with various examples. The following is one example of the instructions for the Issue essay:

> You will be given a brief quotation that states or implies an issue of general interest and specific instructions on how to respond to that issue. You will have 30 minutes to plan and compose a response in which you develop a position on the issue according to the specific instructions. A response to any other issue will receive a score of zero.

Make sure that you respond to the specific instructions and support your position on the issue with reasons and examples drawn from such areas as your reading, experience, observations, and/or academic studies.

Note how important it is to specifically address the assignment provided as part of the Issue prompt; not following ETS's directions will make your grader unhappy and result in a poor score on the essay.

The Argument Essay

The Argument essay requires a different type of response. Instead of presenting your own perspective, your job is to critique someone else's argument. You're supposed to address the logical flaws of the argument, not provide your personal opinion on the subject. The following is one example of the directions for the Argument essay:

You will be given a short passage that presents an argument, or an argument to be completed, and specific instructions on how to respond to that passage. You will have 30 minutes to plan and compose a response in which you analyze the passage according to the specific instructions. A response to any other argument will receive a score of zero.

Note that you are NOT being asked to present your own views on the subject. Make sure that you respond to the specific instructions and support your analysis with relevant reasons and/or examples.

In the Argument essay, the emphasis is on writing a logical analysis of the argument, not an opinion piece. It is absolutely essential that you don't confuse the two essay tasks on the GRE.

ETS graders don't expect a perfect essay; occasional spelling, punctuation, and grammar errors won't kill your score.

HOW DOES THE WORD-PROCESSING PROGRAM WORK?

ETS has created a very simple program that allows students to compose their essays on the screen. Compared to any of the commercial word-processing programs, this one is extremely limited, but it does allow the basic functions: You can move the cursor with the arrow keys, and you can delete, copy, and paste. If you're a computer novice, don't worry. You don't have to use any of these functions. With just the backspace key and the mouse to change your point of insertion, you will be able to use the computer like a regular word-processing program.

Take a look at the image below to see what your screen will look like during the Analytical Writing section of the test:

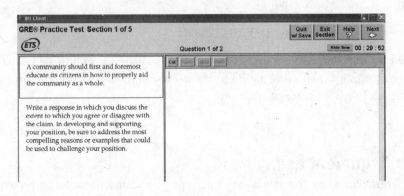

The question will always appear at the top of your screen. Below it, in a box, will be your writing area (in the writing area above, you can see a partially completed sentence). When you click inside the box with your mouse, a winking cursor will appear, indicating that you can begin typing. As we said above, the program supports the use of many of the normal computer keys:

- The "Backspace" key removes text to the left of the cursor.
- The "Delete" key removes text to the right of the cursor.
- The "Arrow" keys move the cursor up, down, left, or right.
- The "Home" key moves the cursor to the beginning of a line.
- The "End" key moves the cursor to the end of a line.
- The "Enter" key moves the cursor to the beginning of the next line.
- "Page up" moves the cursor up one page.
- "Page down" moves the cursor down one page.

You can also use the icons on the right of the screen to copy and paste words, sentences, or paragraphs. To do this, you first have to highlight the desired text by clicking on the starting point with your mouse and holding down the mouse button while you drag it to the ending point. Then click on the "Cut" button. This deletes the text you've selected from the screen, but also stores it in the computer's memory. Next, just move the cursor to wherever you would like the selected text to reappear, and click on the "Paste" button. The selected text will appear in that spot.

If you make a mistake, simply click on the "Undo" button, which will undo whatever operation you have just done. You can undo a cut, a paste, or even the last set of words you've typed in. Unfortunately, unlike many word-processing programs, ETS's program does not have a "Redo" button, so be careful what you decide to undo.

Obviously, the small box on the screen is not big enough to contain your entire essay. However, by hitting the "Page up" and "Page down" keys on your keyboard, or by using the arrows on your keyboard, you will be able to go forward and backward to reread what you have written and make corrections.

Does Spelling Count?

Officially, no. The word-processing program doesn't have a spell checker, and ETS essay readers are supposed to ignore minor errors of spelling and grammar, but the readers wouldn't be human if they weren't influenced by an essay that had lots of spelling mistakes and improper grammar—it gives the impression that you just didn't care enough to proofread.

Because pervasive spelling errors will detract from your score, pick an easier word if you're really uncertain of how to spell a word.

Summary

o Different programs value the essay section in different ways. Check with your program to see how important the essays are.

o Understand the criteria ETS uses when judging your essay. Organization, examples, and language use are important. Perfect grammar and spelling less so.

o On the GRE, longer essays tend to get better scores, so strive to write as much as you can for each essay.

o Make sure you understand the differences in the assignments for the Issue essay and the Argument essay.

o Issue essays ask for your opinion on a topic while argument essays expect you to critique the logic of an argument. The ways in which you're asked to do each of these tasks will vary, so make sure you read each set of directions carefully.

o The word processor ETS provides has only the most basic functions. You can delete, copy, and paste text, but not much more.

Chapter 14
The Issue Essay

The Issue essay of the GRE requires you to present your opinion on the provided topic. This chapter will show you the steps to take in order to write a clear, coherent essay in the limited time provided. You'll learn exactly what sort of things the ETS graders are looking for when they evaluate your essay so you'll know just what to do on test day.

THREE BASIC STEPS

Because you don't have a lot of time to write the essays, you'll need to have a pretty good idea of how you're going to attack them as soon as you sit down at the computer on test day. Our approach to the essays involves three steps. These are:

1.   **Think**. Before you start writing, take a moment to brainstorm some thoughts about the topic.
2.   **Organize**. Take the ideas you've come up with and fit them into the assignment for the prompt.
3.   **Write**. Once you've completed the first two steps, the final step should be a snap.

Thirty minutes is not a lot of time to write an essay, so you have to get it right the first time out. While ETS advises you to leave enough time to proofread and edit your essay, it simply isn't feasible to expect to make any significant changes to your essay during the final minutes of the section. Furthermore, if you get halfway through your essay and realize you're stuck or you're not saying what you need to say, you'll be hard pressed to fix your essay in the time you have left.

It is essential, therefore, to make sure you spend time planning your essay before you start writing. You have to figure out what it is you want to say before you begin; otherwise, you run the risk of writing an incoherent, rambling essay. The first two steps are actually more important to a successful GRE essay than the final step; by spending a little time planning your essay, the actual writing part should be relatively painless.

> The keys to the essay: Think, Organize, Write.

Let's start our discussion of the Issue essay by looking at a typical prompt.

The Prompt

> "True beauty is found not in the exceptional but in the commonplace."
>
> Write an essay in which you take a position on the statement above. In developing and supporting your essay, consider instances in which the statement does and does not hold true.

The prompts are supposed to get you thinking about areas of "general interest," whatever that means. A better way of thinking about the prompt is to look at it as agree/disagree- or pro/con-type statement. Your task in the essay will be to look at both sides of the issue, the pro and the con side, and take a position on the statement. Let's look at how to do that.

You have to know what you want your essay to say before you can start writing.

STEP 1: THINK

"Think" is a pretty broad command, so we need to clarify this step in order to make it more useful. Specifically, we want you to think about three things:

1. **Key Terms**. What are the key words or phrases in the prompt? Do the terms need clarifying before you can properly deal with them in the essay?
2. **Opposite Side**. What would the converse of the statement be?
3. **Examples**. What are some examples that would support the statement? What are some examples that would support the opposite statement?

Let's work through these steps with our sample prompt.

Key Terms

When preparing your essay, you first want to look more closely at the key terms in the prompt. Do they need to be clarified? Are there multiple ways of interpreting the words? In order to make your essay as focused as possible, you might need to limit the key terms to a specific definition or interpretation. If the key terms in the prompt seem pretty straightforward, you still want to note them. By repeatedly returning to these terms in your essay, you'll convey the impression that your essay is strongly organized and on topic.

For the sample prompt above, write down the key terms:

_____

_____

_____

For this prompt, the key terms are *beauty, true, exceptional*, and *commonplace*. We need to think about how we're going to use these terms in our essay. For example, what is *true beauty*? Do we want that to mean just natural beauty or can we consider man-made objects? As for the word *beauty*, do we want to limit our discussion to artistic beauty such as paintings and sculptures, or should we consider poems and literature as well? Should we only discuss natural beauty, such as stars and flowers, or should we consider personal beauty as well, such as models and GRE instructors? As you can see, we could write a lot on this topic, if we had the time. But we don't, so it's important to focus. By defining our key terms, we make the essay a lot more manageable and easier to write in a short amount of time. For this essay, let's include both natural objects and manmade artistic feats, but leave out personal beauty.

Using key terms from the prompt throughout your essay contributes to its overall coherency.

Opposite Side

In order to score well on the Issue essay, you'll have to consider both sides of the prompt. ETS is looking for more than a straightforward "I agree and here's why" or "I disagree and here's why" essay. Rather, the graders want to see you consider both sides of the issue and then defend your position. Take a brief moment to look at the sample prompt, and then write down the converse of the statement.

For this prompt, the opposite side of the argument would be something along the lines of "True beauty is found not in the commonplace, but the exceptional." Note that ETS doesn't have a preference for the pro or con side. So if you find the opposite of the statement more convincing, that's fine. As long as you can support your position with some relevant examples, it doesn't matter what position you take on the prompt. This brings us to the final part of step one—brainstorming examples.

Examples

In many ways, the examples will be the most important part of your essay. Without strong, relevant examples you cannot expect to achieve a high score on the Issue essay. As the instructions state, you should support your position with examples drawn from your reading, experience, observation, and academic studies. In general, the more specific your examples are, the better your essay score. And examples from history, literature, or current events are better than personal observations or experiences. Imagine yourself as an ETS grader (a terrible thought, we know). Which sentence would you respond more favorably to?

"Few observers would doubt the awesome beauty of the ceiling of the Sistine Chapel in Rome, a work of art produced by the great Renaissance artist Michelangelo."

"Few observers would doubt the awesome beauty of the various paintings they see in museums, works of art produced by great artists."

Both sentences essentially say the same thing and use practically the same words. But the first sentence would be graded more favorably by an ETS grader because of the specificity of the example.

Take a moment to jot down some examples for the previous prompt. Make sure you come up with examples for both the original statement and its opposite.

_____

_____

_____

Now take a moment to look over your examples. Are they specific? Are they relevant to the topic? Do they support a position on the topic? The strength of your examples will determine the strength of your argument. It's hard to write a convincing paper with weak examples. Here are some examples that might work for our sample topic, both weaker and stronger:

Okay Example	Better Example
paintings, artwork	Leonardo da Vinci's *Mona Lisa*
buildings, churches	Notre Dame Cathedral in Paris
flowers, natural wonders	Niagara Falls

Avoid hypothetical examples—the more specific your example is, the better.

> Good examples are relevant to the topic and contain specific details.

In each case, the better example is the more specific, more detailed example. Also note that we've avoided any personal examples. While you certainly may feel that your boyfriend or girlfriend is the most beautiful person in the world, that sort of personal example won't resonate with an ETS grader nearly as well as a more academic or global example. Use personal examples only when specifically instructed to by the prompt or as a last resort.

STEP 2: ORGANIZE

Once you've identified the key terms, considered the opposite side of the issue, and generated some examples, it's time to organize your thoughts. Basically, you'll want to do the following:

1. **Separate Your Examples.** How many of your examples support the pro side and how many support the con side? Divide your examples up and see which side has more support.
2. **Write Your Thesis Statement.** After evaluating the strength of your examples, decide what position you will take in your essay, and then write your thesis. Your thesis is the main point that you want your essay to express.

Let's continue the process on the sample prompt.

Separate Your Examples

Do this before you decide on your thesis statement. Even though you might have a strong preference for one position on the issue, you might notice that the examples you brainstormed tend to support the other side of the issue. Don't expend more time trying to think of examples to support your preconceptions; just write your essay supporting the other side! There is no right or wrong response. All that matters is being able to write a strong, coherent essay in a very limited time. Your personal views or beliefs are unimportant to the ETS graders. If we continue with the examples we used earlier, they would probably break down like this:

Pro	Con
natural wonders	*Mona Lisa*
	Notre Dame

Based on some of the examples we've come up with, it looks like we'd be better off supporting the idea that "True beauty is found not in the commonplace, but in the exceptional." While natural wonders like sunsets and flowers are pretty commonplace, we've come up with a lot more exceptional examples. And it looks like we could even argue that it is the exceptional natural wonders, such as Niagara Falls, that are truly beautiful.

Write Your Thesis Statement

Now comes the culmination of all of our work. What point do we want to make about the topic? Write it down here:

_____

Our thesis should probably be something along the lines of this: "While certain commonplace natural objects are examples of beauty, true beauty is most often found in rare, exceptional cases."

Now that we have figured out what we want to say, we can focus on proving why we believe it. But remember, only after working through these steps are we truly ready to write!

It doesn't matter what side of the issue you take on the GRE.

Practice: Steps 1 and 2

Work through steps one and two on the following Issue essay prompts below.

PROMPT 1

> "Genius is nothing more than another term for obsession."
>
> Write an essay in which you take a position on the statement above. In developing and supporting your position, you should consider instances in which the statement is true as well as those in which the statement is false.

On your scratch paper, write the (1) Key Terms, (2) Opposite Side, (3) Examples, and (4) Thesis.

PROMPT 2

> "The proper role of education is to teach facts, not morals."
>
> Write an essay in which you take a position on the statement above. In developing and supporting your position, you should consider cases in which education teaches facts as well as those in which morals are taught.

On your scratch paper, write the (1) Key Terms, (2) Opposite Side, (3) Examples, and (4) Thesis.

Practice: Sample Responses

Obviously, your examples and thesis statements will differ, but these sample responses will give you a good indication of what ETS is looking for.

Prompt 1

Key Terms: Genius and obsession. Are we talking about artistic genius? Or scientific genius? What does the word *obsession* entail? Is it just another word for being crazy?

Opposite Side: "Genius is not just another term for obsession."

Examples: Isaac Newton, who once stuck pins into his own eyes in order to better understand optics; Vincent Van Gogh, who cut off part of his own ear under the stresses of his work; Thomas Edison, who patented over 1,300 different inventions

Thesis: "Many geniuses in both the artistic and scientific fields do demonstrate a form of obsession or mental unbalance."

Prompt 2

Key Terms: What sort of education are we referring to—elementary school, college, business school? What are morals? Are we considering religious viewpoints or just ethical standards?

Opposite Side: "Education should teach morals."

Examples: Law schools, business schools, and medical schools all teach proper ethics for their professions; Trade schools and vocational schools tend to teach only facts; Students can get moral training at home or in a religious institution

Thesis: "Many educational institutions have an obligation to teach morals as well as facts."

STEP 3: WRITE

Now that we know how to prepare for our Issue essay, we can write it. In this section, we'll discuss various templates for essays and show you how you can pre-construct certain portions of your essay. Before we do that though, let's revisit what the readers are looking for from your writing.

What the Readers Want to See

The essay readers will be looking for four characteristics as they skim your Analysis of an Issue essay (at the speed of light). According to ETS, an outstanding essay:

- considers the complexities of the issue
- supports the position with relevant examples
- is clearly well organized
- demonstrates superior facility with the conventions of standard written English, but still with minor flaws.

To put it more simply, the readers are looking for good organization, good supporting examples for whatever position you've taken, and reasonably good use of the English language. We've hopefully taken care of the first two parts, so now we'll deal with the next two.

Essay Essentials

As you learned in sixth-grade composition class, a basic essay has three parts: an introduction, some body paragraphs, and a conclusion. These three things are exactly what ETS wants to see in your Analysis of an Issue essay. Each of these parts has a specific role to play.

1. The **Introduction** should introduce the topic of the essay, discuss the issues surrounding it, and present the essay's thesis.
2. The **Body Paragraphs** should use examples to support the thesis of the essay.
3. The **Conclusion** should summarize the major points of the issue, reiterate the thesis and perhaps consider its implications.

Basically, if you try to think of each paragraph as having a specific job to do, you can pretty much preconstruct each type of paragraph and then fill in the specific details on test day.

The basics of an essay are an introduction, body paragraphs, and a conclusion.

Preconstruction: The Introduction

For the Issue essay, a good introduction accomplishes the following tasks:

> A good introduction:
> 1. Clearly establishes the topic of the paper
> 2. Previews both sides of the issue at hand
> 3. Presents a clear thesis

Let's look at each of these tasks in detail and discuss different ways to accomplish the goals of the introductory paragraph.

Establish the Topic

We want the reader to know what issue the essay is going to talk about. Even though the grader will see the prompt you're writing about, he or she should be able to figure out the prompt just from reading the introduction of your essay. There are a few different ways you can quickly establish the topic, so let's return to our original prompt and preconstruct some approaches.

Don't just restate the prompt! Come up with a strong "hook" for the beginning of your essay.

Here, once again, is our prompt:

> "True beauty is found not in the exceptional but in the commonplace."
>
> Write an essay in which you take a position on the statement above. In developing and supporting your essay, consider instances in which the statement does and does not hold true.

One of the worst ways of establishing the topic is to merely quote the prompt. ETS graders look upon this tactic with disdain, so let's find other ways of starting our essay.

Approach #1: Rhetorical Questions

This is a tried-and-true way of introducing your topic. Instead of simply quoting or paraphrasing the prompt, turn it into a rhetorical question. Here are a few samples:

Where does true beauty lie, in the exceptional or in the commonplace?

Do we find the exceptional more beautiful or the commonplace?

Can we only find beauty in rare, exceptional instances or does it truly lie all around us?

It is immediately clear what topic the essay will explore, from each of these examples of introductory sentences. See if you can come up with a rhetorical question for either this topic or one from the previous drill.

Approach #2: Famous Quotations

Another classic approach to beginning an essay is to use either a well-known saying or a famous quote from someone. Many of the GRE topics are fairly bland, so even if you can't think of a famous quote, there are usually some classic aphorisms you use. Here's what we mean:

"Beauty is Truth and Truth Beauty," or so said the romantic poet John Keats.

A common saying is that beauty is in the eye of the beholder.

Obviously, this type of introduction can be tough to do if something doesn't pop into your head right away. Try to come up with a quote or common saying for this topic or one from the drill.

Approach #3: Anecdote

An anecdote is a brief story. Oftentimes you can grab your reader's attention and introduce the topic with a good anecdote. For example:

It is said that Cezanne, the famed French painter, was so concerned with the beauty of his paintings that he would destroy any of his works that he felt was flawed.

The Romantic poet John Keats was so struck by the beauty of Chapman's translation of Homer's work that he wrote a poem about it.

When using an anecdote you might have to write a sentence or two explaining the relevance of your story. Try out an anecdote for this topic or one of the drill topics.

Approach #4: Fact/Statistic

For some topics, it might be appropriate to start your essay by stating a fact or statistic. ETS graders aren't allowed to penalize you for factual mistakes and they certainly aren't going to fact-check your essay. So don't be afraid if your fact isn't 100 percent accurate. Here's an illustration:

A recent scientific study showed that the faces that people find the most beautiful are those that are the most symmetrical.

Psychologists have demonstrated that people's responses to certain phenomena are based on certain innate mechanisms in the brain.

Give this approach a shot, using this topic or one from the drill.

Approach #5: Definition

One way you may wish to start your essay is by defining one of the key terms from the prompt. For example:

Beauty, by definition, is that which moves us or impacts us significantly.

The "exceptional" typically refers to those things that stand out, which is also a plausible definition for beauty.

The advantage to this approach is that you already spent some time thinking along these lines when you were planning your essay. Come up with a sample introductory sentence for this topic or one of the drill topics.

A good opening line is great to have, but if you're stuck, don't spend an excessive amount of time trying to come up with something clever.

Preview the Issue

Once you've told the reader what the topic is, your next task is to inform the reader of the issues at hand. You want to briefly touch on both sides of the debate, explaining the pros and cons of the prompt. A good way to accomplish this is to make use of strong trigger words—words like *but, despite, while,* and *although.* Here are some examples.

While some people can find beauty in the most common of places, true beauty is only found in the exceptional.

Some would argue that beauty is found everywhere, from the flowers to the stars, but others would state that true beauty is found only in rare, special instances.

Despite the assertions of many that beauty is everywhere, true beauty is found only in exceptional cases.

Although one might argue that many commonplace things are beautiful, it is the exceptional things that possess true beauty.

There can be no doubt that some of the world's most common things are beautiful. And yet, it is often the exceptional objects that possess true beauty.

Practice writing sentences that address both sides of the issue. Use the sample topic or one from the drill.

Present the Thesis

A good thesis tells the reader exactly what your position is and why.

Your final task in the introduction is to present the thesis. Some writers prefer to avoid the first person, refusing to use sentences such as "I believe..." or "I feel..." However, GRE graders will not penalize you for use of the first person. A more important consideration when writing your thesis is giving the reader some indication why you hold your particular position. ETS graders want to see that you've thought about and analyzed the issue. Here are some examples of thesis statements.

I believe that beauty is truly found in the exceptional, not the commonplace, because if common things were beautiful, the very word would lose its meaning.

In my view, beauty is found in the exceptional, not the commonplace. This is because only exceptional things really stand out as special in our minds.

It is clear that true beauty is not to be found in the commonplace but in the exceptional. On closer inspection, even so-called common objects that people consider beautiful are actually exceptional.

After weighing the evidence, it is certain that beauty is the province of the exceptional, not the commonplace. People find true beauty in things that they rarely experience, not the things they experience every day.

For each thesis, you can see that the author is also giving some justification for the viewpoint. This justification will be of course explored more thoroughly in the body paragraphs, but it's good to give the reader a preview of how your essay will take shape. Try writing thesis statements for some of the sample prompts.

Preconstruction: Body Paragraphs

A body paragraph should do the following:

Good body paragraphs:

1. Use a good transition/topic sentence
2. Present an example
3. Explain how the example supports the thesis

Body paragraphs are a little harder to preconstruct because they are the most specific part of the essay. Still, there are some handy tips for creating body paragraphs that an ETS grader will love.

Transition/Topic Sentence

ETS graders love organized essays that flow well. The best way to write an essay like this is to use strong topic sentences and good transitions for each of your body paragraphs. Your topic sentence should serve as a gentle reminder to the reader of what the thesis of the essay is. For example:

One example of beauty found in the exceptional is Leonardo da Vinci's Mona Lisa.

A second instance in which true beauty lies not in the commonplace but in the exceptional is Notre Dame Cathedral in Paris.

Of course, you might want to avoid using simple transitions like "the first example," and "the second example." You can make your writing stronger by leading with the example and making the transition a little more subtle, like so:

Leonardo da Vinci's Mona Lisa *is surely one of the most exceptional, and beautiful, paintings ever created.*

Consider the beauty of Notre Dame Cathedral in Paris, a building that is in no way commonplace.

Or to get even fancier, refer to the previous example in your transition sentence:

Like da Vinci's Mona Lisa, *the cathedral of Notre Dame in Paris is an exceptional, and exceptionally beautiful, object.*

The important point is that each sentence introduces the example and reminds the reader of the purpose of the example, which in this case is to support the notion of beauty as exceptional. In the next few sentences, you'll provide details about your example. It's important that you remember to link the example to your thesis.

Explain How Your Example Supports Your Thesis

Don't just tell the grader about the example; tell the grader why the example is relevant to your thesis.

On the GRE essays, don't get so caught up in providing details for your example that you forget to explain to the reader how or why your example helps your thesis. The purpose of the Issue essay is not to just list out some examples; the purpose is to develop and support a position on the issue. Here's an example of a body paragraph that doesn't quite fulfill that goal:

Like da Vinci's Mona Lisa, *the cathedral of Notre Dame in Paris is an exceptional, and exceptionally beautiful, object. Notre Dame is a stunning example of gothic architecture, famous for the flying buttresses that adorn the sides of the building. The cathedral also has rows and rows of beautiful sculptures recessed into the walls, as well as a gorgeous central stained-glass window. These features make Notre Dame one of the most beautiful cathedrals in the world.*

The writer here did a good job of providing specific details about the example, which ETS graders love. However, the reader failed to explain why Notre Dame supports the view that true beauty is exceptional, not commonplace. Let's fix that:

Like da Vinci's Mona Lisa, *the cathedral of Notre Dame in Paris is an exceptional, and exceptionally beautiful, object. Churches and cathedrals line the streets of most major cities in Western Europe, but few possess the renown of Notre Dame. Notre Dame is a stunning example of gothic architecture, famous for the flying buttresses that adorn the sides of the building. The cathedral also has rows and rows of beautiful sculptures recessed into the walls, as well as a gorgeous central stained-glass window. These features make Notre Dame one of the most beautiful cathedrals in the world. Compared to a common church or cathedral, Notre Dame is truly awe-inspiring; Victor Hugo used the building as the backdrop for his magnificent book* The Hunchback of Notre Dame *and thousands of tourists travel untold miles to view the cathedral. That sort of beauty is not possessed by just any church on the corner.*

This is a stronger body paragraph because it is more explicit in its discussion of the thesis. The author notes that churches and cathedrals are fairly common, but then argues that Notre Dame stands out as an exceptional cathedral. The author concludes the paragraph by showing how Notre Dame is more beautiful than any typical church. Just as a reader should be able to figure out what the topic of the paper is from the introduction, a reader should be able to figure out the thesis from each paragraph.

Write a body paragraph for one of the examples for this sample topic, or one of your examples from the practice. Make sure you have a good topic/transition sentence, specific details for the example, and an explanation of how or why the example is relevant to the thesis.

Preconstruction: Conclusion Paragraphs

Your essay should always have a conclusion, for two reasons. First, a conclusion paragraph is evidence of good organization. It shows the reader that you knew exactly what points you wanted to make, you made them, and now you're ending the essay. And second, an essay that lacks a conclusion seems incomplete, almost as if your writing abruptly ends before it should. This can give the grader a negative impression of your essay. Fortunately, conclusion paragraphs are easy to write. A good conclusion basically:

> A good conclusion:
>
> 1. Alerts the reader that the essay is ending
> 2. Summarizes the main points of the essay

Make sure your essay has a conclusion.

Some test takers even prefer to write their introduction and conclusion first and then fill in the body paragraphs. This strategy has the advantage of making your essay seem complete even if you happen to run out of time writing the body paragraphs.

Alert the Reader

Conclusion paragraphs have their own topic/transition sentences, which generally should contain a word or phrase that tells the reader he or she is reaching the end. Here are some examples:

In conclusion, it's clear that true beauty is found not in the commonplace, but the exceptional.

Ultimately, beauty lies in the exceptional, not the commonplace.

As the bulk of the evidence shows, the exceptional, not the commonplace, possesses true beauty.

Clearly, true beauty is found in exceptional things, not in commonplace ones.

The examples above all support the idea that we find true beauty in exceptional cases, not in commonplace ones.

Write some conclusion sentences for this topic or a sample topic from the somple prompts.

Summarize Main Points

Your conclusion should also summarize the main points of the essay, meaning that it should mention the thesis and how the examples support it. Additionally, you can briefly consider the implications of the thesis. Here are some sample conclusions:

In conclusion, it's clear that true beauty is found not in the commonplace, but the exceptional. The Mona Lisa *and Notre Dame Cathedral are both exceptional examples of fairly commonplace things and it is these exceptions that are noted as truly beautiful. If anything, the commonplace only serves as a contrast to what true beauty really is.*

Ultimately, beauty lies in the exceptional, not the commonplace. While paintings and churches are fairly commonplace, only a small few of them, such as the Mona Lisa *or* Notre Dame, *truly reach the heights of beauty. It is in these exceptions that we find real beauty.*

The examples above all support the idea that we find true beauty in exceptional cases, not in commonplace ones. Common things may seem at first glance to be beautiful, but once we compare these commonplace examples to the truly exceptional ones, we see that the exceptional ones are truly beautiful.

Try your hand at constructing a conclusion paragraph, once again using this topic or one from the sample prompts.

Putting It All Together

Read through this sample essay that's based on the basic five-paragraph model. Then you'll have the chance to try writing a similar essay for a different prompt.

> "True beauty is found not in the exceptional but in the commonplace."
>
> Write an essay in which you take a position on the statement above. In developing and supporting your essay, consider instances in which the statement does and does not hold true.

Beauty, by definition, is that which moves us or impacts us significantly. Some would argue that beauty is found everywhere, from the flowers to the stars. But others would state that true beauty is found only in rare, special instances. After weighing the evidence, it is certain that beauty is the province of the exceptional, not the commonplace. People are moved most by things that they rarely experience, not the things they experience every day.

Those that would argue that true beauty is everywhere might point to the beauty of a flower, or the starlit night. These experiences are certainly common, but do they show that true beauty is commonplace? Flowers might be considered beautiful, but how often does a person stop to look at or appreciate every flower? Flowers are so common that in many cases, they are ignored or viewed as nothing special. However, on those rare occasions—exceptional occasions, one might say—when we want to commemorate an event or express emotion, we notice the beauty of flowers. Thus, it is not the commonplace flower that strikes us as beautiful, but the exceptional situations themselves that move us to appreciate the flower.

Now consider the exceptional. Leonardo da Vinci's Mona Lisa *is surely one of the most exceptional, and beautiful, paintings ever created. Few people who view the painting are not moved by the sheer beauty of it, and the* Mona Lisa *is instantly recognized as a masterpiece of art. And yet, there have been literally millions of paintings produced in human history. Is every single one of them beautiful? Does every one of those paintings have the impact that da Vinci's does? Of course not. In order to find beauty, we must separate the exceptional cases from the common ones. True beauty is such because it stands out from the masses of the average and pedestrian.*

Like da Vinci's Mona Lisa, *the cathedral of Notre Dame in Paris is an exceptional, and exceptionally beautiful, object. Churches and cathedrals line the streets of most major cities in Western Europe, but few possess the renown of Notre Dame, one of the most beautiful cathedrals in the world. Compared to a common church or cathedral, Notre Dame is truly awe-inspiring; Victor Hugo used the building as the backdrop for his magnificent book* The Hunchback of Notre Dame *and thousands of tourists travel untold miles to view the cathedral. That sort of beauty is not possessed by just any church on the corner.*

In conclusion, it's clear that true beauty is found not in the commonplace, but the exceptional. The Mona Lisa *and Notre Dame Cathedral are both exceptional examples of fairly commonplace things and it is these exceptions that are noted as truly beautiful. If anything, the commonplace only serves as a contrast so that we can understand what true beauty really is.*

Your Turn

Try writing a similar essay for the prompt that follows this paragraph. Make sure you consider the opposing side of the argument. Devote a paragraph to looking at an example for the other side of the issue, but make sure you indicate to the reader that there is a flaw in the example or that the example is less than convincing. Set a timer for 30 minutes to practice GRE time constraints.

> "People most respect the powerful not when they exercise their power, but when they refrain from exercising it."
>
> Write an essay in which you develop and support a position on the statement above. In writing your essay, you should consider both when the statement may be true and when it may be false.

How to Score Your Essay

Now it's time to put on your essay-scoring hat and prepare to grade your own essay. If you're lucky enough to have a friend who is also preparing for the GRE, you could switch essays and grade each other's like you used to do in sixth grade. You'll need to be objective during this process. Remember, the only way to improve is to honestly assess your weaknesses and systematically eliminate them.

Set a timer for two minutes. Read the essay carefully but quickly, so that you do not exceed the two minutes on the timer.

Now ask yourself the following questions about the essay:

1. Overall, did it make sense?
2. Did you address the topic directly?
3. Did you address the topic thoroughly?
4. Did your introduction paragraph repeat the issue to establish the topic of the essay?
5. Did you consider both sides of the issue?
6. Did your examples make sense?
7. Did you flesh out your examples with details?
8. Did you explain how your examples supported your thesis?
9. Did your essay have a strong concluding paragraph?
10. Was your essay well organized, using transitions and topic sentences?
11. Did you use language that made the organization of the essay obvious?
12. Did you use correct grammar, spelling, and language, for the most part?

If you could answer "yes" to all or almost all of these questions, congratulations! Your essay would probably receive a score in the 5–6 range. If you continue to practice, and write an essay of similar quality on the real Analysis of an Issue section of the real test, you should score very well.

If you answered "yes" to fewer than 12 of the questions, you have room for improvement. Fortunately, you also know which areas you need to strengthen as you continue to practice.

If you answered "yes" to fewer than 6 of the questions, your essay would probably not score very well on a real GRE. An essay of this quality would not help you in the admissions process and could raise some red flags in the minds of the admissions people. You need to continue to practice, focusing on the areas of weakness that you discovered during this scoring process.

Another Sample Response

Take a look at a high scoring response to the prompt you just practiced on. Your essay might look different and that's fine. This is just one of many ways to successfully complete the Issue essay assignment.

> "The powerful are most respected not when they exercise their power, but when they refrain from exercising it."
>
> Write an essay in which you develop and support a position on the statement above. In writing your essay, you should consider both when the statement may be true and when it may be false.

What aspect of power engenders the greatest respect? Some would argue that power inspires respect only by its ability to change things or bring about results. This camp respects the powerful only when they demonstrate their power by raising a massive army or bestowing charity on the less fortunate. Others believe that the true measure of power lies not in what it is used for, but in how it is restrained. These people believe that people most respect the powerful when they choose not to use their power, such as granting clemency to a criminal on death row or allowing critics of the government to speak out.

Consider first the respect people hold for the exercise of power. One of the mightiest displays of power is the ability to protect and safeguard people and property and this aspect of government is what many people respect. Indeed, in Hobbes's Leviathan, *he argued that one of the reasons people sacrifice themselves for the good of the state is to preserve the power of the state to protect its members from outside attacks. And one of the stated goals of the United States massive military buildup was so that other countries would either "love us or fear us." Thus, it is clear that people have respect for displays of power. Similarly, the ability of the powerful to bestow gifts of charity on the less fortunate is also well respected. The names of philanthropists like Carnegie and Rockefeller are held in high esteem because they used their power to help those less fortunate than themselves.*

On the other hand, the ability to show restraint can also engender respect. Recently, the governor of Illinois decided to commute the death sentences of all the prisoners on death row. Such an act of clemency brought high praise from human rights proponents around the world. Furthermore, the fact that democratic governments allow dissent when they could in many cases censor or squash unfavorable opinions also lends credence to the view that restraint of power is what people respect. For example, the arbitrary arrest and sentencing of political dissidents in Russia has brought much international criticism of the Kremlin, while countries that support freedom of speech and the press are widely respected in the world.

Ultimately, after considering both sides of the issue, it must be concluded that the exercise of power is most respected. This because even in cases of restraint, the entity in power is still exercising its power.

Granting clemency is only possible because the state holds the power of life and death. Allowing dissent is only exceptional because the government has the power to crush it. Thus, it is not the restraint of power that people most respect, it is the exercise of it.

FINAL THOUGHTS: WHAT TO DO WITH YOUR TIME

Now that you know how to construct your essay, you have to practice writing essays in a mere 30 minutes. Here's a guideline for how to use your time:

Your essay doesn't have to be perfect. Focus on the big picture.

- Find key terms, state opposite side, brainstorm examples: 5–7 minutes
- Formulate thesis: 2 minutes
- Write essay: 18–20 minutes
- Proofread: 1–2 minutes

Notice that not a lot of time is allotted for proofreading. Remember that it's okay to have minor spelling and grammatical errors. Your time is better spent making sure you consider both sides of the issue completely and write an effective essay. For tons more practice, you can go to **ETS.org** for the complete list of essay topics.

Summary

- Follow the three simple steps to essay success: Think, Organize, Write.

- One of the keys to high scoring essays is good examples. Make sure your examples are relevant to the topic and as specific as possible.

- Try to use examples drawn from your readings, current events, literature, and history. Avoid personal examples.

- Spice up your writing by employing an interesting "hook" to get your readers attention. Consider using such hooks as rhetorical questions, quotes, anecdotes, facts and statistics, and other attention getting devices.

- A good GRE essay presents a smooth flow of ideas and examples. Make sure you use transitions to help your reader follow the progression of ideas in your essay.

- Templates can be effective ways of organizing your essay, but don't feel restricted to them. Come up with your own template or modify the existing templates as you see fit.

Chapter 15
The Argument Essay

The Argument essay of the GRE asks you to examine and critique the logic of an argument. The arguments you will see in this chapter are similar to the ones you worked with earlier in the book and you will need to use the same approach to breaking these arguments down. This chapter will show you how to organize and write an essay once you've found the premises, conclusion, and assumptions of a GRE argument.

You'll be able to use all the skills we've discussed for the Analysis of an Issue essays on this type of essay as well, but in a slightly different way. Instead of asking for your opinion on a topic, the Analysis of an Argument essay asks you to critique someone else's argument. Before we jump into setting up templates and other pre-construction steps, let's take a look at how Analytical Writing arguments work.

THE PARTS OF AN ARGUMENT

As seen in the Critical Reasoning portion in Chapter 6, an argument, for GRE purposes, is a short paragraph in which an author introduces a topic and uses reasoning or factual evidence to back up his or her opinion about that topic.

A really simplified example of an argument could be:

> *My car broke down yesterday, and I need a car to get to work. Therefore, I should buy a new car.*

The car argument above is composed of three parts:

- The conclusion—the author's opinion and recommendation for action
- The premises—the facts the author uses to back up his or her opinion
- The assumptions—unstated conditions that must be true in order for the argument to make sense

In this argument, the author's conclusion is "I should buy a new car."

The premises the author uses to support this conclusion are that his car broke down yesterday, and that he needs a car to get to work.

The premises must support the conclusion the way table legs support a tabletop. The tabletop is the most obvious and useful part of a table—you see more of it, and you can put things on it. But without the legs to hold it up, it's just a slab of wood on the floor. The same is true for the conclusion of an argument. The conclusion is the part that gets all the attention, since it recommends some course of action, but without the premises to support the conclusion, the conclusion won't hold up.

Conclusion Words

Certain words indicate a conclusion:

- so
- therefore
- thus
- hence
- showed that

- clearly
- then
- consequently
- as a result
- concluded that

When you see these words, you can be pretty sure that you've found the conclusion of the argument.

Premise Words

Certain words indicate premises:

- because
- since
- if
- given that

- in view of
- in light of
- assume

ASSUMPTIONS

An assumption is an unstated premise that supports the author's conclusion. It's the connection between the stated premises and the conclusion. In the example of the table, the assumption is that nails or glue hold the legs and the tabletop together. Without the glue or nails, the table will fall apart. Without the assumption, the argument will fall apart.

Sometimes the assumption is described as the *gap* between the facts that make up the premises and the conclusion. They don't always connect, so the assumption is the gap between them.

Let's take a look back at the car argument:

> *My car broke down yesterday, and I need a car to get to work. Therefore, I should buy a new car.*

The premises are that my car broke down yesterday and I need a car to get to work. The conclusion is that I should buy a new car.

When you first read this argument, you may have had some questions. These questions might have been along the lines of "Why can't the author just rent a car?" or "Why can't the author just fix the car?"

As you read an argument, identifying the premises and conclusion, questions may pop into your head. Those questions are pointing out the gap that leads to the assumption. Here, the gap is between having a broken car and still needing a car to get to work on the one side, and having to buy a new car on the other side.

Therefore, the assumption must be:
There is no other way to have a car.

There are all sorts of smaller assumptions here—that the car can't be fixed, that a car can't be rented, that there's no other car the author can borrow—but those are all covered in the main assumption.

The assumption fills the gap between the premises and conclusion, and, in fact, functions as an unstated premise:
My car broke down yesterday, and I need a car to get to work. There is no other way to have a car. Therefore, I should buy a new car.

Brainstorming for the Argument Essay consists primarily of coming up with a list of assumptions.

Three Common Types of Arguments and Their Assumptions

As outlined in Chapter 6, there are three types of arguments you are likely to see. They are Sampling, Analogy, and Causal. Becoming familiar with these three types will help you identify the assumptions in the argument more quickly when the clock is ticking on the real test.

1. The Sampling Assumption

A sampling argument assumes that A is equal to A, B, and C, or that a small group is representative of a much larger group to which it belongs. To attack a sampling argument, show that one cannot assume that the opinions or experiences of the smaller group are not necessarily representative of the larger group.

2. The Analogy Assumption

An argument by analogy assumes that A = B or that what is true for one entity will be true for another. To attack an argument by analogy, simply show that the two groups or places or individuals are nothing like each other. What is true for one does not have to be true of the other.

3. The Causal Assumption

A causal argument assumes that A causes B, or that if you remove the cause, you will remove the effect. While there may be a strong correlation between A and B, it does not always follow that it is a causal relationship or that A is the cause of B.

To attack a causal relationship, point out that there are other possible causes for B and brainstorm some possible examples.

Well, Great, But Why Do I Care?

You should care about taking apart the argument, and finding the assumptions in particular, because the key to writing a great Argument essay on the Analytical Writing section is ripping apart the argument.

Think about it. The official instructions on the test ask you to "critique" the author's argument. However, if you claim that everything the author says makes sense, you won't be able to write an essay that's more than a few sentences long. This means that in order to write a great essay, you'll need to tear the author's argument apart.

> **Danger:** The most common mistake people make in writing the Argument essay is expressing their own opinions. Don't do this! The Issue essay specifically asks you to give an opinion and then back it up. The Argument essay wants a critique of someone else's opinion, not your own.

WRITING THE ARGUMENT ESSAY

Writing the Analysis of an Argument essay requires a series of steps.

Step 1: Read the topic and identify the conclusion and the premises.

Step 2: Since they're asking you to critique (i.e., weaken) the argument, concentrate on identifying its assumptions. Look for gaps in the argument, weaknesses in the logic, and new information in the conclusion that wasn't present in the premises. Brainstorm as many different assumptions as you can think of. Write these out on your scratch paper or on the computer screen.

Step 3: Select three or four of the strongest assumptions around which to build your essay.

Step 4: Choose a template that allows you to attack the assumptions in an organized way.

Step 5: Write the essay, using all the tools and techniques that you'll be learning in this chapter.

Step 6: Read over the essay and edit it.

You will have 30 minutes to plan and compose a response to the argument topic, so make sure to budget your time wisely.

WHAT THE READERS ARE LOOKING FOR

In the Analysis of an Argument topic section, your job is to critique the argument's line of reasoning and the evidence supporting it and to suggest ways in which the argument could be strengthened. Again, you aren't required to know any more about the subject than would any normal person—but you must be able to spot logical weaknesses. Make absolutely sure you have read and understood the previous section about taking apart the argument and that you can take apart all the arguments in the drills in that section.

Your opinion is not the point in an Analysis of an Argument Essay.

The essay readers will be looking for four things as they skim through your Analysis of an Argument essay at the speed of light. According to a booklet prepared by ETS, "An outstanding argument essay...clearly identifies and insightfully analyzes important features of the argument; develops ideas cogently, organizes them logically, and connects them smoothly with clear transitions; effectively supports the main points of the critique; and demonstrates superior control of language, including diction, syntactic variety, and the conventions of standard written English. There may be minor flaws."

To put it more simply, the readers will be looking for all the same things they were looking for in the Analysis of an Issue essay, plus one extra ingredient: a cursory knowledge of the rules of logic.

Doing the Actual Analysis of the Argument

In any Analytical Writing argument, the first thing you should do is separate the conclusion from the premises.

Let's see how this works with an actual essay topic. The following is the Analysis of an Argument topic you saw before:

Topic:

Save the fancy prose for English class! Your grader cares more that you can identify the parts of the argument than for a clever turn of phrase.

> The director of the International Health Foundation recently released this announcement:
>
> "A new medical test that allows the early detection of a particular disease will prevent the deaths of people all over the world who would otherwise die from the disease. The test has been extremely effective in allowing doctors to diagnose the disease six months to a year before it would have been spotted by conventional means. As soon as we can institute this test as routine procedure in hospitals around the world, the death rate from this disease will plummet."

The conclusion in this argument comes in the first line:

> *A new medical test that allows the early detection of a particular disease will prevent the deaths of people all over the world who would otherwise die from that disease.*

The premises are the evidence in support of this conclusion.

> *The test has been extremely effective in allowing doctors to diagnose the disease six months to a year before it would have been spotted by conventional means.*

The assumptions are the unspoken premises of the argument—without which the argument would fall apart. Remember that assumptions are often causal, analogical, or statistical. What are some assumptions of this argument? Let's brainstorm.

Brainstorming for Assumptions

You can often find assumptions by looking for a gap in the reasoning. "Medical tests allow early detection": According to the conclusion, this medical test leads to the early detection of the disease. There doesn't seem to be a gap here.

"Early detection allows patients to survive": In turn, the early detection of the disease allows patients to survive the disease. Well, hold on a minute. Is this necessarily true?

- First, do we know that early detection will *necessarily* lead to survival? We don't even know if this disease is curable. Early detection of an incurable disease is not going to help anyone survive it.
- Second, will the test be widely available and cheap enough for general use? If the test is expensive or only available in certain parts of the world, people will continue to die from the disease.
- Third, will doctors and patients interpret the tests correctly? The test may be fine, but if doctors misinterpret the results or if patients ignore the need for treatment, then the test will not save lives.

"Death rate will plummet": There's a huge gap here in that there's absolutely no explanation of how merely detecting the disease will immediately cause the death rate from it to plummet. This area is ripe for exploration.

The arguments provided
for the writing assessment
of the GRE typically con-
tain more flaws than those
you worked with in the
multiple-choice section.
The flaws are often easier
to spot as well.

Organizing the Analysis of an Argument Essay

We're now ready to put this into a ready-made template. In any Analysis of an Argument essay, the template structure should be pretty straightforward: You're simply going to reiterate the argument, attack the argument in three different ways (each in a separate paragraph), summarize what you've said, and mention how the argument could be strengthened. From an organizational standpoint, this is pretty easy. Try to minimize your use of the word *I*. Your opinion is not the point in an Analysis of an Argument essay.

A Sample Template

Of course, you will want to develop your own template for the Analysis of an Argument essay, but to get you started, here's one possible structure:

The argument that (restatement of the conclusion) is not entirely logically

convincing, since it ignores certain crucial assumptions.

First, the argument assumes that _____

_____ .

Second, the argument never addresses _____

_____ .

Finally, the argument omits _____

_____ .

Thus, the argument is not completely sound. The evidence in support of the

conclusion _____ .

Ultimately, the argument might have been strengthened by _____

_____ .

The key to succeeding on an Analysis of an Argument essay is to critique the argument clearly..

How Would the Result of Our Brainstorming Fit into the Template?

Here's how the assumptions we came up with for this argument would fit into the template:

> The argument that the new medical test will prevent deaths that would have occurred in the past is not entirely logically convincing since it ignores certain crucial assumptions.
>
> First, the argument assumes that early detection of the disease will lead to an immediate drop in the mortality rate from this disease, yet it does nothing to explain how this will happen, etc.
>
> Second, the argument never addresses the point that the existence of this new test, even if totally effective, is not the same as the widespread use of the test, etc.
>
> Finally, even supposing the ability of early detection to save lives and the widespread use of the test, the argument still depends on the doctors' correct interpretation of the test and the patients' willingness to undergo treatment, etc.
>
> Thus, the argument is not completely sound. The evidence in support of the conclusion that the test will cause death rates to plummet does little to prove that conclusion, since it does not address the assumptions already raised. Ultimately, the argument might have been strengthened if the author could have shown that the disease responds to early treatment, which can be enacted immediately upon receipt of the test results, that the test will be widely available around the world, and that doctors and patients will make proper use of the test.

Customizing Your Analysis of an Argument Template

Your organizational structure may vary in some ways, but it will always include the following elements: The first paragraph should sum up the argument's conclusion. The second, third, and fourth paragraphs will attack the argument and the supporting evidence. The last paragraph should summarize what you've said and state how the argument could be strengthened. Here are some alternate ways of organizing your essay:

Variation 1

1st paragraph: Restate the argument.

2nd paragraph: Discuss the link (or lack thereof) between the conclusion and the evidence presented in support of it.

3rd paragraph: Show three holes in the reasoning of the argument.

4th paragraph: Show how each of the three holes could be plugged up by explicitly stating the missing assumptions.

Variation 2

1st paragraph: Restate the argument and say it has three flaws.

2nd paragraph: Point out a flaw and show how it could be plugged up by explicitly stating the missing assumption.

3rd paragraph: Point out a second flaw and show how it could be plugged up by explicitly stating the missing assumption.

4th paragraph: Point out a third flaw and show how it could be plugged up by explicitly stating the missing assumption.

5th paragraph: Summarize and conclude that because of these three flaws, the argument is weak.

Write Your Own Template for the Argument Topic Here

1st paragraph:

2nd paragraph:

3rd paragraph:

4th paragraph:

5th paragraph:

You Are Ready to Write an Argument Essay

You've separated the conclusion from the premises. You've brainstormed for the gaps that weaken the argument. You've noted how the premises support (or don't support) the conclusion. Now it's time to write your essay. Start typing, indenting each of the four or five paragraphs. Use all the tools you've learned in this chapter. Remember to keep an eye on the time. Again, if you have a minute at the end, read over your essay and do any editing that's necessary.

What To Do with Your Time

Now that you know how to construct your essay, you have to practice writing essays in a mere 30 minutes. Here's a guideline for how to use your time:

- Break down the argument: 3–4 minutes
- Find 2–3 assumptions: 3–4 minutes
- Write essay: 18–20 minutes
- Proofread: 1–2 minutes

Notice that not a lot of time is allotted for proofreading. Remember that it's okay to have minor spelling and grammatical errors. Your time is better spent making sure you consider both sides of the issue completely and write an effective essay.

Practice: Writing an Argument Essay

Practice on the following sample argument topic. If you have access to a computer, turn it on and start up a word-processing program (again, you may want to use a very rudimentary one like Notepad to simulate the ETS program you'll see on the real test). Then set a timer for 30 minutes. In that time, read the topic, brainstorm in the space provided in this book, then type your essay into the computer.

A Sample Argument

> The market for the luxury-goods industry is on the decline. Recent reports show that a higher unemployment rate, coupled with consumer fears, has decreased the amount of money the average household spends on both essential and nonessential items, but especially on nonessential items. Since luxury goods are, by nature, nonessential, this market will be the first to decrease in the present economic climate, and luxury retailers should refocus their attention to lower-priced markets.

Conclusion:

Why? (premises)

Assumptions:

When writing your essay, make sure to use terms like "causative," "analogy," "sampling" and so forth. Nothing impresses an ETS grader like a sentence like "The argument assumes the sample is representative."

Ways you can pull the argument apart:

Ways the argument could be made more compelling:

Now use the template you developed earlier in this chapter to type your essay on the computer.

How to Score Your Essay

It's time to put on your essay-scoring hat and prepare to grade your own essay. (Again, if you're lucky enough to have a friend who is also preparing for the GRE, you could switch essays.) You'll need to be objective about the process. Remember, the only way to improve is to honestly assess your weaknesses and systematically eliminate them.

Set a timer for two minutes. Read the essay carefully but quickly, so that you do not exceed the two minutes on the timer.

Now ask yourself the following questions about the essay:

1. Overall, did it make sense?
2. Did you address the argument directly?
3. Did you critique the argument thoroughly?
4. Did your introduction paragraph repeat the argument to establish the topic of the essay?
5. Did you avoid injecting your own opinion into the essay?
6. Did your essay have three strong paragraphs critiquing the arguments?
7. Did your critiques make sense?
8. Did you flesh out your points to make the weaknesses of the argument explicit?
9. Did the examples apply directly to the topic?
10. Did the essay have a strong conclusion paragraph?
11. Was the essay well organized?
12. Did you use language that made the organization of the essay obvious?
13. Did you use correct grammar, spelling, and language, for the most part?
14. Was the essay of an appropriate length (four to five paragraphs of at least three sentences each)?

If you could answer "yes" to all or almost all of those questions, congratulations! Your essay would receive a score in the 5–6 range. If you continue to practice, and write an essay of similar quality on the Analysis of an Argument essay on the real test, you should score very well.

If you answered "yes" to fewer than 12 of the questions, you have room for improvement. Fortunately, you also know which areas you need to strengthen as you continue to practice.

If you answered "yes" to fewer than 5 of the questions, your essay would not score very well on a real GRE. You need to continue to practice, focusing on the areas of weakness that you discovered during this scoring process.

There are more Argument topics for you to practice in the back of this book, but if you'd like to practice even more, go to **www.gre.org** and view the list of real Argument topics. You cannot possibly practice writing essays on all of these real ETS topics, so don't even try. However, you should spend time reading through them to become familiar with the variety of topics that ETS may give you.

Just Keep Practicing

So now you've read everything you need to know about writing high-scoring essays on the GRE. With a little practice, writing these essays should become second nature, and you'll find yourself sitting at the word processor on test day confident and prepared. Keep it up!

Summary

- o Always start by identifying the conclusion of the argument.

- o Look for the common types of arguments: Sampling, Analogy, and Causal.

- o Brainstorm all of the assumptions that attach the premises to the conclusion.

- o Outline your essay on your scratch paper before you start writing.

- o Leave yourself two minutes to proofread your essay once you are done writing.

Part V
Answers and
Explanations to
Drills and Practice
Sets

CHAPTER 4: TEXT COMPLETIONS

Practice: Finding the Clue (Page 50)

1. Your words: *bad, tortured, negative;* Underline: *reflected in the harrowing nature*

2. Your words: *highest, lofty, tallest;* Underline: *second highest mountain in the world, reaching more than 28,000 feet high*

3. Your words: *dangerous, deadly, deleterious;* Underline: *wind-chill warning, minus 25 degrees Fahrenheit or lower*

4. Your words: *leftovers, remnants, remains;* Underline: *70-year-old from World War II*

5. Your words: *distinct, different, dissimilar;* Underline: *mammoths were hairy with long tusks, while mastodons had low-slung bodies and flatter skulls*

6. Your words: *practical, pragmatic, apolitical;* Underline: *he crafted his policies not with an eye toward their political consequences but instead toward their practical effects*

7. Your words: *amount, volume, preponderance;* Underline: *he imagined that he'd have to read for hours and hours each day to finish it all*

8. Your words: *derived, obtained, borrowed;* Underline: *from the Arabic word "Algol."*

Practice: Clues and Triggers (Page 53)

1. Your words: *poor, disastrous, bad;* Underline: *top talents, ended his career;* Circle: *but*

2. Your words: *praise, accolades, thanks;* Underline: *she brokered a diplomatic solution to a potential crisis;* Circle: *work; she*

3. Your words: *healthful, beneficial, good;* Underline: *detrimental to one's health;* Circle: *While*

4. Your words: *disconnected, separate, apart;* Underline: *technological connectivity;* Circle: *Despite*

5. Your words: *graceful, beautiful, positive;* Underline: *ugliness and clumsiness;* Circle: *Although*

6. Your words: *gauge, sign, portent;* Underline: *use holiday sales to gauge future stock prices;* Circle: *prices; thus*

7. Your words: *negativity, animosity, antagonism;* Underline: *ironic, negative view;* Circle: *while, rarely*

8. Your words: *toxicity, danger, hazards;* Underline: *devastating effects on insects;* Circle: *insects; unfortunately*

Text Completions Drill (Page 56)

1. **B sorrow**

   The trigger *despite* tells you to change direction from the clues *smile* and *jauntily*. The blank must be something sad. Only *sorrow* fits. *Jubilance* and *liveliness* are the opposite of what would fit the blank. *Vision* is not a change of direction from *smile*.

2. **D scant**

   Ruthless is your clue here. Whether they're capitalists or sharecroppers, *ruthless* people would have *little* regard for others. *Mixed* and *inconsistent* imply variations in the capitalists' feelings, so toss those choices. Meanwhile, *undue* and *obtrusive* are extreme and take the sentence in the wrong direction. *Scant* fits best.

3. **C static**

   The semicolon in this sentence acts as a same-direction trigger, which indicates that what follows should continue the idea of "stability versus change." To keep the flow, you'll need replacement words for the opposing pair in the first clause. You already have *different* to stand in for *change*; you'll need a word that describes *stability* to go in the blank. Try *stable* and use POE. An even shorter way to crack this is to use the trigger word *yet*, which tells you that the word in the blank contrasts with *different*. In either case, *static* is the only choice that makes sense.

4. **E prodigious**

   The clue in this sentence is "property values and industrial output…rose exponentially," which tells you the ripples were *large*. *Persistent* doesn't address the rise in values and output, while neither *invaluable* nor *incredulous* makes sense in the blank's context. *Severe*, in contrast, implies a negative economic outcome, something unlikely if values and output were increasing

5. **B stolidity**

   The clue in the sentence is *inured*, which means toughened to the point where one doesn't respond. If the voters are inured, then they would not have a strong reaction, so a good word for the blank might be *stoicism* or *ambivalence*. *Stolidity* is the best answer. Eliminate *amazement*, *exasperation*, and *alarm* because they don't fit. They're not confused by the tax, so eliminate *perplexity*.

6. **A contradiction**

   The clue is "division between child-rearing goals." Therefore, find a word similar to *discrepancy*. *Contradiction* is the closest match for *discrepancy*.

Text Completions Practice Set (Page 63)

1. **E scrumptious**

   The trigger *although* tells you to change direction from the clue "did not appeal." Sean expected the donuts to be gross, but he found them tasty. Look for an answer that means *tasty* or *yummy*. Only *scrumptious* matches. *Unappetizing*, *detestable*, and *bland* are the opposite of *yummy*. Although Sean may have been *gleeful*, the donuts themselves would not be.

2. **A timid** and **F upset**

    Try working with the second blank first. The clue is "using recorded bird calls makes the California gnatcatcher… easier to observe." The trigger *although* reverses the direction of the clue. Therefore, find a word similar to *disturb*. Eliminate *direct* and *increase* because they go in the wrong direction. The clue for the first blank is "easier to observe." Thus, the recorded calls must make the bird less *hard to observe*. Only *timid* goes in the right direction.

3. **C hostile** and **D obvious**

    The word *however* is a trigger that tells you that the sentence changes direction. It's likely that sparring between two lawyers would appear negative in some way and that "the friendship" will be described positively. *Hostile* sparring is a direct contrast to an *obvious* friendship.

4. **B inhibits, E thrived,** and **I abandoned**

    The three blanks work together to complete the sentence. Socialism "emphasizes collective ownership of the means of production," which would likely hurt individual expression. Put *limits* in the first blank; *inhibits* is only choice that goes in the right direction. Given this information, individualism would decrease if socialism persists and likely increase if socialism is given up. Find a pair of words for the second and third blanks that fits one of these options. Only *diminished* and *abandoned* make sense together.

5. **B casual, D employing,** and **I discarding**

    Start with the second blank. The clue "tool users" tells you the blank means *use*. Only *employing* fits. For the first blank, if humans used whatever sticks and stones seemed *convenient*, then they were pretty lazy or impromptu tools users. Only *casual* fits. For the third blank, these casual humans would use the tool, but then get rid of it when they were finished. So, look for a word that means *to throw away*. Only *discarding* fits. *Annihilating* is too extreme.

6. **A flamboyant**

    The colon is a punctuation trigger that indicates that the clue is almost certain to follow. The clue is "attended fashionable parties, wore flashy clothing, and dated other men's wives." You need a word that encapsulates all of this. *Flamboyant* is the best choice.

7. **C maladroit** and **E tyro**

    The clue for the first blank comes in the phrase "the initial sense of awkwardness." Thus, developing a new skill should feel *awkward*, making *maladroit* the best choice. For the second blank, *however* acts as a trigger word before "is usually ephemeral," signaling the reversal of the beginner's awkward phase; taken together with "is usually ephemeral" and "soon gives way to mastery," it becomes even clearer that the last blank needs a word that indicates the status of someone learning a new skill. The only word that comes close is *tyro*.

8. **B tautology** and **E prestidigitation**

    The primary clue for the first blank is the phrase "A is A"; a statement declaring that something is itself is a *tautology*. For the second blank, there are two main clues: The speakers mentioned in the second sentence are said to *substitute in different concepts* in a manner *worthy of a stage magician*. These phrases suggest that the speakers are engaging in a sort of verbal *sleight of hand*, which is also known as *prestidigitation*. *Peregrination* means wandering, while a *peroration* is the concluding part of a speech—and while rhetoric is the subject of this passage, there is no textual support for this choice.

9. **B** quotidian

The clue is "tremendous humanitarian consequence." The trigger is *however*, which reverses the direction of the clue. Therefore, find a word similar to *mundane*. *Fascinating* does not mean *mundane*. If you don't know *quotidian*, you can still use POE to narrow the choices. Choices (A) and (D) clearly do not mean *mundane*, nor do answer choices (C) and (E).

10. **B** complaisant and **D** meddlesome

Begin with the first sentence. The clue is that "Gomez seemed a pleasing combination." Notice the trigger word *and* following *affable*. The clue and trigger together mean that something positive and complementary to affable should go in the first blank. Choose *complaisant*. Whatever goes in the second blank can't be good, because the trigger *however* reverses the nice things said about Gomez in the first sentence, and *officious* is negative. Choose *meddlesome* for the second blank.

CHAPTER 5: SENTENCE EQUIVALENCE

Sentence Equivalence Drill (Page 71)

1. **C** modern and **E** contemporary

The trigger *or* tells you to change direction from the clue *ancient*. Look for words that mean *modern*. *Modern* and *contemporary* are the only words that mean modern. *Antiquated* and *archaic* are the opposite of what's needed. *Perceptive* and *astute* are a good trap pair because they are similar in meaning and fit the incorrect clue of *observer*, but you don't know that ancient observers were not perceptive or astute.

2. **D** innate and **F** instinctive

The blank refers to personality characteristics that interest researchers. The clue is "those that arise through experience." The use of *compared to* indicates that the blank is the opposite of the clue, so the blank has to mean *inborn*. *Innate* and *instinctive* have the same meaning as *inborn*. The other words don't fit the meaning.

3. **A** aberrant and **D** unconventional

The blank refers to Mackenzie King's behavior. The clue is "often used séances to contact his dead pet dog for advice," which would be an *abnormal* behavior. *Aberrant* and *heretical* are the only words with a similar meaning. *Repulsive* and *lackluster* don't fit. *Poised* and *decorous* describe appropriate or formal behavior, so they are more nearly opposites of what's needed.

4. **B** dynamic and **F** fluctuating

The clue *adaptability* and list of examples tell you that the conditions must be *changing*. *Dynamic* and *fluctuating* fit this meaning. None of the other choices fit. *Inveterate* means persisting. *Timorous* and *cowed* mean that the conditions of life are fearful. *Turgid* means complex.

5. **B commandeer** and **F appropriate**

The main clue is that the armed forces were "without an adequate number of vehicles of their own," strongly suggesting that they were looking to get some more. Secondary clues are that time was of the essence—"days after Hurricane Zelda had passed"—and the very fact that the subject of the sentence is *armed forces*, a group capable of taking what it wants. This all adds up to something like *seize* for the blank. *Commandeer* and *appropriate* (the verb, not the adjective) both mean this; none of the other words does.

Sentence Equivalence Practice Set (Page 76)

1. **B *affinity*** and **F *predilection***

The word in the blank is used to describe Jim's feelings for gumdrops. The clues "enjoyed all kinds of candy" and "his absolute favorite" indicates that the blank means *liking*. Both *affinity* and *predilection* mean *liking*. *Odium* and *disregard* go in the wrong direction. *Container* might sound right, but it is not related to the clue. *Nature* does not mean liking.

2. **A *fiasco*** and **B *debacle***

The blank concerns the Wright brothers' first attempt at flying. The clue is that they "subsequent efforts similarly ended in failure." Recycle the clue, and put *failure* in the blank. *Fiasco* and *debacle* are the best matches. *Triumph* and *feat* have the opposite meaning. *Hindrance* isn't close enough, and *precedent* doesn't mean failure.

3. **D *diminishes*** and **F *wanes***

The clue "due to the additional demands" suggests that fuel efficiency is likely to decrease as speed increases. *Diminishes* and *wanes* both mean decreases. Eliminate *equalizes* and *stabilizes* because they mean the fuel efficiency evens out. *Adapts* and *increases* don't fit the clue, and neither has a synonym among the other answer choices.

4. **B *malicious*** and **F *churlish***

The trigger *belied* tells you to change direction from the clue "outwardly amiable disposition." He seems friendly and nice, but he is actually unfriendly and mean, as the actions described in the second part of the sentence attest. *Malicious* and *churlish* fit this meaning. *Gregarious* and *affable* are opposite of unfriendly and mean. *Innocuous* and *insipid* don't go in the right direction—he is bad, not bland.

5. **A *servile*** and **C *obsequious***

This asks what a language with *humble* and *honorific* forms of speech might sound like "to an ear accustomed to more egalitarian phrasings," one from a culture in which one is generally free to address others as equals. Such self-abasing forms of speech might sound *overly deferential* or just *too polite*. This leaves *servile* and *obsequious* as the correct answers, both of which connote excessive humility. *Circumspect* is close, but it has more to do with being careful about revealing information rather than with being careful about showing respect. The other possibilities do describe speech but are otherwise not close to what the sentence calls for.

CHAPTER 6: READING COMPREHENSION

Reading Comprehension Drill (Page 105)

1. **C**

   According to the last paragraph, "To move beyond subsistence level farming, new ways to transport excess crops to market had to be found. The development of canal systems as well as an expanded and improved roadway system facilitated transportation." In other words, the infrastructure of canal systems and roadways allowed excess goods to be more easily transported and made it possible for the revolution to take hold.

2. **A**

   According to the passage, "The term 'revolution' has been reserved by most historians for social upheaval characterized by bloodshed, the use of force, and great technological change." The author goes on to state that he agrees with Cornwall that "the term can be extended to apply to the massive agricultural transformation that took place in the mid- to late- eighteenth century." We can infer from this statement that historians generally did not view agricultural changes as revolutionary. Answer choice (B) is incorrect because the second paragraph notes that the practice of enclosure facilitated the agricultural revolution. Answer choice (C), with the use of the term *disastrous*, is too extreme. No evidence is provided in the passage to support choices (D) or (E).

3. **"To combat soil exhaustion, farmers would be required…"**

   This provides a great lead word to help you find the answer—*communal*. If you search for the word *communal* in the passage, you will see that it states, "Prior to the mid-eighteenth century, farming was a *communal* activity in which the entire village decided what, where, and when to plant." The next sentence tells us the problems inherent in communal farming.

4. **A**

   The author says that "Robert Cornwall cogently argues…," and the rest of the passage explains why Cornwall was right. Thus, you can infer the meaning of *cogently* from the passage; it means *convincingly*. Therefore, the best answer is choice (A).

5. **B**

   Choice (B) is correct. The author states that taxonomic classifications should be used in conjunction with other information about the animal. In choice (B), the team uses both observed and accepted data, which would include classification. Choice (A) is incorrect because the scientists are use only the taxonomic information. Choice (C) is incorrect because the zookeeper uses only observed information, ignoring the taxonomic information.

6. **B**

   The author tries to convey several facts and make a point about the appropriate use of classifications. Because *didactic* means "intended to instruct," that's pretty close. Choice (A) is incorrect because nothing in the passage indicates that the author is upset. Choice (C) is incorrect because the author has a definite opinion on the matter. Choice (D) is incorrect because the author does not sound sad. Choice (E) is incorrect because the passage does not praise anything.

7. **"The appearance and habitat of the moon rat are actually…"**

The author's conclusion is that you have to look at a variety of different types of information to get an accurate picture of the moon rat. The correct sentence mentions that, although the moon rat is similar to the other animals in its family in some ways, it's dissimilar in others. This demonstrates that the classification alone does not give an accurate picture, which leads directly to the conclusion.

8. **A**

Laudatory means expressing praise, which you can surmise from the second paragraph. *Approbative* also means expressing praise, thereby making it the correct answer. Choice (B) is incorrect because *analytical* doesn't mean expressing praise. Choice (C) means not affected by personal or emotional involvement. Choice (D) means an outstandingly clear or typical example of. Choice (E) means leaving no doubt.

9. **"Critics rightly praised the book's vivid accounts of tribal beliefs…"**

The usage of the word "rightly" shows that the author approves of the critical praise Achebe's book received.

10. **B**

The first paragraph of the passage explains why Achebe decided to write *Things Fall Apart*. The second paragraph describes some of the praise Achebe received for his work. The final paragraph explains some of the criticism Achebe received for his work. Answer choice (A) focuses only on the first paragraph and is too specific. The use of the word *prove* in answer choice (C) is too strong. Neither choice (D) nor choice (E) is supported by the passage.

Practice: Identifying Conclusions (Page 111)

1. "it is unlikely that the new defense bill will pass"

2. "grass was not a significant part of the dinosaur diet"

3. "automaker X will have no choice but to file for bankruptcy"

4. "country Y will experience a decrease in obesity-related health problems"

5. "machines will soon outnumber humans as the number-one users of the Internet"

Practice: Finding the Premise (Page 115)

1. **Premise:** A bipartisan group of 15 senators has announced that it does not support the legislation.

2. **Premises:**

   (1) "The earliest known grass fossils date from approximately 55 million years ago"

   (2) "Dinosaurs most likely disappeared from the earth around 60 million years ago"

   (3) "fossilized remains of dinosaur teeth that indicate the creatures were more suited to eating ferns and palms"

3.   Premises:

      (1) "company's poor financial situation"

      (2) "the workers at automaker X are threatening to go on strike"

4.   Premise: "the leading members of the nation's food industry have agreed to provide healthier alternatives, reduce sugar and fat content, and reduce advertisements for unhealthy foods"

5.   Premise: "Recent advances in technology have led to a new wave of 'smart' appliances"

Practice: Locating Assumptions (Page 119)

1.   Conclusion: There will be no decline in enrollment at the University.

      Why?

      Premise: The University plans to hire two highly credentialed biology professors to replace Professor Jones.

      Assumption: That the two new biology professors will be at least as attractive to prospective students as was Professor Jones.

2.   Conclusion: It makes no sense to charge more to customers under 25 years of age who rent cars.

      Why?

      Premise: Most states allow people as young as 16 to have a driver's license and all states allow 18-year-olds the right to vote.

      Assumption: Because people under the age of 25 have the right to vote and drive there is no reason to charge them more to rent a car.

3.   Conclusion: Roughly 12.5 percent of planets in the universe should have life on them

      Why?

      Premise: In our solar system, there are eight planets and at least one of them has life on it.

      Assumption: All planetary systems in the universe have the same proportion of planets with life on them as does our solar system.

4.   Conclusion: The leaders of State A should institute the gas tax.

      Why?

      Premise: 58 percent of voters in Township B approve of a proposed 2-cent gasoline tax.

      Assumption: The opinion of Township B is representative of the opinion of all of State A.

Critical Reasoning Practice Set (Page 133)

1. **A**

   If the conclusion is that it is unlikely that a sufficient number of parts will be available, and the main premise is that the number of factory returns is decreasing, the assumption must be that parts come from factory returns. Choice (A) correctly identifies the gap in the argument. Choice (B) is extreme. Note the use of the word *will*. You don't need anything that strong to hold the argument together. For choice (C), how many people decide to *purchase* a refurbished unit is out of scope because the argument is about the actual process of refurbishing. For choice (D), the manufacturer's predictions are out of scope. For choice (E), be suspicious of the word *every*. You don't need to assume anything that extreme to connect the premise to the conclusion.

2. **A**

   The conclusion is that the apprehension about the dumping of liquid waste from 1983 to 1993 is unwarranted. The premise is that tests performed during the 1960s showed little or no contamination. The argument assumes that the dumping that took place during the 1960s is comparable to the dumping that took place from 1983 to 1993. To weaken the argument, find a reason why the two time periods should not be compared. Choice (A) points out that the amount of dumping during the 1960s was significantly less than that from 1983 to 1993. For choice (B), the greater concentration of contaminants would strengthen the argument. For choice (C), solid waste is out of scope. For choice (D), the "efforts of environmentalists" are beyond the scope of the argument. Choice (E) would strengthen the argument.

3. **C**

   This is an inference , so you're looking for the answer choice that is supported by the argument. We know from the argument that democratic governments have more autonomous departments, and so they require a higher level of cooperation as stated in choice (C). For choice (A), there is no information in the passage about generalized policy. Choice (B) gets the information backwards. There will be more specialized policy makers in democratic governments because democratic governments have more autonomous departments. Choice (D) also gets the information backwards. The argument leads us to believe that an administrator's job is more difficult in a democratic government. For choice (E), efficiency is out of scope

4. **E**

   You need to explain why there were more occurrences of retinal irritations between 1983 and 1991, even though people were exposed to UVRs less frequently. Choice (E) explains that the number of retinal irritations between 1983 and 1991 was not affected by the level of UVRs in that time period. For choice (A), the temporary nature of the irritations is out of scope. For choice (B), the atmospheric elements are out of scope. For choice (C), the decrease in the average level of exposure does not explain the rise in irritations. For choice (D), anything that happened after 1991 is out of scope.

5. **A**

   Choice (A) explains how it can be true that even though running the engine consumes gas, letting the engine run during a short stop uses less gas than does turning the engine off. If more fuel is consumed by restarting the engine than would have been consumed by the running engine, then the scientific study becomes understandable. For choice (B), the amount of fuel consumed to bring the engine up to running speed is out of scope. For choice (C), the decrease in output for the engine is out of scope. For choice (D), the release of gases into the atmosphere is out of scope. For choice (E), why people use their cars is out of scope.

6. **B**

The argument concludes that the improved surgical techniques were responsible for the increased longevity of those diagnosed with stomach cancer. The premises are that more people experience complete remission and that improved surgical techniques were developed. The argument assumes that there was no other cause for the increase in longevity. Choice (B) strengthens the argument by eliminating an alternate cause. If the percentage of advanced stage cancers was the same before and after 1982, a decrease in the cancer rate could not have been the reason for the increase in longevity. For choice (A), people having more surgery in the early stage would provide an alternate cause and weaken—not strengthen—the argument. For choice (C), if a greater percentage were diagnosed, that would provide an alternate cause, and weaken—not strengthen—the argument. For choice (D), the frequency of stomach surgery among the general population is out of scope. For choice (E), other improvements would provide an alternate cause and weaken—not strengthen—the argument.

CHAPTER 7: VOCABULARY FOR THE GRE

Group 1 Exercises: Matching (Page 145)

1. C
2. J
3. E
4. G
5. A

6. L
7. K
8. B
9. N
10. H

11. M
12. I
13. D
14. F

Group 2 Exercises: Matching (Page 149)

1. B
2. M
3. F
4. J
5. N

6. A
7. D
8. E
9. L
10. C

11. H
12. I
13. G
14. K

Group 3 Exercises: Matching (Page 152)

1. D	6. A	11. E
2. G	7. C	12. B
3. K	8. N	13. J
4. I	9. H	14. L
5. M	10. F	

Group 4 Exercises: Matching (Page 155)

1. I	6. B	11. M
2. L	7. J	12. D
3. N	8. A	13. H
4. C	9. G	14. F
5. K	10. E	

CHAPTER 9: NUMBERS AND EQUATIONS

Numbers and Equations Drill (Page 217)

1. **A, B, and D**

   Follow PEMDAS, and simplify each answer choice. For choice (A), $\frac{2}{3} \times 33 - 12 = 22 - 12 = 10$, so choice (A) is correct. Choice (B): $\frac{2}{3} \times 51 - 24 = 34 - 24 = 10$, and choice (B) is correct. Choice (C): $33 - 22 \times 1\frac{1}{2} = 33 - 33 = 0 \neq 10$, so choice (C) is wrong. Choice (D): $51 \div (17 \times 3) + 9 = 51 \div 51 + 9 = 1 + 9 = 10$, and choice (D) is correct. Choice (E): $(51 \div 17) \times 3 + 9 = 3 \times 3 + 9 = 9 + 9 = 18$, so choice (E) is wrong.

2. **A**

   Solve for a by subtracting 7 from both sides of the first equation: $23 - 7 = 16$. Plug $a = 16$ in for the second equation to get $b - 16 = -10$. Add 16 to both sides to find $b = 6$.

3. **27**

Because $9 = 3^2$; the original equation becomes $3^3 \times (3^2)^{12} = 3^x$; or, $3^3 \times 3^{24} = 3^x$; or, $3^{3+24} = 3^x$. Therefore, $x = 27$.

4. **C**

Solve for x by stacking up and adding the two inequalities. In so doing, the y variable from each inequality cancels out, and you get $3x > 36$, or $x > 12$.

5. **A**

You have the relationship among can prices, but no actual numbers, so try plugging in some numbers for can prices. The calculations will be easy if you make the large can cost $5 \times 7 = \$35$, which means that the medium can costs $35 \div 5 = \$7$, and the small can costs $35 \div 7 = \$5$. The amount of money that would buy 200 medium cans is $200 \times \$7 = \$1400$. Because the customer buys the same number of small and large cans, she spends $40 on each small-and-large can combination. Divide $1400 by $40 to get the number of sets she buys ($\$1400 \div \$40 = 35$). She buys 35 sets of small and large cans, which means that she buys 35 small cans, choice (A).

6. **12 and –12**

To isolate $(x + y)$, take the square root of both sides. So, $(x + y) = \pm 4$. Solving the same way for $(x - y)$, you get $(x - y) = \pm 3$. Substituting into the difference of two squares equation $(x^2 - y^2) = (x + y)(x - y)$, you get $(x^2 - y^2) = (\pm 4)(\pm 3)$, or a value of 12 or –12.

7. **B**

Translate the equation. $3a = 6b - 4$. Because the asks for the value of $a - 2b$, go ahead and rearrange your equation so the a and b are on the same side. $3a - 6b = -4$. Next, divide both sides by 3. $\dfrac{3a - 6b}{3} = -\dfrac{4}{3}$.

8. **A**

Simplify each quantity by rationalizing the denominators. For Quantity A, to get rid of the radicals, multiply numerator

and denominator by $(\sqrt{5} + \sqrt{2})$, because $(x - y)(x + y) = x^2 - y^2$. You now have $\dfrac{\sqrt{12}(\sqrt{5} + \sqrt{2})}{\sqrt{5}^2 - \sqrt{2}^2} = \dfrac{\sqrt{60} + \sqrt{24}}{5 - 2}$

$= \dfrac{2\sqrt{15} + 2\sqrt{6}}{3}$. For Quantity B, multiply numerator and denominator by $\sqrt{27}$ to get $\dfrac{(\sqrt{2} + \sqrt{5})(\sqrt{27})}{\sqrt{27}^2} =$

$\dfrac{\sqrt{54} + \sqrt{135}}{27} = \dfrac{3\sqrt{6} + 3\sqrt{15}}{27} = \dfrac{\sqrt{6} + \sqrt{15}}{9}$. Quantity A is $\left(\sqrt{15} + \sqrt{6}\right) \times \dfrac{2}{3}$ and Quantity B is $\left(\sqrt{15} + \sqrt{6}\right) \times \dfrac{1}{9}$,

so Quantity A is greater.

9. **D**

Plug In. If $a = 3$, $b = 6$, $c = 3$, $d = 5$, and $e = 10$, the value of the equation is $\dfrac{(10)\left(3 + \dfrac{6}{3}\right)}{5} = 10$. Half of 10 is your

target of 5. Try doubling each variable to find the one that yields 5. The only one that works is doubling d to 10 so

that the equation is $\dfrac{(10)\left(3 + \dfrac{6}{3}\right)}{10} = 5$.

10. **A, B, and E**

You have variables in the question and variables in the answers, so Plug In. If $x = 6$, then $a = 2$, and if $y = 36$, then $b = 4$. $2(x + y)$ equals 84, so that is your target number. Check your answer choices. A = 48, B = 60, C = 84, D = 84, and E = 96. Since we're looking for the ones that *don't* equal 84, the correct answers are A, B, and E.

CHAPTER 10: REAL WORLD MATH

Real World Math Drill (Page 260)

1. **A**

Plug In for r. If $r = 2$, we can now solve for s. $3(2 + s) = 7$, $2 + s = \dfrac{7}{3}$, $s = \dfrac{7}{3} - 2$. Convert the 2 to a fraction and get

$s = \dfrac{7}{3} - \dfrac{6}{3} = \dfrac{1}{3}$. Go through the answer choices, Plugging In 2 for r. Choice (A) yields the target of $\dfrac{1}{3}$.

2. $\dfrac{1}{6}$

Plugging In your own number is a good way to tackle this. The fractions used in the problem are $\dfrac{1}{3}$ and $\dfrac{1}{2}$, and

multiplying the denominators will produce a good number with which to work. Sadie started with 6 paintings and

gave away one third of them: $6 \times \dfrac{1}{3} = 2$. She has 4 paintings left. She then sold another half of the original 6: $6 \times$

$\dfrac{1}{2} = 3$. So, she's has 1 painting left, or $\dfrac{1}{6}$ of the total.

3. **B, C, and D**

A \$20 scarf can be discounted as much as 50 percent, and \$20 $\times \dfrac{50}{100}$ = \$10, so the minimum sale price of a scarf

is \$20 − \$10 = \$10. The smallest discount is 25 percent, and \$20 $\times \dfrac{25}{100}$ = \$5, so the maximum sale price of a scarf

is \$20 − \$5 = \$15. You have determined the range of possible sale prices for scarves is \$10 to \$15. Now, you need to

eliminate answers that fall outside of that range: Choice (A) is too small, and choice (E) is too large.

4. **C**

To find the value in each column, translate the words into arithmetic. Rewrite Quantity A as $\dfrac{12}{100} \times 35 = \dfrac{12 \times 35}{100}$

and Quantity B as $\dfrac{35}{100} \times 12 = \dfrac{35 \times 12}{100}$. The expression in Quantity A is the same as the expression in Quantity B.

5. **A**

Use the bowtie to compare the quantities: Multiply opposing numerators and denominators, and compare the resulting

products. Think of Quantity B as $\dfrac{10}{1}$. Multiply 2.6 × 1 to get 2.6 on the Quantity A side. Multiply 0.259 × 10 to

get 2.59 on the Quantity B side. Because 2.6 is greater than 2.59, Quantity A is greater.

6. **D**

The population rankings for Year X are: (1) Massachusetts, (2) Connecticut, (3) Maine, (4) Rhode Island, (5) New
Hampshire, (6) Vermont. And for Year Y: (1) Massachusetts; (2) Connecticut; (3) Rhode Island; (4) New Hampshire;
(5) Maine; (6) Vermont. Maine, Rhode Island, and New Hampshire have different rankings from Year X to Year Y.

7. **E**

In Year Y, Vermont's population is 3 percent of 25 million (or 0.75 million), and Massachusetts' population is
37 percent of 25 million (or approximately 9 million). 9 million is what percent of 0.75 million? Now translate:
9 million = $\dfrac{x}{100}$ × 0.75 million: x = 1,200.

8. **D**

In Year X the population of Rhode Island was 10 percent of 15 million, or 1.5 million. In Year Y the population of
Rhode Island was 15 percent of 25 million, or 3.75 million. The increase was 2.25 million, or 2,250,000.

9. **B**

The percent change of Connecticut's percent of total New England population from Year X (24 percent) to Year Y

(27 percent) is: $\dfrac{3}{24}$ = 12.5 percent. The percent change of Massachusetts's percentage of total New England population

from Year X (40 percent) to Year Y (37 percent) is: $\dfrac{3}{40}$ = 7.5 percent. The approximate difference is 5.

10. **D**

You are given that towns A and B each have 3,000 supporters of the referendum and that B and D have an average of 3,500 supporters. Using the average circle you find out that D has 4,000 supporters. You know nothing about C. Because C and D are the two southern–most towns, we cannot tell what their average is. For example, if C had zero supporters, the average of C and D would be 2,000, which is less than Quantity B. If C had 4,000 supporters, the average of C and D would be 4,000, which is greater than Quantity B.

11. **E**

Plug In the answers, starting in the middle with choice (C). If each A employee was given $740, each C employee was given half of that, or $370. Each B employee received one-and-a-half times the C raise, so 1.5 × $370 = $555. Now calculate the total money spent on raises. 50 A employees got $740 each, for a total of 50 × $740 = $37,000. 100 B employees got $555 each, for a total of 100 × $555 = $55,500. 150 C employees got $370 each: 150 × $370 = 55,500. These add up to a total of $148,000, but the problem says that the total raise amount is $500,000. You need a much bigger answer. Rule out choices (A), (B), and (C). Try skipping directly to (E). If the A workers got $2500, the C workers got $1250, and the B workers got $1875. 50 × $2500 = $125,000; 100 × $1875 = $187,500; and 150 × $1250 = $187,500. Because these numbers add up to $500,000, choice (E) is correct.

12. **19**

Plug In $100 for the price the retailer pays for the item. This means the original selling price is 40 percent more, or $140. To find the reduced selling price, subtract 15 percent of $140 from $140 to get $119. The retailer's profit (selling price – cost) is $19. Translating the last line of the , we get $19 = (x ÷ 100) × 100, or 19 percent.

13. **B**

Median means middle. In other words, if you put all the ninth graders in order by score, the middle student would have the median score. Thinking in terms of percentiles, the 50th percentile is the middle, so on the ninth grade pie chart, whatever score includes the 50th percentile when you put the scores in order is the median score. According to the chart, 16 percent of the ninth graders scored below 65, and 37 percent scored between 65 and 69 points. 16 percent + 37 percent = 53 percent. The 50th percentile, then, falls within the group that received 65–69, so 65–69 is the median score.

14. **A**

In 1975 there were 1350 + 950 + 625 + 47, or 3,400 students in grades 9 through 12. 3,400 is 35 percent of School District X, so $3400 = \frac{35}{100} \cdot x$, $x \approx 9700$, so there were 9,700 students.

15. **E**

There were 1,200 ninth graders in 1993. 25 percent of them, or 300, scored in the 70–79 point range. 14 percent, or 168, scored in the 80–89 point range. The difference between 300 and 168 is 132. (E) is the closest choice.

16. **A**

Use the bowtie method to subtract the numbers in Quantity A. This gives you $\dfrac{50-27}{25} = \dfrac{23}{25}$. If you bowtie the

fractions in Quantity B, you get $\dfrac{375+60}{625} = \dfrac{435}{625}$. To compare the two quantities, multiply the fraction in Quantity

A by $\dfrac{25}{25}$. This gives you a value of $\dfrac{575}{625}$ for Quantity A, making it the larger value.

17. **D**

Use several ratio boxes on this problem. Because X has 2 parts of a and 3 parts of b, there are 5 parts total for X, while Y has $1 + 2 = 3$ parts total. Convert these ratios so that they have the same total, which will allow you to compare them. Multiply X by 3 and Y by 5 so that each have 15 total. The new X is 6 parts a and 9 parts b, and the new Y is 5 parts a and 10 parts b. For solution Z there are 2 parts X, so $3 \times 6 = 18$ parts a and $3 \times 9 = 27$ parts b. There are 11 parts of Y in Z, so there are $11 \times 5 = 55$ parts a and $11 \times 10 = 110$ parts b. Thus, solution Z has $18 + 55 = 73$ parts a and $27 + 110 = 137$ parts b, and $73 + 137 = 210$ total in the ratio. Because the actual total is 630, which is 210×3, there must be $73 \times 3 = 219$ parts of a in the final solution of Z.

18. **25**

The library has 160 books on Sunday. Monday's total is $160 - 40$, or 120. Tuesday is $120 + (\dfrac{1}{2} \times 40)$, or 140.

Wednesday is $140 + (\dfrac{1}{2} \times 20) - 20$, or 130. Thursday is $130 + 80 + (\dfrac{1}{6} \times 30)$, or 215. Friday and Saturday see 65

more books leave, so the total for the end of Saturday is $215 - 65 = 150$. Note that the asks for Monday, not the first

Sunday. The percent change from Monday to Saturday is $\dfrac{(150-120)}{120} \times 100$, or 25 percent.

19. **B and D**

Use the Average Pie to find that Jill's mean of 3.75 for 8 evaluations gives her a current total of $3.75 \times 8 = 30$ points. Use the Average Pie to find that if she needs an average of 4.0 for 12 scores, she needs $4.0 \times 12 = 48$ total points. Jill still needs $48 - 30 = 18$ points. Her four remaining scores must total 18 or greater. Only answers (B) and (D) have a total of at least 18.

CHAPTER 11: GEOMETRY

Geometry Drill (Page 296)

1. **A, B, and C**

You need to check if the two angles in each answer choice can be part of a right triangle. A right triangle has a 90-degree angle, and because the sum of all the angles of a triangle is 180 degrees, the sum of the other two angles must equal $180 - 90 = 90$ degrees. In answer choice (A), $20 + 70 = 90$ degrees, so these could be the other two angles in a right triangle. Answer choices (B) and (C) also add up to 90 degrees, and so they are correct as well. In choices (D) and (E), the two angles have a sum greater than 90 degrees, so they are incorrect.

2. **B**

To find the perimeter of the figure, you need to add up all of its external sides. As written, you're missing the measure of one side of the rectangle. Because the side of the rectangle is equal to the hypotenuse of the right triangle, use the triangle to find the missing side. To find the hypotenuse of the right triangle recognize the common right triangle (5:12:13), or use the Pythagorean Theorem ($5^2 + 12^2 = x^2$). The missing sides of the rectangle are each 13. Therefore, the perimeter equals $5 + 12 + 17 + 13 + 17 = 64$. Answer choice (A) is the perimeter without the missing side of the rectangle. If you chose answer choice (D), you included in interior side of the rectangle.

3. **A**

We know that the triangle *EFG* is equilateral because all three angles are equal. That means all of its sides equal 8. From the first equation, we know that the sides of the square also equal 8. The area of the square is $s \times s = 8 \times 8 = 64$, which is larger than Quantity B.

4. **D**

Draw it on your scratch work, and plot the points. Both *a* and *b* must be positive, but their values could be equal or unequal. Region I has (+, +) coordinates, Region II has (−, +) coordinates, Region III has (−, −) coordinates, and Region IV has (+, −) coordinates.

5. **E**

There are variables in the answers, so Plug In. If the shorter piece is 2 yards long, then the longer piece is $3(2) + 2 = 8$ yards and *T* must be $2 + 8 = 10$. The target answer, the length of the longer piece, is 8. Plug In 10 for *T* into all of the answers. Answer choice (E) is the only answer choice that matches your target of 8.

6. **D**

If *CD*, the radius of the smaller circle, is 3, then the diameter of the smaller circle is 6. The diameter of the smaller circle is equal to the radius of the larger circle because the smaller circle touches the center and the edge of the larger circle. The formula for the area of a circle is πr^2, so the area of the larger circle is 36π. To find the area of the semicircle, divide by 2 to find 18π.

7. **24**

Because Karl's turn from due south to due east forms a right angle, you can use the Pythagorean theorem, in which the hypotenuse is 25, one leg is 7, and the other leg is *x*. Therefore, you have $7^2 + x^2 = 25^2$. Solving for *x*, you get $49 + x^2 = 625$, or $x = 24$.

8. **A**

Circumference of a circle is $2\pi r$, which is greater than 6 times the radius. Perimeter of a square is 4 times the length of a side, or $4r$. Try plugging in values for *r*, and you will see that Quantity A is always greater than Quantity B.

9. **C**

The area of the circle is 25π, so the radius of the circle is 5. This means that both *AC* and *BC* have length 5, and angles *A* and *B* are equal to each other. Because angle *C* is 60° and the total angle measure of a triangle is 180°, the sum of angle *A* and *B* must be 120°. Thus, each angle in triangle *ABC* is 60°, making this is an equilateral triangle. An equilateral triangle has equal sides and equal angles, so the only possible length of the triangle legs is 5.

10. A

Remember the third side rule. The third side of a triangle must be less than the sum of the other two sides of a triangle, but greater than the difference. That gives us a clear range for *x*. It must be greater than 6 but less than 12. Quantity A, therefore, is greater than Quantity B; the answer is (A).

11. A

One trick to interpreting geometry problems is to exaggerate whatever is going on in your picture. You can see that the two triangles are almost the same, except that the base length in the triangle to the right is slightly larger. Well, what happens as you keep stretching out that base length? The triangle starts to collapse and its height gets smaller and smaller. Thus, height *f* must be greater than height *g*. This technique works quite well in a number of GRE quant comp geometry problems!

12. B

In order to find the *x*-coordinate of a point on a line, you must first find the slope of the line. Notice that along with points *A* and *B*, the origin is also a point on the line in the figure. Using the coordinates of (0, 0) and *A* (2, 3), the slope is $\frac{(y_2 - y_1)}{(x_2 - x_1)} = \frac{3}{2}$. Because the slope of a line stays constant, you can use the value you just found to solve for the missing *x*-coordinate of point *B*. Using points *A* (2, 3) and *B* (*x*, 4.2), solve $\frac{(4.2 - 3)}{(x - 2)} = \frac{3}{2}$. Cross-multiply to find that $3x - 2 = 2.4$, so $x = 2.8$ or choice (B).

13. A

Use the 3 : 4 : 5 ratio or the Pythagorean theorem to determine that the length of *AB* is 4. Because the area of a triangle equals $\frac{1}{2}$ × base × height, triangle *ABD* has an area of $\frac{1}{2}$ × 3 × 4, or 6. Be wary of answer choice (D), which is the area of the rectangle.

14. B

Because the two angles have the same measure, the wedges of the circle they mark off will have the same area. The triangle is smaller than the wedge, so Quantity B is greater than Quantity A.

15. C

Because *LMNO* is a parallelogram and *c* = 108, angle *LON* must be 180 – 108 = 72. Angle *LON* is the same fraction of the entire circle (360 degrees) that arc *d* is of the entire circumference, $\frac{72}{360} = \frac{1}{5}$. Thus, arc *d* must be $\frac{1}{5}$ of the circumference. So, $\frac{1}{5} \times 15\pi = 3\pi$. If you were stuck on this problem, you could have estimated that *d* looks to be about a fourth or fifth of the circle's circumference. Thus, eliminate answers (A) and (B).

CHAPTER 12: MATH ET CETERA

Et Cetera Drill (Page 316)

1. **C**

   If there is one more red marble than blue, there must be 7 blue marbles and 8 red ones, for a total of 15. The probability of choosing a blue marble is $\dfrac{\text{\# of blue marbles}}{\text{Total \# of marbles}}$, or $\dfrac{7}{15}$. If you selected choice (E), you probably computed the probability of drawing a red marble rather than the probability of drawing a blue one.

2. **D**

   Plug the values into the function. First, find ¥(5): (5 × 10 − 1) = 49. Next, find ¥(3) = (3 × 10 − 1) = 29. Now subtract them: ¥(5) − ¥(3) = 49 − 29 = 20.

3. **A**

   Find all the factors of 78. 78 = 1 × 78 = 2 × 39 = 3 × 26 = 6 × 13. The largest odd factor is 39; the largest prime factor is 13. Quantity A is greater than Quantity B.

4. **20**

   All 5 finalists could be awarded "Best in Show." There are 4 choices left for "Honorable Mention," because a different dog must be chosen. Therefore, the total number of possibilities is 5 · 4, or 20.

5. **A**

   Use the group equation: Group 1 + Group 2 − Both + Neither = Total. So, $40,000 + $30,000 − $15,000 + Neither = $90,000. Thus, $55,000 + Neither = $90,000. So, the company spends $35,000 on other products.

6. **B**

   List out the two-digit prime numbers less than 50: 11, 13, 17, 19, 23, 29, 31, 37, 41, 43, and 47. The numbers in which the tens digit is greater than the units digit are 31, 41, and 43. Because 3 out of the 11 possibilities meet the requirement, choice (B) is correct.

7. **A**

   Plug In the answer choices, starting with (C). With 9 staff members, the elected official has $\dfrac{9!}{5!4!}$ (alternatively, you may have set this up as $\dfrac{9 \times 8}{1 \times 2}$). This works out to 36, which is too large. Try plugging in answer choice (A). With 7 staff members, the elected official has $\dfrac{7!}{5!2!} = 21$ different groups of 5 from which to choose (again, you may have set this up the alternative way as $\dfrac{7 \times 6}{1 \times 2}$).

8. **E**

Plug In: Make $x = 2$ and $y = 3$. Now $x \# y = 2 (2 - 3) = -2$. Watch out for traps: Answer choices (A) and (C) will give you -2, but because the asks for $x \# (x \# y)$, you need to perform the operation again. $2 \# (-2) = 2 [2 - (-2)] = 2 (4) = 8$. Now put $x = 2$ and $y = 3$ into the answer choices to find a match for your target answer, 8. Be sure to eliminate choices (A), (B), (C), and (D) as soon as you realize they are negative. The only answer that matches is choice (E).

9. **B**

Use a ratio box to find that if there are twice as many yellow as green and 12 total, then there are 8 yellows and 4 greens. Two situations would fit the requirements of the problem: pull out a yellow and then green, or pull out a green and then yellow. So, find the probability of each of these situations, then add these two probabilities together. The probability of yellow and then green is $\dfrac{8}{12} \times \dfrac{4}{11} = \dfrac{8}{33}$. The probability of green and then yellow is $\dfrac{4}{12} \times \dfrac{8}{11} = \dfrac{8}{33}$. Add these two probabilities to find $\dfrac{8}{33} + \dfrac{8}{33} = \dfrac{16}{33}$.

10. **B**

You could try to draw this all out, but it would probably be quite a headache. For Quantity A, if you're creating triangles, you're really choosing three points from the set of 10. This is a combination problem—order doesn't matter, because triangle ABC would be the same as triangle BCA. You could use the formula: $\dfrac{10!}{3!(10-3)!} = \dfrac{10!}{3!(7!)} = \dfrac{10 \times 9 \times 8}{3 \times 2 \times 1}$ = 120. Alternatively, if you used the "make slots" method, you'd have: $\dfrac{10 \times 9 \times 8}{3 \times 2 \times 1}$ = 120. For Quantity B, note that quadrilaterals are any four-sided figures, so you're just choosing 4 points from 10. You could use the formula for combinations: $\dfrac{10!}{4!(10-4)!} = \dfrac{10!}{4!(6!)} = \dfrac{10 \times 9 \times 8 \times 7}{4 \times 3 \times 2 \times 1}$ = 210. Alternatively, if you used the "make slots" method, you'd have: $\dfrac{10 \times 9 \times 8 \times 7}{4 \times 3 \times 2 \times 1}$ = 210.

Comprehensive Math Drill (Page 318)

1. **C**

Cross multiply. $\dfrac{0.05}{0.6} = \dfrac{x}{0.18}$, so $0.6x = (0.05)(0.18)$, and $x = \dfrac{(0.05)(0.18)}{0.6} = (0.05)(0.3) = 0.015$.

2. **C**

Simplify the expression in Quantity B: $\dfrac{\frac{x}{5}}{2} = \dfrac{x}{5} \div \dfrac{2}{1} = \dfrac{x}{5} \times \dfrac{1}{2} = \dfrac{x}{10}$. The expressions in Quantity A and in Quantity B are the same.

3. **C**

Remember that the percentages for standard deviation s are 34 percent, 14 percent, 2 percent in both directions from the mean. If the mean is 50, then 34 percent score between 50 and 54, 14 percent score between 54 and 58, and 2 percent score above 58. The same idea applies in the other direction: If the mean is 50, then 34 percent score between 50 and 46, 14 percent score between 46 and 42, and 2 percent score below 42. So, the quantities are both equal to 2 percent.

4. **B**

The equation $y = mx + b$ describes a line where m is the slope and b is the y-intercept—the place where the line crosses the y-axis. Hence, the y-intercept of our line, or P, is (0, 1), which means the length of OP is 1. Because R is on the x-axis, the y-coordinate must be 0, and we can use the line equation to solve for x: $0 = -\frac{5}{6}x + 1$, so $-1 = -\frac{5}{6}x$, and $x = \frac{6}{5}$. That means $OR = \frac{6}{5}$, and Quantity A is greater. Because this is a Quant Comp, though, we can actually compare the Quantities without solving them. If you recognize from the line equation that our slope is $-\frac{5}{6}$, and you remember that slope is defined as $\frac{rise}{run}$, you might also recognize that Quantity A, OR, is our run, and Quantity B, OP, is our rise. Disregarding the negative sign—distance is always an absolute value, and therefore positive—we can see that our rise is less than our run, and Quantity A is greater.

5. **B**

For Quantity A, "pairs" tells you that you're picking two and that order does not matter: This is a combination. You could use the formula: $\frac{20!}{2!(20-2)!} = \frac{20!}{2!(18)!} = \frac{20 \times 19}{2} = 190$. Alternatively, you may have learned the "make slots" way: $\frac{20 \times 19}{1 \times 2} = 190$. For Quantity B, the "rankings" tells you that order matters: This is a permutation. So, you could use the formula: $\frac{10!}{(10-3)!} = \frac{10!}{7!} = 10 \times 9 \times 8 = 720$. Alternatively, the "make slots" way would be $10 \times 9 \times 8 = 720$.

6. **D**

The denominator is the same for both expressions, so we only need to compare numerators to determine which fraction is greater. Plug In to see whether kl is greater than or less than 1. Let $k = 0.5$ and $l = 1.5$, $kl = 0.75$. Eliminate answer choices (B) and (C). Now let $k = 10$ and $l = 10$, $kl = 100$. Eliminate answer choice (A).

7. **A**

Approximate your values. In Column A, $\sqrt{3} + \sqrt{4} \cong 1.7 + 2 = 3.7$. In Column B, $\sqrt{7}$ is less than 3, so Column A is greater.

8. **4**

If Joe starts with $200 and spends $150 on a CD player, he only has $200 – $150 = $50 left. Each CD is $12, so divide $50 by $12. It goes in 4 times with $2 left over. Don't round! Joe can only buy 4.

9. **A**

For triangle ABC, the base is the difference between C and B, 1. Finding the height is a little more difficult. The height of a triangle is any perpendicular line dropped from the highest point to the level of the base. The height does not need to touch segment CB as long as it extends from A to the level of CB. For this triangle, distance from A to the origin is the height, 4. Plugging In the base and height: Area = $\frac{1}{2} \times 1 \times 4 = 2$.

10. **B, C, and D**

To solve this problem, first use PEMDAS: $10(3^2 - 2) = 10(9 - 2) = 10(7) = 70$. The states that 70 is divided by a positive integer, so try dividing 70 by different integers. Choices (B), (C) and (D) could work because you can divide 70 by 1, 2, and 7 respectively. Choice (A) does not work because to get 140, you would have to divide 70 by $\frac{1}{2}$, which is not an integer. Also, 0 is neither positive nor negative, and you cannot divide a number by 0, so choice (E) could not work either.

11. **B and C**

Roberta's rate is 50 miles in 2 hours. Notice that the first number in this proportion is greater than the second. Use that to eliminate choices (A) and (D). For choice (B), $\frac{100}{4} = \frac{50}{2}$, so this is the same as the original proportion. For choice (C), $\frac{400}{16} = \frac{50}{2}$, so this is also the same as the original proportion.

12. **C**

There were seven cities with higher temperatures in Year Y: Baltimore, Detroit, Las Vegas, Minneapolis, New York, Phoenix, and San Francisco.

13. **C**

The lowest average temperature was 34° F in Anchorage, and the highest was 83° F in Las Vegas. Percent change = $\dfrac{\text{difference}}{\text{original}} = \dfrac{49}{34} \approx 144$ percent.

14. **C**

You're averaging the highs and lows for Years X and Y, so the number of things is 4. The bar shows the average of Years X and Y, which reads 60. Multiply 60 by 4 to get the total, 240. Get the average high temperatures for Years X and Y from the straight and dotted lines on the chart. They're about 103 degrees and 97 degrees. The total is 240 = 103 + 97 + low Year X + low Year Y. If you subtract the highs from the total, you're left with 40 degrees as the total for the lows. Because you want the average of the lows, divide this total by 2. The closest answer is 20°.

15. **A, B, and C**

First, simplify the inequality by subtracting 2 from both sides: $|2x - 3| > 5$. Now plug each answer choice into the inequality to see which value of x makes the inequality true. The correct values are those in choices (A), (B), and (C).

16. **A**

The question states that x is an odd integer, so eliminate choice (C) because 0 is not odd. Simplify $x + y + z < z$ by subtracting z from each side: $x + y < 0$. Because x is less than y, x must be negative so that when added to y the answer will be less than zero. Therefore, eliminate choices (D) and (E). Now Plug In the remaining answers to see which value of x will work in the inequality. Choice (A) is the only choice that works.

17. **E**

First, solve for x by multiplying 4 by itself until you get 1024. This means that x equals 5. Substituting 5 for x in the second equation, the reads, "What is $4^6 \times 5^4$?" Because the answers are expressed in terms of 4^n, 5^n, and 10^n, expand out $4^6 \times 5^4$ to get $4 \times 4 \times 4 \times 4 \times 4 \times 4 \times 5 \times 5 \times 5 \times 5$. Now try to express it using 10^n. We need to factor two of the fours and rewrite this as $4 \times 4 \times 4 \times 4 \times 2 \times 2 \times 2 \times 2 \times 5 \times 5 \times 5 \times 5$. Now, convert this back into exponents to get $4^4 \times 2^4 \times 5^4$, or $4^4 \times 10^4$.

18. **D**

First, use the volume formula to find the width: $V = l \times w \times h$. So, $780 = 12 \times w \times 5$. Thus, the width is 13. Next, draw the figure. Notice that the greatest distance is from one corner to the opposite corner, such as from the front left bottom corner diagonally to the rear right top corner. You can use the formula for diagonal of a rectangular solid, $a^2 + b^2 + c^2 = d^2$, in which a, b, and c are the dimensions of the rectangular solid and d is the diagonal, and love that you have a calculator. Thus, $(5)^2 + (12)^2 + (13)^2 = d^2$. So, $25 + 144 + 169 = d^2$, and thus $d = \sqrt{338}$ or $13\sqrt{2}$.

19. **D**

There are six spots to fill. Because no boys can sit on the end of the bench, 3 girls are available to fill one spot at one end of the bench. Once one girl has been chosen to fill that spot, there are 2 girls available to fill the spot on the other end of the bench. Then, there are 4 children (boys and girls) available to fill the other four spots. Because $3 \times 2 \times 4 \times 3 \times 2 \times 1 = 144$, choice (D) is correct.

20. **C**

Use the average pie. If 16 is the average of 3 numbers, their total is 48. You know that one of the numbers is 24, so $p + q + 24 = 48$. Thus, $(p + q) = 24$. You need to find $16(p + q)$, so find $16(24)$. Ballpark that $10(24) = 240$ and $5(24) = 120$. Look for an answer a little more than $240 + 120 = 360$.

Part VI
The Princeton Review GRE Practice Tests and Explanations

TEST INSTRUCTIONS

It's important to become familiar with the instructions for the test now, so that you don't waste time figuring them out on test day.

General Instructions

Each exam consists of six sections—two Analytical Writing sections, two Verbal Reasoning sections, and two Quantitative Reasoning sections. The Analytical Writing sections will always be first. The Verbal and Quantitative Reasoning sections may appear in any order. You will have 35 minutes for each Analytic Writing section, 30 minutes for each Verbal, and 35 minutes for each Quantitative Reasoning section. If desired, you may take a 10-minute break after Section 4. Remember that during the actual test, there may be an additional verbal or quantitative experimental section.

Section 1	30 minutes	Critical Thinking and Analytical Writing
Section 2	30 minutes	Critical Thinking and Analytical Writing
Section 3	30/35 minutes	Verbal or Quantitative Reasoning
Section 4	30/35 minutes	Verbal or Quantitative Reasoning
Section 5	30/35 minutes	Verbal or Quantitative Reasoning
Section 6	30/35 minutes	Verbal or Quantitative Reasoning

When taking a Verbal or Quantitative Reasoning section, you are free to skip questions that you might have difficulty answering and come back to them later during the time allotted for that section. You may also change your response to any question in a section during the time allotted to work on that section. You may not go back to an earlier section of the test after time for that section runs out.

Analytic Writing Instructions

Issue Topic

You will be given a brief statement on an issue of general interest and specific in-structions on how to respond to that issue. You will have 30 minutes to plan and write a response in which you develop a position on the issue. Make sure that you respond to the specific instructions and support your position on the issue with reasons and examples drawn from such areas as your reading, experience, observations, and/or academic studies.

Before you begin writing, you may want to think for a few minutes about the passage and the instructions and then outline your response. Be sure to develop your analysis fully and organize it coherently. Leave a minute or two at the end to reread what you have written and make any revisions you think are necessary.

Argument Topic

You will be given a short passage that presents an argument, or an argument to be completed, and specific instructions on how to respond to that passage. You will have 30 minutes to plan and write a response in which you analyze the passage. Note that you are NOT being asked to present your own views on the subject. Make sure that you respond to the specific instructions and support your analysis with relevant reasons and/or examples.

Before you begin writing, you may want to think for a few minutes about the passage and the instructions and then outline your response. Be sure to develop your analysis fully and organize it coherently. Leave a minute or two at the end to reread what you have written and make any revisions you think are necessary.

Verbal Reasoning Instructions

Each Verbal Reasoning section is 30 minutes long and has 20 questions. For some questions, you will be instructed to choose one or more answer choices. The instructions may or may not specify how many answers you must choose. If the number of answers is specified, you must choose all of the correct answers in order to have your response counted as correct. If the number is not specified, choose all that correctly answer the question. No credit will be given if fewer or more than all of the correct answers are chosen.

Quantitative Reasoning Instructions

Each Quantitative Reasoning section is 35 minutes long and has 20 questions. You may use a five-function calculator—one with addition, subtraction, multiplication, division, and square-root features—during Quantitative Reasoning sections.

For some questions, you will be instructed to choose one or more answer choices. The instructions may or may not specify how many answers you must choose. If the number of answers is specified, you must choose all of the correct answers in order to have your response counted as correct. If the number is not specified, choose all that correctly answer the question. No credit will be given if fewer or more than all of the correct answers are chosen.

Some questions will require you to enter your own answer. If the question provides a single response space, enter a single number. You may enter negative signs and decimal points. If the question tells you to round your answer, do so. Otherwise, enter the entire answer. If the question provides two response spaces, you must enter your answer in the form of a fraction. You are not required to enter fractions in their most reduced form. If there is more than one correct response, you only need to enter one of the correct responses to have your response counted as correct.

Some questions will ask you to fill blanks in the text by clicking to select from a list of choices. Sometimes all of the choices will be used, and sometimes only some of the choices will be used. The correct answer always requires you to put a different choice in every blank.

Note on Numbers and Figures

Numbers: All numbers used are real numbers.

Figures: The position of points, angles, regions, etc. can be assumed to be in the order shown, and angle measures can be assumed to be positive. Lines shown as straight can be assumed to be straight. Figures can be assumed to lie in a plane unless otherwise indicated. Any other figures are not necessarily drawn to scale, unless a note states that a figure is drawn to scale.

Chapter 16
Practice Test 1

SECTION 1: ISSUE TOPIC

Directions:

You will be given a brief quotation that states or implies an issue of general interest and specific instructions on how to respond to that issue. You will have 30 minutes to plan and compose a response in which you develop a position on the issue according to the specific instructions. A response to any other issue will receive a score of zero.

"Governments are justified in circumventing civil laws when doing so is vital to the protection of national security."

Write an essay in which you take a position on the statement above. In developing and supporting your position, you should consider ways in which the statement might or might not hold true.

SECTION 2: ARGUMENT TOPIC

Directions:

You will be given a short passage that presents an argument, or an argument to be completed, and specific instructions on how to respond to that passage. You will have 30 minutes to plan and compose a response in which you analyze the passage according to the specific instructions. A response to any other argument will receive a score of zero.

Note that you are NOT being asked to present your own views on the subject. Make sure that you respond to the specific instructions and support your analysis with relevant reasons and/or examples.

The following is from a recent email by the Diord Corp. Human Resources Manager: "Tobor Technologies found that mental health problems and mental illness were responsible for about 15 percent of employee sick days. Tobor amended its employee insurance plan so that workers receive the same coverage for mental illness as they do for physical illness. In addition, the company hired an on-site psychologist and created a system that allows workers to schedule confidential counseling appointments. After one year, the number of sick days used by employees declined by 10 percent. Diord Corp has had an increase in employee sick days over the past two years, so we should introduce a similar insurance plan and counseling program. These measures will surely reduce employee absenteeism and cause an increase in productivity."

Write a response in which you examine the argument's unstated assumptions, making sure to explain how the argument depends on the assumptions and what the implications are if the assumptions prove unwarranted.

SECTION 3: QUANTITATIVE REASONING

Questions 1 through 7 each consist of two quantities, Quantity A and Quantity B. You are to compare the two quantities and choose the appropriate answer. In a question, information concerning one or both of the quantities to be compared is centered above the two columns. A symbol that appears in both columns represents the same thing in Quantity A as it does in Quantity B.

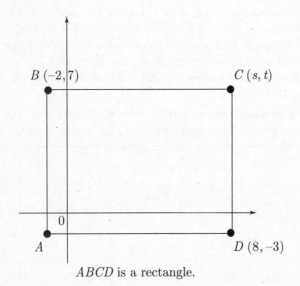

ABCD is a rectangle.

Quantity A	Quantity B
s	t

○ Quantity A is greater.

○ Quantity B is greater.

○ The two quantities are equal.

○ The relationship cannot be determined from the information given.

A certain punch is created by mixing two parts soda and three parts ice cream. The soda is 4 parts sugar, 5 parts citric acid, and 11 parts other ingredients. The ice cream is 3 parts sugar, 2 parts citric acid, and 15 parts other ingredients.

Quantity A	Quantity B
parts sugar in the punch	parts citric acid in the punch

○ Quantity A is greater.

○ Quantity B is greater.

○ The two quantities are equal.

○ The relationship cannot be determined from the information given.

The average (arithmetic mean) of a set of mean daily temperatures for x days is 70 degrees. When a mean daily temperature of 75 degrees is added to this set, the average increases to 71 degrees.

Quantity A	Quantity B
x	5

○ Quantity A is greater.

○ Quantity B is greater.

○ The two quantities are equal.

○ The relationship cannot be determined from the information given.

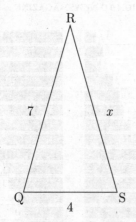

QRS is an isosceles triangle

Quantity A	**Quantity B**
perimeter of QRS	17

○ Quantity A is greater.

○ Quantity B is greater.

○ The two quantities are equal.

○ The relationship cannot be determined from the information given.

The scores for the 500 students who took Ms. Johnson's final exam had a normal distribution. There were 80 students who scored at least 92 points out of a possible 100 total points and 10 students who scored at or below 56.

Quantity A	**Quantity B**
The mean score on the final exam	87

○ Quantity A is greater.

○ Quantity B is greater.

○ The two quantities are equal.

○ The relationship cannot be determined from the information given.

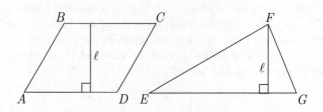

AB is parallel to CD.

AD is parallel to BC.

$2AD = EG$

Quantity A	**Quantity B**
The area of $ABCD$	The area of EFG

○ Quantity A is greater.

○ Quantity B is greater.

○ The two quantities are equal.

○ The relationship cannot be determined from the information given.

$$(3x - 4y)(3x + 4y) = 2$$

Quantity A	**Quantity B**
$9x^2 - 16y^2$	4

○ Quantity A is greater.

○ Quantity B is greater.

○ The two quantities are equal.

○ The relationship cannot be determined from the information given.

If $8a - 2 = 22$, then $4a - 1 =$

○ 2

○ $\dfrac{11}{4}$

○ 11

○ 12

○ 44

SECTION 3: QUANTITATIVE REASONING

Twenty percent of the sweaters in a store are white. Of the remaining sweaters, 40 percent are brown, and the rest are blue. If there are 200 sweaters in the store, then how many more blue sweaters than white sweaters are in the store?

Click on the answer box, then type in a number.
Backspace to erase.

$$\frac{4^{13} - 4^{12}}{4^{11}} =$$

○   0

○   1

○   4

○   12

○   16

Questions 11 through 14 refer to the following graph.

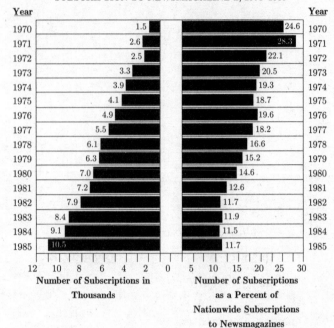

SUBSCRIPTION TO NEWSMAGAZINE x, 1970–1985

Year	Number of Subscriptions in Thousands	Number of Subscriptions as a Percent of Nationwide Subscriptions to Newsmagazines	Year
1970	1.5	24.6	1970
1971	2.6	28.3	1971
1972	2.5	22.1	1972
1973	3.3	20.5	1973
1974	3.9	19.3	1974
1975	4.1	18.7	1975
1976	4.9	19.6	1976
1977	5.5	18.2	1977
1978	6.1	16.6	1978
1979	6.3	15.2	1979
1980	7.0	14.6	1980
1981	7.2	12.6	1981
1982	7.9	11.7	1982
1983	8.4	11.9	1983
1984	9.1	11.5	1984
1985	10.5	11.7	1985

Note: Drawn to scale

NATIONWIDE NEWSMAGAZINE SUBSCRIPTIONS: 1972 TO 1984

Newsmagazine	1972	1975	1978	1981	1984
x	2,500	4,100	6,100	7,200	9,100
y	1,700	3,100	4,600	5,700	7,200
z	3,600	5,800	7,600	9,400	11,400
Others	3,500	8,900	18,500	34,700	51,300

For the year in which Newsmagazine x accounted for 14.6 percent of nationwide newsmagazine subscriptions, what was the number of subscriptions to Newsmagazine x ?

○ 1,020

○ 1,980

○ 6,300

○ 7,000

○ 7,200

SECTION 3: QUANTITATIVE REASONING

In which of the following years did subscriptions to Newsmagazine z account for approximately $\frac{1}{6}$ of the total nationwide magazine subscriptions?

- ○ 1984
- ○ 1981
- ○ 1978
- ○ 1975
- ○ 1972

What was the approximate percent increase in nationwide subscriptions to newsmagazines between 1970 and 1971?

- ○   4%
- ○ 11%
- ○ 26%
- ○ 51%
- ○ 73%

In 1973, what was the approximate number of subscriptions to newsmagazines nationwide?

- ○   3,000
- ○ 13,000
- ○ 16,000
- ○ 20,000
- ○ 67,000

If $a = (27)(3^{-2})$ and $x = (6)(3^{-1})$, then which of the following is equivalent to $(12)(3^{-x}) \times (15)(2^{-a})$?

- ○ $-2245 \times 320 \times 5$
- ○ $\dfrac{2}{5}$
- ○ $\dfrac{5}{2}$
- ○ $24 \times 38 \times 5$
- ○ $2245 \times 320 \times 5$

Sandy has a husband and 2 children. She brings at least 1 member of her family to a diner for lunch every day. The diner offers 10 lunch specials. If no one orders the same thing, how many different orders can Sandy's family make for lunch?

Indicate **all** possible values.

- ☐   45
- ☐   90
- ☐ 120
- ☐ 210
- ☐ 720
- ☐ 5,040

Click on your choice(s).

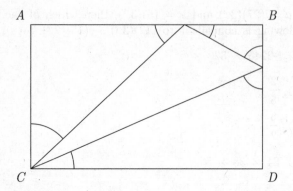

In the figure above, if *ABCD* is a rectangle, what is the sum of the marked angles?

 degrees

Click on the answer box, then type in a number.
Backspace to erase.

If the probability of choosing 2 red marbles without replacement from a bag of only red and blue marbles is $\frac{3}{55}$ and there are 3 red marbles in the bag, what is the total number of marbles in the bag?

- ○ 10
- ○ 11
- ○ 55
- ○ 110
- ○ 165

All first-year students at Red State University must take calculus, English composition, or both. If half of the 2,400 first-year students at Red State University take calculus and half do not, and one-third of those who take calculus also take English composition, how many students take English composition?

- ○ 400
- ○ 800
- ○ 1,200
- ○ 1,600
- ○ 2,000

If $\frac{15!}{3^m}$ is an integer, what is the greatest possible value of *m* ?

- ○ 4
- ○ 5
- ○ 6
- ○ 7
- ○ 8

NO TEST MATERIAL ON THIS PAGE

SECTION 4: VERBAL REASONING

For questions 1 through 4, select one entry for each blank from the corresponding column of choices. Fill all blanks in the way that best completes the text.

Since a large number of the ores frequently located in riverbeds are (i)_____ on the earth's surface, where the processing of chemicals is less costly, recovery of underwater ores is not likely to become a (ii)_____ procedure.

Blank (i)	Blank (ii)
scanty	valuable
abundant	cost-effective
preserved	rejected

It would be (i)_____ for our leaders, given their responsibilities as democratically elected officials, to neglect to do everything they could to (ii)_____ an entirely (iii)_____ problem.

Blank (i)	Blank (ii)	Blank (iii)
irresponsible	forestall	benign
thoughtful	sustain	unimportant
intuitive	cultivate	avoidable

Despite her mentor's advice that she attempt to sound consistently _____ , the graduate student often resorted to using slang when presenting significant parts of her thesis, her habitual speech patterns overriding her years of learning.

lucid
didactic
panegyrical
erudite
rational

Although she felt Steve (i)_____ the subtlety of the delicious stew recipe with his addition of the sweet potato, she thought the pungent onion (ii)_____ the otherwise (iii)_____ taste combination.

Blank (i)	Blank (ii)	Blank (iii)
depleted	exaggerated	delicate
masticated	overwhelmed	zesty
augmented	satiated	detestable

SECTION 4: VERBAL REASONING

For questions 5 through 6, select one entry for each blank from the corresponding column of choices. Fill all blanks in the way that best completes the text.

At first, a still-life painting can appear quite (i)_____ , its focus on such everyday objects as flowers or fruits apparently uninspired. In the hands of (ii)_____ painter, however, careful attention to slight shifts of color and texture can lead to a truly (iii)_____ and exemplary painting.

Blank (i)	Blank (ii)	Blank (iii)
vital	a gauche	unstinting
luxuriant	an adept	sublime
banal	an ascetic	prosaic

The leaders of Ukraine's "Orange Revolution" were a study in contrasts. At the center of the political storm stood Viktor Yushchenko, his once-handsome face turned into a hideous, (i)_____ mask by dioxin poisoning; but, at his side, no one could miss the (ii)_____ Yulia Tymoshenko, soon to become the world's only prime minister to adorn the covers of fashion magazines.

Blank (i)	Blank (ii)
limpid	bonny
fatuous	decorous
teratoid	felicitous

SECTION 4: VERBAL REASONING

Questions 7 through 9 are based on the following reading passage.

In analyzing the poetry of Mona Feather, we are confronted with three different yardsticks by which to measure her work. We could consider her poems as the product of a twentieth-century artist in the tradition of James Joyce, T.S. Eliot, and Wallace Stevens. However, to do so would be to ignore a facet of her that informs every word she writes and that stems from her identity as a woman. Yet, to characterize her solely as a woman poet is to deny her cultural heritage, for Mona Feather is also the first modern poet of stature who is also an American Indian.

Stanley Wilson has argued compellingly that the huge popularity Feather enjoys among the Indian reservation school population of the United States is creating a whole new generation of poetry enthusiasts in an age when the reading of poetry is on the wane. While this is undoubtedly true, Mr. Wilson's praise gives the impression that Feather's readership is limited to her own culture—an impression which hints that Mr. Wilson is himself only measuring her by one criterion. Radical feminist writers have long found in Feather's poetry a sense of self-pride which struck a chord with their own more political philosophies. Her imagery, which always made use of the early Native American traditions in which the woman had an important role, was seen as the awakened sensibility of a kindred spirit.

Yet for all the "feminist" touches in her writing, it would be a disservice to consign Feather to the ranks of politicized writers, for her message is deeper than that. The despair that characterized twentieth-century modern poets is to be found in Mona Feather's work as well; she writes of the American Indians of the 1930s confined to ever-shrinking reservations and finds in that a metaphor for all of modern mankind trapped on a shrinking earth of limited resources.

The primary purpose of the passage is to

○ describe the work of Mona Feather

○ compare Feather with Joyce, Eliot, and Stevens

○ show Feather's roots in her Native American heritage

○ argue that Mona Feather's work can be looked at in several different ways

○ discuss the women's movement in America

The passage implies that the author believes Stanley Wilson's view of Feather is

○ a compelling and complete assessment of her work

○ focused too much on her status as a Native American poet

○ meant to disguise his opinion of Feather as a poet lacking in talent

○ critical of Native American children's literary judgment

○ based on all major themes and images in her poetry

The author mentions James Joyce, T.S. Eliot, and Wallace Stevens in order to

○ compare the political messages in Feather's work to those in the work of other authors

○ highlight the radical differences between male and female poets in the twentieth century

○ contrast Feather's thematic choices with those of her contemporaries

○ enumerate a list of artists whose sensibilities made them Feather's kindred spirits

○ describe a critical context in which Feather's work can be analyzed

SECTION 4: VERBAL REASONING

Questions 10 through 11 are based on the following reading passage.

Among the more interesting elements of etymology is the attempt to derive the meaning of seemingly nonsensical expressions. Take, for instance, the increasingly archaic rural phrase "to buy a pig in a poke." For centuries, the expression has been used to signify the purchase of an item without full knowledge of its condition, and it relates to the common Renaissance practice of securing suckling pigs for transport to market in a poke, or drawstring bag. Unscrupulous sellers would sometimes attempt to dupe purchasers by replacing the suckling pig with a cat, considered worthless at market. An unsuspecting or naïve buyer might fail to confirm the bag's contents; a more urbane buyer, though, would be sure to check and—should the seller be dishonest—"let the cat out of the bag."

Consider each of the choices separately and select all that apply.

Which of the following phrases from the passage would help the reader infer the meaning of the word urbane as used in context?

- [ ] "increasingly archaic rural phrase"
- [ ] "without full knowledge"
- [ ] "unsuspecting or naïve buyer"

Select a sentence in which the author makes deliberate use of a seemingly nonsensical expression.

*For questions 12 through 15, select the **two** answer choices that, when used to complete the sentence, fit the meaning of the sentence as a whole **and** produce completed sentences that are alike in meaning.*

Although she was such a bad-mannered child that she was sent to a boarding school, as an adult she is the very model of _____ .

- [ ] friendliness
- [ ] diffidence
- [ ] propriety
- [ ] reticence
- [ ] decorum
- [ ] brashness

Politicians sometimes appear to act in a manner that is almost _____ ; however, when all the information is released after the fact, it is apparent that they were acting according to a deliberate plan.

- [ ] pithy
- [ ] conventional
- [ ] conformist
- [ ] whimsical
- [ ] flawless
- [ ] capricious

Forced to take an alternate road when a massive oil spill closed the highway, the two-hour detour made their already arduous trip even more _____ .

☐ irksome

☐ onerous

☐ facile

☐ glib

☐ implacable

☐ immutable

Though many of her contemporaries found her odd, Ella Wilkins is now much admired for her _____ spirit, especially her willingness to reject prevailing feminine roles and to travel to foreign lands alone.

☐ forlorn

☐ magnanimous

☐ adventurous

☐ bellicose

☐ desolate

☐ doughty

Microfiber synthetics have been taking the place of natural fibers in an ever-increasing number of clothes because they provide the same durability and deplete fewer natural resources. A shirt made of microfiber synthetics is, however, three times as expensive to produce as a natural-fiber shirt. It follows that the substitution of microfiber synthetic clothes for natural-fiber clothes is, at this time, not recommended from a financial standpoint.

Which of the following statements, if true, most seriously weakens the argument?

◯ A microfiber synthetic shirt costs one-half the price of a natural-fiber shirt to maintain.

◯ The production of microfiber synthetic clothes necessitates garment factories to renovate obsolete machinery and to hire extra workers to operate the new machines.

◯ The upkeep of natural-fiber shirts is far less expensive than the upkeep of any other natural-fiber garment in current production.

◯ While producers anticipate that the cost of microfiber synthetics will remain stable, they recognize that the advent of recycling programs for natural fibers should bring down the costs of natural fibers.

◯ The cost of providing stain guards for microfiber synthetic shirts would probably be greater than what garment producers now spend on stain guards for natural-fiber shirts.

SECTION 4: VERBAL REASONING

Questions 17 through 18 are based on the following reading passage.

Scholars of early Buddhist art agree that Buddha images in human form emerged around the first century A.D. in the regions of Mathura, located in central India, and Gandhara, now part of Pakistan and Afghanistan. Uncertainty exists, however, about whether Mathura or Gandhara has the stronger claim to primacy. Those who believe that anthropomorphic sculptures of the Buddha first appeared in Gandhara point out that earlier Buddhist art was largely aniconic and that *bas relief* was far more common than sculpture. They argue that Greek influence in Gandhara promoted the development of the new style and form of representation of the divine. Other scholars make the case for indigenous development of such representations in Mathura, citing a centuries-long record of iconic art in pre-Buddhist traditions. They don't reject all foreign influence, but they argue that local traditions provided a strong foundation for the development of Buddhist sculpture.

Art historians bolster their arguments by highlighting distinctive features of the sculptures from each region. For example, the artists of Gandhara sculpted their Buddhas in heavy, pleated drapery, similar to that of Greek statues. Wavy lines indicating hair also reflect Greek influence. Mathura Buddhas, on the other hand, are portrayed wearing lighter robes draped in a monastic style, often with part of the shoulder and chest left bare. Elongated earlobes and strong facial features characterize Mathura images of the Buddha, whereas Gandhara images possess more angular features. Sorting out dates and directions of influence has proven difficult, but the totality of evidence suggests that the Buddha image evolved simultaneously in both regions and was shaped by the predominant cultural influences in each region.

Which of the following, if true, would those who believe that anthropomorphic images of Buddha originated in Gandhara be likely to cite as evidence for their viewpoint?

○ Pre-Buddhist subcultures in the Gandhara region created representations of their deities in human form.

○ Mathuran Buddhas' lightweight robes appear to have been modeled on the real robes of people who lived in a warm climate.

○ Gandharan artists were isolated from the larger society and not exposed to influences from outside the region.

○ Rulers from the Mathura region had political ties to Greek rulers and frequently exchanged gifts with them.

○ The hairstyles worn by Gandharan Buddhas are similar to those depicted on Greek pottery from the same period.

According to the passage, Buddhist art

○ first appeared in regions that are now part of India, Pakistan, and Afghanistan

○ experienced a period during which human representations of the Buddha were not common

○ characteristically portrayed figures with elongated earlobes and strong facial features

○ began to appear in the medium of *bas relief* as a result of Greek influence

○ was more influenced by foreign artworks than by indigenous artistic traditions

SECTION 4: VERBAL REASONING

Questions 19 through 20 are based on the following reading passage.

In 1887, Eugene Dubois began his search in Sumatra for the "missing link"—the being that would fill the evolutionary gap between ape and man. He discovered a fossilized human-like thighbone and a section of skull. He confirmed that these fossils were of significant age, based on other fossils in the same area. The thighbone's shape indicated that it belonged to a creature that walked upright. Dubois estimated the size of the creature's skull from the skull fragment and concluded that this creature's brain volume was between that of the higher primates and that of current humans. Although the concept of "missing link" has changed dramatically and a recent dating showed Dubois's fossils to be far too recent for humans to have evolved from this "missing link," the value of his discovery and the debate it generated is unquestionable.

Consider each of the choices separately and select all that apply.

The passage supplies information to answer which of the following questions?

☐ What was the approximate age of the fossils found by Dubois?

☐ Does Dubois's find meet current definitions of the "missing link?"

☐ Do the flaws in Dubois's conclusions invalidate his work?

Select a sentence in which the author reaches a conclusion.

NO TEST MATERIAL ON THIS PAGE

SECTION 5: QUANTITATIVE REASONING

Questions 1 through 8 each consist of two quantities, Quantity A and Quantity B. You are to compare the two quantities and choose the appropriate answer. In a question, information concerning one or both of the quantities to be compared is centered above the two columns. A symbol that appears in both columns represents the same thing in Quantity A as it does in Quantity B.

R is a circle with radius 6.

Quantity A	**Quantity B**
The ratio of the circumference of R to the radius of R	6

○ Quantity A is greater.

○ Quantity B is greater.

○ The two quantities are equal.

○ The relationship cannot be determined from the information given.

Quantity A	**Quantity B**
$\dfrac{.62}{.124}$	$\dfrac{.001}{.0002}$

○ Quantity A is greater.

○ Quantity B is greater.

○ The two quantities are equal.

○ The relationship cannot be determined from the information given.

Quantity A	**Quantity B**
The remainder when 135 is divided by 7	The remainder when 135 is divided by 19

○ Quantity A is greater.

○ Quantity B is greater.

○ The two quantities are equal.

○ The relationship cannot be determined from the information given.

a and b are integers.

$$a^2 = b^3$$

Quantity A	**Quantity B**
a	b

○ Quantity A is greater.

○ Quantity B is greater.

○ The two quantities are equal.

○ The relationship cannot be determined from the information given.

$$ab < 0$$
$$bc > 0$$

Quantity A	**Quantity B**
ac	0

○ Quantity A is greater.

○ Quantity B is greater.

○ The two quantities are equal.

○ The relationship cannot be determined from the information given.

$$|x| = 6$$
$$y = x + 4$$

Quantity A	Quantity B
y	10

○ Quantity A is greater.

○ Quantity B is greater.

○ The two quantities are equal.

○ The relationship cannot be determined from the information given.

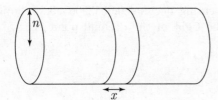

A piece of ribbon is wrapped around a right circular cylinder with radius n. The ribbon, which encircles the cylinder without overlap, has width x and an area equal to the area of the base of the cylinder.

Quantity A	Quantity B
x	n

○ Quantity A is greater.

○ Quantity B is greater.

○ The two quantities are equal.

○ The relationship cannot be determined from the information given.

Set A: $\{1, 2, 7, 8, 15, 2, 3, 5, 6, 13\}$

x is the median of the even numbers in Set A.

y is the median of the prime numbers in Set A.

z is the median of the least and greatest numbers in Set A.

Quantity A	Quantity B
The median of $2x$, y, and z	z

○ Quantity A is greater.

○ Quantity B is greater.

○ The two quantities are equal.

○ The relationship cannot be determined from the information given.

Oil is pumped from a well at a rate of 500 gallons per hour. How many gallons of oil are pumped from the well in 3 hours and 15 minutes?

 gallons

Click on the answer box, then type in a number. Backspace to erase.

A certain pet store sells only dogs and cats. In March, the store sold twice as many dogs as cats. In April, the store sold twice the number of dogs than it sold in March, and three times the number of cats that it sold in March. If the total number of pets the store sold in March and April combined was 500, how many dogs did the store sell in March?

○ 80

○ 100

○ 120

○ 160

○ 180

In the coordinate plane, rectangle $WXYZ$ has vertices at $(-2, -1)$, $(-2, y)$, $(4, y)$, and $(4, -1)$. If the area of $WXYZ$ is 18, what is the length of its diagonal?

○ $3\sqrt{2}$

○ $3\sqrt{3}$

○ $3\sqrt{5}$

○ $3\sqrt{6}$

○ $3\sqrt{7}$

How many three-digit integers can be created from 5 distinct digits?

○ 10

○ 15

○ 20

○ 30

○ 60

At Megalomania Industries, factory workers were paid $20 per hour in 1990 and $10 per hour in 2000. The CEO of Megalomania Industries was paid $5 million per year in 1990 and $50 million per year in 2000. The percent increase in the pay of Megalomania's CEO from 1990 to 2000 was what percent greater than the percent decrease in the hourly pay of Megalomania's factory workers over the same period?

○ 850%

○ 900%

○ 950%

○ 1,700%

○ 1,900%

In the repeating decimal 0.0653906539..., the 34th digit to the right of the decimal point is

○ 9

○ 6

○ 5

○ 3

○ 0

SECTION 5: QUANTITATIVE REASONING

Questions 15 through 17 refer to the following graph.

PRIVATE DONATIONS TO CHARITABLE CAUSES IN COUNTRY x, JAN. 1971–DEC. 1989

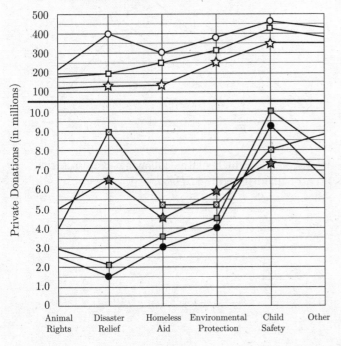

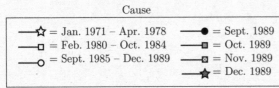

If funds contributed to child safety organizations in September 1989 were distributed evenly to those 38 organizations, approximately how much did each charity receive?

○ $12,000,000

○ $9,400,000

○ $2,500,000

○ $250,000

○ $38,000

From September 1985 to December 1989, what was the approximate ratio of private donations in millions to homeless aid to private donations in millions to animal rights?

○ 20:9

○ 3:2

○ 4:3

○ 9:7

○ 6:5

Which of the following charitable causes received the smallest percent increase in private donations from September 1989 to October 1989?

○ Animal Rights

○ Disaster Relief

○ Homeless Aid

○ Environmental Protection

○ Child Safety

If $3x + 2y = 24$, and $\dfrac{7y}{2x} = 7$, then $y =$

*Click on the answer box, then type in a number.
Backspace to erase.*

If the average (arithmetic mean) of 6, 8, 10, and x is between 7 and 11 inclusive, what is the greatest possible value of x?

○   8

○   11

○   20

○   28

○   44

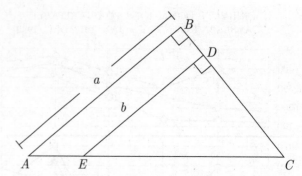

If $AB = BC$, which of the following expresses the area of quadrilateral $ABDE$?

○ $\dfrac{a^2}{2} - \dfrac{b^2}{2}$

○ $\dfrac{a^2}{2} + \dfrac{b^2}{2}$

○ $a^2 - b^2$

○ $\dfrac{a^2}{4} - \dfrac{ab}{2}$

○ $\dfrac{a^2}{4} + \dfrac{ab}{2}$

NO TEST MATERIAL ON THIS PAGE

SECTION 6: VERBAL REASONING

For questions 1 through 5, select one entry for each blank from the corresponding column of choices. Fill all blanks in the way that best completes the text.

Many fashions that were considered daring in their time have been so widely worn and imitated that the (i)_____ style is no longer seen as (ii)_____ .

Blank (i)	Blank (ii)
proposed	outlandish
original	commonplace
revealing	copied

Western culture has so influenced Middle Eastern music that even the latter's roles of composer and performer, at one time inseparable, have now begun to _____ .

divulge
retreat
retrench
diverge
fuse

Kazan was quickly (i)_____ by many of his contemporaries for his transgression, who saw his testimony as treachery, an act of (ii)_____ which stained how they viewed him both as an artist and as a man. It was only by continually making films that he was able to (iii)_____ his perceived sins and achieve some measure of atonement.

Blank (i)	Blank (ii)	Blank (iii)
rebuked	perfidy	exacerbate
lauded	sophistry	deviate
mitigated	redemption	expiate

Although tranquilizers usually have a _____ effect, this is not always the case, especially when the abuse of these drugs results in a failure to induce the much-desired sleep.

soporific
sedulous
coruscating
debilitating
penetrating

As a rule, (i)_____ interpretations of events are rejected by modern science in its attempts to find secular insights into the matrix of causes and effects in our modern world. Paradoxically, this fact does not (ii)_____ the existence of individual scientists who possess views that may be (iii)_____ with a belief in supernatural causes.

Blank (i)	Blank (ii)	Blank (iii)
falsifiable	countenance	at variance
preternatural	enhance	consonant
teleological	preclude	discrepant

The Johnsons were not known for their (i)_____ ; at the very least, none of the family members was fearful of (ii)_____ , of appearing or acting differently from other people.

Blank (i)	Blank (ii)
candor	pettiness
vulgarity	eccentricity
conformity	complaisance

SECTION 6: VERBAL REASONING

Questions 7 through 10 are based on the following reading passage.

According to most scientists, the universe began approximately 10 to 15 billion years ago and has been expanding ever since. This theory, known as the Big Bang theory, is the fairly direct result of Hubble's law, which states that objects farther away from Earth are receding faster than those closer. This expansion implies a singular point which all matter is expanding from.

Complicating the scientific explanation is that the Big Bang cannot be thought of as an explosion from some identifiable source—rather, space and time were created in the Big Bang. Furthermore, the relationship between distance and speed is not precisely linear. So, if one were to think of galaxies as particles created in a big bang, these galaxies have both a local component of motion, as well as playing a role in the overall expansion of the universe.

A further complication is that galactic distances are so great that galactic motion, even if the galaxies are moving at incredible speeds, is difficult to observe. Scientists must therefore rely on a "standard candle," an object of known brightness within the galaxy they wish to observe. Using the inverse square law, scientists can then measure the how far that galaxy is away from our own. For instance, suppose a supernova in galaxy A appears one hundred times as bright as one in galaxy B. By the inverse square law, galaxy B is ten times farther away than galaxy A, assuming, of course, that distance is the only factor affecting brightness.

It can be inferred from the sentence highlighted in the passage that a standard candle is useful to scientists for which of the following reasons?

○ Standard candles do not have their own locus of motion.

○ Standard candles more reliably adhere to the law of inverse squares than do other supernovas.

○ Only standard candles provide a known measure of brightness.

○ Knowledge of an object's brightness of an object allows scientists to measure the speed at which the object is moving toward Earth.

○ Knowledge of an object's brightness allows scientists to accurately measure its distance from Earth.

According to the passage, if two astronomical objects of differing distances from Earth were observed, which of the following would be true of the object closer to Earth?

Select <u>all</u> such statements.

☐ It would not be as bright as the object farther from Earth.

☐ It would be younger than the object farther from Earth.

☐ It would be traveling away from the Earth more slowly than the farther object.

According to the passage, a standard candle may not provide an accurate measure of distance if

○ the galaxy being measured is moving too quickly

○ interstellar dust makes the object measured appear dimmer than it really is

○ if the galaxy being measured has a local component of measurement

○ the particles being measured do not completely accord with a linear motion

○ the galaxies being measured move at different speeds

According to the passage, if two supernovas are observed and one of those supernovas is brighter than the other, scientists can conclude that

○ the brighter supernova is moving closer to our galaxy at a higher speed

○ the precise location of the supernova is measurable

○ the brighter supernova may be closer to our own galaxy

○ the brighter supernova is farther away from Earth by a distance that is roughly inversely proportional to the dim supernova

○ the distance between the supernovas and our own galaxy is inversely proportional

SECTION 6: VERBAL REASONING

Questions 11 through 12 are based on the following reading passage.

Throughout the twentieth century, it was accepted as fact that cells in our brains, called neurons, do not regenerate. Research by neurologist Elizabeth Gould overturned this core doctrine within the span of a few years. Her experiments on rats showed that even after suffering severe trauma, their brains were able to heal themselves by regenerating neurons. Gould's findings have incited a flood of new research into applications that may take advantage of neurogenesis.

One such study examines the role of reduced neurogenesis among individuals suffering from depression. It is speculated that neurogenesis may contribute to an explanation for the so called "Prozac lag." As an antidepressant, the immediate boost of serotonin caused by Prozac should have had instantaneous mood elevating effects. However, patients suffering from depression only begin to experience mood elevation weeks after beginning treatment. The study speculates that during this period, the brain may be regenerating neurons.

The author mentions the "Prozac lag" primarily in order to

○ raise a possible objection to a newly proposed theory

○ present a situation for which a new theory may serve an explanatory role

○ offer evidence that runs counter to a previously held belief

○ suggest a counterexample that undermines a newly proposed theory

○ provide supporting evidence that a newly discovered phenomenon may have unforeseen effects

In the second paragraph, select the sentence in which the author describes an unexpected observation.

SECTION 6: VERBAL REASONING

*For questions 13 through 16, select the **two** answer choices that, when used to complete the sentence, fit the meaning of the sentence as a whole **and** produce completed sentences that are alike in meaning.*

Plato, an important philosopher, is primarily known because he wrote down Socrates's _____ conversations. It is through Plato's record of these dialogues that Socrates's teachings have survived and continue to enlighten seekers of wisdom.

- ☐ inspiring
- ☐ edifying
- ☐ tedious
- ☐ grating
- ☐ rousing
- ☐ didactic

Even the colossal meal failed to _____ her voracious appetite.

- ☐ cadge
- ☐ exacerbate
- ☐ provoke
- ☐ satiate
- ☐ mendicate
- ☐ allay

Slicks of oil on a rain-soaked street are _____ and beautiful, but the lovely rainbows they produce on the asphalt can seem rather ugly when one reflects upon the road hazards they create and the environmental damage they entail.

- ☐ anodyne
- ☐ iridescent
- ☐ monocoque
- ☐ pavonine
- ☐ parietal
- ☐ saturnine

He had not always been so callous, but with time he became _____ to the violence around him.

- ☐ adorned
- ☐ cauterized
- ☐ sensitized
- ☐ ostracized
- ☐ inured
- ☐ attuned

SECTION 6: VERBAL REASONING

When the maker of Megapower, a vitamin supplement, modified its formula two years ago, Tasmania, an island off the coast of New Zealand, suffered a decrease in its export earnings. Tasmania's only export, kiwi fruit, constitutes a substantial portion of the world supply of that fruit. Researchers concluded that the old Megapower formula contained natural kiwi extract, but the new formula does not.

Which of the following, if true, gives the strongest support for the researchers' claim?

- ○ Some South American countries have begun to grow kiwi fruit successfully.

- ○ United States chemists have started development of a synthetic kiwi extract.

- ○ The manufacturers of Megapower chose not to renew their contract with the Tasmanian kiwi growers.

- ○ Imports of kiwi fruit have fallen in the country where Megapower is manufactured.

- ○ There was a marked drop in sales of a number of formerly profitable items that used kiwi as an ingredient.

Questions 18 through 20 are based on the following reading passage.

While art historians do not necessarily agree on the date of the birth of modern art, they do agree that mid-nineteenth century French art shows a clear and distinct break from tradition. Pressed to point to a single picture that represents the vanguard of the modern art movement, art historians will often point to Courbet's *The Painter's Studio.*

The peculiar subtitle of Courbet's work, "Real allegory summing up a seven-year period of my life" confirms that Courbet was striving to do something strikingly original with his work. The argument has been made that the painting struck a blow for the independence of the artist, and that since Courbet's work, artists have felt freed from the societal demands placed upon their work. Paintings prior to Courbet's time were most often focused on depicting events from the Bible, history, or literature. With his singular painting, Courbet promulgated the idea that an artist is capable of representing only that which he can experience through his senses of sight and touch; the true artist will then be compelled to make his representation as simply and directly as possible.

Which of the following would most effectively replace the word promulgated as it is used in the context of the passage?

- ○ displayed

- ○ disseminated

- ○ proclaimed

- ○ concealed

- ○ secreted

Click on the sentence in the passage that best explains the effect of Courbet's work on other artists.

SECTION 6: VERBAL REASONING

The effect that Courbet had on painting is most analogous to which situation?

○ an avant-garde writer who subverts novelistic conventions

○ a machinist who tinkers and improves his invention

○ a watercolor painter who paints in the same style as his peers

○ a scientist who comes up with a unified theory of several discordant scientific ideas

○ a seamstress who makes a ball gown using several different types of fabric

Chapter 17
Answers and Explanations for Practice Test 1

INTERPRETING YOUR RESULTS

After you check your answers on the following pages, fill out this sheet to interpret your results.

Analytic Writing Sections

To evaluate your performance on the Analytic Writing sections, compare your response to the advice and samples in the Analytic Writing chapter.

Verbal Reasoning

Refer to the explanations to check your answers. Count of number of questions you got correct in each Verbal Reasoning section, and calculate the total number correct. Find the section of the Interpretive Guide (below) that corresponds to your total to get an idea of how your performance compares to that of other test takers.

Test 1	# Correct
Section 4	
Section 6	
Total	

Test 2	# Correct
Section 3	
Section 5	
Total	

Quantitative Reasoning

Refer to the explanations to check your answers. Count of number of questions you got correct in each Quantitative Reasoning section, and calculate the total number correct. Find the section of the Interpretive Guide (below) that corresponds to your total to get an idea of how your performance compares to that of other test takers.

Test 1	# Correct
Section 3	
Section 5	
Total	

Test 2	# Correct
Section 4	
Section 6	
Total	

Interpretive Guide

The table below provides a guide for interpreting your performance based on the number of questions you got correct in each subject.

Subject	Well Above Average	Above Average	Average	Below Average
Verbal Reasoning	51–56	40–50	23–39	1–22
Quantitative Reasoning	48–52	40–47	24–39	1–23

Section 3

1. **A**

    Point *C* has the same *x*–coordinate as point *D*, so *s* = 8. Point *C* also has the same *y*-coordinate as point *B*, so *t* = 7. That means that Quantity A is greater.

2. **A**

    The soda has 4 + 5 + 11 = 20 total parts. The ice cream has 3 + 2 + 15 = 20 total parts. You're dealing with the same totals. If you added two parts of soda, then that's 4 × 2 = 8 parts sugar and 5 × 2 = 10 parts citric acid. If you added three parts ice cream, then that's 3 × 3 = 9 parts sugar and 2 × 3 = 6 parts salt. There's 8 + 9 = 17 total parts sugar and 10 + 6 = 16 total parts citric acid. There's more sugar than citric acid.

3. **B**

    If you Plug In 5 for *x*, the total for the 5 days already in the set is 350; after adding the additional 75 degree temperature, the new total is 425, and the new average is $\frac{425}{6}$, which reduces to $70\frac{5}{6}$. Because the additional temperature caused a greater change, there must have been fewer days in the original set. Quantity B is greater.

4. **D**

    Because Δ*QRS* is isosceles, side *RS* must be equal to one of the other sides, and *x* could measure 4 or 7. Thus, the perimeter could be 4 + 4 + 7 = 15, or the perimeter could be 4 + 7 + 7 = 18. You can't tell if the perimeter is greater or less than 17, and, thus, the answer is choice (D). Remember, if it doesn't say "Drawn to scale," you can't assume it is!

5. **B**

    Remember that a normal distribution curve has divisions of 34 percent, 14 percent, and 2 percent on each side of the mean. 80 out of 500 is 16 percent, or 14 percent + 2 percent, and 10 out of 500 is 2 percent. Draw a normal distribution curve and label it. There are three standard deviations between 92 and 56, so 92 − 56 = 36, and 36 ÷ 3 = 12. The mean is 92 − 12 = 80, which is smaller than Quantity B.

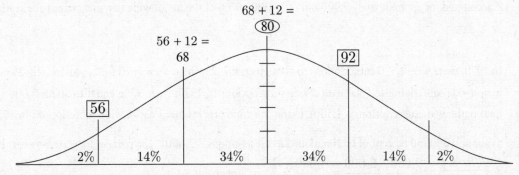

6. **C**

    Plug In numbers for the sides. Let *AD* = 4, so *EG* = 8. Let *l* = 3. The area of *ABCD* = 3 × 4 = 12, and the area of *EFG* = $\frac{1}{2}$ (3 × 8) = 12. The two quantities can be equal, so eliminate answer choices (A) and (B). Try changing your numbers, and you will see that the two quantities will always be equal.

7. **B**

FOIL out the equation given, and you'll get $(3x - 4y)(3x + 4y) = 9x^2 - 16y^2$, so Quantity A is 2. Quantity B is therefore bigger, and the answer is (B).

8. **C**

Solve for a by adding 2 to each side to get $8a = 24$. Divide by 8 to find $a = 3$. Plug $a = 3$ into the second equation to find $4(3) - 1 = 12 - 1 = 11$. Alternatively, you could save yourself some time by noticing that $8a - 2$ is $2(4a - 1)$. If $2(4a - 1) = 22$, divide by 2 to get $4a - 1 = 11$.

9. **56**

Twenty percent of the sweaters in the store are white, so there are $200 \times \dfrac{20}{100} = 40$ white sweaters. There are $200 - 40 = 160$ sweaters remaining. Of the remaining sweaters, $160 \times \dfrac{40}{100} = 64$ are brown. That means that $160 - 64 = 96$ are blue. There are $96 - 40 = 56$ more blue sweaters than white sweaters.

10. **D**

Because 4^{12} is a common factor, you can rewrite the numerator as $4^{12}(4 - 1)$. Now look at the whole fraction: $\dfrac{4^{12}(4 - 1)}{4^{11}}$. You can divide 4^{12} by 4^{11}, leaving you with $4^1(4 - 1)$. Now the calculation should be much easier. $4 \times 3 = 12$, choice (D).

11. **D**

Refer to the second chart, then the first chart. In 1980, Newsmagazine X accounted for 14.6 percent of newsmagazine subscriptions, and it had 7,000 subscriptions.

12. **B**

In 1981, Newsmagazine Z accounted for 9,400 out of 57,000 newsmagazine subscriptions. Therefore, Newsmagazine Z accounted for approximately 9,000 out of 57,000, or $\dfrac{1}{6}$, of the nationwide newsmagazine subscriptions.

13. **D**

In 1970, there were 1,500 subscriptions to Newsmagazine X, which accounted for approximately 25 percent of total nationwide subscriptions. Total nationwide subscriptions in 1970, then, were equal to about 6,000 (25 percent of total nationwide subscriptions = 1,500). Using the same process, total nationwide subscriptions in 1971 were equal to about 9,000 (30 percent of total nationwide subscriptions = 2,600). The percent increase between 1970 and 1971 is $\dfrac{difference}{original}$ or $\dfrac{9,000 - 6,000}{6,000} = \dfrac{3,000}{6,000} = \dfrac{1}{2}$, or 50 percent.

14. **C**

In 1973, Newsmagazine X had 3,300 subscriptions, or 20.5 percent of the total number of newsmagazine subscriptions. Set up the calculation to find the total: $3{,}300 = \dfrac{205x}{100}$. Solve it to find that $x = 16{,}000$.

15. **C**

$a = 27 \times \dfrac{1}{3^2} = 3$, and $x = 6 \times \dfrac{1}{3} = 2$. Find $(12)(3^{-x})(15)(2^{-a}) = (12)(3^{-2})(15)(2^{-3}) = \dfrac{(12)(15)}{(3^2)(2^3)}$. Now, reduce:

$\dfrac{(2 \times 2 \times 3)(3 \times 5)}{(3 \times 3)(2 \times 2 \times 2)} = \dfrac{5}{2}$.

16. **A, C, and D**

This is a combination because who ordered what does not matter; you are only interested in how many different orders it is possible to make. If Sandy brings 1 family member, there are 10 menu items from which 2 are chosen, and the number of combinations is $\dfrac{10!}{2!8!} = \dfrac{10 \times 9}{2 \times 1} = 45$, so choice (A) is correct. If she brings 3 people, the number of combinations is $\dfrac{10!}{3!7!} = \dfrac{10 \times 9 \times 8}{3 \times 2 \times 1} = 120 = 120$, and choice (C) is correct. Finally, if all 4 people are there, the number of combinations is $\dfrac{10!}{4!6!} = \dfrac{10 \times 9 \times 8 \times 7}{4 \times 3 \times 2 \times 1} = 210$, and choice (D) is correct.

17. **270**

There are two ways to do this one. You could plug in values for all the angles, keeping in mind that those inside the triangle must add up to 180°, the ones along AB must add up to 180, the ones along BD must add up to 180°, and the ones at C must add up to 90°. Then add up the marked angles. Alternatively, using the Rule of 180°, add the two straight lines and the right angle (AB, BD and $\angle ACD$) to get 450°, and then subtract the unmarked portions, which are the three angles in the triangle, or 180°: 450° − 180° = 270°.

18. **B**

In this problem, you are choosing a red and then a red. Remember that and tells you to multiply the probabilities. The numerator in the first event will be the 3 red marbles, and the numerator in the second event will be 2 because you've already selected 1 red in the first event: $\left(\dfrac{3}{a}\right)\left(\dfrac{2}{b}\right)$. The denominator will be the total, then 1 less than the total. Because 55 has factors of 11 and 5, and there's a 2 to factor out in the top, you know that the denominator must be $11 \times 5 \times 2$ or 11×10. So, the total must be 11. Alternatively, you could plug in the answers starting with choice (C). If the total is 55, then the probability would be $\left(\dfrac{3}{55}\right)\left(\dfrac{2}{54}\right)$, which does not equal $\dfrac{3}{55}$. The denominator is too large, so try choice (B). If the total is 11, then the probability is $\left(\dfrac{3}{11}\right)\left(\dfrac{2}{10}\right)$, which reduces to $\dfrac{3}{55}$.

19. **D**

Use the Group formula: Total = Group 1 + Group 2 − Both + Neither. In this problem the total is 2,400. The question also states that 1,200 students (half of the total) take calculus, so that is Group 1; one-third of that group (400) take both calculus and English. Because every student takes calculus or English or both, the Neither group is zero. Solve for the number of students who take English by plugging these numbers into the group formula: 2400 = 1200 + Group 2 − 400. The number of students who take English is 1,600, or choice (D).

20. **6**

This is a giant fraction. On the top, you have $15 \times 14 \times 13 \times 12 \times 11...\times 2 \times 1$. On the bottom, you have $3 \times 3 \times 3$ and so on. The question is, how many 3's can you have on the bottom that will cancel out with 3's on the top. So, how many 3's do you have on the top? Well, 15 can be expressed as 3×5, 12 can be expressed as 3×4, 9 can be expressed as 3×3, 6 can be expressed as 3×2, and we have 3. In total, there are six 3's in the expression on top, which means we can have as many as six on the bottom, and they will all cancel out. The correct answer is (6).

Section 4

1. **abundant** and **cost-effective**

   The clue for the second blank is "on the earth's surface, where the processing of chemicals is less costly." Underwater recovery, in contrast, would be more expensive. The second blank describes what's not true of the procedure, so use a word that means low-cost. *Cost-effective* is a close match. Use the same clue for the first blank. If the processing of ores from the surface is less costly, those ores must be plentiful. *Abundant* is a good match.

2. **irresponsible**, **forestall** and **avoidable**

   The keys to the first blank are the clues "given their responsibilities as democratically elected officials" and "neglect to do everything they could." These clues indicate that the first blank should have a negative connotation; a word that means something as simple as bad would eliminate *thoughtful* and *intuitive*, leaving *irresponsible*. Blanks (ii) and (iii) build on the idea set up in the first half of the sentence. The second blank describes the action that would be bad, so use something that means solve. *Sustain* and *cultivate* are the opposites of what's needed for the second blank, leaving *forestall*. The last blank describes the type of problem, and entirely suggests it's a solvable problem. *Avoidable* is close, and it helps the whole sentence make sense.

3. **erudite**

   Despite is a trigger word that implies a contrast between the student's actual behavior when presenting her thesis and her mentor's advice. The student resorted to using slang, language that is informal and unscholarly. Therefore, the word in the blank must mean *formal* or *scholarly*. The only word that fits that description is *erudite*, which is the best choice. The other answer choices can be used to describe speech, but none of these words contrast the mentor's advice with the student's use of slang.

4. **augmented**, **overwhelmed**, and **delicate**

   Start with the second blank. The clue *pungent* tells you this onion did something bad to the delicious stew. *Exaggerated* and *satiated* are positive; *overwhelmed* is the only fit. The trigger *otherwise* tells you to change direction from the third blank's clue of *pungent*. Look for a word that means *subtle* or *soft*. Only *delicate* fits. For the first blank, the clue is that Steve's stinky onion hurt the delicate stew. The trigger *although* tells you to change direction. So, this addition of the sweet potato was good. Only *augmented* fits.

5. **banal**, **an adept**, and **sublime**

   The first clue is *its focus on such everyday objects as flowers or fruits apparently uninspired,* so the first blank has to mean something such as "uninspired." *Banal*, which means predictable, matches this. For the second blank, the painter must pay *careful attention*, so the second blank must mean "careful" or "talented," which matches *an adept*. Since the painting is *exemplary*, the third blank must be *sublime*.

6. **teratoid** and **bonny**

> The first blank requires a synonym for *hideous*; *teratoid* means monstrously deformed, and so works well. *Limpid* means transparent, and *fatuous* means foolish, so those words don't work. For the second blank, both the trigger phrase "a study in contrasts" and the clue about "fashion magazines" suggest that a word that means beautiful is appropriate. Though it might not sound like it, *bonny* does, in fact, mean beautiful. *Felicitous* means well-expressed, and *decorous* means full of propriety, so although they are both positive words, they aren't as fitting here as the credited response is.

7. **D**

> According to the first sentence, her work can be viewed be viewed three different ways. The rest of the passage describes those ways: as the work of a modern poet, of a woman, and of a Native American. Choice (A) is too vague, and the passage doesn't so much describe her work as how it should be viewed. Choices (B) and (C) are too narrow and don't describe the overall purpose. Choice (E) doesn't match the passage.

8. **B**

> In the second paragraph the author states, "Mr. Wilson's praise gives the impression that Feather's readership is limited to her own culture—an impression which hints that Mr. Wilson is himself only measuring her by one criterion," which best fits choice (B). Choices (A) and (E) contradict the passage and are too broad and extreme. Choice (C) contradicts the passage, and choice (D) is not supported.

9. **E**

> The second sentence of the passage claims, "We could consider her poems as the product of a twentieth-century artist in the tradition of James Joyce, T.S. Eliot, and Wallace Stevens." Thus, the author mentions Joyce, Eliot, and Stevens in order to describe one context—twentieth-century poetry—in which Feather's work can be analyzed. Eliminate choice (A) because the author doesn't compare Feather's political messages to those of these authors. Eliminate choice (B) because the author doesn't use these authors to discuss differences between male and female poets. Eliminate choice (C) because the author doesn't contrast Feather's themes with those of these authors. Although Joyce, Eliot, and Stevens were, like Feather, twentieth-century artists, the passage doesn't say that they shared sensibilities, which eliminates choice (E).

10. **C**

> Only answer choice (C) provides a clue to the meaning of *urbane* as used here: The urbane buyer is contrasted with the "unsuspecting or naïve buyer," and so must mean "not unsuspecting" or "not naïve." Choice (A) tantalizingly dangles the word rural before our eyes, trying to take advantage of that word's well-known association with the word urban. *Urban*, though, means *sophisticated*. Moreover, if answer choice (A) were accepted, the strangely illogical proposition that city-dwellers knew best how to buy animals at market would have to be accepted as well. Answer choice (B), thankfully, presents no such difficulties of interpretation and appears in the definition of the obscure expression itself, not in the comparison between unsuspecting and urbane.

11.

> In the last sentence of the passage, the author says, "let the cat out of the bag." This is the only sentence in which the author uses a seemingly nonsensical expression. The second sentence is tempting, but the author isn't actually using the expression.

12. **propriety** and **decorum**

   The clue "was such a bad-mannered child." Time acts as a change-of-direction trigger ("now, as an adult") that indicates the blank should mean something like well-mannered. Only *propriety* and *decorum* mean well-mannered. *Diffidence*, *reticence*, and *brashness* are all traits that would be considered bad-mannered. *Friendliness* does not necessarily mean well-mannered.

13. **whimsical** and **capricious**

   The blank describes how politicians act. The clue is "acting out a deliberate plan." The change-of-direction trigger *however* tells you that they appear not to have a plan. Words that mean unplanned or random should be in the blank. *Whimsical* and *capricious* both fit this meaning. *Conventional* and *conformist* have the opposite meaning. The other two words are unrelated to the blank.

14. **irksome** and **onerous**

   The trigger "even more" tells you to stay in the same direction as the clue. "Forced to take an alternate road," "two-hour detour," and "arduous trip" tell you that the journey was difficult. Put a word that means hard or tiring in the blank. Only *irksome* and *onerous* fit this meaning. *Facile* and *glib* describe something easy, and *implacable* and *immutable* describe something that doesn't change.

15. **adventurous and doughty**

   The trigger *especially* tells you to stay in the same direction as the clue "willingness to reject prevailing feminine roles and travel to foreign lands alone." Thus, she has a bold spirit. Only *adventurous* and *doughty* mean bold. Although she is traveling alone, there is nothing to support that she is lonely, as *forlorn* and *desolate* suggest. *Magnanimous* and *bellicose* do not fit.

16. **A**

   The argument concludes that the substitution of microfiber clothes for those made from natural fabrics is not financially sound. The premise is that microfiber clothes last as long as natural fabric clothes but are three times as expensive to produce. The argument assumes that there are no other factors that need to be considered to evaluate the cost effectiveness of switching. Choice (A) points out another factor that would affect the overall costs and so weakens the argument. Choice (B) helps to explain why the microfiber synthetic shirt is more expensive to produce than a natural fiber shirt, but it does not weaken the argument. In choice (C), comparing natural fiber shirts and other fiber garments is not relevant. Choice (D) strengthens the argument. Choice (E), by pointing out additional costs associated with microfibers, also strengthens the argument.

17. **E**

   The first paragraph presents the Gandhara-first view "…Greek influence in Gandhara promoted the development of the new style and form of representation of the divine." The second paragraph provides evidence Gandharan Buddhas shared certain features with Greek art. Choice (E) provides additional information about those similarities and is the best choice. Choices (A) and (C) undermine the idea that Gandharan artists were responding to outside influences. Choice (B) is irrelevant, and choice (D) provides evidence for outside influences in Mathura.

18. **B**

The first sentence says that "images in human form emerged around the first century A.D.," and the middle of the first paragraph states that "earlier Buddhist art was largely aniconic." You can conclude from these statements that the earliest Buddhist art didn't usually depict the Buddha in human form. Eliminate choice (A); although human representations first appeared in these regions, the passage doesn't say that the first Buddhist art appeared in the same places. The passage doesn't support choices (C), (D), and (E).

19. **B and C**

For choice (A), the passage only says that the age of these fossils was "far too recent for humans to have evolved" from them. This does not given an age for the fossils. The last sentence says that "the concept of 'missing link' has changed dramatically," which answers the question in choice (B). The last sentence also answers the question in choice (C) because it says, "the value of his discovery and the debate it generated is unquestionable."

20. **B and C**

For choice (A) we are told that the fossil is of "significant" age; no actual age is given for the fossil. Cross off (A). While the definition has changed, and this one couldn't have yielded today's humans, the different direction trigger words mean that this is a "missing link." The last sentence of the passage says that the discovery is "invaluable" so whatever "invalidate" means, the discovery still has value. The answers are (B) and (C).

Section 5

1. **A**

   If R has radius 6, then the circumference of R is $2\pi(6)$, or 12π. The ratio of 12π: 6 or $\dfrac{12\pi}{6}$ reduces to 2π, and because π is a little more than 3, 2π is a little more than 6.

2. **C**

   Move the decimal point to the right in the numerator and denominator until each is an integer. Quantity A = $\dfrac{6.2}{1.24} = \dfrac{62}{12.4} = \dfrac{620}{124} = 5$. Quantity B = $\dfrac{.01}{.002} = \dfrac{.1}{.02} = \dfrac{1}{.2} = \dfrac{10}{2} = 5$. The quantities are equal.

3. **C**

   $135 \div 7 = 19$, remainder 2. $135 \div 19 = 7$, remainder 2. Quantity A and Quantity B both equal 2.

4. **D**

   Plug In. Let $a = 8$ and $b = 4$. Quantity A can be greater than Quantity B, so eliminate answer choices (B) and (C). Now let $a = b = 1$. Quantity A can be equal to Quantity B, so eliminate answer choice (A).

5. **B**

   Plug In numbers for a, b, and c. If $a = -2$, $b = 3$, and $c = 4$, then $ac = -8$. Quantity B is greater; eliminate choices (A) and (C). If $a = 2$, $b = -3$, and $c = -4$, then ac is still negative. Quickly consider different numbers, but realize that Quantity A will always be negative.

6. **D**

If $|x| = 6$, then $x = 6$, or $x = -6$. If $x = 6$, then $y = 6 + 4 = 10$. The quantities are equal, so you can eliminate choices (A) and (B). If $x = -6$, then $y = -6 + 4 = -2$, and Quantity B is greater. Eliminate choice (C), and select choice (D).

7. **B**

Plug In for the radius, n, and solve for x. Let's make $n = 3$: the area of the base of the cylinder is now 9π, and the circumference of the base is 6π. The ribbon itself is a rectangle, and we now know both its area, which is the same as the area of the base, and its length, which is the same as the circumference of the base. Now we can solve for x, which is the other side of the rectangle: $6\pi x = 9\pi$, so $x = \dfrac{9\pi}{6\pi}$, or $\dfrac{3}{2}$. Our value for n is greater than our value for x, so Quantity B is greater.

8. **C**

Remember that median is the number that ends up in the middle of the list when you rewrite the list in numerical order. Find x: The even numbers are 2, 2, 6, 8. Because 2 and 6 are in the middle, find their mean: $\dfrac{2+6}{2} = 4$. So, $x = 4$. Find y: the prime numbers are 2, 2, 3, 5, 7, 13. Remember, 1 is not prime. Because 3 and 5 are in the middle, find their mean: $\dfrac{3+5}{2} = 4$. So, $y = 4$. Find z: the least is 1, the greatest is 15. The median of 1 and 15 is $\dfrac{1+15}{2} = 8$. So, $z = 8$. For Quantity A, find the median of 2(4), 4, and 8: so, the median of 4, 8, 8, is 8. Quantity B is also 8.

9. **1,625**

Set up a proportion: $\dfrac{1 \text{ hour}}{500 \text{ gallons}} = \dfrac{3.25 \text{ hours}}{x \text{ gallons}}$. Cross multiply to find that $x = 500 \times 3.25 = 1,625$ gallons.

10. **B**

Plug In the answers, starting with the middle choice. If 120 dogs were sold in March, then 60 cats were sold that month. In April, 240 dogs were sold, along with 180 cats. The total number of dogs and cats sold during those two months is 600, which is too large, so eliminate choices (C), (D), and (E). Try choice (B). If there were 100 dogs sold in March, then 50 cats were sold; in April, 200 dogs were sold along with 150 cats. The correct answer is (B) because $100 + 50 + 200 + 150 = 500$.

11. C

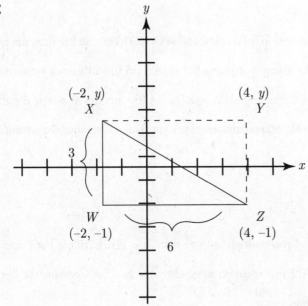

Notice that the length of WZ must be $4 - (-2) = 6$. The area is $l \times w$. $18 = l \times 3$, and the length is 6. Now you have a right triangle with legs of 3 and 6. Use the Pythagorean theorem: $3^2 + 6^2 = c^2$, or $9 + 36 = c^2$. So, $c = \sqrt{45} = \sqrt{9 \times 5} = 3\sqrt{5}$

12. E

Order matters, so this is a permutation problem. You may use the formula: $\dfrac{5!}{(5-3)!} = \dfrac{5!}{2!} = \dfrac{5!}{2} = \dfrac{5 \times 4 \times 3 \times 2 \times 1}{2} = 60$.

Alternatively, you may use the "make slots" method to get $5 \times 4 \times 3 = 60$.

13. D

The percent increase in the CEO's pay was $\dfrac{\$50 - \$5}{5} \times 100\% = 900$ percent. The percent decrease in the factory

workers' pay was $\dfrac{\$20 - \$10}{20} \times 100\% = 50$ percent. To find what percent greater 900 percent is than 50 percent, do

the following: $\dfrac{900\% - 50\%}{50\%} \times 100\% = 1{,}700$ percent, or choice (D).

14. D

This is a pattern problem. The pattern has five digits: 06539. Divide 34 by 5, which gives you a remainder of 4. So the 34th digit will be the fourth in the pattern, which is 3.

15. D

Divide the $9.4 million in private donations received by child safety organizations in September 1989 by the 38 organizations operating at the time. The amount is approximately $250,000.

16. C

From the line graph, you see that homeless aid groups took in about $300 million in private donations, and animal rights groups about $225 million. The ratio of $300 million to $225 million is 4 to 3.

17. **E**

In September 1989, $9.4 million was privately donated to child safety, and in October 1989, $9.9 million was privately donated. Percent change is $\frac{change}{original} \times 100$. The change is equal to 9.9 − 9.4 = 0.5 (the difference between private donations in September 1989 and October 1989). The original is equal to 9.4 (the amount of private donations in September 1989). The percent change is $\frac{.5}{9.4} \times 100$, or approximately 5 percent. This is lower than the percent change in any of the other categories.

18. $\frac{48}{7}$

First, solve for x using the equation $\frac{7y}{2x}$ = 7. Cross-multiply to find that $7y = 14x$. Dividing both sides by 14 yields $\frac{1}{2}y = x$. Substitute this expression into the first equation to get $3(\frac{1}{2}y) + 2y = 24$. Combine the like terms to get $\frac{7}{2}y = 24$, multiply both sides by $\frac{2}{7}$ to find $y = \frac{48}{7}$.

19. **C**

Because the question asks you to find the greatest value of x, make the average the largest it can be; in this case, make it 11. If you multiply the number of things (4) and the average (11), the total will be 44. Notice that choice (E) is 44, but it's a partial answer. To find x, solve 6 + 8 + 10 + x = 44; x = 20, or choice (C).

20. **A**

To find the area of quadrilateral *ABDE*, find the area of right $\triangle ABC$ and subtract the area of right $\triangle EDC$. The base and height of $\triangle ABC$ are both a, so the area equals $\frac{1}{2} \times a \times a$, or $\frac{a^2}{2}$. The base and height of $\triangle EDC$ are both b, so the area equals $\frac{1}{2} \times b \times b$, or $\frac{b^2}{2}$. Therefore, the area of quadrilateral *ABDE* is $\frac{a^2}{2} - \frac{b^2}{2}$.

SECTION 6

1. **original** and **outlandish**

   Try working with the second blank first. The clues are that the fashions were "considered daring" and then "imitated." Starting with the second blank, the sentence suggests that the fashions have changed from what they once were—in other words, daring. *Outlandish* is a good synonym for daring and it makes sense that, in the first blank, the fashions were *original* and then lost their impact because of excess imitation.

2. **diverge**

   Take note of the time trigger "...at one time inseparable...now", which indicates that the combined roles in Middle Eastern music are now not inseparable. You need a word that means divide or separate. *Divulge* starts with the proper root, but its meaning is way off. Meanwhile, neither *retreat* nor *retrench* means divide, while *fuse* is the opposite of what you want. *Diverge* is the best answer.

3. **rebuked**, **perfidy**, and **expiate**

Start with the second blank, which must mean something close to *an act of treachery*. *Perfidy* means this. Since his contemporaries believed Kazan had committed treachery, they would have "harshly criticized" him, so the first blank means rebuked. For the last blank, he was able to achieve *atonement*, which is what *expiate* means.

4. **soporific**

The sentence requires you to figure out the effect that "tranquilizers usually have," and this is provided by the clue in the later part of the sentence, when we read that the "abuse of these drugs results in a failure to induce the much-desired sleep." You can infer that the usual effect of tranquilizers is to produce sleep. *Soporific*, which means sleep-inducing, is the correct answer choice. While *sedulous* might remind you of "sedative," it actually means hard-working.

5. **preternatural**, **preclude**, and **consonant**

The clue for the first blank is "are rejected by modern science in its attempts to find secular insights." Otherworldly interpretations contrast the secular, and the best choice for the first blank is *preternatural*. There would only be a paradox if scientists could hold non-secular beliefs. Therefore, a good word for the second blank is *prevent*, and a good phrase for the last blank would be *in agreement*. *Preclude* is synonymous with prevent, and *consonant* is synonymous with in agreement, making these the best answer choices.

6. **conformity** and **eccentricity**

Try working with the second blank first. The clue is "none of the family members were fearful...of appearing or acting differently from other people." Therefore, find a word for the second blank that means uniqueness. *Eccentricity* fits the bill. Considering the clue, "The Johnson's were not known for their," the two blanks must be opposites. Eliminate *candor* and *vulgarity* based on the clue and the word choice for the second blank, and choose *conformity*.

7. **E**

In the last paragraph, the author discusses the difficulties inherent in measuring intergalactic distances. He notes that scientists use a standard candle in combination with the inverse square law to measure those distances.

8. **C**

The passage states in the third paragraph that brighter objects are closer than dim objects, so eliminate choice (A). The passage never specifies what scientists know about the age of astronomical objects, so eliminate choice (B). The first paragraph says that, according to Hubble's law, *objects farther away from Earth are receding faster than those closer.* This means that the farther object will travel faster, so choice (C) is correct.

9. **B**

According to the last line in the paragraph, "By the inverse square law, galaxy B is ten times farther away than galaxy A, assuming, of course, that distance is the only factor affecting brightness." Therefore, if interstellar dust affects the brightness of an object, the brightness of the object is affected, and the distance scientists measure may be inaccurate.

10. **C**

According to the passage, "By the inverse square law, galaxy B is ten times farther away than galaxy A, assuming, of course, that distance is the only factor affecting brightness." Therefore, assuming that all other factors affecting brightness can be known, we can conclude that the brighter of the supernovas will be closer to Earth.

11. **B**

    "Prozac lag" is a phenomenon for which there is currently no explanation, but neurogenesis may offer a solution. Answer (A) contradicts this. The passage offers "prozac lag" as supporting evidence of a new theory, not disproving an old one, as choice (C) suggests, or disproving a new one, as choice (D) states. Answer (E) goes too far by discussing "unforeseen effects." Choice (B) is the best option.

12. **However, patients suffering from depression only begin to experience mood elevation weeks after beginning treatment.**

    The second paragraph has five sentences, so this question has five answer choices. For an "unexpected observation," a good place to start would be to check the trigger words. The fourth sentence starts with the word "however." While the effects should occur immediately, these don't occur until weeks after starting treatment. The answer is the fourth sentence.

13. **edifying** and **didactic**

    The blank describes Socrates's conversations. The clue is "Socrates's teachings have survived and continue to enlighten seekers of wisdom," so the blank must mean instructional. *Edifying* and *didactic* are the closest in meaning. *Tedious, grating, inspiring* and *rousing* could all be used to describe Socrates's conversations, but they do not match the clue.

14. **satiate** and **allay**

    You would expect "the colossal meal" to fill someone up, but the sentence says that "failed to…her voracious appetite." Thus, she was not full, and the meal failed to satisfy. *Satiate* and *allay* are the best match. *Cadge* and *mendicate* mean the meal begged her hunger. *Exacerbate* and *provoke* go in the wrong direction.

15. **iridescent** and **pavonine**

    The clue for this sentence is "the lovely rainbows they produce," which suggests that the blank should be filled by a word meaning colorful. Both *iridescent* and *pavonine* mean exactly that. Even if you don't agree that the blank necessarily refers to rainbows of color, the missing word does have to agree with *beautiful* due to the trigger and, and none of the other four options does: *anodyne* means eliminating physical pain, *monocoque* means constructed in one piece, *parietal* mean college-related, and *saturnine* means gloomy.

16. **B** and **E**

    The clue for this sentence is *callous,* so the blank must mean "used to," or "didn't notice." Choices (B), *cauterized,* and (E), *inured,* mean this. (F) is incorrect because he didn't notice the violence more, but rather noticed it less.

17. **D**

    The conclusion of the argument is the old formula for Megapower contained natural kiwi extract, while the new formula does not. The evidence is that Tasmania suffered a decrease in its kiwi exports. The assumption is that Megapower is not getting kiwi fruit from another country. Choice (D) strengthens the argument by pointing out that kiwi imports have fallen in the country that produces Megapower, which would reinforce that assumption that the manufacture is not getting kiwis from another country. Choice (A) would weaken the argument by providing a potential alternate source for kiwi fruit. Choice (C) weakens the argument by providing evidence that the manufacturer of Megapower could be getting kiwi fruit from another source. Choices (B) and Choice (E) are not relevant to the conclusion.

18. **C**

While the word *promulgate* can take on the meanings given in answer choices (A), (B), or (C), within the context of the sentence it is clear that Courbet is taking a stand on what he believes art should be. Therefore, answer choice (C) is closest to the correct meaning.

19. **"The argument has been made that the painting struck a…"**

While the rest of the passage enumerates Courbet's ideas on painting, only this sentence points to the effect that Courbet's work may have had on other artists when it states that "since Courbet's work artists have felt freed from the societal demands placed on their work."

20. **A**

According to the passage, Courbet broke with convention by "striving to do something strikingly original." Only answer choice (A) provides that sense of defying a convention to do something original.

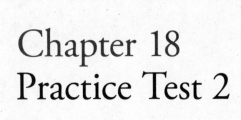

Chapter 18
Practice Test 2

SECTION 1: ISSUE TOPIC

Directions:

You will be given a brief quotation that states or implies an issue of general interest and specific instructions on how to respond to that issue. You will have 30 minutes to plan and compose a response in which you develop a position on the issue according to the specific instructions. A response to any other issue will receive a score of zero.

"Studying foodways—what foods people eat and how they produce, acquire, prepare, and consume them—is the best way to gain deep understanding of a culture."

Write an essay in which you take a position on the statement above. In developing and supporting your position, you should consider ways in which the statement might or might not hold true.

SECTION 2: ARGUMENT TOPIC

Directions:

You will be given a short passage that presents an argument, or an argument to be completed, and specific instructions on how to respond to that passage. You will have 30 minutes to plan and compose a response in which you analyze the passage according to the specific instructions. A response to any other argument will receive a score of zero.

Note that you are NOT being asked to present your own views on the subject. Make sure that you respond to the specific instructions and support your analysis with relevant reasons and/or examples.

Fossil evidence indicates that the blompus—an extremely large, carnivorous land mammal—inhabited the continent of Pentagoria for tens of thousands of years until its sudden decline and ultimate extinction about twelve thousand years ago. Scientists have determined that the extinction coincided with a period of significant climate change and with the arrival of the first humans. Some scholars theorize that the climate change so altered the distribution of plants and animals in the environment that the food chain upon which the blompus depended was irretrievably disrupted. Others contend that predation by humans is the more plausible explanation for the rapid population decline.

Write a response in which you discuss specific evidence that could be used to decide between the proposed explanations above.

SECTION 3: VERBAL REASONING

For questions 1 through 6, select one entry for each blank from the corresponding column of choices. Fill all blanks in the way that best completes the text.

The (i)_____ with which a statement is conveyed is frequently more important to the listener in determining the intended meaning than the actual words (ii)_____ . For example, a compliment, when delivered sarcastically, will be perceived by the receiver as fairly insulting.

Blank (i)	Blank (ii)
inflection	implied
pitch	repudiated
accuracy	utilized

Though a film studio produces works that are (i)_____ and artistic, its priorities often dictate that creativity be (ii)_____ to a secondary position since the creative process can (iii)_____ the organization and hierarchy necessary to running a large company.

Blank (i)	Blank (ii)	Blank (iii)
expressive	compared	respond to
tedious	uplifted	conflict with
tiresome	relegated	coexist with

Science and religion each have core tenets that are considered _____ ; however, because some scientific tenets are in conflict with some religious ones, these tenets cannot all be correct.

historic
axiomatic
disputable
ubiquitous
empirical

Although most medical, preventative ointments commonly in use would have (i)_____ an infection, the particular one Helen applied to her sores actually, much to her dismay, (ii)_____ her (iii)_____ .

Blank (i)	Blank (ii)	Blank (iii)
surrendered to	contributed to	medicine
exacerbated	detracted from	salve
staved off	disbursed with	affliction

A single (i)_____ remark can easily ruin the career of a politician, so most are quickly trained to avoid such offhand remarks and instead stick to prepared talking points. This training can result in a lack of (ii)_____, however, and elicit in merely (iii)_____ , lukewarm responses from crowds.

Blank (i)	Blank (ii)	Blank (iii)
elated	spontaneity	ardent
glib	equanimity	tepid
pedantic	rigidity	morose

Oscar Wilde's *The Importance of Being Earnest* satirizes the _____ nature of upper crust British society; its characters take trivial concerns seriously while glibly dismissing important ones.

maladaptive
insincere
unusual
insignificant
shallow

SECTION 3: VERBAL REASONING

Questions 7 through 8 are based on the following reading passage.

In 1798, economist Thomas Robert Malthus stated in his "Essay on the Principle of Population" that "population increases in a geometric ratio, while the means of subsistence increases in an arithmetic ratio." However, Malthus's dire prediction of a precipitous decline in the world's population has not come to pass. The miscalculations in what has come to be known as the Malthus Doctrine are partly due to Malthus's inability to foresee the innovations that allowed vast increases in worldwide wheat production.

In the late nineteenth century, the invention of the tractor staved off a Malthusian disaster. While the first tractors were not particularly powerful, the replacement of animals by machinery meant that land that had been devoted to hay and oats could now be reclaimed for growth of crops for human consumption. Nevertheless, the Malthusian limit might still have been reached if crop yield had not been increased.

A natural way to increase crop yield is to supply the soil with additional nitrogen. In 1909, chemist Fritz Haber succeeded in combining nitrogen and hydrogen to make ammonia, the white powder version of which, when added to the soil, improves wheat production. Haber nitrogen, however, was not widely used until later in the twentieth century, largely due to farmers' resistance to spreading an unnatural substance on their crops. Haber's invention had a further drawback: If applied in incorrect quantities, the wheat crop would grow taller and thicker, eventually toppling over and rotting.

Interestingly, in the late twentieth century the discovery of genetic engineering, which provides a means of increasing rice and maize production, met with equal resistance, this time from the environmental movement. Even without direct genetic engineering, it is likely that science will discover new methods to improve agricultural production.

According to the passage, which is of the following is true about Haber nitrogen?

○ Haber nitrogen is more effective at increasing the yield of wheat crops than that of maize or oat crops.

○ Undesired effects can result from the application of surplus quantities of Haber nitrogen.

○ Haber nitrogen was the first non-naturally occurring substance to be applied to crops as fertilizer.

○ Haber nitrogen may not be effective if applied at an improper time in wheat's growth cycle.

○ Farmers were quick to adopt Haber nitrogen because it made their crops grow taller and thicker.

The passage implies all of the following EXCEPT

○ world food production has kept pace with world population growth

○ technological innovation is one factor that allowed for an increase in crop production

○ complex genetic structure can hinder the efficacy of scientifically induced genetic mutation

○ the Malthusian limit might well have been reached if new methods to increase crop production had not been found

○ a Malthusian disaster would have been ensured if it were not for the invention of genetic engineering

SECTION 3: VERBAL REASONING

Which of the following, if it were to happen, would best accord with Malthus's contention as it is stated in the first paragraph?

- ○ By 2040 the world's population increases marginally, and food production keeps pace with demand.

- ○ By 2040 the world's population decreases marginally, and food production outstrips demand.

- ○ By 2040 the world's population remains unchanged, and food production declines slightly.

- ○ By 2040 the world's population has significantly increased, and food production has increased slightly.

- ○ By 2040 the world's population has significantly decreased, and food production has decreased slightly.

Replacing the word precipitous with which one of the following, would least affect the overall meaning of the sentence?

- ○ anticipated

- ○ deliberate

- ○ gradual

- ○ risky

- ○ sharp

Questions 11 through 12 are based on the following reading passage.

The dearth of natural resources on the Australian continent is a problem with which government officials there have long struggled. As long distance travel has become less of an obstacle, the tourism industry has become ever more important to the national economy. Tourism represents more than 10 percent of national export earnings annually, and in less developed regions such as the Western Territory, the percentage is much higher.

Unfortunately, this otherwise rosy prospect has one significant cloud on the horizon. In recent years, there has been a move towards returning some of the land to the Aboriginal people. As Western society and culture have flourished on Australian soil, tribal people have been forced ever farther inland in an attempt to maintain their traditional ways of living, a desire that the government has striven to respect.

One of the central beliefs of the Aboriginal religion is that certain natural formations have spiritual significance and must be treated accordingly. Strict guidelines determine who may visit these sites and at what times. Unfortunately, many of these sites are the very natural wonders tourists flock to see. If non-Aboriginal people are forbidden to visit these natural wonders, many may choose not to vacation in a region that sorely needs the income generated by tourism.

The Australian government has dealt with this dilemma thus far by trying to support both sides. The Aboriginal council is still trying to put an end to such use of certain sites, however, and it remains to be seen whether philanthropic or economic desires will ultimately triumph.

In the context of the passage, which of the following most closely matches the meaning of the phrase "otherwise rosy prospect has one significant cloud on the horizon"?

- ○ A colorful sunset is marred by a dark storm cloud.

- ○ A generally promising future has a potential problem.

- ○ The view is beautiful but partially blocked.

- ○ The future of the Aboriginal people is doubtful.

- ○ Although the situation looks good, in reality it is hopeless.

Consider each of the choices separately and select all that apply.

According to the passage, which of the following is a cause of the current dispute between the Aborigines and the Australian government?

- ☐ economic hardships in certain regions of the country

- ☐ the influx of European value systems

- ☐ limited natural resources in most of Australia

SECTION 3: VERBAL REASONING

*For questions 13 through 14, select the **two** answer choices that, when used to complete the sentence, fit the meaning of the sentence as a whole **and** produce completed sentences that are alike in meaning.*

George was a mercurial character; one moment he was optimistic about his prospects, and the next he was _____ .

- ☐ immoral
- ☐ hopeful
- ☐ witty
- ☐ morose
- ☐ dour
- ☐ buoyant

Growing up in a wealthy suburb, she felt quite the _____ as she began her first job as a llama caretaker on a rural farm.

- ☐ tyro
- ☐ concierge
- ☐ agronomist
- ☐ cultivator
- ☐ neophyte
- ☐ curator

William Shakespeare's *Macbeth* was based upon a highly _____ version of events that the playwright wrought from Raphael Holinshed's *Chronicles of England, Scotland, and Ireland*; King Duncan's death at the hand of Macbeth comprises the play's only historical truth.

- ☐ anachronistic
- ☐ effusive
- ☐ embellished
- ☐ prosaic
- ☐ serpentine
- ☐ colored

While comic book artists such as Neal Adams demonstrated a more thorough mastery of human anatomy than did the generation that preceded them, some readers wondered whether the superheroes they drew were really supposed to be so _____ that every detail of their musculatures would be visible through their clothing.

- ☐ thewy
- ☐ sinewy
- ☐ superfluous
- ☐ pneumatic
- ☐ flocculent
- ☐ atrophied

SECTION 3: VERBAL REASONING

One of the most curious structures in cellular biology is the telomere, a length of repeated bases located at the end of every chromosome that, unlike the rest of the DNA strand, carries no useful genetic information. While the telomere seems on the surface to be nothing more than a useless afterthought of DNA, a closer look proves that it is not only important, but also crucial to the functioning of any organism. Indeed, without this mundane structure, every cell division would be a step into senescence, and the onset of old age would begin at birth.

Scientists have found that during cell division not every base of the DNA strand can be replicated, and many, especially those near the end, are lost. If, instead of telomeres, our chromosomes stored valuable genetic information at the end of the DNA strand, then cell division would cause our cells to lose the ability to code for certain information. In fact, many ailments associated with normal old age begin only after the telomere buffer has been exhausted through years of cell division.

Consider each of the choices separately and select all that apply.

Which of the following can reasonably be inferred based on the passage?

☐ The length of the telomere buffer generally shortens with time.

☐ Scientists once believed that telomeres served no useful purpose.

☐ If DNA degradation were absent, then telomeres would be less important to human health.

The passage suggests that if telomere buffers did not exist

○ problems associated with aging would begin earlier in life

○ people would age so rapidly that almost no one would live past childhood

○ cellular senescence would probably be prevented by DNA bases

○ chromosomes would lose the ability to store genetic codes

○ DNA strands would contain only useful genetic information

SECTION 3: VERBAL REASONING

Questions 19 through 20 are based on the following reading passage.

Music education in America emerged in the early eighteenth century out of a desire to ensure that church goers could sing the weekly hymns in tune. In 1721, John Tufts, a minister, penned the first textbook for musical education entitled *An Introduction to the Singing of Psalm Tunes.* Tufts's pedagogical technique relied primarily on rote learning, omitting the reading of music until a student's singing abilities had improved.

In the same year that Tufts's publication emerged, Reverend Thomas Walter published *The Ground Rules of Music Explained,* which, while also focusing on preparing students to sing religious music, took a note-based approach by teaching students the rudiments of note reading from the onset. The "note versus rote" controversy in music education continued well into the mid-nineteenth century. With no curriculum to guide them, singing school teachers focused on either the rote or note method with little consistency.

19 of 20

The author discusses Tufts's pedagogical technique in order to

○ suggest that rote learning is superior to note learning

○ present a contrast with Walter's educational technique

○ argue that rote learning improves a student's singing ability

○ show the origin of Walter's educational techniques

○ show that rote learning was inconsistently practiced

20 of 20

Select the sentence in the passage that best describes the endurance of the tension between pedagogical techniques.

SECTION 4: QUANTITATIVE REASONING

Questions 1 through 8 each consist of two quantities, Quantity A and Quantity B. You are to compare the two quantities and choose the appropriate answer. In a question, information concerning one or both of the quantities to be compared is centered above the two columns. A symbol that appears in both columns represents the same thing in Quantity A as it does in Quantity B.

1 of 20

Quantity A	Quantity B
0.15	$\dfrac{3}{20}$

○ Quantity A is greater.

○ Quantity B is greater.

○ The two quantities are equal.

○ The relationship cannot be determined from the information given.

2 of 20

5 is r percent of 25

s is 25 percent of 60

Quantity A	Quantity B
r	s

○ Quantity A is greater.

○ Quantity B is greater.

○ The two quantities are equal.

○ The relationship cannot be determined from the information given.

3 of 20

g and h are positive integers such that the value of g is twice the value of h.

Quantity A	Quantity B
The ratio of g to 1	The ratio of 1 to h

○ Quantity A is greater.

○ Quantity B is greater.

○ The two quantities are equal.

○ The relationship cannot be determined from the information given.

4 of 20

Quantity A	Quantity B
The average (arithmetic mean) of 67, 78, x, and 101	The average (arithmetic mean) of 66, 79, x, and 102

○ Quantity A is greater.

○ Quantity B is greater.

○ The two quantities are equal.

○ The relationship cannot be determined from the information given.

5 of 20

In each of the years 1989 and 1990, the total weight of recycled newspapers in a certain country increased by .79 million tons over the previous year.

Quantity A	Quantity B
Percent increase in the weight of recycled newspapers in 1989 over 1988	Percent increase in the weight of recycled newspapers in 1990 over 1989

○ Quantity A is greater.

○ Quantity B is greater.

○ The two quantities are equal.

○ The relationship cannot be determined from the information given.

SECTION 4: QUANTITATIVE REASONING

Quantity A	Quantity B
The total weight of m peanuts at a weight of $n + 3$ mg each	The total weight of n almonds at a weight of $m + 3$ mg each

○ Quantity A is greater.

○ Quantity B is greater.

○ The two quantities are equal.

○ The relationship cannot be determined from the information given.

Quantity A	Quantity B
$5^{27}(575)$	$5^{28}(115)$

○ Quantity A is greater.

○ Quantity B is greater.

○ The two quantities are equal.

○ The relationship cannot be determined from the information given.

Alejandro has a six-sided die with faces numbered 1 through 6. He rolls the die twice.

Quantity A	Quantity B
The probability that both rolls are even	The probability that neither roll is a multiple of 3

○ Quantity A is greater.

○ Quantity B is greater.

○ The two quantities are equal.

○ The relationship cannot be determined from the information given.

If $4(r - s) = -2$, then what is r, in terms of s ?

○ $\dfrac{-s}{2}$

○ $s - \dfrac{1}{2}$

○ $s - \dfrac{3}{2}$

○ $s + 2$

○ $2s$

At Tenderloin Pharmaceuticals, 25 percent of the employees take the subway to work. Among those who ride the subway, 42 percent transfer from one subway line to another during their commutes, and the rest do not transfer. What percent of all employees transfer lines?

[   ] percent

Click on the answer box, then type in a number. Backspace to erase.

To make bread dough, a baker mixes flour, eggs, yeast, and salt by weight in the ratio of 11 : 9 : 3 : 2, respectively. How many pounds of yeast are there in 20 pounds of the mixture?

○ $1\dfrac{3}{5}$

○ $1\dfrac{4}{5}$

○ 2

○ $2\dfrac{2}{5}$

○ $8\dfrac{4}{5}$

SECTION 4: QUANTITATIVE REASONING

$(\sqrt{5} - \sqrt{3})^2 =$

- ○ $2 - 2\sqrt{15}$
- ○ $2 - \sqrt{15}$
- ○ $8 - 2\sqrt{15}$
- ○ 2
- ○ $8 - 2\sqrt{5}$

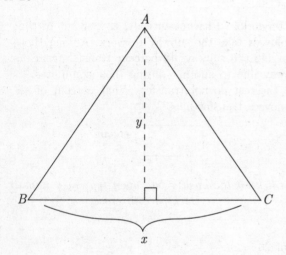

$\triangle ABC$ has an area of 108 cm². If x and y are both integers, which of the following could be the value of x ?

Indicate **all** possible values.

- ☐ 4
- ☐ 5
- ☐ 6
- ☐ 8
- ☐ 9

Click on your choice(s).

Questions 14 through 16 refer to the following graphs.

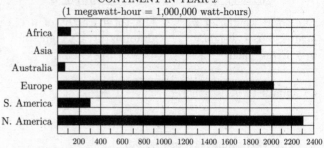

WORLD ELECTRICITY PRODUCTION BY
CONTINENT IN YEAR x
(1 megawatt-hour = 1,000,000 watt-hours)

Electricity Production in Megawatt - hours
<u>Note</u>: Drawn to scale

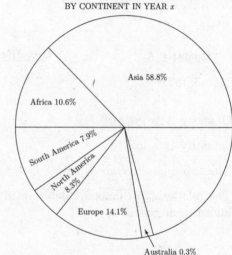

DISTRIBUTION OF WORLD POPULATION
BY CONTINENT IN YEAR x

<u>Note</u>: Not drawn to scale

In Year x, on which continent did electricity production most closely equal electricity production in Europe?

- ○ Africa
- ○ Asia
- ○ Australia
- ○ South America
- ○ North America

SECTION 4: QUANTITATIVE REASONING

In Year x, for which continent was the ratio of electricity production to population the greatest?

○ Africa

○ Asia

○ Australia

○ Europe

○ North America

In Year x, if South America had a population of approximately 368 million, what was the approximate population, in millions, of Africa?

○ 494

○ 470

○ 274

○ 150

○ 39

The average (arithmetic mean) weight of 5 crates is 250 pounds. The 2 lightest crates weigh between 200 and 205 pounds each, and the 2 heaviest weigh between 300 and 310 pounds each. If the weight of the fifth crate is x pounds, then x is expressed by which of the following?

○ $220 \leq x \leq 250$

○ $230 \leq x \leq 260$

○ $240 \leq x \leq 270$

○ $250 \leq x \leq 270$

○ $260 \leq x \leq 280$

A mathematician has devised a theorem that produces a series of numbers $s_1, s_2 \ldots s_x$ according to the principles $s_1 = 2$, $s_2 = 2$, $s_3 = 2$, and for $x \geq 4$, $s_x = 2s_{x-1} + s_{x-2}$. Which of the following equals s_6?

○ 30

○ 34

○ 37

○ 38

○ 40

Y is a point on line segment XZ such that $XY = \frac{1}{2} XZ$. If the length of YZ is $4a + 6$, and the length of XZ is 68, then $a =$

Click on the answer box, then type in a number. Backspace to erase.

Talk show host Ralph Burke has exactly one guest on his show each day, and Burke's show airs every Monday through Friday. Burke always schedules politicians on Mondays and Wednesdays, actors on Tuesdays and athletes on Thursdays, but can have a guest of any one of these three kinds on Friday. No guest appears more than once per week on Burke's show. If Burke has five politicians, three actors and six athletes he could invite, and if no politician is also an actor or an athlete and no actor is also an athlete, how many different schedules of guests from Monday to Friday could Burke create?

○ 30

○ 1,200

○ 3,600

○ 4,500

○ 6,300

SECTION 5: VERBAL REASONING

For questions 1 through 4, select one entry for each blank from the corresponding column of choices. Fill all blanks in the way that best completes the text.

Despite what _____ philosophies of child-rearing suggest, there is no imperative that the day-to-day action of raising a child be simple, unambiguous and unchanging—no requirement, in other words, ensures that life follow philosophy.

inexact
aggressive
random
shameless
systematic

Several cultures throughout the world and many informal subcultures within the United States (i)_____ the Winter Solstice, the (ii)_____ day of the year, as a time to welcome back the lengthening of each day.

Blank (i)	Blank (ii)
condemn	lengthiest
burke	shortest
fête	coldest

The novel emphasizes the innate (i)_____ of all humans, showing how each and every character within the narrative is, ultimately, (ii)_____ . This motif becomes tiresome due to its (iii)_____ , however, as character after character is bribed, either explicitly or implicitly, into giving up his or her supposedly cherished beliefs.

Blank (i)	Blank (ii)	Blank (iii)
zealousness	adroit	redundancy
corruptibility	cunning	triviality
optimism	venal	subtlety

Although pirating software, such as borrowing a friend's copy of an installation CD or downloading software from unapproved sources is (i)_____ , many people continue to do so (ii)_____ , almost as if they were unaware of the potential consequences if they were caught.

Blank (i)	Blank (ii)
uncommon	savagely
illegal	sensibly
difficult	unabashedly

Having squandered his life's savings on unprofitable business ventures, the _____ entrepreneur was forced to live in squalor.

former
unlikely
insolvent
perturbed
eccentric

Teachers of composition urge their students to (i)_____ in their writing and instead use clear, simple language. Why use (ii)_____ vocabulary when a (iii)_____ phrasing conveys one's meaning so much more effectively?

Blank (i)	Blank (ii)	Blank (iii)
exscind obloquy	recreant	arcane
eschew obfuscation	redolent	limpid
evince ossification	recondite	droll

SECTION 5: VERBAL REASONING

Questions 7 through 8 are based on the following reading passage.

That axon malfunction plays a role in neurological disorders has never been in question by neurobiologists, but the nature of the relationship has been a matter of speculation. Enter George Bartzokis. Bartzokis's neurological research at UCLA suggests that many previously little understood disorders such as Alzheimer's disease may be explained by examining the role of the chemical compound myelin.

Myelin is produced by oligodendrocyte cells as a protective sheathing for axons within the nervous system. As humans mature and their neurochemistries grow more complex, oligodendrocyte cells produce increasing amounts of myelin to protect the byzantine circuitry inside our nervous systems. An apt comparison may be to the plastic insulation around copper wires. Bereft of myelin, certain areas of the brain may be left vulnerable to short circuiting, resulting in such disorders as ADHD, schizophrenia, or autism.

Consider each of the choices separately and select all that apply.

It can be inferred from the passage that the author would be most likely to agree with which of the following statements regarding the role of myelin?

- ☐ The levels of myelin in the brain can contribute to the neurological health of individuals.

- ☐ Increasing the levels of myelin in the brain can reverse the effects of neurological damage.

- ☐ The levels of myelin in the brain are not fixed throughout the lifetime of an individual.

In the context in which it appears, byzantine most nearly means

- ○ devious
- ○ intricate
- ○ mature
- ○ beautiful
- ○ electronic

The cost of operating many small college administrative offices is significantly reduced when the college replaces its heavily compensated administrative assistants with part-time work-study students whose earnings are partially subsidized by the government. Therefore, large universities should follow suit. They will certainly realize more financial gains than do the small colleges.

In the above argument it is assumed that

- ○ replacing administrative assistants with work-study students is more cost-effective for small colleges than for large universities

- ○ large universities usually depend upon small colleges for development of money-saving strategies

- ○ the financial gains realized by large universities would not be as great were they to use non-work-study students in place of the administrative assistants

- ○ work-study students could feasibly fulfill a similar or greater proportion of administrative assistant jobs at large universities than they could at small colleges

- ○ the smaller the college or university, the easier it is for that college or university to control costs

SECTION 5: VERBAL REASONING

The nineteenth century marked a revolutionary change in the way that wealth was perceived in England. As landed wealth gave way to monied wealth, investments became increasingly speculative.

A popular investment vehicle was the three-percent consol which took its name from the fact that it paid three pounds on a hundred pound investment. The drawback to the consol was that once issued, there was no easy way for the government to buy back the debt. To address the problem, the British government instituted a sinking fund, using tax revenue to buy back the bonds in the open market. The fact that the consol had no fixed maturity date ensured that any change in interest rate was fully reflected in the capital value of the bond. The often wild fluctuation of interest rates ensured the consol's popularity with speculative traders.

Which of the following best describes the relationship of the first paragraph of the passage to the passage as a whole?

- ○ It provides a generalization which is later supported in the passage.

- ○ It provides an antithesis to the author's main argument.

- ○ It briefly compares two different investment strategies.

- ○ It explains an investment vehicle that is later examined in greater detail.

- ○ It provides a historical framework by which the nature of the nineteenth century investor can more easily be understood.

In the second paragraph, select the sentence that describes a solution to a problem.

*For questions 12 through 15, select the **two** answer choices that, when used to complete the sentence, fit the meaning of the sentence as a whole **and** produce completed sentences that are alike in meaning.*

Owing to a combination of its proximity and _____ atmosphere, Mars is the only planet in our solar system whose surface details can be discerned from the Earth.

- ☐ viscous
- ☐ ossified
- ☐ rarefied
- ☐ estimable
- ☐ copious
- ☐ meager

Using the hardships of the Joad family as a model, John Steinbeck's *The Grapes of Wrath* effectively demonstrated how one clan's struggles epitomized the _____ experienced by an entire country.

- ☐ reticence
- ☐ adversity
- ☐ repudiation
- ☐ quiescence
- ☐ verisimilitude
- ☐ tribulation

SECTION 5: VERBAL REASONING

The Mayan pyramid of Kukulkan is more than just _____ edifice; this imposing structure was built to create a chirping echo whenever people clap their hands on the staircase. This echo sounds just like the chirp of the Quetzal, a bird which is sacred in the Mayan culture.

- ☐ a venerable
- ☐ a humble
- ☐ a beguiling
- ☐ an august
- ☐ a specious
- ☐ a prosaic

Some wealthy city-dwellers become enchanted with the prospect of trading their hectic schedules for a bucolic life in the countryside, and they buy property with a pleasant view of farmland—only to find the stench of the livestock so _____ that they move back to the city.

- ☐ bovine
- ☐ pastoral
- ☐ noisome
- ☐ atavistic
- ☐ olfactory
- ☐ mephitic

Questions 16 through 18 are based on the following reading passage.

Often the most influential developments initially appear to be of minor significance. Take stirrups. Without them, horse and rider are, in terms of force, separate entities; lances can be used from horseback, but only by throwing or stabbing, and mounted warriors gain only height and mobility. A lance couched under the rider's arm, unifying the force of rider and weapon, would throw its wielder backwards off the horse at impact. Stirrups unify lance, rider, and horse into a force capable of unprecedented violence. This development left unusually clear archaeological markers: Lethality assured, lances evolved barbs meant to slow progress after impact, lest the weight of body pull rider from horse. The change presaged the dominance of mounted combat, and increasingly expensive equipment destroyed the venerable ideal of freeman warriors. New technology demanded military aristocracy, and chivalric culture bore its marks for a millennium.

The primary purpose of the passage is to

- ○ discuss the influence of a recent archeological discovery
- ○ explore the social significance of a technological innovation
- ○ assess the state of research in a given field
- ○ lament the destruction of certain social ideals
- ○ explicate the physics of combat artillery

It can be inferred from the passage that the author believes which of the following about medieval innovations in military technology?

- ○ Their study merits additional research.
- ○ They had more lasting influence than did those of the ancient world.
- ○ Most of them had equally far-reaching repercussions.
- ○ Prior to their application, the military value of horses was considered insignificant.
- ○ Many of them are archaeologically ambiguous.

SECTION 5: VERBAL REASONING

Click on the sentence in the passage in which the author cites the physical effects of a technological innovation being discussed as an example of a previous generalization.

Questions 19 through 20 are based on the following reading passage.

Few mathematical constructs seem as conceptually simple as that of randomness. According to the traditional definition, a number is random if it is chosen purely as the result of a probabilistic mechanism such as the roll of a fair die. In their groundbreaking work regarding complexity and the limitations of formal systems, mathematicians Gregory Chaitin and A.N. Kolmogorov force us to consider this last claim more closely.

Consider two possible outcomes of throwing a fair die three times: first, 1, 6, and 2; second 3, 3, and 3. Now let us construct two three-member sets based on the results. Though the first set—{1,6,2}—intuitively seems more random than the second—{3,3,3}, they are each as likely to occur, and thus according to the accepted definition, must be considered equally random. This unwelcome result prompts Chaitin and Kolmogorov to suggest the need for a new standard of randomness, one that relies on the internal coherence of the set as opposed to its origin.

Which of the following best describes the organization of the passage as whole?

○ A concept is introduced; a traditional definition is put forward; a thought experiment is described; a new definition is proposed; the traditional definition is amended as a result.

○ A concept is introduced; a traditional definition is supported by authorities; a thought experiment is described; the implications of the experiment are discussed.

○ A concept is introduced; a traditional definition is considered and rejected; a thought experiment is described; a new definition is proposed.

○ A concept is introduced; a traditional definition is called into question; a thought experiment is described; the implications of the experiment are discussed.

○ A concept is introduced; authorities are called in to reevaluate a definition; a thought experiment is described; the implications of the experiment are considered and rejected.

Consider each of the choices separately and select all that apply.

Which of the following is an inference made in the passage above?

☐ The results of the same probabilistic mechanism will each be as likely as the other to occur.

☐ According to the traditional definition of randomness, two numbers should be considered equally random if they result from the same probabilistic mechanism.

☐ Different probabilistic mechanisms are likely to result in similar outcomes.

NO TEST MATERIAL ON THIS PAGE

SECTION 6: QUANTITATIVE REASONING

Questions 1 through 7 each consist of two quantities, Quantity A and Quantity B. You are to compare the two quantities and choose the appropriate answer. In a question, information concerning one or both of the quantities to be compared is centered above the two columns. A symbol that appears in both columns represents the same thing in Quantity A as it does in Quantity B.

1 of 20

$$\frac{x}{6} + 2 = \frac{6}{2}$$

$$\frac{y}{3} + 2 = \frac{9}{3}$$

Quantity A	**Quantity B**
$\dfrac{(x-1)}{y}$	$\dfrac{(y-1)}{x}$

○ Quantity A is greater.

○ Quantity B is greater.

○ The two quantities are equal.

○ The relationship cannot be determined from the information given.

2 of 20

Quantity A	**Quantity B**
The distance that Bob drives in 3 hours at a speed of 44 miles per hour	The distance that Inez drives in 2 hours and 30 minutes at a speed of 50 miles per hour

○ Quantity A is greater.

○ Quantity B is greater.

○ The two quantities are equal.

○ The relationship cannot be determined from the information given.

3 of 20

$$0 < x < y < 1$$

Quantity A	**Quantity B**
$\dfrac{x}{y}$	$\dfrac{y}{x}$

○ Quantity A is greater.

○ Quantity B is greater.

○ The two quantities are equal.

○ The relationship cannot be determined from the information given.

4 of 20

$$y > 0$$

Quantity A	**Quantity B**
$0.98(8.21)y$	$\dfrac{821y}{98}$

○ Quantity A is greater.

○ Quantity B is greater.

○ The two quantities are equal.

○ The relationship cannot be determined from the information given.

5 of 20

12.5 percent of k is 80.
k is y percent of 80.

Quantity A	**Quantity B**
y	650

○ Quantity A is greater.

○ Quantity B is greater.

○ The two quantities are equal.

○ The relationship cannot be determined from the information given.

SECTION 6: QUANTITATIVE REASONING

Set $P = \{a, b, c, d, e, f, g\}$

Set $Q = \{a, b, c, d, e, f\}$

$a, b, c, d, e, f,$ and g are distinct integers

Quantity A   **Quantity B**

Range of Set P Range of Set Q

○ Quantity A is greater.

○ Quantity B is greater.

○ The two quantities are equal.

○ The relationship cannot be determined from the information given.

Series F is defined as $F_n = F_{(n-1)} + 3$ and $F_1 = 10$.

Quantity A   **Quantity B**

The sum of F_4 through F_{10} The sum of F_6 through F_{11}

○ Quantity A is greater.

○ Quantity B is greater.

○ The two quantities are equal.

○ The relationship cannot be determined from the information given.

A number, n, is multiplied by 6. The product is increased by 24. Finally, the entire quantity is divided by 3. Which of the following expresses the final result in terms of n ?

○ $\dfrac{n}{3} + 8$

○ $\dfrac{n + 24}{2}$

○ $2n + 8$

○ $3n + 24$

○ $16n$

The average (arithmetic mean) of a and b is 10, and the average (arithmetic mean) of c and d is 7. If the average (arithmetic mean) of a, b, and c is 8, what is the value of d ?

Click on the answer box, then type in a number. Backspace to erase.

In the coordinate plane, square $ABCD$ has vertices at A (3, 7), B (3, 12), C (8, 12), and D (8, 7). What is the area of $ABCD$?

○ 16

○ 20

○ 25

○ 30

○ 36

Houses Sold in July		
Week	Peter	Dylan
Week 1	4	9
Week 2	6	3
Week 3	10	10
Week 4	4	2

The table above shows the number of houses sold per week for the month of July by two real estate agents, Peter and Dylan. What is the difference between the median number of houses sold per week by Dylan and the median number of houses sold per week by Peter?

○ 0

○ 1

○ 2

○ 5

○ 6

SECTION 6: QUANTITATIVE REASONING

Questions 12 through 14 refer to the following graph.

In 1995 there were 95 million television households in the United States. If, in 1983, there were 80 percent of the number of television households in 1995, then approximately how many television households in millions viewed Program *y* in 1983 ?

- ○ 80
- ○ 76
- ○ 15
- ○ 12
- ○ 10

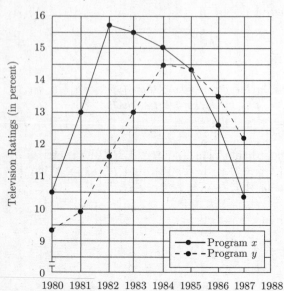

TELEVISION RATINGS* IN THE UNITED STATES
1980–1987

*Ratings equal the percent of television households in the United States that viewed the program.

Approximately what was the average number of television households in the United States that viewed Program *x* from 1981 through 1985 inclusive?

- ○ 12.7%
- ○ 14.8%
- ○ 15.6%
- ○ 18.5%
- ○ It cannot be determined from the information given.

For how many of the years shown did the ratings for Program *y* increase over the ratings for Program *y* the previous year?

- ○ Two
- ○ Three
- ○ Four
- ○ Five
- ○ Six

At Flo's Pancake House, pancakes can be ordered with any of six possible toppings. How many different ways are there to order pancakes with three toppings?

- ○ 20
- ○ 40
- ○ 54
- ○ 120
- ○ 720

SECTION 6: QUANTITATIVE REASONING

The area of triangle KLM is equal to the area of rectangle $ABCD$. If the perimeter of $ABCD$ is 16, what is the length of LM ?

- ○ $\frac{3}{2}$
- ○ 3
- ○ $\frac{16}{5}$
- ○ 5
- ○ 6

Each of the 576 houses in Tenantville is owned by one of the following landlords: Matt, Gavin, Angela, or Susan. Matt and Angela together own twice as many houses as Gavin and Susan own. If Gavin owns 100 more houses than Susan owns, and Matt owns 100 more houses than Angela owns, how many houses does Susan own?

- ○ 46
- ○ 142
- ○ 146
- ○ 192
- ○ 242

One-quarter of the cars that an automobile manufacturer produces are sports cars, and the rest are sedans. If one-fifth of the cars that the manufacturer produces are red and one-third of the sports cars are red, then what fraction of the sedans is red?

Click on the answer boxes, then type numbers. Backspace to erase.

A candy jar has 4 lime, 10 cherry, 8 orange, and x grape candies. Tom randomly selects a candy from the jar. The probability that he selects an orange candy is greater than 20 percent. Which of the following could be the value of x ?

Indicate **all** possible values.

- ☐ 10
- ☐ 14
- ☐ 18
- ☐ 22
- ☐ 24
- ☐ 28

Click on your choice(s).

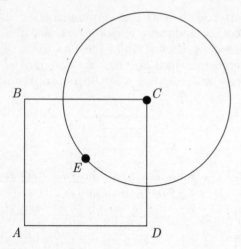

Square $ABCD$ and a circle with center C intersect as shown. If point E is at the center of $ABCD$ and if the radius of circle C is k, then what is the area of $ABCD$, in terms of k ?

○ $\dfrac{k^2}{2\pi}$

○ $\dfrac{\pi k^2}{2}$

○ πk^2

○ k^2

○ $2k^2$

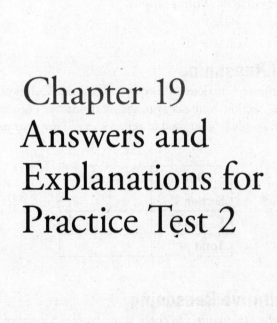

Chapter 19
Answers and
Explanations for
Practice Test 2

INTERPRETING YOUR RESULTS

After you check your answers on the following pages, fill out this sheet to interpret your results.

Analytic Writing Sections

To evaluate your performance on the Analytic Writing sections, compare your response to the advice and samples in the Analytic Writing chapter.

Verbal Reasoning

Refer to the explanations to check your answers. Count of number of questions you got correct in each Verbal Reasoning section, and calculate the total number correct. Find the section of the Interpretive Guide (below) that corresponds to your total to get an idea of how your performance compares to that of other test takers.

Test 1	# Correct
Section 4	
Section 6	
Total	

Test 2	# Correct
Section 3	
Section 5	
Total	

Quantitative Reasoning

Refer to the explanations to check your answers. Count of number of questions you got correct in each Quantitative Reasoning section, and calculate the total number correct. Find the section of the Interpretive Guide (below) that corresponds to your total to get an idea of how your performance compares to that of other test takers.

Test 1	# Correct
Section 3	
Section 5	
Total	

Test 2	# Correct
Section 4	
Section 6	
Total	

Interpretive Guide

The table below provides a guide for interpreting your performance based on the number of questions you got correct in each subject.

Subject	Well Above Average	Above Average	Average	Below Average
Verbal Reasoning	51–56	40–50	23–39	1–22
Quantitative Reasoning	48–52	40–47	24–39	1–23

Section 3

1. **inflection** and **utilized**

   For the first blank, the trigger "more important" tells you to change direction from "actual words." Also, *sarcastically* is an example of tone. Look for a choice that means tone. *Inflection* fits tone. *Pitch* is non-verbal, but it does not match the example of sarcastically. *Accuracy* does not fit. For the second blank, look for a word that means *conveyed* or *spoken*. *Utilized* is the best match. *Implied* and *repudiated* don't fit.

2. **expressive**, **relegated**, and **conflict with**

   Try working with the first blank first. The clue is *artistic*, and the trigger *and* indicates the first blank should be a word that is the same as artistic. *Expressive* is the best choice; neither *tedious* nor *tiresome* works. Though changes the direction of the sentence—though the studio likes the creative/artistic aspect, something negative must be happening to creativity—it's brought down to a secondary position. Eliminate *uplifted* and *compared* for blank (ii) because they are not negative, and choose *relegated*. Turning to the third blank, "organization and hierarchy" are in opposition to *creativity*, and *conflict with* makes the most sense.

3. **axiomatic**

   You are given the clue that the beliefs "are in conflict" and "cannot all be correct." Therefore, whatever goes into the blank must be synonymous with *correct* or something we can infer correctness from. The correct answer is *axiomatic*, which means self-evident or universally true. *Disputable* is the opposite of what the sentence requires, and *ubiquitous*, and *historic* are not synonymous with self-evident. Although *empirical*, meaning derived from observation, might fit science, it is not a good fit for religion.

4. **staved off**, **contributed to**, and **affliction**

   The clue "Although most medical, preventative ointments commonly in use," tells you that most ointments would prevent an infection, but the one Helen used did not. Recycle the clue, and put a word that means prevent in the first blank; *staved off* is the best match. Work with the second and third blanks together. The ointment did not prevent an infection, and the clue "much to her dismay" tells you that something bad happened. The only pair that makes sense together is *contributed to* and *affliction* because they tell you that the ointment made her problem worse.

5. **glib**, **spontaneity**, and **tepid**

   For the first blank, the clue is *offhand remarks,* so the blank means something like "offhand." *Glib,* which means "superficial or showing a lack of concern," is the closest match for this. Sticking to *prepared talking points* can result in a lack of "excitement" or "naturalness," which *spontaneity* matches. For the last blank, you know the crowd's responses are *lukewarm,* so the answer for that blank is *tepid.*

6. **shallow**

   The clue is the entire clause that follows the semicolon, "its characters take trivial concerns seriously while glibly dismissing important ones." Look for a word that means superficial or petty to go in the blank. The only one that fits is *shallow*.

7. **B**

The third paragraph states that if too much Haber nitrogen were applied, "the wheat crop would grow taller and thicker, eventually toppling over and rotting." Losing a crop would be an undesirable effect, making choice (B) the best answer. Eliminate choice (A) because the passage doesn't compare the effects of Haber nitrogen on different kinds of crops. The passage doesn't provide any information to support choices (C) and (D). Choice (E) contradicts the passage, which says the farmers were wary of the substance.

8. **E**

According to the first paragraph, there has been no sharp decline in the world's population and, therefore, we can surmise that food production has been sufficient to allow for the existing population growth, as in answer choice (A). In the second paragraph, the author mentions the invention of the tractor as one of the factors that allowed more crops to be grown for human consumption. This reflects the technological innovation in answer choice (B). In the last paragraph, the author notes that the complexity of the wheat genome has hindered attempts at genetic alteration. Thus, answer choice (C) is implied as well. The author notes that increases in crop production through the invention of the tractor and ammonia prevented Malthus's predictions from being realized, and this rules out answer choice (D). The extent of the impact of genetic engineering is not clear. We don't know that a Malthusian disaster would have been a *certainty* without genetic engineering. Therefore, the correct answer is choice (E) because it is not implied.

9. **D**

The first paragraph states that Malthus believed that "population increases in a geometric ratio, while the means of subsistence increases in an arithmetic ratio." More simply put, Malthus argued that population growth happens at a significantly faster rate than food production. Only answer choice (D) demonstrates this.

10. **E**

The first paragraph presents Malthus's prediction about what would happen if population growth were to outstrip food production. If there were too many people and not enough food, you would expect a significant or rapid population decline. Look for a word to replace *precipitous* that is similar to significant or rapid. *Sharp* is the best word.

11. **B**

The "rosy prospect" refers to the previous paragraph's discussion of the booming tourism industry in Australia, which implies a positive future, and the "cloud on the horizon" refers to the conflict between the rights of the Aborigines and the need for the money from tourism, a potential problem. Choice (A) incorrectly interprets the quote as referring to a literal *horizon and prospect*. Choice (C) is also too literal, taking *prospect* to mean view. Choice (D) is incorrect because, although this may be true based on later information in the passage, it is not an accurate interpretation of this phrase. Choice (E) is too strong because the future is described as generally good, not hopeless.

12. **A, B, and C**

All three statements are given as sources of the conflict. Choice (A), economic hardship, is mentioned in the third paragraph. Due to financial difficulties, many regions are unwilling to give up the income derived from tourists visiting Aboriginal lands. Choice (B) is discussed in the second paragraph. The expansion of Western culture is the reason that the Aborigines have moved inland and abandoned other sacred sites. Choice (C) is mentioned in the first sentence. Tourism is described as particularly important due to the "dearth of natural resources."

13. **morose** and **dour**

The first part of the clue is "mercurial character," which means George's moods change frequently. The second part of the clue is "one moment he was optimistic about his prospects," and the trigger is "the next he was." Thus, the blank should be the opposite of optimistic; look for words that mean pessimistic. *Morose* and *dour* are both similar to pessimistic. *Hopeful* and *buoyant* have the opposite meaning, and *witty* and *immoral* are not related.

14. **tyro** and **neophyte**

The clue is that she "began her first job." Also, the contrast of "wealthy suburb" and "llama caretaker on a rural farm" suggests that she'd feel out of place or lacking in experience at her first job. Look for words that mean beginner. *Tyro* and *neophyte* are the only words that mean beginner. *Agronomist* and *cultivator* are traps for people who focused too heavily on the farm. *Concierge* and *curator* are traps for people who focused too heavily on caretaker.

15. **embellished** and **colored**

The clue "King Duncan's death at the hand of Macbeth comprises the play's only historical truth" tells you that the version of events related in Macbeth was not very accurate. Does *anachronistic* mean inaccurate? No; cross it out. What about *effusive*? No. In contrast, *embellished* works well, but *prosaic* and *serpentine* do not. Finally, *colored*—which, like embellished, means misrepresented or distorted—fits the blank nicely.

16. **thewy** and **sinewy**

The word that goes into the blank describes superheroes, who the clue phrase describes as having "every detail of their musculatures would be visible through their clothing." Clearly, something like muscular is called for, and *thewy* and *sinewy* both fit the bill. The other four words don't fit: *superfluous* means unnecessary, *pneumatic* means full of air, *flocculent* means covered in wool, and *atrophied* means shriveled due to disuse.

17. **A and C**

Answer choice (A) is correct because the passage states that during cell division many of the DNA bases are lost, also we know that over the course of many cell divisions the telomere buffer may disappear entirely. Choice (B) is not correct because we have no information about what scientists used to think about telomeres. Choice (C) is correct because we are told that one function of telomeres is to mitigate the loss of DNA bases. If no bases are lost, then this role is not important any more.

18. **A**

The first paragraph says that without telomere buffers "every cell division would be a step into senescence, and the onset of old age would begin at birth," and the last sentence of the passage states that "many ailments associated with normal old age begin only after the telomere buffer has been exhausted through years of cell division." If the protection offered by the buffers didn't exist, you could expect problems related to aging to start sooner, as choice (A) suggests. Choice (B) goes too far; though the passage speaks on the onset of old age at birth, we can't be sure that almost no one would live past childhood. The passage provides no support for choices (C), (D), or (E).

19. **B**

The passage as a whole provides a short history of two types of early musical education, the rote method and the note method. Nowhere in the passage does the author come out in favor of either method, thereby ruling out choices (A) and (C). Given that Reverend Walter taught music by the note method he developed, answer choice (D) doesn't make sense. While it is true that rote learning was inconsistently practiced, as choice (E) states, this does not answer the question.

20. "The 'note vs. rote' controversy in music education…"

The use of the word "controversy" in the final paragraph is the only indication the author gives that the decision between "note" or "rote" as a musical learning technique was in any way contentious.

Section 4

1. **C**

   Converting the decimal to a fraction: 0.15 becomes $\frac{15}{100}$, which reduces to $\frac{3}{20}$. You could also just punch this into your calculator and find that $\frac{3}{20}$ is 0.15. The two quantities are equal.

2. **A**

   Translate and solve each expression. The expression "5 is r percent of 25" becomes $5 = \frac{r}{100} \times 25$. So, $r = 20$. The expression "s is 25 percent of 60" becomes $s = \frac{25}{100} \times 60$. So, $s = 15$, and Quantity A is greater.

3. **A**

   Plug In for this question. Let $h = 3$, which makes $g = 6$. Quantity A equals $\frac{6}{1} = 6$ and Quantity B equals $\frac{1}{3}$. Quantity A can be greater than Quantity B, so eliminate answer choices (B) and (C). Because g and h are positive integers, Quantity A will always be greater than 1 and Quantity B will always be less than or equal to 1. Quantity A will always be greater than Quantity B.

4. **B**

   The average is the sum divided by the number of elements. Because three elements make up both averages, you can simply compare the sum of each set. $67 + 78 + 101 + x = 246 + x$, and $66 + 79 + 102 + x = 247 + x$. Thus, Quantity B is greater.

5. **A**

   Although the amount of increase was the same in both years, the percent increase was greater from 1988 to 1989. For example, say there were 10 million tons in 1988. The percent increase was $\frac{.79}{10}$. Then in 1989 there were 10.79 tons, so the percent increase from 1989 to 1990 was $\frac{.79}{10.79}$. Quantity A must be greater.

6. **D**

   Plug In. Make $m = 2$ and $n = 3$. For Quantity A, the weight of 2 peanuts at $3 + 3$ mg each is $2 \times 6 = 12$ mg. For Quantity B, the weight of 3 almonds at $2 + 3$ mg each is $3 \times 5 = 15$ mg. Eliminate choices (A) and (C). Plug In again to see if you can get a different result. Keep $m = 2$, and change n to 2. For Quantity A, the weight of 2 peanuts at $2 + 3$ mg each is $2 \times 5 = 10$ mg. For Quantity B, the weight of 2 almonds at $2 + 3$ mg each is $2 \times 5 = 10$ mg. Eliminate choice (B), and choose choice (D).

7. **C**

   Because $575 \div 5 = 115$, you can rewrite Quantity A as $5^{27}(5)(115)$, or $5^{28}(115)$. The quantities are equal.

8. B

For Quantity A, there are three ways to get an even number (these are: 2, 4, 6). So, the probability of "rolling an even" and then "rolling an even" is $\frac{3}{6} \times \frac{3}{6} = \frac{1}{4}$. For multiple independent events, multiply the probabilities. For Quantity B, there are 4 ways to not get a multiple of 3 (these are: 1, 2, 4, 5). The probability of "not rolling a multiple of 3" then "not rolling a multiple of 3" is $\frac{4}{6} \times \frac{4}{6} = \frac{4}{9}$. Quantity B is greater than Quantity A.

9. B

There are variables in the answer choice, so Plug In. If $r = 2$, then $4((2) - s) = -2$. Divide both sides by 4 to find $2 - s = -0.5$. So, $s = 2.5$. The target answer is r, which is 2. Go to the answer choices and Plug In 2.5 for s. Answer choice (B) is the only answer choice that matches your target of 2.

10. 10.5

25 percent is .25, and 42 percent is .42. Multiply the quantities to find 42 percent of 25 percent: $.25 \times .42 = .105$. Change the product into a percentage by multiplying by 100: 10.5 percent of employees transfer lines.

11. D

Set up a ratio box:

	Flour	Eggs	Yeast	Salt	Total
Ratio	11	9	3	2	25
Multiply by			$\frac{4}{5}$		$\frac{4}{5}$
Actual			$2\frac{2}{5}$		20

Because the ratio total is 25, and the actual total is 20, the "multiply by" number is $\frac{4}{5}$. Yeast is 3, so $3 \times \frac{4}{5} = \frac{12}{5} = 2\frac{2}{5}$. Be sure to use labels in your ratio box.

12. C

For this question, you can FOIL: $(\sqrt{5})^2 - (\sqrt{3})(\sqrt{5}) - (\sqrt{5})(\sqrt{3}) + (\sqrt{3})^2$. This simplifies to $5 - 2\sqrt{15} + 3$, or $8 - 2\sqrt{15}$.

13. A, C, D, and E

Plug the information given into the formula for the area of a triangle to learn more about the relationship between x and y: $A = \frac{bh}{2} = \frac{xy}{2} = 108$. The product of x and y is 216, so x needs to be a factor of 216. The only number in the answer choices that is not a factor of 216 is 5. The remaining choices are possible values of x.

14. **B**

Europe's electricity production (2,000 megawatt-hours) most closely matches that of Asia (1,900 megawatt-hours).

15. **C**

The ratio for Australia is 100 to 0.003, or $\dfrac{100}{0.003}$. This is approximately equal to $\dfrac{33.333}{1}$, or 33,333 : 1.

16. **A**

Africa's population is 10.6 percent on the pie chart; South America's is 7.9 percent. Right away, you can eliminate all of the answer choices that are smaller than 368. Now you are left with choices (A) and (B). Because the question gives you South America's population (368 million), you can use a proportion to find the population of Africa. The proportion would look like this: $\dfrac{.079}{368} = \dfrac{.106}{x}$, where x is equal to the population of Africa. Cross-multiplying gives you $.079 \times x = .106 \times 368$, and $x = 493.7$.

17. **A**

If the average of 5 crates is 250, then their total $= 5 \times 250 = 1,250$. To find the high end of the range for the fifth crate, make the other crates as light as possible: Make the two lightest crates 200 each, for a total of 400, and the two heaviest crates 300 each, for a total of 600; together, those four crates weigh 1,000 pounds, leaving 250 pounds for x. Because only choice (A) sets 250 pounds as the high end, you can eliminate choices (B), (C), (D), and (E).

18. **B**

Substitute 6 for x in the equation, $s_x = 2s_{x-1} + s_{x-2}$ and work carefully from there. $s_6 = 2\,s_{6-1} + s_{6-2}$, which simplifies to $s_6 = 2s_5 + s_4$. However you don't know s_5 or s_4. Use the equation to find these missing terms. $s_4 = 2s_3 + s_2$ and the problem tells you s_2 and s_3 are equal to 2. $s_4 = (2 \times 2) + 2$, which is 6. Now you need to find s_5. Using the equation, you get $s_5 = (2 \times 6) + 2$, which is 14. Now that you know s_5 and s_4, go back to your original equation, $s_6 = 2s_5 + s_4$, and $s_6 = (2 \times 14) + 6$, which is 34.

19. **7**

Always draw a figure when one is not provided. In this case, line segment XZ has a length of 68. Point Y is the midpoint of the segment, and $2XY = XZ$. To find the lengths of these segments, divide 68 by 2. Segment $YZ = 34$. Because $YZ = 4a + 6$, you know that $34 = 4a + 6$, and $a = 7$.

20. **C**

Make a spot for each day, and fill in the number of guests who could occupy that spot. Burke has 5 choices for Monday, 3 choices for Tuesday, 4 choices for Wednesday (because one politician was chosen on Monday), 6 choices for Thursday, and 10 choices for Friday (because 4 of the 14 potential guests have already been chosen). Multiply these to arrive at 3,600 different schedules.

Section 5

1. **systematic**

The clue is "simple, unambiguous, and unchanging." The trigger word is "in other words." The trigger word maintains the direction of the clue. Therefore, find a word that means regimented. *Systematic* is the best match.

2. **fête** and **shortest**

For the first blank, the clue of "welcome back" tells you to look for a word that means welcome or celebrate. *Fête* is the only choice that fits. The clue for the second blank is "welcome back the lengthening," which suggests that the Solstice must be a short day. *Lengthiest* is the opposite of *shortest*. Although it is wintertime, you don't know that the solstice is necessarily the coldest day of the year.

3. **corruptibility, venal**, and **redundancy**

The first two blanks are related, but there isn't a strong clue for either one in the first part, so let's start with the third blank. Since the motif is *tiresome,* the third blank must mean something close to "repetitive." *Redundancy* matches this. At the end of the paragraph, each character is *bribed...into giving up...beliefs.* So the first two blanks must mean "bribable." *Corruptibility* in the first blank and *venal* in the second both match this.

4. **illegal** and **unabashedly**

For the first blank, the clues "pirating software" and "downloading software from unapproved sources" describe unauthorized activities, and *illegal* is the best fit. *Uncommon* and *difficult* are incorrect because the sentence says that "many people continue to do so." If people are doing something despite its illegality and "almost as if they were unaware of the potential consequences if they were caught," you could describe them as acting *brashly. Unabashedly* is the best fit.

5. **insolvent**

The phrase "squandered his life's savings on unprofitable business ventures" tells you that the entrepreneur had no money left. The blank needs a word that means broke. *Former* and *unlikely* are tempting choices, but they don't match broke. Eliminate them. *Eccentric* also doesn't match, while *perturbed* only describes the entrepreneur's possible feelings. *Insolvent* agrees with the clue, so keep it.

6. **eschew obfuscation, recondite**, and **limpid**

The key clue is that the teachers urge students to "use clear, simple language." The trigger *instead* indicates that the phrase that goes into the blank will present an alternative to using clear, simple language, while the and indicates that the phrase will nevertheless agree with the clue. Something like avoid difficult language would be best: difficult language is the alternative to clear, simple language, but the two phrases still agree because the difficult language is something to avoid. Thus, *eschew obfuscation* is best: *eschew* means avoid, while *obfuscation* means the act of hiding the meaning of something. *Exscind obloquy* means to cut out critical language, while *evince ossification* means to show excessive rigidity, neither of which is appropriate here. The second blank needs a word that means difficult or obscure because teachers call into question the use of difficult vocabulary; recondite means obscure and hard to understand. *Recreant* means cowardly; *redolent* means fragrant. The final blank requires a word like *clear* because that is the type of language that "conveys one's meaning so much more effectively." *Limpid* means easily understood, and so is correct.

7. **A and C**

Answer choice (A) is supported because the passage says that myelin protects the brain's circuitry. Answer choice (C) is supported by the fact that "as humans mature" increasing levels of myelin need to be produced. While the passage suggests that a lack of myelin leaves the brain vulnerable, that doesn't mean that increasing the levels of myelin will reverse damage.

8. **B**

In the passage, *byzantine* refers to the "circuitry inside our nervous systems." Previously, the circuitry is described as growing more complex, so you need to find a word with a similar meaning. Answer choice (A) is an alternate meaning for byzantine, but is not supported by the passage. Answer choices (C), (D), and (E) do not have meanings similar to complex.

9. **D**

The argument concludes that large universities should utilize work-study students rather than administrative assistants. The premise is that a similar strategy realizes a cost savings at small colleges. This is an argument by analogy. Hence, the argument assumes that there are similar conditions at small colleges and at large universities. Choice (D) says that students at universities are just as qualified to take over the administrative roles as they are in small colleges. In other words, the administrative jobs at universities are not appreciably different than those at colleges. For choice (A), whether the practice would be of greater benefit to the small colleges is out of scope. For choice (B), whether large universities usually depend on small colleges for ideas is out of scope. For choice (C), the issue of non-work-study students is out of scope. For choice (E), whether anyone has an easier ride than anyone else is out of scope.

10. **A**

The first paragraph acts as an introduction to the rest of the passage. The author notes that in the nineteenth century "investments became increasingly speculative." In the last paragraph, the author explains that due to fluctuating interest rates, the consol was popular with speculative investors. There is no support in the passage for (B), (C), or (D). Although the first paragraph provides a historical framework, as suggested in answer choice (E), it does not provide a way "by which the nature of the nineteenth-century investor" could be understood.

11. **To address the problem, the British government instituted a sinking fund, using tax revenue to buy back the bonds in the open market.**

The second paragraph has five sentences so this question has five answer choices. The third sentence begins, "To address the problem...." This is a clear indication that the sentence describes a solution to a problem. The correct answer is the third sentence.

12. **rarefied** and **meager**

What sort of atmosphere would make Mars the only planet "whose surface details can be discerned from the Earth?" You need a word that means transparent or thin for the blank. *Viscous* takes you in the wrong direction, so toss it. The next choice, *ossified*, makes no sense; toss that one, too. In contrast, *rarefied* works well, so hang onto it. Meanwhile, a *copious* atmosphere would definitely not be easy to see through, so cross out that choice. *Meager* fits nicely and agrees with *rarefied*, making those two the best answers.

13. **adversity** and **tribulation**

The clue is "Using the hardships of the Joad family as a model." Recycle *hardships*, and use POE. Does *reticence* mean hardships? No; cross it out. *Adversity* works, so leave it. Do the same for the remaining choices. Only *tribulation* agrees with hardships, so that's the other correct answer.

14. **a venerable** and **an august**

The blank is a description of the pyramid. The clue is "imposing structure" because this is the only other description of the pyramid. *Venerable* and *august* are the only words that match *imposing*.

15. **noisome** and **mephitic**

The word that fills the blank must describe "the stench of the livestock," which is so malodorous that it drives the newcomers back to the city; it must mean something like, well, stinky! Both *noisome* and *mephitic* are appropriate choices. The other words don't work; if you were tempted by *olfactory*, realize that it simply means "related to the sense of smell" and does not actually describe a particular scent.

16. **B**

Answer choice (B) correctly sums up the purpose of the passage: It explores the social significance—the creation of a military aristocracy and chivalric culture—of a technological innovation—the stirrup. Choice (A) is incorrect because nothing in the passage suggests that this discussion has a basis in recent discovery. Answer choice (C) is too broad for the limited subject matter discussed. Choice (D) is too extreme. Answer choice (E) is incorrect because the physics, while important in connecting the stirrup to its social effects, isn't really the point of the passage—and, in any event, the physics relates to cavalry, not artillery.

17. **E**

Answer choice (E) is supported by the passage because the sixth sentence suggests that the development of the barbed lance serves as an "unusually clear" marker. Choice (A) is incorrect because no additional subjects for research are brought up in the passage. Choices (B) and (C) both require comparisons beyond the scope of the information in the passage: No other technology, ancient or medieval, was discussed. Answer choice (D), finally, is an extreme overstatement: Although the stirrup increased the military value of the horse, nowhere is it suggested that it had previously been considered militarily insignificant.

18. **"Stirrups unify lance, rider, and horse into a force capable…"**

The "previous generalization" is the one in the first sentence, and the "technological innovation" being discussed is, of course, the stirrup, which comes in the second sentence. The question really asks about the stirrup's physical effects, which are discussed in the fifth sentence. The third and fourth sentences describe the situation prior to the development of stirrups. The sixth sentence shifts emphasis and explains that the innovation left a record. The final two sentences explain how the innovation changed the military and social landscape—the cultural effects, in other words, rather than the physical ones.

19. **D**

Choice (D) describes the organization of the passage. Answer choice (A) can be eliminated because the traditional definition is never amended. Answer choice (B) can be eliminated because the authorities do not support the traditional theory. Answer choice (C) can be eliminated because no new definition is proposed. Answer choice (E) can be eliminated because the "implications of the experiment" are not rejected.

20. **A and B**

The author's dismissal of the traditional definition of randomness rests upon the premises that the results of the same probabilistic mechanism will all have the same likelihood of occurring, and, as such, should be considered equally probable. The passage never mentions how the results of different probabilistic mechanisms relate to each other, so eliminate choice (C).

Section 6

1. **A**

Solve for x in the top equation, $\frac{x}{6} + 2 = \frac{6}{2}$, by reducing the right side: $\frac{x}{6} + 2 = 3$. Subtract 2 from both sides, and multiply both sides by 6 to find that $x = 6$. Solve for y in the second equation, $\frac{y}{3} + 2 = \frac{9}{3}$, by reducing the right side: $\frac{y}{3} + 2 = 3$. Subtract 2 from both sides, and multiply both sides by 3 to find that $y = 3$. Using 6 for x and 3 for y, Quantity A becomes $\frac{5}{3}$, and Quantity B becomes $\frac{2}{6} = \frac{1}{3}$.

2. **A**

Use the equation distance = rate × time. Bob's time is 3 hours, and his rate is 44 miles per hour, so his distance is $3 \times 44 = 132$ miles. Inez's time is 2.5 hours, and her rate is 50 miles per hour, so her distance is $2.5 \times 50 = 125$ miles.

3. **B**

When a fraction's numerator and denominator are both positive, the fraction is greater than 1 if the numerator is greater than the denominator and less than 1 if the denominator is greater than the numerator. Because y is greater than x, Quantity B is greater than 1, and Quantity A is less than 1. Plugging in numbers makes this apparent. Let $x = \frac{1}{4}$ and $y = \frac{1}{2}$. $\dfrac{x}{y} = \dfrac{\frac{1}{4}}{\frac{1}{2}} = \frac{1}{4} \times \frac{2}{1} = \frac{1}{2}$, and $\dfrac{y}{x} = \dfrac{\frac{1}{2}}{\frac{1}{4}} = \frac{1}{2} \times \frac{4}{1} = \frac{4}{2} = 2$. No matter what numbers you try, the result will be the same.

4. **B**

Use your calculator. $0.98(8.21)y = 8.0458y$, and $\dfrac{821y}{98} = 8.37y$. Plug In different values for y, and you'll find that Quantity B is always greater than Quantity A.

5. **A**

Translate: $\dfrac{125}{100}k = 80$, so $\dfrac{1}{8}k = 80$, and $k = 640$. Use this information in the other equation: $k = 640 = \dfrac{y}{100} \times 80$, and solve for y: $y = \dfrac{10}{8} \times 640 = 800$. Quantity A is greater than Quantity B.

6. **D**

Plug In values for each set. If $P = \{1, 2, 3, 4, 5, 6, 7\}$ and $Q = \{1, 2, 3, 4, 5, 6\}$, the range of Q is smaller. Eliminate choices (B) and (C). If you change P to $\{1, 2, 3, 4, 5, 7, 6\}$, and Q to $\{1, 2, 3, 4, 5, 7\}$, the range of Q is equal to that of P. Eliminate choice (A), and select choice (D).

7. **A**

One way to attack this problem is to list out F_1 to F_{11}: 10, 13, 16, 19, 22, 25, 28, 31, 34, 37, 40. Notice that F_6 through F_{10} are included in both quantities, so focus on what's different, Quantity A is $F_4 + F_5$ and Quantity B is F_{11}. Quantity A is 19 + 22 = 43, and Quantity B is 40. Alternatively, you know that F_4 has had 3 changes from F_1. So, $F_4 = F_1 + 3(3) = 10 + 9 = 19$. F_5 has had 4 changes from F_1, so $F_5 = F_1 + 3(4) = 10 + 12 = 22$. F_{11} has had 10 changes from F_1, so $F_{11} = F_1 + 3(10) = 10 + 30 = 40$.

8. **C**

Plug In a number for n. Let $n = 5$. Because $5 \times 6 = 30$, the product is 30. Add 24 to get 54. Divide by 3 to get 18 as your target. If you Plug In 5 for n in each answer choice, only choice (C) matches the target: $2n + 8 = 2(5) + 8 = 18$.

9. **10**

If the average of a and b is 10, then $a + b = 20$. Likewise, if the average of c and d is 7, then $c + d = 14$. If the average of a, b, and c is 8, then $a + b + c = 24$. Because $a + b = 20$, $c = 4$. If $c = 4$, then $d = 10$.

10. **C**

To find the area of a square, you need the length of a side. To find a side, find the distance between two vertices. If A is at $(3, 7)$ and B is at $(3, 12)$, then length of a side is equivalent to the difference in the y-coordinates: $12 - 7 = 5$. So, side AB has a length of 5. Square this to find the area: $5^2 = 25$.

11. **B**

Get Dylan's median by putting his weekly sales into increasing order and finding the middle value. Dylan's set is {2, 3, 9, 10}, and his median is the average of 3 and 9, or 6. Next, do the same thing for Peter's sales numbers. Peter's set is {4, 4, 6, 10}, so his median the average of 4 and 6, which is 5. The difference between the medians is $6 - 5 = 1$.

12. **C**

From 1981 through 1984, Program y's ratings were higher than they were in the previous year.

13. **E**

There were 95 million times 80 percent, or 76 million, television households in 1983. Thirteen percent of them viewed Program y. 76 million times 13 percent (.13) is 9.88 million, or approximately 10.

14. **E**

You don't know if the number of television-viewing households changes from year to year (though it is likely that it does). Therefore, you can't assume that a 13.2 percent rating in 1981 indicates a smaller number of viewing households than a 14.3 percent rating in 1985. You can't answer this question without information about the number of television households in each year from 1981 to 1985.

15. **A**

Because order doesn't matter, use the combination formula. To order 3 out of 6 toppings = $\dfrac{6 \times 5 \times 4}{3 \times 2 \times 1} = 20$.

16. **E**

   Because you know the perimeter of the rectangle, you can figure out that both BC and $AD = 5$. Thus, the area of the rectangle is $3 \times 5 = 15$. The area of the triangle is therefore also 15. Because the area of a triangle $= \frac{1}{2}bh$, you can put in the values you know to find $15 = \frac{1}{2}(b \times 5)$ and solve for the base, which is 6. LM is the base of the triangle, so $LM = 6$.

17. **A**

   Plug In the answer choices, starting with choice (C). If Susan owns 146, Gavin owns 246, and together they own 392. Matt and Angela together would own 784, and the total number of houses would be 1,176. Choice (C) is too large, so also cross off (D) and (E). Try a smaller number. For choice (A), if Susan owns 46, Gavin owns 146, and together they own 192. Matt and Angela together would own 384 and the total number of houses would be 576.

18. $\dfrac{7}{45}$

   Plugging In your own number is a great way to tackle this question. Multiply the denominators of $\frac{1}{4}$, $\frac{1}{5}$, and $\frac{1}{3}$ together to get 60, which will be an easy number with which to work. Make the total number of cars 60. $60 \times \frac{1}{4} = 15$ sports cars, and $60 - 15 = 45$ sedans. The number of red cars is $60 \times \frac{1}{5} = 12$. The number of red sports cars is $15 \times \frac{1}{3} = 5$, which means that there are $12 - 5 = 7$ red sedans. The fraction of the sedans that are red is $\frac{7}{45}$.

19. **A and B**

   Plug In the answer choices. Start with one of the middle values, such as choice (C). If there are 18 grape candies, then there are 40 total candies in the jar. The probability of selecting an orange candy is $\frac{8}{40}$ or 20 percent. The question states that the probability of selecting an orange candy is greater than 20 percent, so choice (C) cannot work. Values larger than 18 also do not work because when the denominator becomes larger than 40, the probability becomes less than 20 percent. The only choices that could work are (A) and (B).

20. **E**

   Plug In for k, and let $k = 3$. CE is a radius and also half of the square's diagonal. If k is 3, then CE is 3, and the diagonal is 6. The diagonal of a square is also the hypotenuse of a 45°-45°-90° triangle. To get the hypotenuse from a side, you multiply by $\sqrt{2}$; so, to get a side from the hypotenuse, divide by $\sqrt{2}$. The sides of the square are each $\frac{6}{\sqrt{2}}$. To find the area, square the side to find $\left(\frac{6}{\sqrt{2}}\right)^2 = \frac{6^2}{\sqrt{2}^2} = \frac{36}{2} = 18$. Plug $k = 3$ into the answers to find one that yields your target of 18. Choice answer (E) yields the target of 18.

Appendix: Accommodated Testing

If you plan to request accommodations, you need to get a copy of the Request for Nonstandard Testing Accommodations form. You can download it at **www.gre.org** or request it by phone at 609-771-7780 (TTY: 609-771-7714). You can also write to:

GRE Disability Services
P.O. Box 6054
Princeton, NJ
08541-6054

Some of the available accommodations include the following:

- Extended testing time (There are no untimed tests.)

- Additional rest breaks

- Test reader

- Sign language interpreter

- Enlarged font

- Kensington Trackball mouse

- Audio Recording

- Braille

This is not an exhaustive list. You should contact ETS to learn your full set of options.

Accommodations are granted for a variety of reasons, but most commonly for learning disabilities (especially if you have a documented history of learning disabilities) and certain physical disabilities (such as substantial visual impairment).

Processing a request for accommodations takes time, so you should submit your request as early as possible (at least six weeks before you intend to take the test). The request must include the following:

- A completed CBT Authorization Voucher Request form and the proper test fee

- A completed Nonstandard Testing Accommodations form

- A Certificate of Eligibility if you currently use or have used accommodations at your college, university, or place of employment; have documentation on file that meets the ETS documentation criteria; and are requesting only those accommodations specified in Part III of the Request for Nonstandard Testing Accommodations form

- Documentation of your disability if you do not have a Certificate of Eligibility

Those who have a disability that is not specifically listed in Part 1 of the Nonstandard Testing Accommodations form, or who are requesting any accommodation not specifically listed in Part III of the form, or who are requesting more than 50 percent extended testing time (time-and-a-half), or who have not previously used the accommodations they are requesting, or whose disability has been diagnosed within the last 12 months, must submit documentation to ETS.

The documentation you submit must meet the following criteria:

- Clearly state the diagnosed disability.

- Describe the functional limitations resulting from the disability.

- Be current: within the last five years for a learning disability, last six months for psychiatric disabilities, or last three years for all other disabilities. (This does not apply to physical or sensory disabilities of a permanent or unchanging nature.)

- Include complete educational, developmental, and medical history relevant to the disability.

- Include a list of all test instruments used in the evaluation report and relevant subtest scores used to document the stated disability. (This does not apply to physical or sensory disabilities of a permanent or unchanging nature.)

- Describe the specific accommodations requested.

- State why the disability qualifies you for the requested accommodations.

- You must type or print this information on official letterhead and have it signed by an evaluator qualified to make the diagnosis (it should include information about license or certification and area of specialization).

If you have a learning disability, ADHD, or a psychiatric disability, you should refer to the ETS website at **www.ets.org/disability** for more documentation requirements.

If your request is approved, ETS will send a letter confirming the accommodations that have been approved for you. The letter will include your voucher number and appointment authorization number. Do not call to schedule a test date until you receive this information.

Most tests that are administered with accommodations are not flagged as such by ETS in the score report. However, when a testing accommodation affects one of the measured test constructs, ETS includes a statement with the score report indicating that the test was taken under nonstandard conditions. Contact ETS to find out more about how your specific accommodation will appear on your score report.